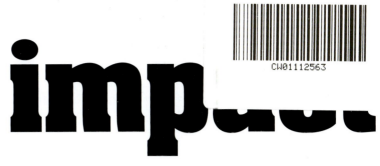

impact

LESSON PLANNER

1

NATIONAL GEOGRAPHIC
L E A R N I N G

Australia · Brazil · Mexico · Singapore · United Kingdom · United States

Impact, *a new five-level series from National Geographic Learning, helps teenage learners to better understand themselves, each other and the world they live in. Impact features real-world content, stunning photographs and video from authentic sources, and inspiring stories from National Geographic Explorers, challenging teenagers not only to understand their world but also to engage with it. By encouraging self-expression, global citizenship and active participation,* Impact *motivates students to explore who they are and who they want to be – all while learning English.*

The Unit Opener uses **high-interest photographs** to engage students, present the unit theme and provide opportunities for discussion.

Image **captions** help students understand the image and make connections with the unit theme.

Unit 1

Life in the City

'Geography is about curiosity, exploration and discovery. It gives you the power to see places in new ways, search for your own answers and make sense of the world.'
Daniel Raven-Ellison

8

A red fox exploring Bristol, UK

TO START

1. Look at the photo. If you saw this in person, would it surprise you? Why or why not?

2. The animal in the photo is exploring. Do you explore? Why is it good to explore a new place?

3. What is your favourite place? What do you do there? Why is this place special to you?

9

Each unit highlights one **National Geographic Explorer** to inspire future global citizens and promote 21st-century skills and values. Students first meet the unit explorer with a quote connected to the unit theme.

Discussion questions activate prior knowledge and lead students into the unit.

A **guiding question** promotes critical thinking, helps students access prior knowledge and introduces the context of the main vocabulary presentation.

Target vocabulary is presented in meaningful contexts to help students build fluency and confidence to discuss relevant real-world topics.

1 What makes Astana different from other cities? Discuss. Then listen and read. ∩ 002

The city of Astana is truly a **unique** place. It was **constructed** in 1997 to replace the city of Almaty as the **capital** of Kazakhstan. Almaty was in the south-eastern corner of the country, but the president of Kazakhstan wanted a new capital. So Astana was built right in the middle of the country. As a result, this modern city is **surrounded by** nothing but rural areas.

The unusual **architecture** of Astana makes it look like a space-age city. There are amazing **skyscrapers** and eye-catching buildings. A cultural centre looks like a big, blue eye. A university building has the **shape** of a dog bowl.

Another unusual building, the Bayterek **Tower**, is a **symbol** of the city. This tall structure is 105 m. (345 ft.) high and looks like an enormous tree with a golden egg inside.

A Japanese architect named Kisho Kurokawa won first prize in a competition to **design** and **plan** the new capital. He included many parks and public spaces to connect urban life with nature.

Astana has pleasant summers. But the weather can get very cold in the winter, with temperatures dropping to -40°C (-40°F). Because of its extreme climate, Astana offers a lot of **indoor** entertainment. A popular entertainment centre is the Khan Shatyr, or

king's tent, the world's largest tent. Inside, there is a river for boating, a park, an indoor running track, a waterslide and even a sandy beach with palm trees! The **residents** of Astana can enjoy a variety of outdoor activities even when it's well below freezing.

The Khan Shatyr

The Bayterek Tower in central Astana

10 VOCABULARY

2 LEARN NEW WORDS Listen and repeat. 🔊

3 Work in pairs. Compare Astana to the place where you live. What do you like and dislike about each place? Would you like to live in Astana? Why or why not?
VOCABULARY 11

Students **work in pairs or groups** to practise the new words.

All target vocabulary is presented on the **audio** in isolation, in a contextualised sentence, as well as in the context of the main presentation.

Student's Book Walkthrough

New vocabulary is practised in **meaningful contexts** involving National Geographic Explorers and real-world topics.

Students learn **new target vocabulary** and a **vocabulary strategy** that gives students tools to learn new words on their own.

The **Speaking Strategy** page presents phrases and model dialogues that help students express themselves fluently.

4 **Read and write the words from the list.** Make any necessary changes.

| architecture | capital | outdoors | plan |
| resident | skyscraper | surrounded by | unique |

Daniel Raven-Ellison has a very _____ job: he's a guerrilla geographer. He loves exploring places and making discoveries. Daniel says that we are _____ interesting things just waiting to be discovered. According to him, _____ of a place should keep exploring. They can make new discoveries even if they've lived in the same place their whole lives. Daniel _____ all kinds of exciting adventures. In one adventure, he climbed more than 3,300 floors of the many tall _____ in London. In another, he walked across Mexico City, the _____ of Mexico. He photographed everything he saw in front of him every eight steps. He took photos of _____, streets and public spaces. He's done the same thing in 12 other cities!

5 **LEARN NEW WORDS** Listen to these words and match them with the definitions. Then listen and repeat. 🎧004 005

| rural | unusual | urban |

_____ 1. different or uncommon
_____ 2. relating to the countryside
_____ 3. relating to the city

6 **YOU DECIDE** Choose an activity.

1. **Work independently.** Go on a discovery walk outdoors. Find things that are hard, soft, sticky, brown, pink, small, big or smelly. Take photos and present your experience to the class.

2. **Work in pairs.** Think of two adventures you can have near your home. Why would you choose these adventures? What can you learn from them?

3. **Work independently.** Walk through your school building and take photographs every eight steps. What interesting things do you see? Create a photo book of your discoveries.

Daniel Raven-Ellison

SPEAKING STRATEGY 🎧006

Active listening

Really?	You're kidding!
Wow!	Seriously?
No way!	That's incredible!

1 **Listen.** How do the speakers show they're listening actively? Write the words and phrases you hear. 🎧007

2 **Read and complete the dialogue.**

Dad: Meiling, look at this. I found this old map of our city. It's more than 100 years old.

Meiling: _____ Let me see.

Dad: This building was a hospital. It's a music hall now.

Meiling: _____

Dad: I know! And this was the old library.

Meiling: _____ Now it's a tall skyscraper.

Dad: And look. This was a park.

Meiling: _____ It's my school now!

Dad: Hey, let's go for a walk. We can take the map and look for other changes.

Meiling: Great idea! I'll bring my camera and take some photos.

3 **Work in groups.** Take turns. Choose a card. Read the question and the possible answers. Group members guess the correct answer and use active listening to respond to the real answer.

One million? That's amazing!

Go to page 153.

4 **Work in pairs.** Think of an interesting place, thing or event in your neighbourhood, and describe it to your partner. Your partner should use the words and phrases above to show active listening. When you finish, swap roles.

You Decide activities allow students to make decisions and become active participants in learning. They're encouraged to think critically and creatively as they discover who they are and who they want to be.

Games provide a fun context for communication.

Grammar boxes include natural examples of real-world language. Expanded grammar boxes with explanations are provided in the Workbook and on the Classroom Presentation Tool.

Additional target vocabulary is presented in meaningful contexts and applied in the grammar practice.

Present simple: Talking about facts

I **live** near the High Line.
She **works** next to the High Line.
Cars **don't drive** on the High Line.

You **go** to concerts on the High Line.
The High Line **doesn't allow** pets.
We **walk** through the High Line's gardens.

1 **Listen.** You will hear eight facts about the High Line. For each fact, circle the present simple form you hear. Ⓐ009

1.	grow	grows	don't grow	5.	need	needs	don't need
2.	visit	visits	doesn't visit	6.	enjoy	enjoys	don't enjoy
3.	open	opens	doesn't open	7.	sell	sells	doesn't sell
4.	close	closes	doesn't close	8.	get	gets	don't get

2 **Read.** Complete the sentences with the correct present simple form of the verbs in brackets.

1. The High Line _____ open all night. (not stay)
2. The High Line _____ special chairs for relaxing. (have)
3. A tour guide _____ about the High Line's gardens. (talk)
4. Musicians _____ concerts on Saturday afternoons. (give)
5. Visitors _____ to walk along the High Line. (not pay)

3 **Work in pairs.** Take turns saying facts about the High Line. Use the present simple.

1. the High Line / have / a play area for children
2. you / not / need / a ticket for the High Line
3. many different animals / live / on the High Line
4. guides / give / free tours to visitors
5. he / attend / exercise classes on the High Line
6. I / want / to visit the High Line

The High Line in New York City, USA

14 GRAMMAR

4 **LEARN NEW WORDS** Read about the Cheonggyecheon Stream park in Seoul, Korea. Then listen and repeat. Ⓐ010 011

bridge
pavement
stream

Cheonggyecheon Stream

In 2003, the mayor of Seoul decided to remove a **motorway** over an underground **stream**. He wanted the area around the stream to be an urban green space for people to enjoy. Today, the six-kilometre (four-mile) park on either side of the Cheonggyecheon Stream provides a place for people to relax.

At the park, visitors attend traditional festivals and concerts. They enjoy cultural events, look at art, and watch water and light shows. Many people just walk along the **pavements** or over one of 22 **bridges**, each with its own design and meaning.

5 **Read and complete the sentences.** Make any necessary changes.

| bridge | motorway | pavement | stream |

1. The Cheonggyecheon Stream was covered by a _____ .
2. Now visitors go for walks on the _____ near the water.
3. People enjoy water shows over the _____ .
4. Each of the _____ has a unique look and meaning.

6 **Work in groups.** Name an interesting outdoor place where you live. How do people enjoy this place? What can you see and do at this place? Use the present simple.

GRAMMAR 15

Grammar is practised in **context** with multiple opportunities for real communication using **all four language skills.**

Student's Book Walkthrough

New target vocabulary is presented in the reading and gives students an opportunity to make predictions about the reading topic.

Reading strategies promote comprehension and help students become independent readers.

Readings feature engaging, relevant topics covering a variety of **cross-curricular areas**.

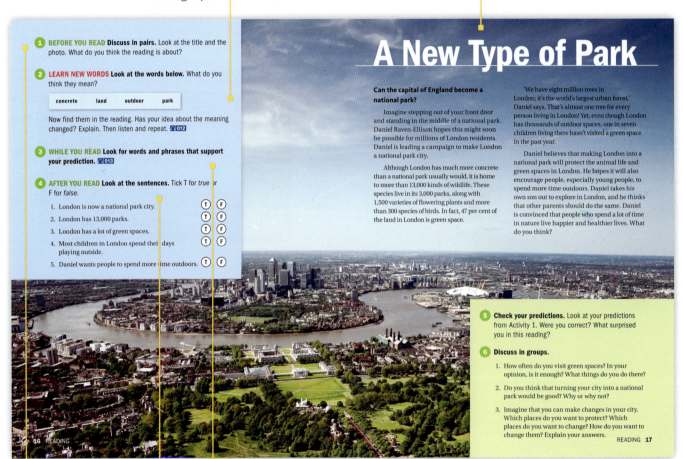

1. **BEFORE YOU READ** Discuss in pairs. Look at the title and the photo. What do you think the reading is about?

2. **LEARN NEW WORDS** Look at the words below. What do you think they mean?

concrete	land	outdoor	park

Now find them in the reading. Has your idea about the meaning changed? Explain. Then listen and repeat. 🔊 012

3. **WHILE YOU READ** Look for words and phrases that support your prediction. 🔊 013

4. **AFTER YOU READ** Look at the sentences. Tick T for *true* or F for *false*.

1. London is now a national park city. T F
2. London has 13,000 parks. T F
3. London has a lot of green spaces. T F
4. Most children in London spend their days playing outside. T F
5. Daniel wants people to spend more time outdoors. T F

16 READING

A New Type of Park

Can the capital of England become a national park?

Imagine stepping out of your front door and standing in the middle of a national park. Daniel Raven-Ellison hopes this might soon be possible for millions of London residents. Daniel is leading a campaign to make London a national park city.

Although London has much more concrete than a national park usually would, it is home to more than 13,000 kinds of wildlife. These species live in its 3,000 parks, along with 1,500 varieties of flowering plants and more than 300 species of birds. In fact, 47 per cent of the land in London is green space.

'We have eight million trees in London; it's the world's largest urban forest,' Daniel says. That's almost one tree for every person living in London! Yet, even though London has thousands of outdoor spaces, one in seven children living there hasn't visited a green space in the past year.

Daniel believes that making London into a national park will protect the animal life and green spaces in London. He hopes it will also encourage people, especially young people, to spend more time outdoors. Daniel takes his own son out to explore in London, and he thinks that other parents should do the same. Daniel is convinced that people who spend a lot of time in nature live happier and healthier lives. What do you think?

5. **Check your predictions.** Look at your predictions from Activity 1. Were you correct? What surprised you in this reading?

6. **Discuss in groups.**

1. How often do you visit green spaces? In your opinion, is it enough? What things do you do there?

2. Do you think that turning your city into a national park would be good? Why or why not?

3. Imagine that you can make changes in your city. Which places do you want to protect? Which places do you want to change? How do you want to change them? Explain your answers.

READING 17

Before reading activities help students make predictions about the reading.

While reading activities guide students and help them stay focused.

After reading activities provide students with opportunities to react and respond to the text, and to make connections between the reading and their lives.

Meaningful, relevant and timely topics are presented through videos from **National Geographic** and other sources, as well as animated **infographic videos** created specifically for this series.

Before watching activities help students make predictions about the video.

While watching activities guide students and help them stay focused.

After watching activities provide students with opportunities for discussion and reflection.

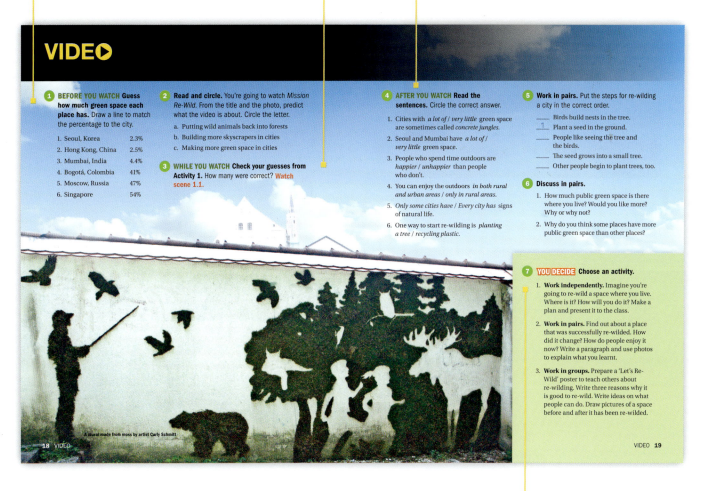

VIDEO

1 **BEFORE YOU WATCH** **Guess how much green space each place has.** Draw a line to match the percentage to the city.

1. Seoul, Korea   2.3%
2. Hong Kong, China   2.5%
3. Mumbai, India   4.4%
4. Bogotá, Colombia   41%
5. Moscow, Russia   47%
6. Singapore   54%

2 **Read and circle.** You're going to watch *Mission Re-Wild*. From the title and the photo, predict what the video is about. Circle the letter.

a. Putting wild animals back into forests
b. Building more skyscrapers in cities
c. Making more green space in cities

3 **WHILE YOU WATCH** **Check your guesses from Activity 1.** How many were correct? Watch scene 1.1.

4 **AFTER YOU WATCH** **Read the sentences.** Circle the correct answer.

1. Cities with *a lot of / very little* green space are sometimes called *concrete jungles*.
2. Seoul and Mumbai have *a lot of / very little* green space.
3. People who spend time outdoors are *happier / unhappier* than people who don't.
4. You can enjoy the outdoors *in both rural and urban areas / only in rural areas*.
5. *Only some cities have / Every city has* signs of natural life.
6. One way to start re-wilding is *planting a tree / recycling plastic*.

5 **Work in pairs.** Put the steps for re-wilding a city in the correct order.

____ Birds build nests in the tree.
__1__ Plant a seed in the ground.
____ People like seeing the tree and the birds.
____ The seed grows into a small tree.
____ Other people begin to plant trees, too.

6 **Discuss in pairs.**

1. How much public green space is there where you live? Would you like more? Why or why not?
2. Why do you think some places have more public green space than other places?

7 **YOU DECIDE** **Choose an activity.**

1. **Work independently.** Imagine you're going to re-wild a space where you live. Where is it? How will you do it? Make a plan and present it to the class.
2. **Work in pairs.** Find out about a place that was successfully re-wilded. How did it change? How do people enjoy it now? Write a paragraph and use photos to explain what you learnt.
3. **Work in groups.** Prepare a 'Let's Re-Wild' poster to teach others about re-wilding. Write three reasons why it is good to re-wild. Write ideas on what people can do. Draw pictures of a space before and after it has been re-wilded.

A mural made from moss by artist Carly Schmitt

18 VIDEO

VIDEO 19

A **You Decide activity** supports learner autonomy and allows flexibility in the classroom by offering opportunities for individual, pair or group work.

Student's Book Walkthrough

Grammar boxes include natural examples of real-world language. Expanded grammar boxes with explanations are provided in the Workbook and on the Classroom Presentation Tool.

Students learn the basics of **academic writing** and are introduced to a variety of writing genres.

Models written at the student level provide examples for students to follow.

GRAMMAR 014

In and *on*: Expressing location

Lion City is **in** eastern China.
There are many beautiful bridges **in** Lion City.
Lion City is **in** the water.

China is **on** the continent of Asia.
Lion City is one of the most unique places **on** Earth.
Lion City is not **on** a mountain.

1 **Listen.** Write *in* or *on* in the spaces below. 015

1. There are many ancient cities _____ Asia, such as Shi Cheng, also known as Lion City.

2. Shi Cheng is an ancient city located _____ China.

3. Visitors to Shi Cheng today can't walk _____ its streets to admire it.

4. It isn't _____ a mountain or _____ an island. It's _____ the water!

5. _____ Shi Cheng, there are 265 archways crossing over its streets.

6. There are beautiful sculptures of lions, dragons and birds _____ these archways.

2 **Work in pairs.** Listen to the passage again. Write two additional facts about Shi Cheng. Use *on* and *in* in your sentences. 016

_____

_____

3 **Work in groups.** Take turns using the spinner. Make sentences using *in* or *on*.

About seven billion people live on Earth.

Go to page 155.

20 GRAMMAR

WRITING

In descriptive writing, we try to create a picture for the reader. We use describing words to help the reader clearly imagine what we're writing about. Examples of describing words include:

beautiful   colourful   new   short   sweet-smelling   yellow

1 **Read the model.** Work in pairs to find and underline all of the describing words the writer uses to talk about the garden.

Last year, the empty space opposite my bus stop was a sad, empty, ugly space, with only a couple of dead bushes and one short tree. Then some hard-working gardeners in the neighbourhood changed that. They were tired of looking at that sad space while waiting for the bus, so they made it into a beautiful garden. Now, on a sunny summer day you can look across the street and see colourful vegetable plants and sweet-smelling flowers while you wait for the bus. Yellow butterflies fly from plant to plant, and tiny birds sing in the green trees. I love taking the bus now!

2 **Work in pairs.** Draw a picture of the garden described in Activity 1. Compare your drawing with a partner's. How are they the same? How are they different?

3 **Write.** Think of a beautiful place in your neighbourhood. Use describing words to write a paragraph about this place.

WRITING 21

Grammar is practised **in context** through engaging activities and **games**.

Step-by-step **pre-writing and drafting support** is provided in the Workbook.

Optional worksheets guide students through the five steps involved in **process writing**: pre-writing, drafting, revising, editing and publishing.

The **Mission** page features National Geographic Explorers as role models who embody the **21st-century skills and values** teenagers need to become successful global citizens.

A variety of **projects** build 21st-century skills through independent research, discussion and presentations using a variety of media.

NATIONAL GEOGRAPHIC

Explore Your World

'There are amazing adventures to be had right outside our doors.'

Daniel Raven-Ellison
National Geographic Explorer, Guerrilla Geographer

1. **Watch scene 1.2.**

2. Daniel thinks it's best for students to experience geography rather than just read about it. What other school subjects can you explore outside the classroom? How can you explore them?

3. How much of your town or city have you explored? What else is there to learn about where you live? Keep a journal of outdoor adventures you have in your area.

22 MISSION

Make an Impact

YOU DECIDE Choose a project.

1 **Conduct a survey.**
- Ask your friends how much time they spent indoors and outdoors in the past week.
- Calculate the average amount of indoor and outdoor time.
- Present your findings to the class. Give suggestions for spending more time outdoors.

2 **Plan and conduct a scavenger hunt.**
- Work as a group to prepare a list of items to find in a local green space.
- Work independently to find the items on the list.
- Discuss which items on the list were the easiest and the most difficult to find.

3 **Write a newspaper article.**
- Think of someone who has lived in your neighbourhood for a long time. Write questions to ask them about your neighbourhood.
- Interview that person. Find maps and photos to show the changes that he or she describes.
- Write a newspaper article to summarise the interview and show the changes.

PROJECT 23

A **quote** by the Explorer and a **Meet the Explorer** video help students connect with these inspirational people who are making a difference in the world.

You Decide project choices allow students to take charge of their own learning and choose their preferred way to use the language they learnt to synthesise and reflect on the unit topic.

Student's Book Walkthrough

Express Yourself appears every two units. It actively engages students in discussions to synthesise what they learnt in the preceding units and make connections beyond the unit themes.

This section exposes students to a wide range of **creative expression**, from poems and film scripts, to presentations and personal narratives.

Express Yourself

1 Read and listen to the online travel review. 🎧 031

GoTravel REVIEWS

🧳🧳🧳🧳🧳 JGirl, Seoul

GONDOLA TOURS OF VENICE

🧳🧳🧳🧳🧳 210 reviews

'Our gondolier saved my holiday!'

Well, I'm in Venice, Italy, with my family! Venice is incredible! The city is hundreds of years old, and it's built on WATER. People get around on special boats called *gondolas*, and today I had my first gondola ride!

A gondolier controls the gondola using an oar and his own strength. (These gondoliers are REALLY strong.) The gondolier's job is to describe Venice's culture and history as he takes you through the city's canals. Our gondolier was so good at telling stories I almost forgot I was sharing the ride with my parents.

That might sound exciting, and it was, but of course I was with … my dad. And Dad thought it would be funny to wear a striped shirt to match the gondolier's shirt. How *embarrassing*!

My parents loved looking at the beautiful bridges, churches and palaces along the route. I really enjoyed listening to our gondolier talk about his work. He told us that it takes years of study and practice to get the job. Who knew? He also told us that of all the gondoliers in Venice, only one is a woman! I think I need to change that! It's time to start training for my dream job! Maybe my dad will let me borrow his shirt. ;)

Gondola Tours of Venice gave me a great tour of a beautiful city – and an interesting idea for my future career! I recommend the gondola tour to anyone who's interested in learning about unusual places and unusual jobs … especially if they're stuck on a boat with their parents!

2 **Work in groups.** Discuss the review.

1. Does JGirl's review make you want to visit Venice and go on a gondola ride? Why or why not?

2. Do you think the review gives enough information? Is it funny and interesting? What else would you like to know about Venice or about Gondola Tours of Venice?

3 **Connect ideas.** In Unit 1, you learnt about exploring and unusual places. In Unit 2, you learnt about unusual jobs. What connection can you see between the two units?

4 **YOU DECIDE** **Choose an activity.**

1. Choose a topic:
   - an unusual place
   - an unusual job

2. Choose a way to express yourself:
   - a review
   - an advertisement
   - an interview

3. Present your work.

Gondolas in Venice, Italy

40

41

Students **choose** a form of creative expression to find their own voice and reflect on the themes they have studied.

Unit 1

Syllables and stress

1 **Listen.** Words in English have one or more parts. These parts make up *syllables*. A syllable has a vowel sound and can also have one or more consonant sounds. Listen. Notice the numbers of syllables in these words. 🎧 116

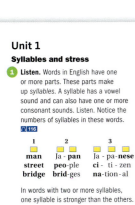

1	2	3
man	Ja - **pan**	Ja - pa - **nese**
street	**peo** - ple	**ci** - ti - zen
bridge	**brid** - ges	**na** - tion - al

In words with two or more syllables, one syllable is stronger than the others. The vowel in that syllable is pronounced more loudly and clearly. This is the stressed syllable. Listen again and notice the stressed syllable in the two- and three-syllable words above.

Unit 2

Intonation in questions

1 **Listen.** Notice how the voice goes up or down at the end of the questions. 🎧 119

Does a pastry chef wear a uniform?

Do pastry chefs work every day?

How do you create beautiful desserts?

Where do pastry chefs work?

The voice rises at the end of questions asking for an answer of *yes* or *no*.

The voice falls at the end of questions that ask for information. These questions start with the words *who*, *what*, *when*, *where*, *why* and *how*.

2 **Listen and repeat.** Do the word pairs have the same number of syllables? Write *Y* for *yes* or *N* for *no*. Then listen again and circle the stressed syllable. 🎧 117

1. __Y__ London — England
2. __N__ surround — surrounded
3. __N__ Mexico — America
4. __Y__ travel — travelled
5. __Y__ pavement — streetlight
6. __N__ explore — exploration

3 **Work in pairs.** Write the words in the correct column. Then listen to the completed table to check your answers. 🎧 118

architecture	capital	design	entertainment
planned	resident	sign	unique

Introductions: Formal and informal

3 **Listen and read.** 🎧 142

Formal

Gabi: Mr Moore, I'd like to introduce you to Ben.
Mr Moore: Hello, Ben. It's a pleasure to meet you.

Making an introduction	Responding
• I'd like you to meet Ben.	• I'm very pleased to meet you.
• I'd like to introduce you to Ben.	• It's a pleasure to meet you, Ben.
• Please allow me to introduce Ben. He's a student at my school.	• Hello, Ben. I'm glad to meet you.
• I don't think we've met. May I introduce myself? I'm Ben.	• Hello, Ben. I'm Mr Moore. Pleased to meet you.

4 **Listen and read.** 🎧 143

Informal

Ben: Hi. My name is Ben. Nice to meet you.
Gabi: Hi, Ben. I'm Gabi. Very nice to meet you, too.

Making an introduction	Responding
• Hi. I'm Ben.	• Hi, Ben. My name is Gabi. Nice to meet you.
• Hi there. My name is Ben. Nice to meet you.	• Hello. I'm Gabi. Very nice to meet you, too.
• Hi, Ben. This is Gabi. She's in my class.	• Hi, Gabi. Nice to meet you.
• This is Ben. He's a student in my school.	• Hi, Ben. I'm Gabi. It's nice to meet you.

Asking for permission

5 **Listen and read.** 🎧 144

Isabella: Mum, can I go to the cinema on Fri...
Mum: Sure. Who are you going with? And...
Isabella: I'm going with Mia and Valerie. Is it...
Mum: I'm afraid not. But I can take you.

Asking for permission	Giving permission
• Can I/we ...?	• Sure.
• May I/we ...? (formal)	• No problem.
• Is it OK if I/we ...?	• Of course.
• Do you mind if I/we ...?	• Go ahead.
• Would you mind if ...?	
• Would it be OK if ...?	

Pronunciation activities provide practice with stress, intonation, reductions and connected speech to help students better understand speakers of English and be better understood.

A **speaking** section presents common language functions such as asking for and giving permission, apologising, interrupting politely and making presentations.

A variety of **games** allows students to practise concepts and develop fluency – all while having fun.

Workbook

The **Workbook** contains activities that reinforce and consolidate the material in the Student's Book and include listening, reading, writing, grammar and vocabulary practice.

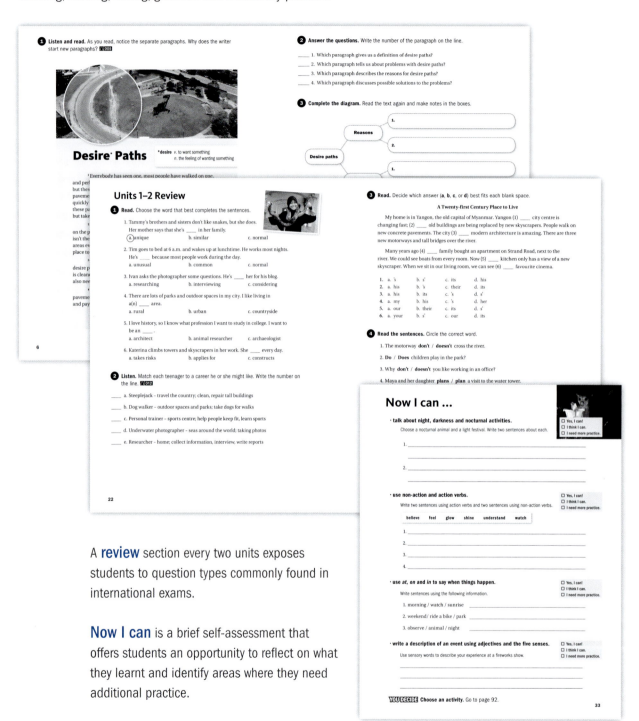

A **review** section every two units exposes students to question types commonly found in international exams.

Now I can is a brief self-assessment that offers students an opportunity to reflect on what they learnt and identify areas where they need additional practice.

Each unit ends with a **You Decide activity** that provides options for targeted skill practice.

Workbook **audio** is available for streaming and download at **NGL.Cengage.com/impact**.

Online Workbook and Student Website

The Online Workbook, hosted on MyELT, includes **interactive activities** to support each section from the Student's Book:

- Vocabulary
- Speaking Strategy
- Grammar
- Reading
- Video
- Writing

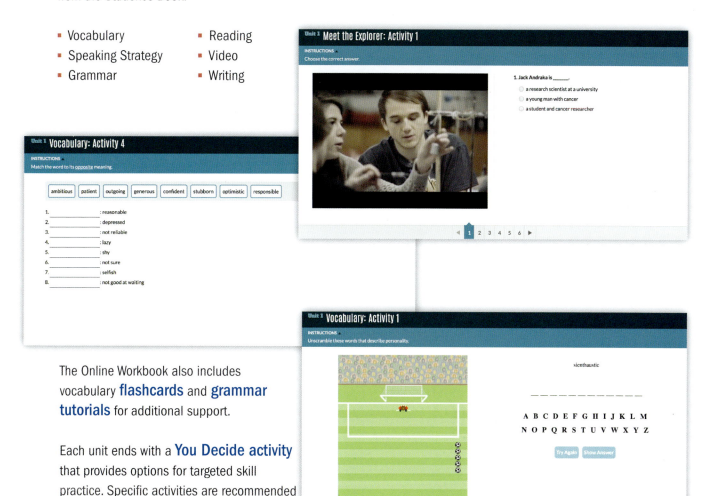

The Online Workbook also includes vocabulary **flashcards** and **grammar tutorials** for additional support.

Each unit ends with a **You Decide activity** that provides options for targeted skill practice. Specific activities are recommended based on the Now I can self-assessment.

Student resources, including audio for Student's Book and Workbook activities, are available at **NGL.Cengage.com/impact**.

Teacher's Resources

The **Lesson Planner**, with DVD, Audio CD and Teacher's Resource CD-ROM, provides everything needed to successfully plan, teach and supplement lessons.

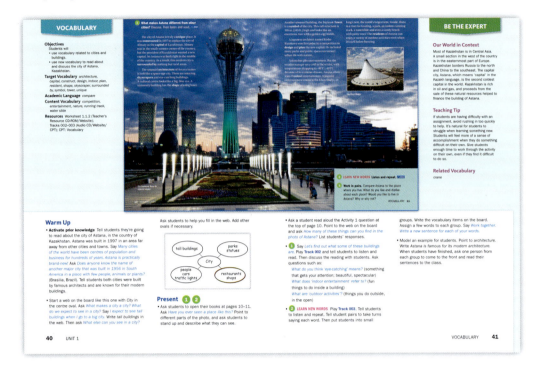

The Lesson Planner includes:

- a professional development section that introduces the key principles of the course;
- a detailed scope and sequence;
- step-by-step instructions for carrying out lessons;
- reduced Student's Book pages with answers at point of use;
- Student's Book audio scripts;
- extension activities to supplement the Student's Book, including instructions to use the worksheets on the Teacher's Resource CD-ROM;
- teaching tips and professional development support at point of use;
- suggestions for formative assessment.

The **Teacher's Resource CD-ROM** includes:

- unit-by-unit pacing guides for easy lesson planning;
- printable worksheets for extension activities and process writing support;
- printable graphic organisers;
- video scripts;
- Workbook audio scripts;
- pronunciation activities answer keys.

The *Impact* **DVD** and the **Audio CD** contain all of the multimedia to support the Student's Book.

The **Classroom Presentation Tool** integrates all of the *Impact* resources, including video, audio, Student's Book pages and interactive activities, making it easy to carry out lessons in any classroom with an interactive whiteboard or a computer and projector.

The **Assessment CD-ROM with *ExamView*®** includes activity banks to generate customised unit quizzes, mastery tests and final exams, as well as a pre-test and placement test.

The **Teacher's Resource Website** includes the Student's Book and Workbook audio, the Professional Development Video, as well as all the printable materials contained in the Teacher's Resource CD-ROM.
NGL.Cengage.com/impact

Video

Main Video The main video in each unit introduces a key concept of the unit theme in a unique way, either through **live action National Geographic content** or through an original animation designed specifically for this course.

The videos cover meaningful, relevant and timely topics such as:

- Group behaviour
- Art in the open
- Forming teen identity
- Pushing your limits

Meet the Explorer When students reach the Mission page of each unit, they'll learn more about the National Geographic Explorer featured in the unit. A quote by the Explorer and a Meet the Explorer video help students connect with these inspirational people who are making a difference in the world. These **short one-minute clips** reinforce unit objectives, develop critical thinking skills and allow students to hear from each explorer in his or her own words.

Tan Le
TECHNOLOGY ENTREPRENEUR / INVENTOR
NATIONAL GEOGRAPHIC 2013 EMERGING EXPLORER

The videos are available on a DVD bound with the Lesson Planner, on the Online Workbook and on the Classroom Presentation Tool.

To ensure that teachers are able to improve their classroom practice and get the most out of the *Impact* teaching resources, Dr Joan Kang Shin and Dr Jodi Crandall have developed the *Impact* Professional Development Video.

The ***Impact* Professional Development Video**, available on the Teacher's Resource Website, is hosted by Dr Joan Kang Shin and it features interviews with teachers around the world. The video provides useful insights and practical advice on the following topics:

- Characteristics of young teens
- 21st-century skills
- Global citizenship
- Learning language through content
- Student choice and classroom management
- Strategy instruction
- Classroom routines
- Effective use of media in the classroom
- Assessment
- Teaching writing

Professional development topics are also covered at point-of-use throughout the Lesson Planner.

About the Author

Lesley Koustaff

Lesley Koustaff has been teaching students and writing ELT materials for all levels for over 30 years. Lesley hopes that by involving students in their learning throughout *Impact*, they will be interested, engaged and motivated every step of the way. Lesley has conducted educational workshops all over Asia, the United States, Central and South America and Turkey. She earned her Masters in Teaching from The School for International Training in Vermont.

About the Series Editors

Dr JoAnn (Jodi) Crandall

Dr JoAnn (Jodi) Crandall is Professor Emerita and former Director of the Language, Literacy and Culture PhD Program, and Co-Director of the MA TESOL Program at the University of Maryland, Baltimore County (UMBC). She has worked in all areas of ESL/EFL including teaching, curriculum and materials development, standards development and teacher training.

Dr Joan Kang Shin

Dr. Joan Kang Shin is an Associate Professor of Education at George Mason University and the Academic Program Coordinator of the Teaching Culturally & Linguistically Diverse & Exceptional Learners (TCLDEL) program. Dr. Shin specialises in teaching ESL/EFL to young learners and teenagers and has provided professional development programs and workshops to EFL teachers in over 100 countries around the world.

Teaching with *Impact*

National Geographic Learning's *Impact* is an exciting new series for young teens that aims to help students to better understand themselves, one another and the world they live in. The series integrates real-world content, the work and stories of National Geographic Explorers, a wide variety of cross-curricular concepts and engaging projects into a unified course of English language instruction. It uses a content-based, communicative approach to learning English, with grammar and vocabulary taught and practised in context, and multiple opportunities for authentic communication using all language skills. In every thematically organised unit, students are immersed in a topic that they explore from different curricular perspectives, using the skills of listening, speaking, reading and writing.

Young teens are actively exploring their own identities and grappling with big ideas daily. *Impact* encourages teens to consider how their learning might relate to their current or future lives and to the roles they may play in the world as adults. *Impact* challenges teens to think about their places in their communities, in their countries and in the world at large. By addressing issues of local and global importance, *Impact* stimulates students to use 21st-century skills, such as problem-solving, critical thinking and other higher-order thinking skills. In every unit of *Impact*, students use their skills to delve deeply into topics of immediate concern to them as citizens of the 21st century.

Impact reflects key concepts and principles of English-language teaching and learning as they apply to adolescent learners of English:

- Learning is a process of constructing meaning. Active learners work to make sense of their world through interaction in personal, social and academic contexts.

- All English learners, and especially teens, need multiple opportunities for questioning and communicating meaning about topics that concern them, at a level that is appropriate to their emotional, social and intellectual stages of development.

- Learners benefit greatly from the support of knowledgeable persons (teachers, adults and peers) to help them successfully incorporate and understand new information.

- Learning is most effective when the learner is challenged to go one step beyond his or her current stage of cognitive and language development.

- Activities that encourage students to think critically about issues and that engage them in problem solving are most effective; these activities link language learning with other curricular areas.

Characteristics of Young Teens

Young teens are going through a number of changes: physical, social and cognitive. For teens, life is both exciting and confusing. They're engaged in discovering who they are and who they want to be, and in exploring the qualities that make them unique, as well as those qualities they share with their peers.

Teens combine childlike playfulness with a nearly adult ability to think critically. They're engaged in questioning, analysing and comparing points of view, and they are likely to express strong opinions about topics related to their lives. *Impact* encourages them to discuss and express their views using a variety of print and communications media, such as videos, posters, stories, comic strips, raps, poems and songs.

Adolescent English learners have already learnt at least one language and are cognitively more efficient language learners than younger children. They can infer and confirm grammar, vocabulary and language use when given sufficient opportunities to use the language to communicate. They also need to take part in activities that create language awareness and foster an understanding of, and an interest in, how language functions.

Many young people are concerned about their places in the world and their roles as global citizens. They're developing a sense of social responsibility. They're also developing a personal sense of values and looking for role models. National Geographic Explorers are people who have made a difference in the world and who challenge young teens to do the same. Eight Explorers and their work are featured in each level of *Impact*. They're presented as potential role models who can encourage teens to explore their world (Daniel Raven-Ellison), to discover the future (Bethany Ehlmann), to be curious (Katy Croff-Bell) and to test their limits (Cory Richards).

Real-World Content

Students learn language and content at the same time, so it's natural and authentic to incorporate academic content into the English classroom. Integrating grade-appropriate content from science, geography, history and other subjects complements what students are learning in their other courses, helps them develop the academic English they may need for future study and motivates them to use English in meaningful ways.

Because technology plays such a large role in the lives of teens – mobile phones, laptops, social media, texting and more are part of their everyday lives – *Impact* provides opportunities for adolescent English learners to explore the influence of media and technology in their lives. In Level 2, for example, in *Your Virtual Self* (Unit 3), students explore the many ways in which technology extends our human abilities. Explorer Amber Case, a cyborg anthropologist, challenges teens (and adults!) to think about the positive and negative aspects of our reliance on technology.

In *Everybody's Doing It* (Unit 3), students in Level 3 learn about the various ways that animals and humans organise into groups, and how those groups affect behaviour. They compare groups that they choose to belong to with others that are involuntary, and discuss the importance of groups in their lives.

Other units focus on contemporary issues such as the environmental impact of entertainment. As they read *The Footprint of Fun* (Unit 4) in Level 4, for example, students consider how they can reduce their carbon footprints and take part in sustainable activities while still enjoying themselves in public settings.

Multicultural Outlook

Today's teens live in a world made much smaller through technology and the role of English as a global language. *Impact* brings that world into the classroom, introducing teens to the diversity of global customs, traditions and ways of life. Learning about cultures other than their own helps young people develop a multicultural outlook and learn to communicate successfully with others who are using English as a global language, both in person and through social media. And of course, as we've come to expect with National Geographic and its global reach and extensive research, we can rely on the accuracy of all content, as well as the stunning photographs and visuals that accompany the text and engage and motivate adolescent learners.

In *Impact*, teens

- learn about robots and how they are used in many different aspects of life, from hospitals to the home. (Foundation Level)

- read about people with unusual and amazing jobs, who work in some of the world's most extreme and dangerous environments. (L1)

- discover that colour affects people's emotions all over the world, and is often used to express and represent one's self. (L2)

- explore the different ways in which young people in various cultures express themselves through fashion, from special T-shirts and eco-friendly clothing to hair and body accessories. (L3)

- learn how to become digital humanitarians and help others during times of conflict or crisis by employing techniques used in crisis mapping and crowdsourcing. (L4)

Cultural Connections

In addition to learning about other cultures, *Impact* provides teens with opportunities to make connections between their own and other traditions and customs. Students reflect upon their own cultures and discuss connections with their peers. The process helps them build a stronger understanding and appreciation of themselves and their place in the world. It also helps them to learn to use English to communicate and describe their values and traditions to others around them.

In Foundation level, students read about education in countries around the world. They learn about different types of schools and reflect on their own learning experiences.

After reading about the growth of the Internet and the use of electronic gadgets in Level 1, for example, teens are asked about the impact that technology has on their lives. In Level 2, after reading about Tristram Stuart's campaign to encourage consumers not to reject that extra lumpy potato or misshaped carrot, students are asked to think about food waste and ugly food.

In Level 3, students read about the many different ways people around the world have developed animation, from cartoons to films, video games, mobile phone emojis and special effects in live-action films. In Level 4, after reading about public art, teens are urged to think about how they can use art to express their feelings and ideas.

National Geographic Explorers

As noted, each unit of *Impact* presents inspiring stories about National Geographic Explorers, global citizens who are actively working in many different fields, helping students explore content from different relevant perspectives. Each unit opener presents a quote from the unit Explorer, meant for students to reflect upon and discuss in the context of their own lives.

These Explorers convey, through their work and their words, a sense of global values. They model universal values such as acting responsibly, respecting others, appreciating the environment and believing in the value of collaboration. Each unit in *Impact* includes a 'Mission' page dedicated to the Explorer's work and message for teens, as well as a short 'Meet the Explorer' video in which the Explorer shares his or her perspectives and challenges with students.

Impact gives students a window into the work of Explorers such as Jack Andraka, who at only 15 years of age invented an inexpensive and quick way to detect certain types of cancer. It took him 4,000 attempts to find the protein he needed for his experiment, and 200 attempts to find a research scientist who would accept his project. He hopes to inspire other young people to pursue their passions, no matter the odds, as he asks, 'Why not you?'

Explorer Jenny Daltry, in a unit on misunderstood animals, many of which are endangered species, urges teens to 'keep an open mind'. Iain Couzin, a behavioural ecologist, studies the value of collaboration. As he notes, whether we're talking about 'invasive cells to schooling fish to human cultures, groups can accomplish what solitary individuals cannot'.

Explorer Jimmy Chin, a photographer and climber, reminds teens to be prepared, and to avoid situations where the risks are high and their level of control is low. In a unit about exploration, Corey Jaskolski remarks on the importance of learning by doing and 'showing people the world in a different light, in a new format – something that they can engage with and be excited about'.

Students meet Bethany Ehlmann, an Explorer and planetary geologist who works to help the Curiosity rover navigate on Mars. Bethany hopes that she and others can someday study signs of life not only on Mars but also in other worlds. She encourages students to 'discover the future'.

There are other role models in *Impact* in addition to the Explorers. From successful teenage fashion designers who have donated part of their earnings to charities or environmental organisations, to a young girl who has regularly attended space camps from the age of seven in the hope of becoming an astronaut, users of *Impact* also read and learn about young people like themselves who are making a difference.

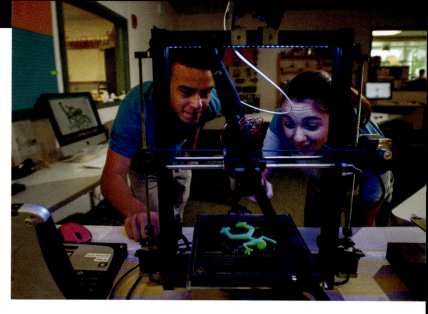

21st-century Skills

In our increasingly interconnected world, exposure to 21st-century topics and ideas is essential to student success. In addition to key subjects such as English, world languages, arts, mathematics, economics, science, geography and history, 21st-century students must also develop an awareness and understanding of topics such as:

- Global awareness

- Financial, economic, business and entrepreneurial literacy

- Civic literacy

- Health literacy

- Environmental literacy

- Learning and innovation skills

Impact provides students with rich opportunities to think deeply and critically about all of these topics and others. With the help of National Geographic Explorers, students explore ideas that span the globe and affect people of all ages and backgrounds. They ask and answer questions about food consumption and waste, unusual occupations, crisis management, the performing arts, planetary geology and collective behaviour, among many other topics.

In the process, *Impact* helps teens develop the skills that have been called the *4Cs*, and which are considered essential for success in the 21st century:

- Creativity and innovation

- Critical thinking and problem solving

- Communication

- Collaboration

Students are engaged in *thinking critically* about the choices they make and the problems that confront them. Together, they develop fact sheets, posters, videos or even advertisements that *communicate* their views to their peers and others. They consider the ways in which groups affect their behaviour and how, by *collaborating*, they can solve problems or accomplish goals. They analyse, compare and offer their own views. They also engage with a range of media and technology in order to *create* their own narratives. Students using *Impact* are challenged in every lesson and activity to think creatively, critically and innovatively, and to communicate and collaborate as a matter of course.

We live in a technology- and media-driven environment characterised by immediately available information and constantly evolving technology. Learning and innovation skills beyond the *4Cs* are needed for the complex life and work environments students will face in today's world. In addition to the ability to collaborate and to make individual contributions, students must also be able to master a range of functional skills such as:

- Life and career skills

- ICT (Information and Communication Technology) literacy

- Information literacy

- Media literacy

With *Impact*, teens develop new ways of thinking, new ways of working, new skills for living fuller and more responsible lives, and a range of ICT skills that they can use in their education and careers.

Skills and Strategies

In addition to the 4*Cs*, the four domains of listening, speaking, reading and writing, and the ICT skills necessary for success in the 21st century, today's students need to develop content knowledge and social and emotional competencies to navigate complex life and work environments, and skills and strategies to help them navigate their academic environments.

Each unit of *Impact* includes direct, explicit strategy instruction to help students effectively use English for academic and future success, and to express their views in appropriate ways.

Impact helps adolescent English learners navigate language challenges by presenting real-world situations that 21st-century students encounter every day. All speaking strategies are presented and practised in authentic contexts. For example, students might compare and contrast their parents and discuss how alike or unlike they are, or they may tell a surprising story to a partner, parts of which might be true or untrue, with the partner using expressions of surprise, such as 'That's amazing!' or 'Wow! Really?' to respond.

Speaking strategies in *Impact* include:

- Extending the conversation
- Asking for help with schoolwork
- Expressing strong opinions
- Asking for repetition and clarification
- Expressing surprise or disbelief
- Arguing and conceding
- Offering, accepting and declining advice
- Expressing interpretation and understanding

Supporting Reading Instruction

Reading is arguably the single most important skill for academic success. At this stage in their learning, adolescents are exposed to longer and more complex texts in all of their academic subjects. *Impact* provides an explicit focus on developing effective reading strategies that will not only be helpful when reading English texts, but will also help students become more effective readers of content in their own or other languages.

Each Reading lesson in your *Impact* Lesson Planner is presented in a three-step instructional plan: **Before reading**, **While reading** and **After reading**. During the lesson, students are directed to use a range of strategies before, while and after they read.

Before reading Students may be asked to talk with a partner about what they already know about a topic and related vocabulary, or, based on the title and photo, to predict what the text will be about or what they expect to learn from it.

While reading Students are given prompts that help them self-monitor and focus while they read. As effective readers, they're asked, for example, to notice details that support their beliefs, to look for similarities and differences, or to notice the order in which events happened.

After reading Readers may be asked to work in small groups to discuss a main idea, to recall important facts, to discuss the relationship of the text to their own lives, or to evaluate or comment on the text. They might be asked to identify possible good ideas not included in the reading.

Reading strategies in *Impact* include:

- Comparing and contrasting
- Scanning a text
- Making a personal connection
- Visualising
- Identifying a sequence of events
- Drawing conclusions
- Summarising
- Identifying an author's purpose

Vocabulary

A balanced approach to vocabulary instruction includes explicit instruction of a limited number of well-chosen words, along with instruction in

strategies with which students can acquire words independently. *Impact* does both by introducing high-utility and academic vocabulary thematically, in context, within reading and listening activities, and by supporting students as they develop strategies for learning the vocabulary they need to communicate in English about a range of topics drawn from science, history, art and other areas of interest.

Vocabulary strategies in *Impact* include:

- The study of word parts such as prefixes, suffixes and word roots (including Greek and Latin roots)

- Using a dictionary to learn the most common meaning of a word, how to pronounce it, etc.

- Recognising common English collocations

- Identifying multiple-meaning words

- Using context clues to discover meaning

Research has shown that at least seven to twelve exposures are needed to begin to 'know' a word in terms of its literal definition, its relationship to other words, its connotations and its power of transformation into other forms. Students who can master these different aspects of knowing a word have deep vocabulary knowledge, and students who are familiar with many words have breadth of vocabulary knowledge. *Impact* helps students develop broad, deep vocabulary knowledge by providing multiple exposures to target vocabulary in contextualised activities that include pair and group work, in addition to independent Workbook practice, audio activities, whiteboard activities and videos.

Vocabulary is a fundamental part of communicating and being understood, especially in another language. The sheer number of English words to be learnt – about a million – represents a major challenge for students. Social and academic vocabularies consist not simply of single words, but also of set phrases or chunks of words, many of which are learnt together and frequently used together. In order to succeed academically and socially, adolescent English learners must master both social and academic English. While an average English speaker learns about 1,000 words a year, at least until the age of 20, a non-English-speaking student who is trying to learn the language may be lucky to achieve 25% of that rate.

Impact presents the language students need for academic and social success in highly contextualised, real-world settings. It supports vocabulary development with direct, explicit instruction in vocabulary strategies. Students learn to use common collocations in English, to break words into their component parts in order to work out their meanings, to identify the Greek and Latin roots of many English words, and to consult reference sources to find out how to correctly pronounce a new word or to confirm its meaning.

Types of Language in Impact

Target vocabulary High-utility, theme-related vocabulary that can be related to students' lives, relationships and studies at school. Target vocabulary is assessed.

Academic vocabulary The language of the classroom. Academic language plays an increasingly prominent role as students read to learn about science, social studies, maths and other areas of academic interest.

Content vocabulary Useful, theme-related vocabulary that allows students to discuss thematic content.

Related vocabulary Useful vocabulary that students might need at point of use, for example,

to describe a photo in the book.

Although *Impact* provides contextualised vocabulary and complete lesson plans for all vocabulary instruction, it's helpful for teachers to become familiar with simple routines that can be used to introduce or present new vocabulary words to students.

A simple vocabulary routine

- Display and pronounce the word. Images are powerful aids to comprehension.

- Introduce the meaning of the word with a student-friendly explanation (vs. a standard dictionary definition).

- Illustrate with examples and sample sentences.

- Check for understanding by asking students to actively use vocabulary.

- Encourage wordplay.

Pronunciation

Impact includes a pronunciation topic in each unit. The pronunciation syllabus covers basic topics like the pronunciation of schwa, reductions and pronunciation of -*ed* endings. There is a strong focus on discourse-level suprasegmental features, such as stress, intonation and connected speech. The goal is to help students to be better understood by and to better understand English speakers.

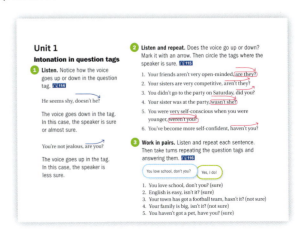

Impact's Videos

Video is a powerful tool that can help bring the world into the classroom – and bring the classroom to life! Because video allows students to view and listen to authentic representations of content, it can be a powerful tool for teachers and an especially useful aid for language learners.

In each unit of *Impact*, students encounter two short videos:

- **Main video** The main video in each unit introduces a key concept of the unit theme in a unique way, either through live-action National Geographic content or through an original animation created for this series. Each main video reviews target unit vocabulary and grammar, and exposes students to authentic communication. Corresponding Student's Book pages and activities provide opportunities for students to discuss and critically engage with the material.

- **Meet the Explorer** When students reach the 'Mission' page of each unit, they'll learn even more about the National Geographic Explorer whose mission both drives the unit theme and encourages students to be active participants in their learning. These short one-minute clips reinforce unit objectives, develop critical thinking skills and allow students to hear from each explorer in his or her own words.

The videos in *Impact* introduce students to real people using English in real ways. They provide a richer environment for learning and engage 21st-century teens who are motivated by content that both informs and entertains. More importantly, building students' media and digital literacy skills prepares them to use English both inside and outside the classroom.

Classroom Management

Classroom atmosphere Effective teachers take care to build a fair, safe and supportive classroom climate. As supportive adults rather than friends, they aim for positive relationships with all their students and consciously avoid favouritism. They have high but reasonable expectations and model the values they hope to inspire in their students – kindness, patience, fairness and respect.

Classroom rules and expectations The establishment of rules is particularly important because students need rules to function successfully. Brainstorm classroom rules with your students at the beginning of the year so that they know what's expected of them and feel responsible for following the rules. It's important to share and communicate rules clearly and simply, and to make sure they're consistently enforced with age-appropriate rewards and sanctions.

Managing You Decide activities A balance of independence and support is important to adolescent learners. They respond well to having a choice of activities and to deciding whether they want to work independently or in pairs or groups.

When given choices, adolescents also need clear direction and support from peers and teachers.

By providing students with real choices in activities and projects, *Impact* actively supports learner autonomy.
You Decide activities are an important feature of *Impact* and carry an important message: given the right support and materials, students can and shoud be accountable and responsible for their own learning.

Writing

Impact introduces students to a variety of writing genres and gives them multiple opportunities to express themselves in writing. Young teens are systematically introduced to academic writing starting in Level 1. They move from descriptive paragraphs to other types of paragraphs, and on to short essays.

In Levels 2–4, students are introduced to common academic writing genres, including Classification, Cause and Effect, Narration, Biography, Persuasion, Review, and Compare and Contrast, among others.

Scaffolded support For each writing assignment in the Student's Book, students are guided step by step in the Workbook. A complete model is provided for the writing task in each unit, so that learners have clear, meaningful examples of what they're expected to do.

Worksheets Optional Genre worksheets provide support for the academic writing genres presented in *Impact*. These include the genres listed above. Optional Process Writing worksheets guide students through the five steps: Pre-writing, Writing a First Draft, Revising, Editing and Proofreading, and Publishing.

In addition, common real-world genres are presented throughout the course in You Decide activities and projects, in Express Yourself, in the Workbook and in all course components. These include blogs, letters, presentations, travel reviews, poems, film scripts and brochures.

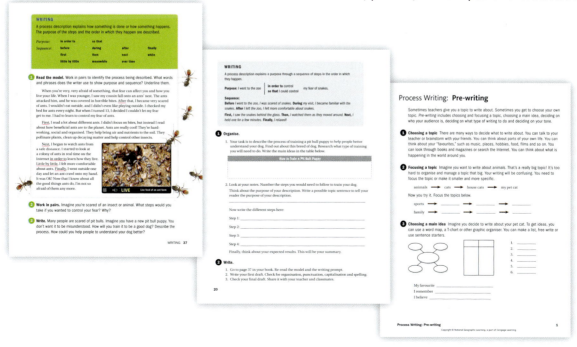

Assessment in *Impact*

Assessment should always mirror learning. Tests should reflect curriculum objectives and provide students with opportunities to demonstrate what they know and what they can do, in tasks and formats that are similar to what they've experienced in class. Tests should also contribute to learning on the part of both teacher and student. Assessment results should provide teachers with information on which to base subsequent instruction, especially modifications that are needed for some or all students. And, of course, the results should provide information to learners on their current strengths and weaknesses, as well as their progress in learning English.

Assessment should include a variety of techniques that correspond to learners' abilities and learning styles. That is to say, assessments should provide opportunities for learners who are not primarily linguistically, logical-mathematically or spatially inclined to demonstrate other types of intelligence or learning styles. All learners should have multiple chances to demonstrate their skills, abilities and knowledge.

Assessment should motivate learners and build learner confidence. Teachers work hard to include a variety of motivating and engaging activities in their lessons, and they're conscientious about providing praise and constructive feedback to their students in class. Students should have the same opportunities for fun, engagement and motivating feedback in assessments.

Finally, it's important to note that tests should take place over time in order to collect evidence of growth. Assessment should not be approached as an occasional but necessary, fear-inducing evil. Indeed, the more frequently students are assessed through a variety of ways, the less test anxiety they may have, and the more practised and confident they may feel.

Impact Assessment Options *Impact* ensures that students engage in a wide variety of communicative activities in each thematic unit, and many of these themes and activity types are correspondingly reflected in the assessment process. *Impact* provides many opportunities for both formal and informal assessment of different types. The *Impact* assessment programme includes various kinds of written tests: placement tests and level pre-tests, eight unit quizzes, two mastery tests and final tests, together with an Audio CD for listening and speaking assessment.

Formal assessment in *Impact* is provided in the form of *ExamView*® test banks. Banks include test items that allow teachers to create a pre-test for use at the beginning of the school year, unit quizzes, mastery tests and a final exam. A placement test is also provided. In addition, with the use of the Assessment CD-ROM with *ExamView*®, all of the quizzes and tests are easily generated and customisable to the needs of each teacher's students. **Formative assessment** opportunities appear at the end of each lesson and align directly to that lesson's objectives.

Accurate assessment reflects not only what students can recognise and produce on a written test, but also what they can perform or do as they actually use the language in real or realistic contexts. *Impact* therefore provides a wealth of opportunities for **informal assessment**. These include pair and group work, review pages in the Student's Book, Workbook activities and the Classroom Presentation Tool, among others. Many of the products students create, including end-of-unit projects, may also be assembled as part of a **portfolio assessment** system.

Pacing Guides

2–3 hours per week

Use Warm Up and Consolidate sections from the Lesson Planner or replace with your own Warm Up and Consolidate activities.

Week 1	Week 2	Week 3	Week 4	Week 9*
Unit Opener: Introduce the Unit **Vocabulary:** Warm Up; Present; Practise; Apply; Consolidate **Resources** · Student's Book · Workbook/Online Workbook · Audio (Audio CD/Website/CPT) · Classroom Presentation Tool: Unit Opener and Vocabulary **Speaking Strategy:** Warm Up; Present; Practise; Apply; Consolidate **Resources** · Student's Book · Online Workbook · Audio (Audio CD/Website/CPT) · Classroom Presentation Tool: Speaking Strategy	**Grammar 1:** Warm Up; Present; Practise; Apply; Consolidate **Resources** · Student's Book · Workbook/Online Workbook · Audio (Audio CD/Website/CPT) · Classroom Presentation Tool: Grammar 1 **Reading:** Warm Up; Before You Read; While You Read; After You Read; Consolidate **Resources** · Student's Book · Workbook/Online Workbook · Audio (Audio CD/Website/CPT) · Classroom Presentation Tool: Reading	**Video:** Before You Watch; While You Watch; After You Watch **Resources** · Student's Book · Online Workbook · Video (DVD/Online Workbook/CPT) · Classroom Presentation Tool: Video **Grammar 2:** Warm Up; Present; Practise; Apply; Consolidate **Resources** · Student's Book · Workbook/Online Workbook · Audio (Audio CD/Website/CPT) · Classroom Presentation Tool: Grammar 2	**Writing:** Warm Up; Present; Read the Model; Plan; Write **Mission:** Mission **Project:** Prepare **Resources** · Student's Book · Workbook/Online Workbook · Process Writing / Genre Writing Worksheets (Teacher's Resource CD-ROM/Website) · Video (DVD/Online Workbook/CPT) · Classroom Presentation Tool: Writing **Project** (continued): Share **Assessment** **Resources** · Student's Book · Classroom Presentation Tool: Project and Review Games · Unit Quiz (*ExamView*®)	**Express Yourself:** Present; Practise; Connect; Prepare **Resources** · Student's Book · Audio (Audio CD/Website/CPT) · Classroom Presentation Tool: Express Yourself **Express Yourself** (continued): Share **Resources** · Classroom Presentation Tool: Express Yourself *Express Yourself gives students an opportunity to synthesise what they have learnt and focus on creative expression after every two units. The Express Yourself for Units 1 and 2 will be covered in Week 9.

Pacing Guides

3–4 hours per week

Extend activities, including Extend Worksheets, are optional.

Week 1	Week 2	Week 3	Week 4	Week 9*
Unit Opener: Introduce the Unit; Extend **Vocabulary:** Warm Up; Present; Practise **Resources** · Student's Book · Extend Worksheets (Teacher's Resource CD-ROM/Website) · Audio (Audio CD/Website/CPT) · Classroom Presentation Tool: Unit Opener **Vocabulary** *(continued)***:** Apply; Extend; Consolidate **Resources** · Student's Book · Workbook/Online Workbook · Extend Worksheets (Teacher's Resource CD-ROM/Website CPT) · Classroom Presentation Tool: Vocabulary **Speaking Strategy:** Warm Up; Present; Practise; Apply; Extend; Consolidate **Resources** · Student's Book · Workbook/Online Workbook · Extend Worksheets (Teacher's Resource CD-ROM/Website CPT) · Audio (Audio CD/Website/CPT) · Classroom Presentation Tool: Speaking Strategy	**Grammar 1:** Warm Up; Present; Practise **Resources** · Student's Book · Workbook/Online Workbook · Audio (Audio CD/Website/CPT) · Classroom Presentation Tool: Grammar 1 **Grammar 1** *(continued)***:** Apply; Extend; Consolidate **Resources** · Student's Book · Workbook/Online Workbook · Audio (Audio CD/Website/CPT) · Classroom Presentation Tool: Grammar 1 **Reading:** Warm Up; Before You Read; While You Read **Resources** · Student's Book · Workbook/Online Workbook · Audio (Audio CD/Website/CPT) · Classroom Presentation Tool: Reading	**Reading** *(continued)***:** After You Read; Extend; Consolidate **Resources** · Student's Book · Workbook/Online Workbook · Extend Worksheets (Teacher's Resource CD-ROM/Website) · Classroom Presentation Tool: Reading **Video:** Before You Watch; While You Watch; After You Watch **Resources** · Student's Book · Online Workbook · Video (DVD/Online Workbook/CPT) · Classroom Presentation Tool: Video **Grammar 2:** Warm Up; Present; Practise; Apply; Extend; Consolidate **Resources** · Student's Book · Workbook/Online Workbook · Extend Worksheets (Teacher's Resource CD-ROM/Website) · Audio (Audio CD/Website/CPT) · Classroom Presentation Tool: Grammar 2	**Writing:** Warm Up; Present; Read the Model; Plan; Write **Resources** · Student's Book · Workbook/Online Workbook · Process Writing / Genre Writing Worksheets (Teacher's Resource CD-ROM/Website) · Classroom Presentation Tool: Writing **Writing** *(continued)***:** Revise; Edit and Proofread; Publish **Mission:** Mission **Project:** Prepare **Resources** · Student's Book · Process Writing / Genre Writing Worksheets (Teacher's Resource CD-ROM/Website) · Video (DVD/Online Workbook) · Classroom Presentation Tool: Writing **Project** *(continued)***:** Share **Assessment** **Resources** · Student's Book · Classroom Presentation Tool: Project · Unit Quiz (*ExamView®*)	**Express Yourself:** Present; Practise; Connect **Resources** · Student's Book · Audio (Audio CD/Website/CPT) · Classroom Presentation Tool: Express Yourself **Express Yourself** *(continued)***:** Prepare **Cumulative Review** **Resources** · Student's Book · Classroom Presentation Tool: Express Yourself · Cumulative Review Worksheets (Teacher's Resource CD-ROM/Website) **Express Yourself** *(continued)***:** Share **Resources** · Student's Book · Classroom Presentation Tool: Express Yourself · Unit Quiz (*ExamView®*) *Express Yourself gives students an opportunity to synthesise what they have learnt and focus on creative expression after every two units. The Express Yourself for Units 1 and 2 will be covered in Week 9.

Pacing Guides

5–6 hours per week

Week 1	Week 2	Week 3	Week 4	Week 9*
Unit Opener: Introduce the Unit; Extend **Resources** · Student's Book · Extend Worksheets (Teacher's Resource CD-ROM/Website) · Classroom Presentation Tool: Unit Opener **Vocabulary:** Warm Up; Present; Practise **Resources** · Student's Book · Workbook/Online Workbook · Audio (Audio CD/Website/CPT) · Classroom Presentation Tool: Vocabulary **Vocabulary** *(continued)*: Apply; Extend; Consolidate **Resources** · Student's Book · Workbook/Online Workbook · Extend Worksheets (Teacher's Resource CD-ROM/Website) · Classroom Presentation Tool: Vocabulary **Speaking Strategy:** Warm Up; Present; Practise; Apply; Extend; Consolidate **Resources** · Student's Book · Online Workbook · Extend Worksheets (Teacher's Resource CD-ROM/Website) · Audio (Audio CD/Website/CPT) · Classroom Presentation Tool: Speaking Strategy	**Grammar 1:** Warm Up; Present; Practise **Resources** · Student's Book · Workbook/Online Workbook · Audio (Audio CD/Website/CPT) · Classroom Presentation Tool: Grammar 1 **Grammar 1** *(continued)*: Apply; Extend; Consolidate **Resources** · Student's Book · Workbook/Online Workbook · Audio (Audio CD/Website/CPT) · Classroom Presentation Tool: Grammar 1 **Reading:** Warm Up; Before You Read; While You Read **Resources** · Student's Book · Workbook/Online Workbook · Audio (Audio CD/Website/CPT) · Classroom Presentation Tool: Reading **Reading** *(continued)*: After You Read; Extend; Consolidate **Resources** · Student's Book · Workbook/Online Workbook · Extend Worksheets (Teacher's Resource CD-ROM/Website) · Classroom Presentation Tool: Reading	**Video:** Before You Watch; While You Watch; After You Watch **Resources** · Student's Book · Online Workbook · Video (DVD/Online Workbook/CPT) · Classroom Presentation Tool: Video **Grammar 2:** Warm Up; Present; Practise; Apply; Extend; Consolidate **Resources** · Student's Book · Workbook/Online Workbook · Extend Worksheets (Teacher's Resource CD-ROM/Website) · Audio (Audio CD/Website/CPT) · Classroom Presentation Tool: Grammar 2 **Writing:** Warm Up; Present; Read the Model; Plan; Write **Resources** · Student's Book · Workbook/Online Workbook · Process Writing / Genre Writing Worksheets (Teacher's Resource CD-ROM/Website) · Classroom Presentation Tool: Writing **Writing** *(continued)*: Revise; Edit and Proofread; Publish **Resources** · Student's Book · Workbook/Online Workbook · Process Writing / Genre Writing Worksheets (Teacher's Resource CD-ROM/Website) · Classroom Presentation Tool: Writing	**Mission:** Mission **Project:** Prepare **Resources** · Student's Book · Extend Worksheets (Teacher's Resource CD-ROM/Website) · Video (DVD/Online Workbook/CPT) · Classroom Presentation Tool: Mission and Project **Unit Review** **Resources** · Unit Review Worksheets (Teacher's Resource CD-ROM/Website) · Classroom Presentation Tool: Review Games **Project** *(continued)*: Share **Resources** · Student's Book · Classroom Presentation Tool: Project **Assessment** **Resources** · Unit Quiz (*ExamView®*)	**Express Yourself:** Present; Practise; Connect **Resources** · Student's Book · Audio (Audio CD/Website/CPT) · Classroom Presentation Tool: Express Yourself **Express Yourself** *(continued)*: Prepare **Resources** · Student's Book · Classroom Presentation Tool: Express Yourself **Express Yourself** *(continued)*: Share **Resources** · Student's Book · Classroom Presentation Tool: Express Yourself **Cumulative Review** **Resources** · Cumulative Review Worksheets (Teacher's Resource CD-ROM/Website) *Express Yourself gives students an opportunity to synthesise what they have learnt and focus on creative expression after every two units. The Express Yourself for Units 1 and 2 will be covered in Week 9.

Scope and Sequence

1 Life in the City

2 Amazing Jobs

	1 Life in the City	**2 Amazing Jobs**
THEME	Exploring your city or town	Unusual and interesting careers
LANGUAGE OBJECTIVES	· Talk about cities and the different types of life in the city · Show that you're listening actively · Use the present simple to talk about the facts · Use *in* and *on* to express location · Write about a place using describing words	· Talk about jobs and the routines they involve · Show that you can extend the conversation · Use the present simple tense to ask and answer questions about job routines · Use possessives to show ownership · Write a descriptive paragraph about someone's routine
VOCABULARY	architecture, capital, construct, design, indoor, plan, resident, shape, skyscraper, surrounded by, symbol, tower, unique, rural, unusual, urban, bridge, motorway, pavement, stream, concrete, land, outdoor, park **Vocabulary Strategies:** · Prefix *un-* · Use context	adventure, archaeologist, career, clue, consider, explore, job, office, passion, profession, study, take risks, train, work, choice, dangerous, researcher, apply for, employee, interview, schedule, skills, advisor, commute, create, photographer, scientist **Vocabulary Strategies:** · Suffixes *-er, -or,* and *-ist* · Identify word parts (suffixes)
SPEAKING STRATEGY	Active listening	Active listening
GRAMMAR	**Present simple:** Talking about facts *I live near the High Line.* **In and on:** Expressing location *Lion City is in eastern China.* *China is on the continent of Asia.*	**Present simple questions and answers:** Talking about routines *Do pastry chefs work every day?* *Yes, they do./No, they don't.* **Possessives:** Showing ownership *This dentist's job isn't done in an office.*
READING	*A New Type of Park* Can the capital of England become a national park? **Reading Strategy:** Make predictions	*Adventures Near and Far* These explorers love working in extreme places. **Reading Strategy:** Compare and contrast
VIDEO	*Mission Re-Wild*	*Searching for Life in Iceland's Fissures*
MISSION	**Explore Your World** National Geographic Explorer: **Daniel Raven-Ellison**, Guerilla Geographer	**Do What You Love** National Geographic Explorer: **Guillermo de Anda**, Underwater Archaeologist
WRITING	Genre: **Descriptive paragraph** Focus: Use adjectives	Genre: **Descriptive paragraph** Focus: Identify and include elements of a paragraph
PROJECT	· Survey · Scavenger hunt · Newspaper article	· Job advert · Comic strip · Job fair
PRONUNCIATION	Syllables and stress	Intonation in questions
EXPRESS YOURSELF	Creative Expression: **Travel review** *Gondola Tours of Venice* Making connections: Unusual places and unusual jobs	

3 Secrets of the Dark

4 Living Together

	3 Secrets of the Dark	4 Living Together
THEME	The world at night	Animal and human interactions
LANGUAGE OBJECTIVES	· Talk about night, darkness and nocturnal activities · Ask for and give help with schoolwork · Use the present continuous to say what is happening now · Use *at*, *on*, and *in* to talk about when things happen · Write about an event using sensory details	· Talk about interactions between animals and humans · Ask for and give reasons · Use modals to describe obligation and advice · Use *can*, *can't*, *could*, and *couldn't* to describe ability in the present and past · Write about a relationship between an animal and a human, and edit and proofread writing

VOCABULARY

3 Secrets of the Dark

active
dark
darkness
festival
go to sleep
headlight
horizon
light up
north
south
sunrise
sunset

daylight
healthy
streetlight

asleep
awake
east
time zones
west

dawn
fascinate
glow

observe
pattern

Vocabulary Strategies:
· Compound words
· Use a dictionary: Most common meaning

4 Living Together

access
afraid of
behaviour
conflict
disappear
frighten
habitat
interact
learn
need
smart
wild
wildlife

hunt
mistreat
relationship
survival

defend
injured
predator
prey
rescue

avoid
chemical

domestic
feeling
sniff

Vocabulary Strategies:
· Prefix *mis-*
· Identify collocations

	3 Secrets of the Dark	4 Living Together
SPEAKING STRATEGY	Asking for help and helping with schoolwork	Asking for and giving reasons
GRAMMAR	**Present continuous:** Saying what is happening now *While I'm reading in bed at night in Mexico, my friend Akiko is reading at school in Japan!* **At, on, and in:** Saying when things happen *at eight o'clock, on Monday(s), in the winter.*	**Modals:** Describing obligation and advice *We have to protect rhinos.* *We shouldn't ignore the rhino problem.* **Modals:** Describing ability in present and past *What can we do about it?* *How could they avoid cars?*
READING	*In the Dark of the Ocean* There are incredible creatures living in the darkness. **Reading Strategy:** Scan the text	*Four-Legged Heroes* Animals with Amazing Abilities **Reading Strategy:** Identify problems and solutions
VIDEO	*What Glows Beneath*	*The Elephant Whisperers*
MISSION	**Understand and Protect** National Geographic Explorer: **David Gruber**, Marine Biologist	**Start Small** National Geographic Explorer: **Amy Dickman**, Animal Conservationist
WRITING	Genre: **Descriptive paragraph** Focus: Use sensory writing	Genre: **Descriptive paragraph** Focus: Proofread
PROJECT	· Poster · Blog entry · 'Day-and-night' video	· Poster or brochure · Presentation · Video interview
PRONUNCIATION	Present continuous: Stress of the verb *be*	*Can* and *can't*
EXPRESS YOURSELF	Creative Expression: **Graphic story** *Sleeping with a Lion* Making connections: Interactions between humans and animals at night	

5
What We Wear

6
Mix and Mash

	5 What We Wear	6 Mix and Mash
THEME	Clothing and accessories throughout history	Mash-ups
LANGUAGE OBJECTIVES	· Compare modern clothes with the clothes people wore in the past · Ask for opinions and agree or disagree · Use the past simple tense of regular verbs to describe the past · Use the past simple tense of irregular verbs to describe the past · Write a description of a uniform that has changed over time	· Talk about mash-ups · Clarify a point · Use adjectives to compare two or more things · Use countable and uncountable nouns to talk about amounts · Write a paragraph of exemplification about animal mash-ups
VOCABULARY	casual wear accessory century bracelet dress up denim necklace fashion fabric outfit formal replace wealth heel tights jeans **Vocabulary Strategies:** look bride · Prefix -re practical decorate · Use a dictionary: suit paint Pronunciation sweatshirt pierce tie tattoos uniform	audio video **Vocabulary Strategies:** cool · Words with DJ combine multiple meanings edit download · Use context: fan electronic Examples include hit mix opinion imagine perform imitate record modern recording original song weird traditional
SPEAKING STRATEGY	Asking for opinions; Agreeing and disagreeing	Clarifying a point
GRAMMAR	**Past simple:** Saying what happened *Ancient Greek women preferred golden hair to dark hair.* **Past simple:** Saying what happened *Doctors wore special protective suits.*	**Adjectives:** Comparing two or more things *Underwater hockey is more difficult than field hockey.* **Countable and uncountable nouns:** Talking about amounts *Some meals are a mix of food from different cultures.*
READING	*Jewellery Talks* How accessories help tell our stories **Reading Strategy:** Make a personal connection	*A Feast for the Eyes* Using food to create art **Reading Strategy:** Visualise
VIDEO	*What to Wear*	*What's in a Mash-Up?*
MISSION	**Learn to Adapt** National Geographic Explorer: **Andrés Ruzo**, Geoscientist	**Be Unique** National Geographic Explorer: **Josh Ponte**, Musical Explorer/Filmmaker
WRITING	Genre: **Descriptive paragraph** Focus: Publish	Genre: **Paragraph of exemplification** Focus: Introduce examples
PROJECT	· Design · Scavenger hunt · Presentation	· Food art · Hybrid sport · Comic strip
PRONUNCIATION	The -ed ending	Linking: Consonant + vowel sounds
EXPRESS YOURSELF	Creative Expression: **Feature article** *Get Steampunked* Making connections: Fashion mash-ups	

7
Cool Apps and Gadgets

8
Into the Past

	7 Cool Apps and Gadgets	8 Into the Past
THEME	Useful and interesting technology	Exploring the distant past
LANGUAGE OBJECTIVES	· Talk about the uses of technology · Make and respond to requests · Use superlatives to talk about extremes · Use *will* and *going to* to talk about the future · Write a review of a product	· Talk about the distant past · Use new phrases to check for understanding · Use the present perfect to describe a past action that still continues · Use *there + to be* to talk about existence · Write a classification paragraph about local festivals
VOCABULARY	app chat connect gadget game Internet look up mobile search send share smartphone useful Wi-Fi incredible possible tablet text battery camera keyboard microphone screen borrow find function invent **Vocabulary Strategies:** · Suffix *-ible* · Identify parts of speech	adult ancestor believe bone civilisation continue diet discover origin site skeleton skull species advanced back descendant helpful advice chess king piece queen age chore culture education teenager **Vocabulary Strategies:** · Suffix *-ful* · Context clues: Definitions and examples
SPEAKING STRATEGY	Making and responding to requests	Talking about likes and dislikes
GRAMMAR	**Superlatives:** Talking about extremes *The newest version of this game is going to be amazing.* ***Will* and *going to*:** Talking about the future *People won't talk to each other on smartphones anymore.*	**Present perfect:** Describing a past action that still continues *Games have always been a popular activity.* ***There + to be*:** Expressing existence at different points in time *There have always been sun celebrations around the world.*
READING	*Thinking Outside the Box* Creative teens can make a difference! **Reading Strategy:** Identify main idea and details	*Growing Up: Then and Now* How kids' lives have changed over the years **Reading Strategy:** Identify cause and effect
VIDEO	*From Gadgets to Apps*	*A Journey Back in Time*
MISSION	**Always Keep Learning** National Geographic Explorer: **Manu Prakash**, Biophysicist	**Understand the Past** National Geographic Explorer: **Alberto Nava Blank**, Underwater Cave Explorer/Cartographer
WRITING	Genre: **Product review** Focus: Use examples	Genre: **Classification paragraph** Focus: Writing a concluding sentence
PROJECT	· Presentation · Robot design · Outdated gadget museum	· Mancala game · Biographical poster · Sketch
PRONUNCIATION	The two-vowel rule	The schwa (/ə/) sound
EXPRESS YOURSELF	Creative Expression: **Letter for a time capsule** *Transportation of Tomorrow* Making connections: Past, present and future technology	

In This Unit

Theme This unit is about cities and the interesting green spaces in them waiting to be explored.

Content Objectives
Students will
- examine cities – the cities they know and ones they may never have heard of – and the interesting and surprising places in them.
- read about a plan to make London a national park city and discuss how they might change their own cities.
- discuss a geographer's ideas about discovering new things in familiar places.

Language Objectives
Students will
- talk about cities and the different types of life in the city.
- show that they're listening actively.
- use the present simple tense to talk about facts.
- use *in* and *on* to express location.
- write about a place using describing words.

Vocabulary
pages 10–11 *architecture, capital, construct, design, indoor, plan, resident, shape, skyscraper, surrounded by, symbol, tower, unique*
page 12 *rural, unusual, urban*
page 15 *bridge, motorway, pavement, stream*
page 16 *concrete, land, outdoor, park*
Vocabulary Strategies Base words and the prefix *un-*; Using a dictionary

Speaking Strategies Active listening

Grammar
Grammar 1 Use the present simple to talk about facts
Grammar 2 Use the prepositions *in* and *on* to express location

Reading *A New Type of Park*
Reading Strategy Making predictions

Video Scene 1.1: *Rewild;*
Scene 1.2: Meet Daniel Raven-Ellison

Writing Description of a place

National Geographic
Mission Explore Your World

Project
- Survey
- Scavenger hunt
- Newspaper article

Pronunciation Syllables and stress

Pacing Guides 1.1.1, 1.1.2, 1.1.3

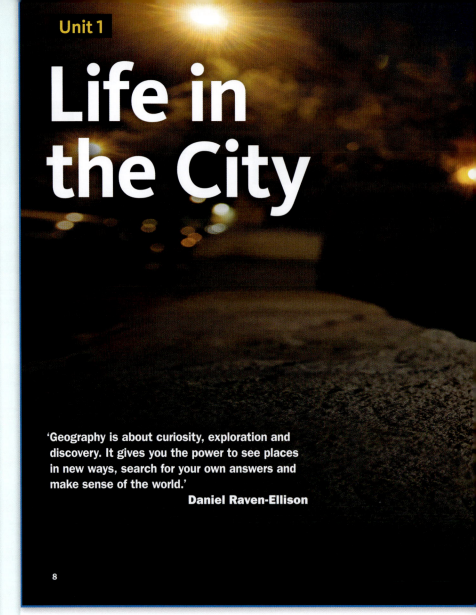

Life in the City

'Geography is about curiosity, exploration and discovery. It gives you the power to see places in new ways, search for your own answers and make sense of the world.'

Daniel Raven-Ellison

8

Introduce the Unit

- **Build background** Ask *Who has seen a wild animal in a city?* List the animals students have seen. Ask *Were you surprised to see a (fox) there? What did you think it was doing?* Explain that it's not unusual to see wild animals in cities. Wild animals explore towns and cities in order to find food in gardens and dustbins. There are also usually fewer predators in cities.

- **TO START** Ask students to open their books at pages 8–9. Ask *What animal is this a photo of?* (a fox) *Where is the fox?* (in the city) *What is the fox doing?* Discuss the image and the fact that the fox appears to be looking over a wall. Say *Imagine you're that fox.* Ask *What are you looking at? Are you scared? Curious?*

- Read the first question in item 1 on page 9 aloud to students. Ask students to share any experiences they may have had with foxes. Make sure you ask students who've never seen any urban wildlife to give their answers, too.

- Tell students that Bristol is a city in England in the UK. Then ask questions to encourage further discussion of the photo:

A red fox exploring Bristol, UK

Objectives
Students will
• describe and discuss a photo.
• discuss exploring and their favourite places.

Resources Worksheet 1.1.1 (Teacher's Resource CD-ROM/Website); CPT: Unit Opener

Materials globe or map of the world (optional)

BE THE EXPERT

About the Photo

Bristol is the largest city in southwestern England, in the UK. Situated near the Atlantic coast, it's been a sea-trading centre since the Middle Ages. Foxes have been living in Bristol for decades, and efforts to control their population in the city have been unsuccessful. Some city residents consider the foxes to be pests, while others have come to enjoy their presence.

One man who spent months photographing urban foxes in Bristol said, 'The next time you see an urban fox in your city or village, take the time to watch this animal and show it respect as it is wild and should not be approached. Maybe you too will fall in love with this beautiful, adaptable and resourceful animal'.

Teaching Tip

Some students may remember an experience better if they act it out. Help students to remember details by asking such questions as *What happened first? Then what happened? When was it most exciting? How did it end?* Then tell students to act out the event. Help them describe it in words.

TO START

1. Look at the photo. If you saw this in person, would it surprise you? Why or why not?

2. The animal in the photo is exploring. Do you explore? Why is it good to explore a new place?

3. What is your favourite place? What do you do there? Why is this place special to you?

9

Where is the UK? (Europe)
Can you name other big cities around the world? (London, São Paulo, New York, Berlin, Mexico City, Delhi, Buenos Aires, Beijing)
Do you think there's wildlife in those cities?

• Invite a student to read item 2 aloud. Explain to students that when you explore, you discover things you didn't know before and expand your knowledge of the world.

• Draw students' attention to the quote on page 8 by Daniel Raven-Ellison. Read the quote aloud. Then say *Let's think about what Daniel means.*

• Read the questions in item 3 aloud and invite students to share their thoughts on their favourite places and why they're special to them.

Extend

• Hand out **Worksheet 1.1.1**. Put students into pairs. Explain that students will be thinking and writing about exploring and comparing their ideas with a partner.

Objectives
    Students will
    • use vocabulary related to cities and buildings.
    • use new vocabulary to read about and discuss the city of Astana, Kazakhstan.

Target Vocabulary *architecture, capital, construct, design, indoor, plan, resident, shape, skyscraper, surrounded by, symbol, tower, unique*

Academic Language *compare*

Content Vocabulary *competition, entertainment, nature, running track, water slide*

Resources Worksheet 1.1.2 (Teacher's Resource CD-ROM/Website); Tracks 002–003 (Audio CD/Website/CPT); CPT: Vocabulary

1 What makes Astana different from other cities? Discuss. Then listen and read. ∩ 002

The city of Astana is truly a **unique** place. It was **constructed** in 1997 to replace the city of Almaty as the **capital** of Kazakhstan. Almaty was in the south-eastern corner of the country, but the president of Kazakhstan wanted a new capital. So Astana was built right in the middle of the country. As a result, this modern city is **surrounded by** nothing but rural areas.

The unusual **architecture** of Astana makes it look like a space-age city. There are amazing **skyscrapers** and eye-catching buildings. A cultural centre looks like a big, blue eye. A university building has the **shape** of a dog bowl.

The Bayterek Tower in central Astana

10 VOCABULARY

Warm Up

• **Activate prior knowledge** Tell students they're going to read about the city of Astana, in the country of Kazakhstan. Astana was built in 1997 in an area far away from other cities and towns. Say *Many cities of the world have been centres of population and business for hundreds of years. Astana is practically brand-new!* Ask *Does anyone know the name of another major city that was built in 1956 in South America in a place with few people, animals or plants?* (Brasilia, Brazil). Tell students both cities were built by famous architects and are known for their modern buildings.

• Start a web on the board like this one with *City* in the centre oval. Ask *What makes a city a city? What do we expect to see in a city?* Say *I expect to see tall buildings when I go to a big city.* Write *tall buildings* in the web. Then ask *What else can you see in a city?*

Ask students to help you fill in the web. Add other ovals if necessary.

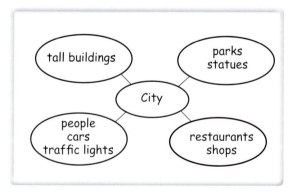

Present

• Ask students to open their books at pages 10–11. Ask *Have you ever seen a place like this?* Point to different parts of the photo, and ask students to stand up and describe what they can see.

Another unusual building, the Bayterek **Tower**, is a **symbol** of the city. This tall structure is 105 m. (345 ft.) high and looks like an enormous tree with a golden egg inside.

A Japanese architect named Kisho Kurokawa won first prize in a competition to **design** and **plan** the new capital. He included many parks and public spaces to connect urban life with nature.

Astana has pleasant summers. But the weather can get very cold in the winter, with temperatures dropping to -40°C (-40°F). Because of its extreme climate, Astana offers a lot of **indoor** entertainment. A popular entertainment centre is the Khan Shatyr, or king's tent, the world's largest tent. Inside, there is a river for boating, a park, an indoor running track, a waterslide and even a sandy beach with palm trees! The **residents** of Astana can enjoy a variety of outdoor activities even when it's well below freezing.

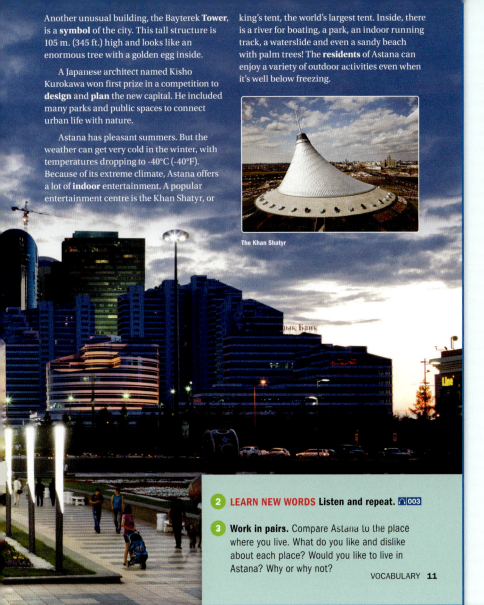

The Khan Shatyr

2 **LEARN NEW WORDS** Listen and repeat. 🎧 003

3 **Work in pairs.** Compare Astana to the place where you live. What do you like and dislike about each place? Would you like to live in Astana? Why or why not?

VOCABULARY **11**

Our World in Context

Most of Kazakhstan is in Central Asia. A small section in the west of the country is in the easternmost part of Europe. Kazakhstan borders Russia to the north and China to the southeast. The capital city, Astana, which means 'capital' in the Kazakh language, is the second coldest capital in the world. Kazakhstan is rich in oil and gas, and proceeds from the sale of these natural resources helped to finance the building of Astana.

Teaching Tip

If students are having difficulty with an assignment, avoid rushing in too quickly to help. It's natural for students to struggle when learning something new. Students will feel more of a sense of accomplishment when they do something difficult on their own. Give students enough time to work through the activity on their own, even if they find it difficult to do so.

Related Vocabulary

crane

• Ask a student to read aloud the Activity 1 question at the top of page 10. Point to the web on the board and ask *How many of these things can you find in the photo of Astana?* List students' responses.

• **1** Say *Let's find out what some of these buildings are.* Play **Track 002** and tell students to listen and read. Then discuss the reading with students. Ask questions such as:

What do you think 'eye-catching' means? (something that gets your attention; beautiful, spectacular)

What does 'indoor entertainment' refer to? (fun things to do inside a building)

What are 'outdoor activities'? (things you do outside, in the open)

• **2** **LEARN NEW WORDS** Play **Track 003**. Tell students to listen and repeat. Tell student pairs to take turns saying each word. Then put students into small groups. Write the vocabulary items on the board. Assign a few words to each group. Say *Work together. Write a new sentence for each of your words.*

• Model an example for students. Point to *architecture.* Write *Astana is famous for its modern architecture.* When students have finished, ask one person from each group to come to the front and read their sentences to the class.

VOCABULARY

Objectives

Students will

- practise using vocabulary related to cities and how one geographer explores them.
- use a vocabulary strategy to learn new vocabulary.

Target Vocabulary *rural, unusual, urban*

Vocabulary Strategy Base words and the prefix *un-*

Academic Language *compare, relating to*

Content Vocabulary *adventure*

Resources Online Workbook/Workbook pages 2–3; Worksheet 1.1.2 (Teacher's Resource CD-ROM/Website); Tracks 004–005 (Audio CD/Website/CPT); CPT: Vocabulary

Materials cameras, drawing materials

---

4 **Read and write the words from the list.** Make any necessary changes.

architecture	capital	outdoors	plan
resident	skyscraper	surrounded by	unique

Daniel Raven-Ellison has a very _____ unique _____ job: he's a guerrilla geographer. He loves exploring places and making discoveries. Daniel says that we are _____ surrounded by _____ interesting things just waiting to be discovered. According to him, _____ residents _____ of a place should keep exploring. They can make new discoveries even if they've lived in the same place their whole lives. Daniel _____ plans _____ all kinds of exciting adventures. In one adventure, he climbed more than 3,300 floors of the many tall _____ skyscrapers _____ in London. In another, he walked across Mexico City, the _____ capital _____ of Mexico. He photographed everything he saw in front of him every eight steps. He took photos of _____ architecture _____, streets and public spaces. He's done the same thing in 12 other cities!

5 **LEARN NEW WORDS** Listen to these words and match them with the definitions. Then listen and repeat.

rural	unusual	urban

_____ unusual _____   1. different or uncommon

_____ rural _____   2. relating to the countryside

_____ urban _____   3. relating to the city

6 **YOU DECIDE** Choose an activity.

1. **Work independently.** Go on a discovery walk outdoors. Find things that are hard, soft, sticky, brown, pink, small, big or smelly. Take photos and present your experience to the class.

2. **Work in pairs.** Think of two adventures you can have near your home. Why would you choose these adventures? What can you learn from them?

3. **Work independently.** Walk through your school building and take photographs every eight steps. What interesting things do you see? Create a photo book of your discoveries.

Daniel Raven-Ellison

12 VOCABULARY

Practise ③ ④ ⑤

- **③** Put students into pairs. Say *Think about Astana and its unique buildings. Think about the place where you live.* Ask *Are the two places alike in any way?* Ask pairs to read and complete Activity 3 on page 11. Say *Try to use your new words as you talk about the two places.*

- **④** Ask students to turn to page 12. Choose several students to read the words in the word box aloud and use them to make sentences. Then point to the photo of Daniel Raven-Ellison. Say *Daniel is called a 'guerrilla geographer' because he explores places in unusual ways.* Tell students to complete Activity 4 independently. Ask someone to come to the front and read the completed paragraph aloud.

- **⑤** **LEARN NEW WORDS** Read the words in the box. Tell students they've heard and read these words before. Challenge student pairs to find the words in context in the reading on pages 10–11. Then play **Track 004** while students listen. Ask students to pronounce each new word and use it in a sentence. Then play **Track 005**, and ask students to listen and repeat. Review word meanings, then tell students to complete Activity 5 independently.

- **Vocabulary Strategy** Write *unusual* on the board. Cover the prefix *un-*. Ask *What word is left if you take away u–n?* (*usual*) Tell students *usual* is the base word. Uncover *un* and circle it. Say *This word part is called a prefix. Prefixes have their own meanings, and when a prefix is added to a base word, it changes the base word's meaning. Un- means 'not'. Usual means 'normal'. When* un- *is added to* usual, *it changes the word to* unusual, *and the meaning to 'not normal'.* Ask *What other word can you see in Activity 5 that begins with* un-? (*uncommon*) Write the following examples on the board. Then ask students to suggest other words with *un-* and add them to the board. Discuss their meanings.

Apply

- **6** **YOU DECIDE** Tell students to silently read the Activity 6 options on page 12. Say *All of these activities have to do with exploring and making discoveries. Before choosing, think about each activity, what you need to do it and what you might learn from it.*

- Students who choose options 1 and 2 can do the activities after school. For students who want to take photographs in the school building, you may need to obtain permission beforehand and possibly arrange for someone to supervise the students. Allow time for students to present their discoveries to the class. Tell each student to answer the questions, *What did you learn from your experience? What was your most surprising discovery?*

Extend

- Tell students who chose options 1 and 3 to display their photos all together. Divide the class into small groups. Give groups time to compare the photos for both activities. Tell them to take notes. Ask *Were any of the photographs of the same things? What were they? Did they choose good examples of things that were hard, soft, smelly, interesting and so on? Were you surprised by any of the students' choices? Why?* Tell groups to discuss their ideas. Finally, invite the individuals themselves to explain why they chose the things they photographed.

- If time allows, hand out **Worksheet 1.1.2.** Explain that students will use vocabulary items to write about and discuss capital cities and their buildings.

Consolidate

- Write the following words on the board: *skyscraper, egg, tree, dog bowl, symbol, tent, eye, tower.*

- Say *Draw a picture of a new building for your city or town. Choose ideas from the board to include in your drawing. Give the building a name and write a short sentence saying what kind of building it would be.* Invite students to present their work. Then ask the class to discuss which drawing includes the most ideas from the board.

Objective

Students will
• use active listening words and phrases.

Speaking Strategy Active listening

Academic Language *active listening*

Content Vocabulary *music hall*

Resources Worksheet 1.1.3 (Teacher's Resource CD-ROM/Website); Tracks 006–007 (Audio CD/Website/CPT); CPT: Speaking Strategy

SPEAKING STRATEGY ∩ 006

Active listening

Really?	You're kidding!
Wow!	Seriously?
No way!	That's incredible!

1 **Listen.** How do the speakers show they're listening actively? Write the words and phrases you hear. ∩ 007

2 **Read and complete the dialogue.**

Possible answers:

Dad: Meiling, look at this. I found this old map of our city. It's more than 100 years old.

Meiling: _____ *Seriously?* _____ Let me see.

Dad: This building was a hospital. It's a music hall now.

Meiling: _____ *That's incredible!* _____

Dad: I know! And this was the old library.

Meiling: _____ *You're kidding!* _____ Now it's a tall skyscraper.

Dad: And look. This was a park.

Meiling: _____ *Wow! That's amazing!* _____ It's my school now!

Dad: Hey, let's go for a walk. We can take the map and look for other changes.

Meiling: Great idea! I'll bring my camera and take some photos.

3 **Work in groups.** Take turns. Choose a card. Read the question and the possible answers. Group members guess the correct answer and use active listening to respond to the real answer.

One million? That's amazing!

How many ants are there for every person in the world?
A. one thousand
B. one million
C. six million

Go to page 153.

4 **Work in pairs.** Think of an interesting place, thing or event in your neighbourhood, and describe it to your partner. Your partner should use the words and phrases above to show active listening. When you finish, swap roles.

SPEAKING **13**

Warm Up

• **Activate prior knowledge** Say *Pretend for a minute that you know nothing about Astana, and I told you I read about a city that has one building that looks like a big blue eye and another that looks like a dog bowl. What might you say to me?* (Really? You're kidding!) List appropriate responses on the board.

• **Model** Ask a student to come to the front and role-play a short conversation describing the Bayterek Tower or the Khan Shatyr in Astana. Use some of the language on the board to respond. Show expression in your voices.

Really?	Seriously?
You're kidding!	No way!
That's incredible!	Wow!

Present 1

• Point to the expressions on the board. Say *This is how we respond when someone tells us something so surprising or unusual that we're not sure it's true.* Say *When we respond in one of these ways to what someone is saying, we show we're listening carefully.* Ask students to open their books at page 13. Play **Track 006**.

• Play **Track 006** again. Tell students to listen and read. Then put students into pairs, and tell them to role-play conversations in which one partner tells the other something surprising. Write *interesting, amazing* and *unbelievable* on the board, and tell students they can also use these words in an expression like 'That's incredible!'

• 1 Say *Now listen as one person tells another some interesting information about Daniel Raven-Ellison.*

You'll hear some of the active listening words and phrases we've talked about. Write them down. Play **Track 007**. When students have finished listening and writing, tell them to review the expressions as a class.

Practise

• Once students seem comfortable using the active listening words and phrases, draw their attention to Activity 8. Ask students to work independently to complete Meiling's responses with the expressions they've heard and read.

• Ask several students to read their completed dialogues aloud. Tell them to take turns as Meiling and her father. Ask *Did the partners' voices show strong feeling? Did Meiling use active listening in her responses? What words and phrases did she use?*

Apply

• Put students into groups. Then tell students to cut out the cards on page 153. Each group will use one set of cards, shuffled and placed face down. Say *After group members guess, the person who picked the card reads the answer. Use active listening words and phrases to respond.*

• Say *You've used active listening words and phrases to respond to surprising or interesting facts about other places. Now you'll tell a partner something about where you live.* Ask a student to read the directions for Activity 4 aloud. Then put students into pairs. If students need help, suggest some topics: an unusual building or statue, or an annual parade or other event.

Extend

• Divide the class into small groups. Give each group a set of the cards from Activity 3, but don't include the ant and spider cards. Each group should set them face down in a pile. Say *Let's see how good your memories are! You'll take a card and make a new question using the information on the card.*

• Model making new questions, but tell students not to call out the answers. Say, for example, *What city has a train called the 'Doorway Railway'?* Tell students to take turns until all the cards have been used and answered correctly.

• If time allows, hand out **Worksheet 1.1.3**. Explain that students will use the worksheet to role-play a conversation with a partner for additional practice using active listening words and phrases.

Consolidate

• Prepare index cards with the following written on them: *Astana, unusual, architecture, design, tower, unique.* Put students into pairs and give each partner two or three cards, but not the same ones. Tell pairs to take turns saying a sentence with an interesting fact about Astana, including the word on their card, and any other vocabulary words that make sense.

Strategy in Depth

Speakers want listeners to demonstrate active listening by responding appropriately to what they're saying. Active listening can be conveyed non-verbally as well as verbally. Non-verbal indications of active listening include making eye contact, smiling, nodding in agreement, and using facial expressions to show interest, surprise or disbelief.

Verbal expressions of active listening can be a fun way for students to practise language. They provide opportunities to speak in dramatic or humorous tones or to express strong feeling.

Formative Assessment

Can students
• use active listening words and phrases?

Ask students to respond to the following:

Did you know that Yakutsk, Russia, is the coldest city in the world? The lowest temperature recorded there was 84 degrees below zero! (-64.4 °C or -83.9 °F) People can't wear glasses outside in the winter because the metal freezes to their skin. If they tried to take them off, their skin would come off, too!

Objectives

Students will

- recognise the form, meaning and use of the present simple.
- use the present simple to talk about facts.
- identify and use words associated with an urban park in South Korea.

Grammar Present simple: Talking about facts

Target Vocabulary *bridge, motorway, pavement, stream*

Academic Language *fact, present simple form*

Content Vocabulary *cultural, green space, mayor, traditional, water and light shows*

Pronunciation Syllables and stress

Resources Online Workbook/Workbook pages 4–5; Tracks 008–011, Tracks 116–118 (Audio CD/Website/CPT); CPT: Grammar 1 and Pronunciation; Pronunciation Answer Key (Teacher's Resource CD-ROM/Website)

Materials pieces of card

GRAMMAR 🔊008

Present simple: Talking about facts

I **live** near the High Line.
She **works** next to the High Line.
Cars **don't drive** on the High Line.

You **go** to concerts on the High Line.
The High Line **doesn't allow** pets.
We **walk** through the High Line's gardens.

1 **Listen.** You will hear eight facts about the High Line. For each fact, circle the present simple form you hear. 🔊009

1. (grow)   grows   don't grow
2. (visit)   visits   doesn't visit
3. open   (opens)   doesn't open
4. close   closes   (doesn't close)

5. need   needs   (don't need)
6. (enjoy)   enjoys   don't enjoy
7. (sell)   sells   doesn't sell
8. (get)   gets   don't get

2 **Read.** Complete the sentences with the correct present simple form of the verbs in brackets.

1. The High Line _____doesn't stay_____ open all night. (not stay)
2. The High Line _____has_____ special chairs for relaxing. (have)
3. A tour guide _____talks_____ about the High Line's gardens. (talk)
4. Musicians _____give_____ concerts on Saturday afternoons. (give)
5. Visitors _____don't pay_____ to walk along the High Line. (not pay)

3 **Work in pairs.** Take turns saying facts about the High Line. Use the present simple.

1. the High Line / have / a play area for children
2. you / not / need / a ticket for the High Line
3. many different animals / live / on the High Line
4. guides / give / free tours to visitors
5. he / attend / exercise classes on the High Line
6. I / want / to visit the High Line

The High Line in New York City, USA

14 GRAMMAR

Warm Up

- **Build background** Say *I live in (name of city/town). I live near (landmark).* (Name a landmark or major street.) Point to a few students, and ask them where they live or what they live near. Say *Turn to the person next to you. Tell each other where you live and what you live near.* Then say *These are the places where we live right now. We might've lived somewhere else in the past, but this is where we live now, in the present.*

Present

- Ask students to open their books at page 14 and draw their attention to the photo at the bottom of the page. Ask a student to read the caption. Say *The High Line is a park named after a railway that used to run on tracks there.* Ask *Can you see anything unusual about the park?* Point out to students that the park is elevated, or set above the streets, and forms a straight, narrow path above the city, compared to other parks that are spread out over a wide space.

4 **LEARN NEW WORDS** Read about the Cheonggyecheon Stream park in Seoul, Korea. Then listen and repeat. 🎧 010 011

Cheonggyecheon Stream

In 2003, the mayor of Seoul decided to remove a **motorway** over an underground **stream**. He wanted the area around the stream to be an urban green space for people to enjoy. Today, the six-kilometre (four-mile) park on either side of the Cheonggyecheon Stream provides a place for people to relax.

At the park, visitors attend traditional festivals and concerts. They enjoy cultural events, look at art, and watch water and light shows. Many people just walk along the **pavements** or over one of 22 **bridges**, each with its own design and meaning.

5 **Read and complete the sentences.** Make any necessary changes.

bridge	motorway	pavement	stream

1. The Cheonggyecheon Stream was covered by a _____motorway_____ .
2. Now visitors go for walks on the _____pavements_____ near the water.
3. People enjoy water shows over the _____stream_____ .
4. Each of the _____bridges_____ has a unique look and meaning.

6 **Work in groups.** Name an interesting outdoor place where you live. How do people enjoy this place? What can you see and do at this place? Use the present simple.

GRAMMAR **15**

- Play **Track 008** as students listen. Then read the title of the table aloud and point out the words in the sentences in dark print. Say *All these words are present simple verbs.* Present simple *means the verbs describe an action or situation that exists now, in the present time.* Point to and read the third sentence on the left.

- Say *The present simple also describes actions or situations that regularly exist, such as the fact that cars don't drive on the High Line, or, as in the second sentence on the right, you can't bring pets on the High Line.* Play **Track 008** again and tell students to listen and read.

- Write some uses of the present simple on the board and walk through them with students. Tell students that scientific facts fall into the category of things that are always true. Share some examples: *Earth revolves around the Sun. Water boils at 100°C. The lack of gravity makes astronauts float in space.*

Our World in Context

The last train ran on the High Line in 1980, and the first section of the High Line park opened to the public in 2009. The park is an example of a piece of industrial infrastructure being converted into a public green space. The High Line landscape functions like a 'green roof'. The park pathways have open spaces, so rainwater can drain onto the gardens, cutting down on the amount of water that runs into the city sewage system.

The landscape of the park incorporates many of the plants that grew out of the abandoned rail bed during the twenty-five years or so after the trains stopped running, and before work began on the park. These self-seeded grasses and trees inspired the park's designers to focus on native plant species and keep the look of the park wild and natural.

Grammar in Depth

In addition to expressing an action or situation that exists in the present time, other key uses of the present simple include the following:

- Habitual actions in the present: *I walk on the High Line every day.*
- Scientific facts: *Water freezes at 0°C.*
- Scheduled events in the future: *What time does the tour start tomorrow?*
- To describe states of being and feelings:
  I love trains. / The flowers smell good.

The present simple is also used in questions and answers about routines, as in *Does he work at the park? Yes, he does.* This use will be covered in Unit 2.

Teaching Tip

You can use the time that students spend in group activities to re-teach struggling students. Notice which students seem to have the most difficulty with new grammar or vocabulary, and put them together in one group. Then, at the beginning of an activity, sit down with this group and give them additional instruction. This allows time for you to provide extra support and correct misunderstandings without drawing attention to struggling students in front of the class.

Uses of the present simple

To describe an action or situation that exists now	You <u>read</u> now.
To describe an action or situation that happens regularly	You <u>read</u> every day.
To describe something that is true now and will always be true	<u>Reading</u> is necessary for learning.
To describe a feeling	I <u>love</u> books!

• Tell pairs to practise reading the sentences in the table on page 14 to each other.

Practise

• **1** Say *Now we'll listen to some facts about the High Line.* Ask *Can anyone tell us what a fact is?* Make sure students understand that a fact is a statement that can be proved. Point to a window. Say *It's (sunny) today. Is that a fact?* (yes) *Why?* (Because we can look outside and see that the sun is shining.) Say *Pizza is the best food. Is that a fact?* (no) *Why?* Make sure students understand that it's not a fact because it expresses an opinion, or a personal feeling about something that not everyone agrees with.

• Play **Track 009** once and ask students to listen. Play the track again and tell students to complete the activity. Say *Pay attention to the form of each verb. Circle the form you hear.* Ask *Does it end in s or not? Is it a negative form?*

• **2** Draw students' attention to Activity 2. Read the instructions aloud. Say *Let's do the first one together.* Read item 1. Say *I have to fill in the blank with the correct form of the verb* not stay. Not *tells me I need a negative form, and it has to be the present simple. I can't say The High Line not stay open all night. That's wrong. I need to add an auxiliary, or helping, verb.* Ask different students to provide the answer. Tell students to complete Activity 2.

• **3** Say *Now you'll work in pairs to say more facts about the High Line. Look at Activity 3. Take turns to form the present simple.* Model item 1 with a student. Point out that the singular noun, *the High Line,* requires the present simple form *has* not *have.* Say *Write down each correct verb.* Then ask pairs to read their facts to the class.

Apply

• **4** **LEARN NEW WORDS** Say *Look at page 15. Now we're going to read about another park. It's in Seoul, South Korea. Remember the High Line used to be a railway. This park had an unusual beginning, too.* Point to the stream in the photo. Say *This is a stream. The water used to be hidden under a motorway.* Point to the bridge and the pavement in the photo. Write the new words on the board: *motorway, stream, pavement* and *bridge.* Invite students to describe what else they can see in the photo. Play **Track 010** and tell students to follow in their books. Say *Listen for the words on the board.* Then play **Track 011**. Ask students to listen and repeat.

• **5** Read aloud the instructions for Activity 5. Tell students to read the words in the box. Say *Before you fill in the words, read each sentence carefully. Find the part of the reading that talks about the same thing. Look at the photo. Think to yourself, 'Do I have to change the word in the box to a plural form?'* Ask students to read the completed sentences.

• **6** Put students into small groups. Say *You're going to talk about a place near where you live.* Read the instructions aloud. Say *Remember that one of the uses of the present simple is to talk about things that happen regularly.* Tell students to read paragraph 2 of the reading as a model of this use of the present simple. Say *Read paragraph 2 of the reading. Pay attention to the present simple verbs.*

Extend

- Ask students to write a short paragraph based on their group discussions. They can write about the place they talked about or another outdoor place they know. Say *Use the vocabulary to describe the place, and use the present simple when you can.* Ask students to read their paragraphs. Hang students' work in an 'Interesting Places to Visit' display in the classroom.

Consolidate

- Choose verbs from the following list to write on pieces of card, one to a card: *cross, live, not live, drive, ride, go, enjoy, visit, walk, look, stay* and *not walk.* Give each student a card. Take one yourself. Display the following list:

bridge	motorway	indoor	outdoor
park	resident	rural	pavement
skyscraper	stream	tower	urban

- Tell students to sit in a circle. Say *I'm going to pick a word from the board and make a sentence using the word and the correct present simple form of the present simple verb on my card.* Read the verb on your card. Say *My card says (not walk). I choose the word (skyscraper). My sentence is: People don't walk up the stairs in a skyscraper; they take the lift.*

- Continue around the circle until everyone has had a chance to say a sentence. Once a word on the board has been used, erase it from the list.

BE THE EXPERT

Pronunciation

Go to Student's Book page 144. Use Audio Tracks 116–118.

Syllables and stress In words with more than two syllables, one syllable has primary stress. This means that the vowel sound in that syllable is louder and longer than the vowels in other syllables. In longer words, there can be both primary and secondary stress (ed u CA tion). Most dictionaries indicate primary and secondary stress.

Word stress in English is variable, but there are some patterns and general rules you may want to share with your students:

- Most, but not all, two syllable nouns have stress on the first syllable (e.g. **moun**tain, **tea**cher, **stu**dent, **bro**ther, **cof**fee, **swea**ter, **pen**cil).
- Most compound nouns also have stress on the first syllable (e.g., **mot**orway, **pave**ment, **sky**scraper, **lap**top).
- When endings, or *suffixes,* are added to words, the stress sometimes shifts to a different syllable (e.g., **mu**sic, mu**si**cian; **nat**ional, nation**al**ity; **pho**to, pho**tog**rapher).

Formative Assessment

Can students

- recognise the form, meaning and use of the present simple?

  Ask *Can you name some things you do every day?*

- use the present simple to talk about facts?

  Ask students to supply the correct present simple form of *show:*

  A tour guide at the High Line _____ visitors the best views of the city. (shows)

- identify and use words associated with an urban park in South Korea?

  Ask students to fill in the blanks:

  People enjoy the park by walking along the stream on the _____ or over the stream on the _____. (pavements, bridges)

Workbook For additional practice, assign Workbook pages 4–5.

Online Workbook Grammar 1

Objectives

Students will

- interpret information from a reading about London and its green spaces.
- use new words from the reading.
- discuss opinions about green spaces in cities.

Reading Strategy Making predictions

Target Vocabulary *concrete, land, outdoor, park*

Vocabulary Strategy Using a dictionary

Academic Language *alphabetical order, predict, prediction*

Content Vocabulary *campaign, convinced, encourage*

Resources Online Workbook/Workbook pages 6–7; Worksheet 1.1.4 (Teacher's Resource CD-ROM/ Website); Tracks 012–013 (Audio CD/ Website/CPT); CPT: Reading

Materials drawing materials; set of classroom dictionaries

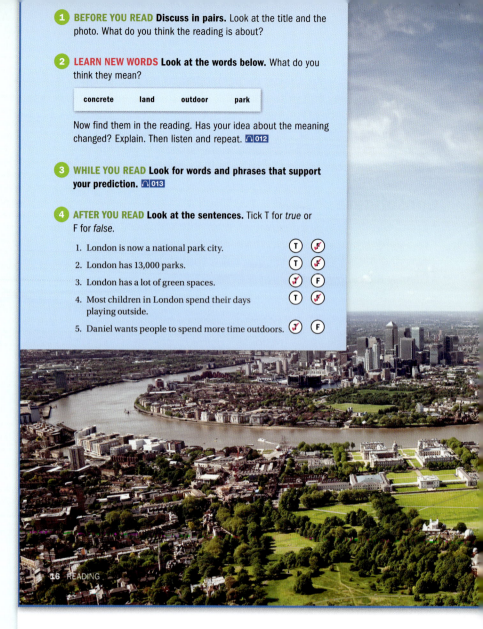

1. **BEFORE YOU READ** **Discuss in pairs.** Look at the title and the photo. What do you think the reading is about?

2. **LEARN NEW WORDS** **Look at the words below.** What do you think they mean?

> | concrete | land | outdoor | park |

Now find them in the reading. Has your idea about the meaning changed? Explain. Then listen and repeat. 🎧 012

3. **WHILE YOU READ** Look for words and phrases that support your prediction. 🎧 013

4. **AFTER YOU READ** **Look at the sentences.** Tick T for *true* or F for *false*.

1. London is now a national park city. T **F**
2. London has 13,000 parks. T **F**
3. London has a lot of green spaces. **T** F
4. Most children in London spend their days playing outside. T **F**
5. Daniel wants people to spend more time outdoors. **T** F

16 READING

Warm Up

- **Build background** Explain that a national park is a large area of land protected by the government because of its natural beauty, plants and wildlife. Ask *Has anyone ever been to a national park? Where was it? What did you see there?* Then ask *Do a lot of people normally live in national parks? Are there tall buildings and lots of businesses there? Would you describe a national park as urban or rural?* Discuss things students associate with national parks.

- Say *Let's make a word web about national parks. What words from our discussion should we add?* Invite students to suggest words. You may want students to copy the word web into their notebooks.

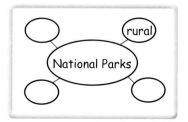

A New Type of Park

Can the capital of England become a national park?

Imagine stepping out of your front door and standing in the middle of a national park. Daniel Raven-Ellison hopes this might soon be possible for millions of London residents. Daniel is leading a campaign to make London a national park city.

Although London has much more concrete than a national park usually would, it is home to more than 13,000 kinds of wildlife. These species live in its 3,000 parks, along with 1,500 varieties of flowering plants and more than 300 species of birds. In fact, 47 per cent of the land in London is green space.

'We have eight million trees in London; it's the world's largest urban forest,' Daniel says. That's almost one tree for every person living in London! Yet, even though London has thousands of outdoor spaces, one in seven children living there hasn't visited a green space in the past year.

Daniel believes that making London into a national park will protect the animal life and green spaces in London. He hopes it will also encourage people, especially young people, to spend more time outdoors. Daniel takes his own son out to explore in London, and he thinks that other parents should do the same. Daniel is convinced that people who spend a lot of time in nature live happier and healthier lives. What do you think?

5 **Check your predictions.** Look at your predictions from Activity 1. Were you correct? What surprised you in this reading?

6 **Discuss in groups.**

1. How often do you visit green spaces? In your opinion, is it enough? What things do you do there?

2. Do you think that turning your city into a national park would be good? Why or why not?

3. Imagine that you can make changes in your city. Which places do you want to protect? Which places do you want to change? How do you want to change them? Explain your answers.

READING **17**

Before You Read

- **1** Ask students to open their books at pages 16–17. Discuss the photo. Then say *Read Activity 1.* Explain to students that when you look closely at the title of a reading, the photos, captions and other images it includes, you try to guess what it will be about. Say *This is called making a prediction.*

- Say *Now make predictions. Discuss with a partner what you think the reading will be about.* When students are ready, review their predictions as a class. Then say *Here's my prediction: From the title and the photo, I predict that the reading will be about an idea for a different kind of national park.* Write some of the predictions on the board. Tell students to keep their predictions in mind as they read *A New Type of Park.*

- **2** LEARN NEW WORDS Read the words in the box. Ask students to repeat. Point to *park*. Say *We've been talking a lot about parks – both urban and rural parks. Can you see any parks in the photo?* Ask *How would you define the word park?* Tell students to write down what they think the four words mean.

Reading Strategy

Making predictions Making predictions is a reading strategy students can use before, during and after they read. They should be encouraged to check their predictions as they read – correcting or revising them as new information is acquired – and to continue to make new predictions about what will happen next. When they make predictions, students become active readers and are more likely to remember what they read.

Vocabulary Strategy

Using a dictionary A dictionary contains a lot of information. Learning to use it efficiently will help your students find what they need quickly and thereby increase their language skills. Guide words at the top or bottom of the page give the first and the last words listed on that page. The entries in most dictionaries contain the following information: syllabication, phonetic spelling, parts of speech, definitions, and the history or origin of the word (its etymology). Many dictionaries will also contain additional information. Consult each dictionary's table of contents to see what it includes.

Teaching Tip

Graphic organisers are helpful in teaching reading strategies. They give students a picture of how the ideas and events they read about are related to each other. Organisers come in many different forms: webs, charts, tables, and circles connected to other circles with lines or arrows. You can make your own organisers or use the ones provided on the Teacher's Resource CD-ROM. Always model the correct use of organisers, and explain how they connect to learning strategies.

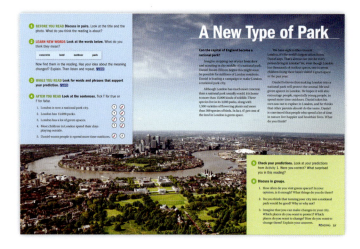

A New Type of Park

• Say *One way to work out the meaning of an unfamiliar word when you read is to look at the words around it. They might provide clues to the unknown word's meaning.* Ask students to look at paragraph 2. Say *If you didn't know what park meant, the sentences in paragraph 2 can help you work out that a park is a 'green' place with wildlife, plants and birds.*

• Tell students to find the other three words in the reading. When students have finished, say *Now that you've seen the words in the reading, do you want to change any of your definitions? Finally, play* **Track 012**. *Ask students to listen and repeat.*

• **Vocabulary Strategy** Tell students they can always look up an unknown word in a dictionary. Open a dictionary and point out the guide words. Say *At the top or bottom of each page, you'll find the first and last words that are on that page. These guide words will help you find the word you want.*

• Remind students that the words in a dictionary are listed in alphabetical, or ABC, order. Say *Look at the spelling of the word you're looking for. The guide words will show you the right page. For example, if you're looking up park, you wouldn't look on a page with the guide words paper clip and parachute. Why not?* Pass out dictionaries and ask student pairs to practise using guide words to look up one or two words.

While You Read 3

• **3** Say *Now you're going to listen to* A New Type of Park. *Play* **Track 013**, and tell students to listen and read.

• Say *Now read again. But before you do* (point to the board), *think about the predictions you made. As you read this time, look for words and phrases that relate to your predictions. Do they support your ideas about what the reading would be about? In other words, do they show that your predictions were right? Play* **Track 013** *again or allow students to read in silence.*

After You Read

• **4** Tell students to read the activity instructions. Do the first item together. Say *This sentence says that London is a national park city right now.* Ask *Is that true?* Say *I don't think so, but I'll check the reading. My first clue is the question in dark print at the beginning of the text.*

• Ask *How does this question help me decide whether item 1 is true or false?* (It asks if London 'can become' a national park city. That means it's not one yet.) Ask *What other clues can you find in paragraph 1?* (The text says Daniel Raven-Ellison 'hopes' London will become a national park city; he's leading a campaign, or planned set of activities, to make it happen.) Ask students to complete the activity. Review the answers as a class.

• **5** Ask *Now that you've read* A New Type of Park, *how many of you found support for your predictions? What details from the reading support them?* Say *I predicted the reading would be about an idea for a different kind of city park. Well, that's partly true. The reading is about a new kind of park – but the park isn't in the city. It is the city!* Discuss the support students found for their predictions.

• Ask *What surprised you most about the reading?* Say *I was most surprised by the fact that London has 3,000 parks and eight million trees! That's a lot.* Discuss students' responses.

- **6** Put students into small groups. Tell groups to read the activity questions. Appoint a group member to act as secretary, and write down notes from the discussion about each question. Provide ideas if students are struggling with their discussions.

Discussion prompts

What do you do in green spaces?	• play sports, swim • go to outdoor concerts
Is making a city a national park a good or bad idea?	<u>Good</u> • It would get special protection. <u>Bad</u> • It would be crowded with tourists.
How would you change your city?	• add more parks and pools • clean up rubbish

Extend

- Draw students' attention to the photo of London on pages 16–17. Point to the river, the tall buildings and the green spaces. Say *Work by yourself, or with a partner who lives in the same area as you do. Make a drawing of your neighbourhood. Show any large buildings. Show any rivers, streams, parks or gardens. If you think there should be more green spaces, show where you would put them. Write what you would like them to be.*

- **Worksheet** If time allows, you may want to hand out **Worksheet 1.1.4** in class. Students will use the worksheet to explore more words related to cities and green spaces.

Consolidate

- Write on the board: *architecture, bridge, concrete, design, land, outdoor, rural, skyscraper, stream, unusual* and *urban.* Divide the class into small groups. Say *We've read about and seen photos of two cities – Astana and London – and two parks – the High Line and Cheonggyecheon Stream.* Assign each group one of two topics: Cities or Parks. Tell the Cities groups to discuss what they like about Astana and London. Tell the Parks groups to discuss what they like about the High Line and the park in Seoul.

- Say *I want each group to make a list of things that you think the best city or park should include.* Tell groups to look at the photos again and review the readings and sentences about their topics. Say *Use the vocabulary items.* Invite groups to share their lists.

Objectives

Students will
- discuss urban green spaces and how to create more of them.
- apply the message of the video to their personal lives.

Content Vocabulary *moss, mural, shade, soil*

Resources Video scene 1.1 (DVD/ Website/CPT); Online Workbook; CPT: Video

Materials art materials

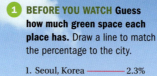

1 **BEFORE YOU WATCH** Guess how much green space each place has. Draw a line to match the percentage to the city.

1. Seoul, Korea ——— 2.3%
2. Hong Kong, China — 2.5%
3. Mumbai, India — 4.4%
4. Bogotá, Colombia — 41%
5. Moscow, Russia — 47%
6. Singapore — 54%

2 **Read and circle.** You're going to watch *Mission Re-Wild*. From the title and the photo, predict what the video is about. Circle the letter.

a. Putting wild animals back into forests
b. Building more skyscrapers in cities
c. Making more green space in cities

3 **WHILE YOU WATCH** Check your guesses from Activity 1. How many were correct? Watch scene 1.1.

A mural made from moss by artist Carly Schmitt

18 VIDEO

Before You Watch

- Put students into small groups. Ask *Where can you go when you want to see green, open space with trees and grass? Is there a place nearby, or do you have to go beyond your neighbourhood?* Tell groups to discuss the green spaces they go to. Then say *Make a list of all the local green spaces you know.* Ask *How many places did you list?*

- Ask students to open their books at pages 18–19. Read the photo caption and discuss the mural. Tell students that moss is a plant that likes shade and can grow with only a little moisture. Say *It doesn't even need soil!* Ask *What animals can you see in the mural? How do you think the artist created the mural?*

- **1** Read the instructions for Activity 1 aloud. Tell students to complete the activity. When they've finished, ask them to share which cities they think have the most and the least green space.

- **2** Read Activity 2 aloud. Remind students that when you predict, you make a guess about what a reading or a video will be about by reading the title and looking at any pictures that are part of it. Ask *What do you think re-wild means?* Tell students it means to make something that used to be wild or natural, wild again. Then ask them to do the activity.

While You Watch

- **3** Say *Now we're going to watch Mission Re-Wild. Before we do, look again at what you guessed for Activity 1. You'll see the answers in the video. See how many you got right.* Play **Video scene 1.1**.

- If students have trouble following the video or understanding the text, pause the video and allow them to ask questions. Try replaying the video with and without sound, and invite students to describe and comment on what they can see.

54   UNIT 1

4 AFTER YOU WATCH Read the sentences. Circle the correct answer.

1. Cities with *a lot of* / *very little* green space are sometimes called *concrete jungles*.

2. Seoul and Mumbai have *a lot of* / *very little* green space.

3. People who spend time outdoors are *happier* / *unhappier* than people who don't.

4. You can enjoy the outdoors *in both rural and urban areas* / *only in rural areas*.

5. *Only some cities have* / *Every city has* signs of natural life.

6. One way to start re-wilding is *planting a tree* / *recycling plastic*.

5 Work in pairs. Put the steps for re-wilding a city in the correct order.

3 Birds build nests in the tree.

1 Plant a seed in the ground.

4 People like seeing the tree and the birds.

2 The seed grows into a small tree.

5 Other people begin to plant trees, too.

6 Discuss in pairs.

1. How much public green space is there where you live? Would you like more? Why or why not?

2. Why do you think some places have more public green space than other places?

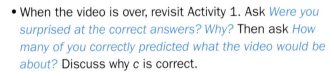

7 YOU DECIDE Choose an activity.

1. **Work independently.** Imagine you're going to re-wild a space where you live. Where is it? How will you do it? Make a plan and present it to the class.

2. **Work in pairs.** Find out about a place that was successfully re-wilded. How did it change? How do people enjoy it now? Write a paragraph and use photos to explain what you learnt.

3. **Work in groups.** Prepare a 'Let's Re-Wild' poster to teach others about re-wilding. Write three reasons why it is good to re-wild. Write ideas on what people can do. Draw pictures of a space before and after it has been re-wilded.

VIDEO **19**

Teaching Tip

As students work on projects, make sure they apply unit vocabulary and language rather than work silently. Ask students to read instructions aloud and talk to one another about the parts of a project and the process they'll follow. Circulate as students work, and ask them questions about what they're doing or making.

Related Vocabulary

bobcat, moose, owl

Formative Assessment

Can students
• discuss urban green spaces and how to create more of them?

Ask *What will you do to help create more green space in your neighbourhood? What will be your main purpose for doing it?*

Online Workbook Video

• When the video is over, revisit Activity 1. Ask *Were you surprised at the correct answers? Why?* Then ask *How many of you correctly predicted what the video would be about?* Discuss why c is correct.

After You Watch 4 5 6 7

• **4** Explain the instructions to students. Tell them to circle their answers. Then review the answers as a class. Replay the video if necessary.

• **5** Put students into pairs. Read aloud the instructions for Activity 5. Say *You need to write a number next to each statement to show what step it is in the process of re-wilding a city. The first step is numbered for you. Now number the other steps in order.* Then ask students to come to the front of the class and read the steps in the correct order.

• **6** Tell partners to read and discuss the Activity 6 questions. Say *Remember your list of green spaces in your area. Are there enough of them?* Prompt students to discuss question 2. Ask *What might affect the amount of green space a place has? What about the climate, the number of people who live there and other uses for the land?* Invite pairs to share their ideas.

• **7 YOU DECIDE** Read aloud the three options. Ask *What purpose do all of these activities have in common?* (re-wilding places to create more green space) Say *Think about which activity suits your talents or interests. If you like to solve problems, maybe option 1 is for you.*

• Explain that students who like to do research might like option 2. Those who like art projects and want to educate people about the importance of green spaces should consider option 3. Say *Remember to decide on specific tasks for each group member.*

Objectives
Students will
- use *in* and *on* to express location.
- recognise when a phrase requires *in* and when it requires *on*.

Grammar *In* and *on*: Expressing location

Academic Language *location*

Content Vocabulary *ancient, archway, continent, sculpture*

Resources Online Workbook/Workbook pages 8–9; Worksheet 1.1.5 (Teacher's Resource CD-ROM/ Website); Tracks 014–016 (Audio CD/ Website/CPT); CPT: Grammar 2

Resources pencils and paper clips

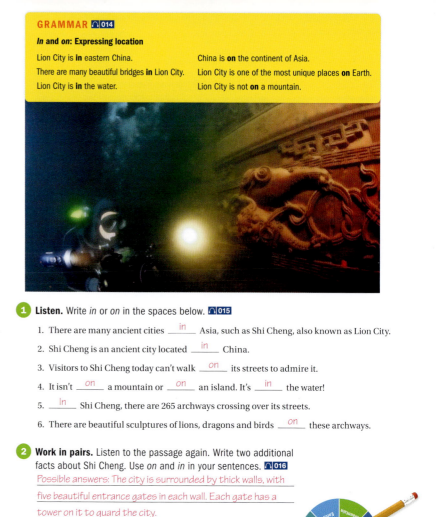

GRAMMAR 🎧 014

In and *on*: Expressing location

Lion City is **in** eastern China.
There are many beautiful bridges **in** Lion City.
Lion City is **in** the water.

China is **on** the continent of Asia.
Lion City is one of the most unique places **on** Earth.
Lion City is not **on** a mountain.

1 **Listen.** Write *in* or *on* in the spaces below. 🎧 015

1. There are many ancient cities __in__ Asia, such as Shi Cheng, also known as Lion City.
2. Shi Cheng is an ancient city located __in__ China.
3. Visitors to Shi Cheng today can't walk __on__ its streets to admire it.
4. It isn't __on__ a mountain or __on__ an island. It's __in__ the water!
5. __In__ Shi Cheng, there are 265 archways crossing over its streets.
6. There are beautiful sculptures of lions, dragons and birds __on__ these archways.

2 **Work in pairs.** Listen to the passage again. Write two additional facts about Shi Cheng. Use *on* and *in* in your sentences. 🎧 016
Possible answers: The city is surrounded by thick walls, with five beautiful entrance gates in each wall. Each gate has a tower on it to guard the city.

3 **Work in groups.** Take turns using the spinner. Make sentences using *in* or *on*.

About seven billion people live on Earth.

Go to page 155.

Warm Up

- **Build background** Place a book on a table or desk. Ask *Where's the book?* (It's on the table.) Put a pencil or other classroom object into a container, such as a drawer or backpack. Ask *Where's the pencil?* (It's in the drawer.) Then make a gesture with your arms to indicate the room you and the students are in. Ask *Where are we right now?* Say *We use the word* in *to say where we are. Sometimes, we use at. But we wouldn't say 'We're* on *the classroom' or 'We're* on *school'.*

- Display these sentences: *We're* in *the classroom. The book is* on *the table.* Point to each one and say *In usually means inside, or enclosed within, a place or an area. On usually means that there's contact with the surface of something.*

Present

- Say *Short words, such as* in *and* on, *have specific meanings when you talk about location – a place where someone or something is. Turn to page 20.* Say *We're going to hear sentences using* in *and* on *to talk about location.* Play **Track 014**. Tell students to listen and read silently.

- Play **Track 014** again. Then ask students to read the sentences aloud. Next, ask partners to take turns reading the sentences to each other. Ask two students to stand up. Say *(Shen), you read the first sentence on the left. Then (Myra), you read the first sentence on the right. Take turns until you have read all the sentences.*

- Explain to students that when talking about geographic locations, certain rules apply: Say *Use* in *with countries, cities, regions, mountain ranges and oceans.* Write some phrases on the board. Then say *Use* on *with a particular geographical feature, such as a continent, a planet, an island or a mountain.* Add more phrases.

in California	in Asia	in the Andes	in the Pacific Ocean
on the continent of Asia	on Mars	on the island of Jamaica	on Mt. Everest

Practise

- **1** Ask students to look at the sentences in Activity 1. Say *You're going to hear about a unique place in China. Listen to the information and fill in each gap with* in *or* on. Play **Track 015** and ask students to do the activity. Review the answers as a class.

- **2** Put students into pairs. Say *Now, you'll hear about Shi Cheng again.* Say *What new facts about the underwater city do you hear?* Play **Track 016**. Say *Now listen again and write.* Replay **Track 016** and tell student pairs to complete the activity. Invite pairs to come to the front of the class and share their work.

Apply

- **3** Tell students to turn to page 155. Say *Use the words in the section the spinner lands on to create a sentence that includes* in *or* on. *Play until the words in every section of the spinner have been used. Don't repeat a sentence someone else has already said.* Remind students to politely correct one another if they hear *in* or *on* used incorrectly.

Extend

- Put students into pairs to play a new version of the game. Demonstrate with a student partner. Spin the spinner. Say *The spinner has landed on (a mountain).* Prompt your partner to ask you, *Where is the (mountain)?* Say *I have to answer with* in *or* on. *I'll say 'The mountain is in the Andes'. Now it's my partner's turn to spin.* Explain that each time one partner says the place the spinner has landed, the other partner must ask *Where is (the place)?* Explain that for the moon, South America, the ocean and Earth, the response should be such phrases as *in the solar system, in the universe, on Earth,* and so on.

- Hand out **Worksheet 1.1.5.** to practise using *in* or *on* correctly to write about location.

Consolidate

- Write *Astana, the High Line, London* and *Lion City.* Say *You're going to take turns asking and answering questions about these locations.* Model with two students. Ask the first student *Where is Astana?* He/She should respond *Astana is in Kazakhstan.* Then turn to the other student and ask, for example, *Where is Kazakhstan?* He/She responds, *Kazakhstan is in Asia.*

- Give students a few minutes to think of some questions. Say *You must be able to use* in *or* on *in the answers.* Ask students to stand in a circle to play. Say *If you use* in *or* on *incorrectly, you have to sit down.*

Grammar in Depth

When dealing with Geography, specific rules for the use of *in* and *on* apply:

- Use *in* with specific countries, cities, regions/states, mountain ranges and oceans.

- Use *on* with certain geographical features, such as continents, islands, specific mountains and planets.

English prepositions pose a big challenge to EFL students. A single preposition may be used in different contexts in one language, while two different prepositions would be used in another language. Always encourage students to learn prepositional phrases as meaningful language chunks rather than to try to remember rules, for which there are often exceptions or idiomatic usages.

Teaching Tip

Remind students that making revisions and improvements to their work is part of the learning process. When students give feedback to one another, make sure they use positive language. It's important that students receive feedback in a positive way. Remind them that such feedback is not a personal criticism. These suggestions can make their work even better.

Formative Assessment

Can students

- use *in* and *on* to express location?

  Ask students to describe where they live.

- recognise when a phrase requires *in* and when it requires *on*?

  Ask students to complete the sentences with *in* or *on*:

  In 1969, the first humans landed _____ the Moon.

  They took off from Florida _____ the United States.

Workbook For additional practice, assign Workbook pages 18–19.

Online Workbook Grammar 2

WRITING

Objectives

Students will
- apply elements of descriptive writing.
- use describing words.
- analyse a model of descriptive writing.
- produce a paragraph of descriptive writing.

Writing Description of a place

Academic Language *compare, descriptive writing*

Resources Online Workbook/Workbook page 10; Process Writing Worksheets 1–5, Genre Writing Worksheet: Description (Teacher's Resource CD-ROM/Website); CPT: Writing

Materials drawing materials

WRITING

In descriptive writing, we try to create a picture for the reader. We use describing words to help the reader clearly imagine what we're writing about. Examples of describing words include:

beautiful   **colourful**   **new**   **short**   **sweet-smelling**   **yellow**

1 **Read the model.** Work in pairs to find and underline all of the describing words the writer uses to talk about the garden.

Last year, the empty space opposite my bus stop was a sad, empty, ugly space, with only a couple of dead bushes and one short tree. Then some hard-working gardeners in the neighbourhood changed that. They were tired of looking at that sad space while waiting for the bus, so they made it into a beautiful garden. Now, on a sunny summer day you can look across the street and see colourful vegetable plants and sweet-smelling flowers while you wait for the bus. Yellow butterflies fly from plant to plant, and tiny birds sing in the green trees. I love taking the bus now!

2 **Work in pairs.** Draw a picture of the garden described in Activity 1. Compare your drawing with a partner's. How are they the same? How are they different?

3 **Write.** Think of a beautiful place in your neighbourhood. Use describing words to write a paragraph about this place.

WRITING **21**

Warm Up

- **Activate prior knowledge** Say *Think about what you say when you tell a friend about an interesting place. You want your friend to be able to imagine the place in his/her mind.* Ask *How do you help him/her do that?*

- Discuss how to describe a place to someone who's never seen it. You start by saying where the place is and what type of place it is. You describe how the place looks: *colourful, busy, scary*; how it sounds: *filled with loud music* or *the voices of people*; how it smells: *fragrant like baking bread* or *unpleasant like exhaust fumes*; and how it makes you feel: *excited, nervous* or *happy*.

- Say *We describe people and things, too. We do it all the time. You describe your new teacher to your parents, the goal you scored to your brother, the new jacket you want from your grandmother, the film you saw, the day you had at school.*

- Say *Turn to the person next to you. Take turns describing some object in the classroom to each other. How can you make your partner 'see' the object in his/her mind? Can he/she identify it from your description?* Tell students to avoid saying what the object is used for; just describe its physical features – its size, colour, shape, texture, smell and sound, if either applies.

- When students have finished, ask *Did your partner describe the object well? Were you able to identify it? Are there other words your partner could have used?* Discuss your descriptions.

Present

- Say *Open your books at page 21.* Say *You've shared descriptions with one another; now we're going to see how to write one.* Read aloud the text in the green box. Then ask different students to stand up and repeat the describing words aloud. Say *Let's write some other describing words on the board.* Write some words, categorising them as shown. Then ask students to suggest others, and add them to the chart.

Colour	Size	Shape	Smell	Texture	Other qualities
red	big	round	sour	rough	rural
bright	tiny	boxy	smoky	smooth	modern
shiny	huge	uneven	flowery	bumpy	eye-catching

Read the Model

- Say *Now we're going to look at a model of descriptive writing. First, let's look at the photo.* Ask *What do you call looking at a picture that goes with a text and trying to guess what the text will be about?* (making a prediction) Ask students to predict what the text will be about.

- Read the instructions for Activity 1 aloud. Say *Read the text. Then work with a partner to underline all the describing words you can see.* As pairs work, tell them to pay attention to what the words they underline are describing.

- **Model** When students have finished, model how to analyse the writer's descriptions. Read the first sentence aloud. Say *In this sentence, the writer is describing the land around the bus stop. I underlined* empty, dead *and* short. Empty *describes* land, dead *describes* bushes *and* short *describes* tree. *I ask myself, 'What kind of picture does this bring to mind?' It's not a very pretty one – empty land, dead bushes and a short tree. I imagine a brown, bare, depressing place.* Tell pairs to use the same process to work through the rest of the model.

- Next, ask pairs to read the Activity 2 instructions. Before they begin drawing, tell them to read the text again. Say *As you read, picture the garden again in your mind.* Then tell students to work on their own to make a rough drawing of the garden. Say *Look at your drawing and decide if you want any other details in it. Then revise your drawing and colour it in. When you're satisfied, compare it with your partner's drawing. Do your drawings look similar? Did you show the same things? Use the same colours?*

- **Worksheet** If your students need a reminder of the elements of the Descriptive Writing genre, you may want to hand out **Genre Writing Worksheet 7 (Description)** and review it together.

Writing Support

Organising descriptions logically When writing a description, it's important to organise details in a logical way. When describing an event, chronological order helps the reader to understand the order in which things happened. Spatial order is helpful when describing an object or a place. You can also describe something from top to bottom or bottom to top, from left to right or right to left, or from the outside in or the inside out.

Problems will occur for the reader when you deviate from the organisation you've established. Avoid describing events out of order, and when describing things, don't jump from one description to another and then back again.

Teaching Tip

Remind students of the vocabulary and grammar you'll be looking for in their writing assignments. Before they begin writing, review target vocabulary and important grammar structures that will help them complete the activity. Model example sentences so that your expectations are clear to students.

Related Vocabulary

community garden, plot

Workbook For scaffolded Writing support, assign Workbook page 10.

Online Workbook Writing

WRITING

In descriptive writing, we try to create a picture for the reader. We use describing words to help the reader clearly imagine what we're writing about. Examples of describing words include:

beautiful   colourful   new   short   sweet-smelling   yellow

1 **Read the model.** Work in pairs to find and underline all of the describing words the writer uses to talk about the garden.

Last year, the empty space opposite my bus stop was a sad, empty, ugly space, with only a couple of dead bushes and one short tree. Then some hard-working gardeners in the neighbourhood changed that. They were tired of looking at that sad space while waiting for the bus, so they made it into a beautiful garden. Now, on a sunny summer day you can look across the street and see colourful vegetable plants and sweet-smelling flowers while you wait for the bus. Yellow butterflies fly from plant to plant, and tiny birds sing in the green trees. I love taking the bus now!

2 **Work in pairs.** Draw a picture of the garden described in Activity 1. Compare your drawing with a partner's. How are they the same? How are they different?

3 **Write.** Think of a beautiful place in your neighbourhood. Use describing words to write a paragraph about this place.

WRITING **21**

Plan **3**

- **3** Say *It's time to plan your own writing. First, read the instructions.* Say *Think about beautiful places you might describe. Your next step is pre-writing. Let's review. What are some of the things we do when we pre-write?* (brainstorm, freewrite, make lists, use a graphic organiser, use sentence starters)

- Say *Now decide what you want to use for pre-writing.* If you have time in class, allow students to work on this step. If not, assign it as homework.

- **Worksheets** If your students need a reminder of any of the steps of process writing, you may want to hand out **Process Writing Worksheets 1–5** and review them together.

- **Workbook** Refer students to Workbook page 10 to help them organise and plan their writing.

Write

- After students have finished their pre-writing, tell them to work on their first drafts. If you don't have enough time in class, assign the first draft as homework.

Revise

- After students have finished their first drafts, tell them to review their writing and think about their ideas and organisation. Tell them to quietly read their drafts aloud to themselves. Ask each student to consider the following: *Is the main idea easily identifiable? Does the description develop in a logical way? What seems good? What needs more work?*

Edit and Proofread

- Invite students to consider elements of style, such as sentence variety, parallelism and word choice. Then tell them to proofread for mistakes in grammar, punctuation, capitalisation and spelling.

Publish

- Publishing includes handing in pieces of writing to the teacher, sharing work with classmates, adding pieces to a class book, displaying pieces on a classroom wall or in a hallway, and posting on the Internet.

Writing Assessment		1	2	3	4
Use these guidelines to assess students' writing. You can add other aspects of their writing you'd like to assess at the bottom of the table. 4 = Excellent 3 = Good 2 = Needs improvement 1 = Re-do	**Writing** Student uses a variety of descriptive words that are appropriate for a description of a beautiful place.				
	Grammar Student uses the present simple and *in* and *on* when appropriate.				
	Vocabulary Student uses a variety of word choices, including words taught in this unit.				

NATIONAL GEOGRAPHIC

Explore Your World

'There are amazing adventures to be had right outside our doors.'

Daniel Raven-Ellison
National Geographic Explorer, Guerrilla Geographer

1. **Watch scene 1.2.**

2. Daniel thinks it's best for students to experience geography rather than just read about it. What other school subjects can you explore outside the classroom? How can you explore them?

3. How much of your town or city have you explored? What else is there to learn about where you live? Keep a journal of outdoor adventures you have in your area.

22 MISSION

Objectives
Students will
• discuss exploring and making new discoveries in their own cities and towns.

Academic Language *journal*

Resources Video scene 1.2 (DVD/ Website); Worksheet 1.1.6 (Teacher's Resource CD-ROM/Website); Online Workbook: Meet the Explorer; CPT: Mission

Teaching Tip

Giving opinions in the classroom gives students experience with expressing and hearing different viewpoints. It's good to have rules for expressing opinions. Work with the class to develop a list of rules, for example, *Listen when someone speaks. Don't interrupt. Give good reasons for your opinions. Show respect for opinions that are different from your own.*

Online Workbook Meet the Explorer

Mission

• Say *Turn to page 22 in your books.* Read aloud the Mission. Ask *What places have you explored? Where are they located?* Ask students to share experiences they've had exploring places either alone, with their families, or with a club or organisation. Ask *What does 'your world' mean?* Discuss with students that it means not only planet Earth and all the faraway places in it, but also the local world outside your door. Remind students that exploration leads to discovery and knowledge.

• Ask a student to stand up and read the quote from Daniel Raven-Ellison. Ask *Do you agree with Daniel? What do you think it would be like to go exploring with him?*

• **Activity 1** Say *Now let's watch a video about Daniel Raven-Ellison.* Play **Video scene 1.2.** Tell students to pay attention to Daniel's ideas about geography as a

tool for solving problems and exploration, and as a way to gain knowledge about the world and its people.

• **Activity 2** Say *Geography is the study of the earth and its places and features, so it makes sense to learn about geography outside. But what about history? What about science?* Put students into small groups to discuss other subjects they can explore outside.

• **Activity 3** Say *You've talked to one another about interesting places in your neighbourhoods, and written a description of a beautiful place there.* Ask *What more can you learn about where you live?* Make sure students understand what a journal is and how to use it. If possible, show them an example of a nature journal.

• **Worksheet** Hand out **Worksheet 1.1.6.** Explain that students will use the worksheet to think and write about Daniel Raven-Ellison's ideas and their own thoughts about exploration and discovery.

Make an Impact

YOU DECIDE Choose a project.

1 Conduct a survey.

· Ask your friends how much time they spent indoors and outdoors in the past week.

· Calculate the average amount of indoor and outdoor time.

· Present your findings to the class. Give suggestions for spending more time outdoors.

2 Plan and conduct a scavenger hunt.

· Work as a group to prepare a list of items to find in a local green space.

· Work independently to find the items on the list.

· Discuss which items on the list were the easiest and the most difficult to find.

3 Write a newspaper article.

· Think of someone who has lived in your neighbourhood for a long time. Write questions to ask them about your neighbourhood.

· Interview that person. Find maps and photos to show the changes that he or she describes.

· Write a newspaper article to summarise the interview and show the changes.

Objective
Students will
• choose and complete a project related to their neighbourhoods.

Content Vocabulary *calculate, scavenger hunt, survey*

Resources Assessment: Unit 1 Quiz; Workbook pages 11 and 90; Worksheet 1.1.7 (Teacher's Resource CD-ROM/Website; CPT: Make an Impact and Review Games

Assessment Go to page 254.

Unit Review Assign Worksheet 1.1.7.
Workbook Assign pages 11 and 90.
Online Workbook Now I can

Prepare
• **YOU DECIDE** Ask students to choose a project.

• **Activity 1** Ask students to consider how many friends they'll need to survey to make the results meaningful. Say *Asking just two or three friends about their activities is not enough to make an impact. To convince people to change their habits, you need results from a large enough group to make people pay attention!* Explain that students shouldn't just survey people that they know spend a lot of time indoors – or outdoors. That will not give an accurate picture of the average person's habits.

• **Activity 2** Make sure everyone knows what a scavenger hunt is. Help students identify a place for the hunt and create a checklist of things to find. Suggest items related to the senses, something in a certain colour, or birds and animals students are likely to see and be able to identify.

• **Activity 3** Help students create 5–7 interview questions, such as what year did the person first come to the area, how has the landscape changed over the years, has the amount of green space increased or decreased, what technological development has had the biggest impact on residents' lives, and so on.

Share
• Schedule time to allow groups to present their final projects to the class. Students may want to invite the person interviewed for option 3 to come to the presentation and answer questions students may have. You may also want to invite students to submit the interview article to a local newspaper, website or blog.

Track 002 ② **Listen and read.** See Student's Book pages 10–11.

Track 003 ② **LEARN NEW WORDS** **architecture** / This city's architecture is very detailed. **capital** / Astana is the capital of Kazakhstan. **construct** / They're going to construct the new museum this year. **design** / It takes time and knowledge to design a building. **indoor** / Watching films is a popular indoor activity. **plan** / A Japanese architect planned the city of Astana. **resident** / Residents of a city can enjoy its green spaces. **shape** / The stadium has a round shape. **skyscraper** / Shanghai is a city with tall skyscrapers. **be surrounded by** / The fountain in the garden is surrounded by trees. **symbol** / The cherry blossom tree is a symbol of Japan. **tower** / The clock tower is over one hundred metres tall. **unique** / Astana is known for its unique buildings.

Track 004 ⑤ It is unusual to find a lot of people living in a rural area. Instead there are usually just a few houses or farms surrounded by a lot of land. But in 1997 the President of Kazakhstan created a large urban area right in the middle of the countryside. Before long what used to be empty space was filled with skyscrapers and parks. Now the population of the capital city is 750,000 and growing!

Track 005 ⑤ **LEARN NEW WORDS** **rural** / A rural area is far from a city. **unusual** / Astana is unique because of its unusual architecture. **urban** / Green spaces in a city connect urban life with nature.

Track 006 **SPEAKING STRATEGY** See Student's Book page 13.

Track 007 ① **S1**: Hi, Ronaldo. What are you reading? **S2**: Hey, Caroline. It's a really cool article about this geographer, Daniel Raven-Ellison. He does some amazing stuff. **S1**: Really? A geographer? **S2**: Well, they call him a guerrilla geographer because he explores urban areas in really unusual ways. **S1**: That's interesting. **S2**: Listen to this! He recently climbed 52,252 steps over ten days. That's more than 10,000 metres – higher than Mount Everest! **S1**: No way! That's incredible! Where did he climb all those stairs? **S2**: In apartment buildings, skyscrapers, offices and shopping centres in London. **S1**: You're kidding! Why did he do it? **S2**: He wants to show people that you don't need to go to Mount Everest to have an adventure. You can be physically active and stay healthy where you live. **S1**: Wow! You know, he's right. OK, I'm ready. Are you? **S2**: Ready to do what? **S1**: To start exploring. Let's get our adventure started!

Track 008 **GRAMMAR** See Student's Book page 14

Track 009 ①

1. More than 300 kinds of plants grow along the High Line.

2. Almost five million people visit the High Line each year.

3. The High Line opens at seven o'clock.

4. It doesn't close during the winter when it's cold.

5. You don't need money to enter the High Line. It's free.

6. Residents of New York enjoy the High Line's art exhibits.

7. Special vendors sell snacks on the High Line.

8. You get great views of New York from the High Line.

Track 010 ④ In 2003, the mayor of Seoul decided to remove a motorway over an underground stream. He wanted the area around the stream to be an urban green space for people to enjoy. Today, the six-kilometre park on either side of the Cheonggyecheon Stream provides a place for people to relax.

At the park, visitors attend traditional festivals and concerts. They enjoy cultural events, look at art and watch water-and-light shows. Many people just walk along the pavements or over one of 22 bridges, each with its own design and meaning.

Track 011 ④ **LEARN NEW WORDS** **bridge** / A car goes over a bridge to cross a river. **motorway** / People drive on motorways to get to cities. **pavement** / It's safer to walk on the pavement than in the street. **stream** / A stream is smaller than a river.

Track 012 ② **LEARN NEW WORDS** **concrete** /Some houses and buildings are made of concrete. **land** / Cities take up a lot of land. **outdoor** / In summer a lot of people enjoy outdoor meals. **park** / A park is a great place to visit if you live in a city.

Track 013 ③ **WHILE YOU READ** See Student's Book pages 16–17.

Track 014 **GRAMMAR** See Student's Book page 20.

Track 015 ① There are a lot of ancient cities in Asia, but one city stands out because it's so unusual – and wet! This interesting city is in China, and it's about 1,300 years old. It's a small city called Lion City, or Shi Cheng in Mandarin. Today, no visitors walk on the streets of Shi Cheng to see its beautiful architecture. Shi Cheng isn't on a mountain, or on an island. It's 26 to 40 metres deep in Thousand Island Lake. To visit Shi Cheng, people have to dive underwater.

The city is surrounded by thick walls, with five beautiful entrance gates in each wall. Each gate has a tower on it to guard the city. In Shi Cheng, there are also 265 amazing archways. There are beautiful carvings of lions, dragons and birds on these archways.

Track 016 ② See **Track 015**.

Amazing Jobs

In This Unit

Theme This unit is about unusual jobs, including jobs that involve adventure, danger and extreme physical activity.

Content Objectives
Students will
- examine some unusual professions and discuss the work they involve and what it takes to succeed in them.
- compare and contrast two people whose work takes them to extraordinary places but also involves taking risks.
- discuss an underwater archaeologist whose work combines science and diving.

Language Objectives
Students will
- talk about jobs and the routines they involve.
- show that they can extend a conversation.
- use the present simple tense to ask and answer questions about job routines.
- use possessives to show ownership.
- write a descriptive paragraph about someone's routine.

Vocabulary
pages 26–27 *adventure, archaeologist, career, clue, consider, explore, job, office, passion, profession, study, take risks, train, work*
page 28 *choice, dangerous, researcher*
page 31 *apply for, employee, interview, schedule, skills*
page 32 *adviser, commute, create, photographer, scientist*
Vocabulary Strategy Base words and the suffixes *-er, -or* and *-ist*

Speaking Strategy Extending the conversation

Grammar
Grammar 1 Use present simple questions and answers to talk about routines
Grammar 2 Use possessives

Reading *Adventures Near and Far*
Reading Strategy Compare and contrast

Video Scene 2.1: *Searching for Life in Iceland's Fissures;* Scene 2.2: Meet Guillermo de Anda

Writing Description of a daily routine

National Geographic Mission Do What You Love

Project
- Job advert
- Comic strip
- Job fair

Pronunciation Intonation in questions

Pacing Guides 1.2.1, 1.2.2, 1.2.3

NASA astronauts working underwater on a Hubble space telescope model

24

Introduce the Unit

- **Build background** Say *Let's talk about jobs.* Ask *What kind of job would you like after you've completed your education?* Say *Turn to the person next to you and talk about the jobs you might like.*

- Ask *What jobs did you talk about?* Write them on the board. Point to a few of the more common jobs and say *There are jobs that we come into contact with every day, such as teacher or bus driver. Then there are jobs that are less common but familiar, such as doctor, athlete or actor. There are other jobs that you may not have heard of. We're going to talk about some of those jobs.*

- **TO START** Ask students to open their books at pages 24–25. Read aloud question 1 on page 25. Discuss students' responses. Then ask a student to read aloud the caption on page 24. Explain that the astronauts are training to repair the Hubble telescope, which has been orbiting Earth since 1990, taking pictures of stars, planets and galaxies.

- Ask questions such as the following to encourage further discussion of the photo:

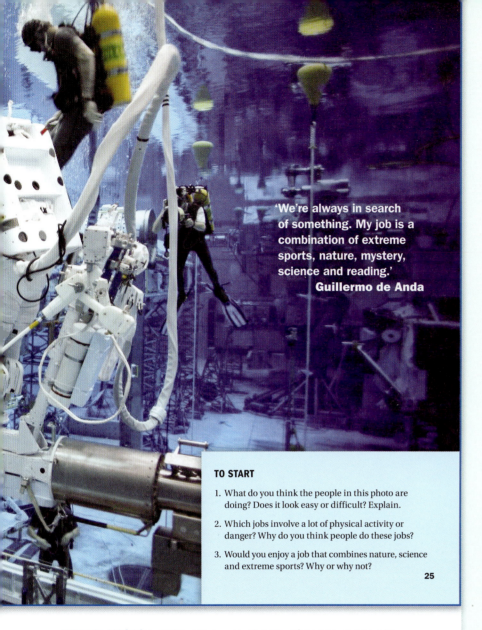

'We're always in search of something. My job is a combination of extreme sports, nature, mystery, science and reading.'
Guillermo de Anda

TO START

1. What do you think the people in this photo are doing? Does it look easy or difficult? Explain.

2. Which jobs involve a lot of physical activity or danger? Why do you think people do these jobs?

3. Would you enjoy a job that combines nature, science and extreme sports? Why or why not?

25

Objectives

Students will
- describe and discuss a photo.
- discuss different kinds of jobs, including jobs that involve danger or extreme physical activity.

Resources Worksheet 1.2.1 (Teacher's Resource CD-ROM/Website); CPT: Unit Opener

BE THE EXPERT

About the Photo

The photo shows astronauts working on a model of the Hubble Space Telescope in a huge water tank at the Johnson Space Center in Houston, Texas. The astronauts are practising how to inspect and repair Hubble, which was launched in 1990 and is still operating in space. The only way Hubble can be inspected is during a spacewalk, and floating underwater simulates the effects of weightlessness that astronauts must contend with during telescope-servicing missions. The astronauts must be able to work quickly and efficiently, so practice is critical.

Teaching Tip

When grouping students, consider their fluency with English. Less fluent or less proficient students benefit from listening to, and speaking with, more fluent students. Make it a practice to group students of different proficiency levels together. To encourage less fluent students to use English, ask them to repeat questions and answers. In group settings, when one student voices an idea, encourage others in the group to restate it.

Related Vocabulary

fins, scuba diver, tank

What is NASA? (a USA agency in charge of space research) *Why do you think the astronauts are training underwater?* You may want to share the information in About the Photo with students.

- Invite a student to read question 2 aloud. Then discuss students' ideas about why people do these jobs.

- Read aloud the quote on page 25. Say *Name some extreme sports.* (rock climbing, mountain biking, snowboarding, whitewater rafting) Ask *How are these sports alike?* (They're all outdoor sports; they have a high level of danger and physical activity.)

- Read aloud question 3 and discuss. Ask *What other jobs might involve nature, science and extreme sports?* Prompt students with such jobs as marine biologists, workers on oil rigs, archaeologists and forest firefighters. Ask students to share their thoughts on these kinds of jobs.

Extend

- Hand out **Worksheet 1.2.1**. Explain that student pairs will consider the meaning of *amazing* and discuss what makes a job amazing.

VOCABULARY

Objectives

Students will

- use vocabulary related to the work of an underwater archaeologist.
- use new vocabulary to discuss different kinds of jobs.

Target Vocabulary *adventure, archaeologist, career, clue, consider, explore, job, office, passion, profession, study, take risks, train, work*

Content Vocabulary *artefacts, detective, Mayan*

Resources Worksheet 1.2.2 (Teacher's Resource CD-ROM/Website); Tracks 017–018 (Audio CD/Website/CPT); CPT: Vocabulary

Materials drawing materials

1 What is unusual about Guillermo de Anda's job?
Discuss. Then listen and read. 017

What do underwater **adventure**, detective work and Mayan history have in common? They're all part of the unusual **profession** of Guillermo de Anda. He's a college professor and an underwater **archaeologist**. Guillermo's **job** is to **explore** flooded underground areas known as *cenotes*. 'It's unusual **work** for a lot of people,' Guillermo says about his job. 'It's hard, but it's a lot of fun as well.'

Guillermo dives to learn more about Mayan culture. About 2,000 years ago, the Maya lived in the Yucatán Peninsula of Mexico, the area Guillermo explores. Guillermo dives there now to look for ancient Mayan artefacts underwater. He **studies** them for **clues** about how the Maya lived.

The inside of a cenote

26 VOCABULARY

Warm Up

- **Build background** Explain that Guillermo de Anda has the unusual job of studying underwater caves. Say *I didn't know there were caves underwater! I've never been in a real cave, but I've got some ideas about what they're like.* Begin a word web for *cave.* Say *When I think of a cave, I think of a dark, damp space.* Write that in the web. Then ask *What do you think of?* Invite students to help you complete the web.

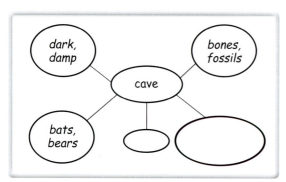

- Review the word web and ask students to come up to the board and use the information to make up sentences. Model an example. Say *Early humans lived in caves. They drew pictures on the walls that you can still see today.*

Present

- **1** Ask students to open their books at the photo on pages 26–27. Point out that it shows someone being lowered into a cavern or deep hole. Then draw their attention to the diagram at the bottom left of page 26. Ask *What does this diagram show?* Point out that it's a diagram of what the photo shows and that it gives more information. Ask *What's the green section?* (water) *What's in the water?* (a cave)

- **2** **LEARN NEW WORDS** Ask students to listen as you read Guillermo's words on page 25 about his job. Ask *Does this photo give you an idea of what Guillermo does for a living?* Then write *extreme sports, nature,*

Guillermo doesn't spend all of his time underwater. Like many people, he does much of his work in an **office**. He's also a researcher and a teacher. Sometimes, Guillermo takes his archaeology students underwater with him. He wants to **train** them to explore the cenotes. He thinks underwater archaeology is a good **career** choice for his students to **consider**. 'Very few archaeologists know how to dive in caves. We need more,' he says.

Guillermo and his team are **taking risks** each time they enter a cave. They go over 60 m. (200 ft.) underground to dark places filled with bats, snakes and scorpions. Some of the caves they explore are thousands of metres wide. It's not always easy for the team to remember the way out! Even though it can be dangerous, Guillermo has a **passion** for what he does. 'We go back into history when we're in the field,' he says. 'I never stop learning.'

Entering a cenote

2 **LEARN NEW WORDS** Listen and repeat. 🎧 018

3 **Work in pairs.** What makes Guillermo's job unusual? What parts of his job aren't unusual? Would you like to have his job? Why or why not?

VOCABULARY **27**

Our World in Context

The Maya are a Mesoamerican people living in southern Mexico, Guatemala, and northern Belize. Ancient Mayan civilisation reached its peak in the early centuries of the Common Era (CE). The Maya practised agriculture, built cities with great stone buildings and pyramid temples, and created striking artefacts of jade, gold and copper. They excelled in hieroglyphic writing, calendar making and mathematics.

The modern Maya still live within the boundaries of their old empire in Central America. The region that makes up this area now consists of the countries of Belize, Honduras, El Salvador, Guatemala, and five states in Mexico. Guatemala is considered to be the birthplace of the Mayan civilisation and consequently still has a very active Mayan population.

Teaching Tip

Encourage students to speak, even when they aren't sure of the answer or don't have all of the vocabulary they need. If you ask a question and no one responds, ask students to tell you single words they can use to answer the question. You can also invite students to ask you a question about the vocabulary they need in order to respond.

---

mystery, science, and *reading* on the board. Say *Discuss with a partner which of the things on the board are shown in the photo.*

- **1** Ask students to answer the question in Activity 1. Then play **Track 017** and ask students to listen and read. Discuss the reading with students. Ask questions such as:
  Who are the Maya? You may want to share information from Our World in Context with students.
  What are cenotes?
  What are some of the risks of exploring underwater caves?

- **2** **LEARN NEW WORDS** Play **Track 018**. Ask students to listen and repeat. Then invite student pairs to take turns saying each word. Clarify for students the differences between *career, job, profession* and *work.* Write the words and say *The meanings of these words are similar, but there are slight differences.*

Add the meanings and example sentences. Review with students.

job	what you do for a living now	*My job is teaching.*
career	long-term job	*I hope to have a career in nursing.*
work	activities you do at your job	*Part of my work is training people.*
profession	job that requires special training and study	*The profession of doctor requires years of study.*

- Put students into pairs. Say *Say a sentence to your partner that gives a clue to the meaning of a new word. But leave out the target word for your partner to fill in.* Model an example with a student partner. Say *I wouldn't mind a job with a little danger because I love (blank)!* Say the sentence again for your partner, this time asking him/her to fill in the blank with *adventure.*

VOCABULARY **67**

VOCABULARY

Objectives

Students will
- practise using vocabulary related to unusual jobs.
- use a vocabulary strategy to learn new vocabulary.

Target Vocabulary *choice, dangerous, researcher*

Vocabulary Strategy: Base words and the suffixes *-er, -or* and *-ist*

Academic Language *base words, suffixes*

Content Vocabulary *dive, remotely*

Resources Online Workbook/Workbook pages 12–13; Worksheet 1.2.2 (Teacher's Resource CD-ROM/Website); Tracks 019–020 (Audio CD/Website/CPT); CPT: Vocabulary

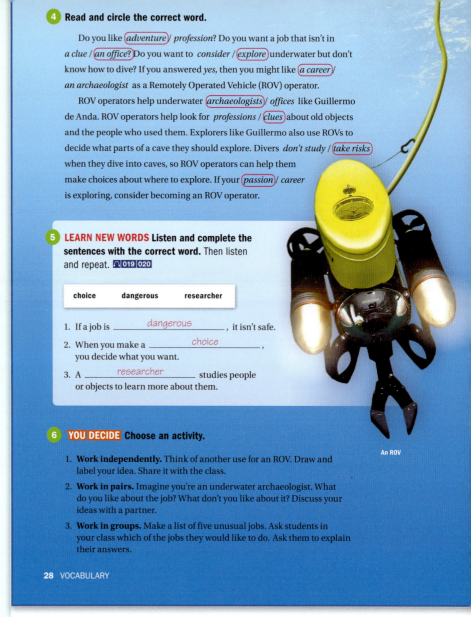

4 Read and circle the correct word.

Do you like *adventure*/ *profession*? Do you want a job that isn't in *a clue* / *an office*? Do you want to *consider* / *explore* underwater but don't know how to dive? If you answered *yes*, then you might like *a career*/ *an archaeologist* as a Remotely Operated Vehicle (ROV) operator.

ROV operators help underwater *archaeologists*/ *offices* like Guillermo de Anda. ROV operators help look for *professions* / *clues* about old objects and the people who used them. Explorers like Guillermo also use ROVs to decide what parts of a cave they should explore. Divers *don't study* / *take risks* when they dive into caves, so ROV operators can help them make choices about where to explore. If your *passion*/ *career* is exploring, consider becoming an ROV operator.

5 **LEARN NEW WORDS** Listen and complete the sentences with the correct word. Then listen and repeat. 🎧 019 020

choice	dangerous	researcher

1. If a job is _____dangerous_____, it isn't safe.

2. When you make a _____choice_____, you decide what you want.

3. A _____researcher_____ studies people or objects to learn more about them.

6 **YOU DECIDE** Choose an activity.

1. **Work independently.** Think of another use for an ROV. Draw and label your idea. Share it with the class.

2. **Work in pairs.** Imagine you're an underwater archaeologist. What do you like about the job? What don't you like about it? Discuss your ideas with a partner.

3. **Work in groups.** Make a list of five unusual jobs. Ask students in your class which of the jobs they would like to do. Ask them to explain their answers.

28 VOCABULARY

An ROV

Practise ③ ④ ⑤

- **3** Put students into pairs. Read the instructions for Activity 3 aloud. Say *Look again at the things that make Guillermo de Anda's job unusual. Remember, though, that he doesn't spend all his time in caves. Think about what is not unusual about his job.* Tell partners to complete the activity together.

- **4** Ask students to turn to page 28. Point out the photo of the ROV and make sure students understand what 'Remotely Operated Vehicle' means. Then model reading the first sentence and choosing the correct word aloud. Tell students to complete Activity 4 independently.

- **5** **LEARN NEW WORDS** Invite students to read aloud the three words in the box. Tell them to find the words in the text on page 27. Then play **Track 019** as students listen. Ask them to complete the sentences. Play **Track 020**. Ask students to listen and repeat. Then review the words and their meanings, and ask students to use each word in a sentence.

- **Vocabulary Strategy** Write *research* and *researcher* on the board. Underline the *-er* ending in *researcher*. Tell students *-er* is a word part called a suffix. Explain that suffixes have their own meanings, and when a suffix is added to the end of a base word, it changes the word's meaning.

- Say *The suffix -er means 'one who performs a certain action'. What do you think researcher means?* (a person who does research) *Two other suffixes that mean the same thing as -er are -or and -ist.* Write the words *instruct > instructor* and *archaeology > archaeologist* on the board and work through them with students.

Apply 6

- 6 **YOU DECIDE** Tell students to silently read the three Activity 6 options. Make sure students who are considering the first activity understand that they need to think of something that a ROV could do better or more easily than a person. Ask them to consider whether they would change the design of the ROV pictured in their books.

- Ask pairs to review what an underwater archaeologist does. Ask: *Do you like to swim? How do you feel about snakes and bats? What about being in a small space for a long time? Would you like doing research and teaching?*

- Help students doing the third activity think of unusual jobs. If possible, give them time to do an online search of unusual jobs. Tell them to come up with a list of jobs requiring different kinds of skills.

Extend

- Say *When you have a passion for something, you have a strong interest in it. Guillermo is passionate about archaeology. I'm passionate about learning.* Ask *What are you passionate about?* Then say *Think about a job that would let you follow your passion. Write a description of it. Use the vocabulary words.* Explain to students they can make up the job as long as it's believable. Invite students to share their jobs.

- If time allows, hand out **Worksheet 1.2.2**. Explain that students will use the new vocabulary words to consider jobs, adventure and taking risks.

Consolidate

- Write the following jobs on the board: *animal trainer, astronaut, ice sculptor, personal shopper*. Ask students to stand up and say what they know about each job or what they think each job might involve. Then write the following categories on the board: *adventure, danger, physical activity, training*. Ask *Which of these applies to these jobs?* Ask students to put their hands up for each category.

- Then invite students to vote for the job they think is the most adventurous, the most dangerous, involves the most activity. Ask who would like to have any of the jobs to say why.

Vocabulary Strategy

Base words and the suffixes *-er*, *-or* and *-ist* Inflectional endings, such as *-s* and *-es* do not change the word's meaning. By contrast, when the suffixes *-er*, *-or* and *-ist* are added to a word, the new word has a new meaning and is usually a different part of speech. The new meaning remains related to the meaning of the base word.

Other words with these suffixes include:

act	>	actor
bake	>	baker
cartoon	>	cartoonist
direct	>	director
geography	>	geographer
office work	>	office worker

Formative Assessment

Can students

- use vocabulary related to the work of an underwater archaeologist?

  Ask students to describe Guillermo de Anda's work.

- use new vocabulary to discuss different kinds of jobs?

  Ask students to use vocabulary words to complete the sentence frames:

  If you like _____, then being an archaeologist might be the career for you. (adventure)

  The work of a _____ involves hours of studying data. (researcher)

Workbook For additional practice, assign Workbook pages 12–13.

Online Workbook Vocabulary

SPEAKING STRATEGY

Objective
Students will
• use questions to extend a conversation.

Speaking Strategy Extending the conversation

Academic Language *conversation, extend*

Content Vocabulary *cruise ship*

Resources Worksheet 1.2.3 (Teacher's Resource CD-ROM/Website); Tracks 021–022 (Audio CD/Website/CPT); CPT: Speaking Strategy

Materials pencils and paper clips

SPEAKING STRATEGY 🎧 021

Extending the conversation

Topic	Extending the conversation
I'd like to be an explorer.	And you? What about you? What do you think?
I can speak Spanish.	Can you?
He knows how to dive.	Do you?

1 **Listen.** How do the speakers extend the conversation? Write the phrases you hear. 🎧 022

2 **Read and complete the dialogue.**
Possible answers:

Elena: I'd love to work on a cruise ship and travel the world.
What about you?

Sarah: Not me. The travelling would be fun, but I think it's *really* hard work.
What do you think?

Elena: You're right, it may be hard work. But I like exploring new places.
Do you?

Sarah: I do, but remember, you have to look after people. It's not a holiday!

Elena: You're right, but I love people, so it's OK. And I speak Spanish, English and Mandarin, so I can talk to people from lots of different places.
Can you?

Sarah: No, I can only speak English. You know, I think I'll be a travel writer. That way, I can travel without looking after other people!

3 **Work in pairs.** Spin the wheel. Read the sentence aloud, giving correct information about yourself. Then extend the conversation.

> It would be really cool to work in an airport. What do you think?

4 **Discuss in pairs.** How does this strategy help you to communicate better? What are some other words or phrases you know that will help you learn more about the person you're talking to?

Go to page 155.

Warm Up

• **Activate prior knowledge** Say *When you talk to someone, it's called having a conversation. When you're with someone you know well, talking is easy. There are times, though, when conversation isn't so easy.* Ask *What are some of those times? What about when you meet someone for the first time? What do you talk about?*

• Explain that if you and the person have a common interest, it makes conversation a little easier. Invite a student and model having a conversation about the student's neighbourhood (or some other familiar topic). Say *(Tina), I live in (area). Where do you live?* Ask the student to respond. Then say *I know that neighbourhood. I buy (bread) there all the time. Do you?* Ask the student to respond. Then say *I wonder (what it's like to be a baker). What do you think?*

Present

• Write on the board: *Do you?* and *What about you?* Say *When you ask questions like these in a conversation, you're giving the other person a chance to talk and tell you something about him/herself.*

• Tell students to turn to page 29. Read aloud the first statement on the table at the top of the page, followed by the first question on the right. Invite a student to stand up and repeat the statement. Prompt him/her to follow that with the second question on the right. Ask another student to repeat the process, using the third question on the right. Finally, play **Track 021**.

• **1** Say *Now listen as two people talk about jobs. Pay attention to the questions they each use to extend the conversation. Write them down.* Play **Track 022**. When students have finished listening and writing, invite them to share what they wrote. Review as a class.

Practise

- Once students seem comfortable using questions to extend the conversation, ask them to complete Activity 2 independently. Tell them that more than one question can be used to complete each part of the dialogue, but they should make sure each question sounds right. Tell students to read their completed dialogues aloud, taking turns to be Elena and Sarah.

Apply

- Tell pairs to cut out and assemble the spinner on page 155. Read aloud the game instructions as pairs look at their spinners. Say *Take turns. Choose one of the words or phrases in brackets to complete a sentence on the spinner. Then use a question to extend the conversation.* Invite a student to read the speech bubble on page 29 to model.

- 4 Read Activity 4 instructions aloud. Say *Discuss with a partner how extending a conversation helps you improve your conversation skills.* When students have completed their discussions, ask them to share some of their ideas, words and phrases with the class.

Extend

- Put students into new pairs, preferably pairing a less fluent student with one more proficient in English. Say *Now, have a conversation! Use your notes from Activity 4.* If necessary, suggest some topics to help partners get started: *learning how to do something, going to a presentation by a scientist, watching a video, trying something new.* Then write sentence frames such as the ones below:

> I'm excited about _____! Are you?
>
> We'll be going to _____. Will you?
>
> I think I want to _____. What do you want?
>
> I could _____. Could you?

- If time allows, hand out **Worksheet 1.2.3**. Pairs can use the worksheet for further practice in extending the conversation and using the new vocabulary.

Consolidate

- Write the following on the board: *adventure, archaeologist, career, dangerous, job, office, researcher, study, take risks* and *work.*

- Tell students to stand in a circle. Say *Use the words on the board in order. Make a sentence to say to the next person in the circle. Then use one of the phrases you learnt to extend the conversation.* Point to *adventure.* Model for students: *I'd like a job with adventure! How about you?* When all the words have been used, add new vocabulary words. Play until every student has had a turn.

Strategy in Depth

Learning how to extend a conversation helps students improve their language skills. Tell students this simple strategy is a good way to prevent a conversation from ending too quickly. Another form of conversation extender is the follow-up question. It may be helpful for students to practise with questions starting with the five *W*s: *who, what, when, where* and *why,* and also *how.* Examples include:

> *What did you do next?*
> *Why do you say that?*
> *How did that happen?*
> *When did that happen?*
> *Who were you with?*
> *What did you say?*
> *Where did that happen?*

Formative Assessment

Can students
- use questions to extend a conversation?

  Ask students to complete the sentence frame and extend the conversation:

  I think I'd like a job _____.
  _____?

Objectives

Students will
- use present simple questions and answers to talk about routines.
- recognise and use words associated with applying for jobs.

Grammar Present simple questions and answers: Talking about routines

Target Vocabulary *apply for, employee, interview, schedule, skills*

Pronunciation Intonation in questions

Resources Online Workbook/Workbook pages 14–15; Tracks 023–027, Tracks 116–118 (Audio CD/Website/CPT); CPT: Grammar 1 and Pronunciation; Pronunciation Answer Key (Teacher's Resource CD-ROM/Website)

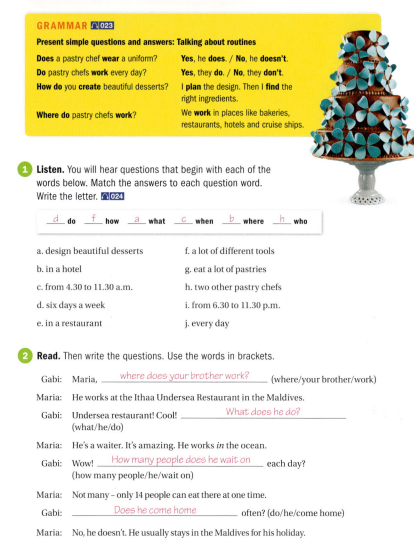

GRAMMAR 🎧 023

Present simple questions and answers: Talking about routines

Does a pastry chef **wear** a uniform? — **Yes**, he **does**. / **No**, he **doesn't**.

Do pastry chefs **work** every day? — **Yes**, they **do**. / **No**, they **don't**.

How do you **create** beautiful desserts? — I **plan** the design. Then I **find** the right ingredients.

Where do pastry chefs **work**? — We **work** in places like bakeries, restaurants, hotels and cruise ships.

1 **Listen.** You will hear questions that begin with each of the words below. Match the answers to each question word. Write the letter. 🎧 024

| _d_ do | _f_ how | _a_ what | _c_ when | _b_ where | _h_ who |

a. design beautiful desserts   f. a lot of different tools

b. in a hotel   g. eat a lot of pastries

c. from 4.30 to 11.30 a.m.   h. two other pastry chefs

d. six days a week   i. from 6.30 to 11.30 p.m.

e. in a restaurant   j. every day

2 **Read.** Then write the questions. Use the words in brackets.

Gabi: Maria, _where does your brother work?_ (where/your brother/work)

Maria: He works at the Ithaa Undersea Restaurant in the Maldives.

Gabi: Undersea restaurant! Cool! _What does he do?_ (what/he/do)

Maria: He's a waiter. It's amazing. He works *in* the ocean.

Gabi: Wow! _How many people does he wait on_ each day? (how many people/he/wait on)

Maria: Not many – only 14 people can eat there at one time.

Gabi: _Does he come home_ often? (do/he/come home)

Maria: No, he doesn't. He usually stays in the Maldives for his holiday.

30 GRAMMAR

Warm Up

- **Build background** Write *routine* on the board. Ask *What does routine mean?* Discuss with students that it can mean a series of things you do at a particular time. Say *For example, I've got a morning routine.* Describe your morning routine, using the present simple. Then say *It's a routine because I do these same things, in the same order, every morning that I work at school.* Ask students describe their morning routines.

- Say *Another kind of routine is one that is associated with a specific activity. When astronauts repair the Hubble telescope, they have a routine, or set of steps, they follow to make sure they check every part.* Explain that a routine can also refer to things that are associated with a particular job – for example, it's part of a nurse's routine to wear a uniform, to give out medication, to assist at operations, and so on.

- Say *Remember, in Unit 1 we learnt to use the present simple to talk about situations that exist now, as in 'I live on (street)'. Well, we also use the present simple to describe actions that are part of a routine. That's why we say 'Nurses wear uniforms and give out medication'.*

3 **LEARN NEW WORDS** **Exploration Cruises is looking for new employees.** Listen to their advert. Read the information. Then listen and repeat. 🎧 **025 | 026**

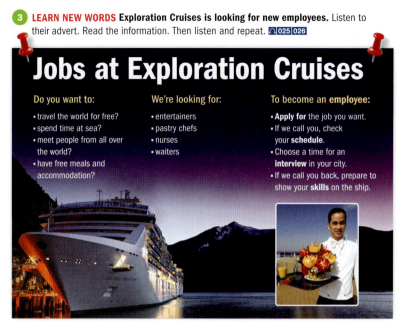

Jobs at Exploration Cruises

Do you want to:
- travel the world for free?
- spend time at sea?
- meet people from all over the world?
- have free meals and accommodation?

We're looking for:
- entertainers
- pastry chefs
- nurses
- waiters

To become an employee:
- **Apply for** the job you want.
- If we call you, check your **schedule**.
- Choose a time for an **interview** in your city.
- If we call you back, prepare to show your **skills** on the ship.

4 **Listen.** You will hear an interview with the captain of a cruise ship. Write sentences to answer the questions. 🎧 **027**   *Possible answers:*

1. How many employees work on the ship?
   One thousand employees work on the ship.

2. What is the captain's schedule like?
   The captain has a busy schedule.

3. What is one skill the captain has?
   The captain controls the ship/uses maps and new technology/works well with others.

4. Does the captain like his job?
   Yes, he does.

5. Does the captain work all year round?
   No, he doesn't.

5 **Work in pairs.** Think of two other questions to ask the captain about his routine. Role-play the rest of the interview.

GRAMMAR **31**

Grammar in Depth

For a review of the uses of the present simple, see the Grammar 1 instruction and Grammar in Depth note in Unit 1.

Talking about routines is one instance when students should be encouraged to respond with short answers. For example, the preferred response to a question such as 'Does he work in a restaurant?' is 'Yes, he does.' Although a simple 'Yes' or the longer 'Yes, he works in a restaurant' are correct, responding with the longer sentence may, in English, suggest annoyance with the question.

Pronunciation

Go to Student's Book page 144. Use Audio Tracks 119–120.

Intonation in questions Intonation is the way we use our voices when speaking; it's the 'music' of the language. For English speakers, there is typically a rising intonation at the end of *yes/no* questions and a falling intonation at the end of *wh-* questions.

Present

- Tell students to open their books at page 30 and look at the table. Say *Here are some questions and answers about the routine of a pastry chef, which is a baker who makes fancy desserts.* Read aloud the questions in the table one at a time and point to individual students to read each answer. Then point out and read aloud the present simple verbs in bold. Ask students to repeat. Play **Track 023** as students listen. Then ask student pairs to take turns asking and answering the questions in the table.

- Write some jobs on the board. Tell partners to choose jobs and ask and answer questions about the job routines. Say *Remember to use present simple verbs in your questions and answers.* When they've worked for several minutes, invite pairs to repeat their dialogues for the class.

firefighter	teacher	football player
doctor	astronaut	underwater archaeologist

GRAMMAR 1   **73**

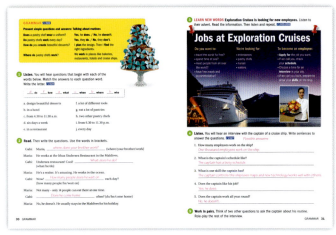

Practise

- Say *Now we're going to hear a conversation between a pastry chef and someone who wants to know about that job. Let's listen.* Play **Track 024**. When students have listened to the entire dialogue, read Activity 1 instructions aloud. Ask students to read the question words in the box. Ask *Did you hear any of these words in the dialogue? Let's listen again.*

- Play the track again, but this time pause the dialogue periodically after a question to make sure students understand the activity. Model the activity for students.

- Begin **Track 024**. Pause it after the first question. Write *What do you do as a pastry chef?* Ask *What word does the question begin with?* (what) Say *Find the word in the box.* Then play the answer. Ask *What letter should you put on the line next to* what *in the box?* (a)

- Continue the track, pausing it once or twice to repeat the process above. Play the track a third time if necessary. Make sure students understand that there are activity items in their books that they will not hear in the audio. Check answers as a class.

- Tell students the next activity is a conversation about a man who works as a server, another word for *waiter,* in a restaurant that's underwater. The roof and sides are made of a strong clear plastic, so the diners can look at the water and sea life surrounding them as they eat. Tell them the Maldives is a nation in the Indian Ocean made up of hundreds of islands. Review the activity instructions with students. Lead them through the first item.

- Say *Remember, we use present simple verbs when we talk about routines.* Check answers as a class.

Apply

- Point to the photo on page 31. Invite students to describe it. Ask different students to stand up and read the first two sections of text in the photo. Give assistance as needed. (*Accommodation* refers to the rooms people stay in at a hotel or on a cruise ship.) Ask *What words do you see that end in one of the suffixes we learnt about?* (entertainers, waiters) *What are the base words?* (entertain, wait) Finally, invite students to define each word.

- **LEARN NEW WORDS** Read Activity 3 instructions aloud. Ask *What is an ad?* Explain that *ad* is a shortened form of *advertisement* and means a notice in a newspaper, on a poster, or online about a product, a job or an event. Say *Now we'll learn some new words that will help you talk about jobs and what people need to do to get one.* Play **Track 025** while students listen. Then say *We'll listen to the new words again in sentences. We'll repeat each one alone and in a sentence.* Play **Track 026**.

- Read the instructions for Activity 4. Say *First, we'll listen. Pay attention to the captain's answers to the interviewer's questions. Make notes. Then I'll play the track again and you'll write your answers.* Play **Track 027**. When students have finished listening, tell them to use present simple verbs in their answers, and explain to them that there's no one correct way to answer some of the questions.

- Play **Track 027** again as students write. You may want to pause the audio after the captain answers each question to give students time to write their answers. Invite students to share their answers.

- **5** Put students into pairs and ask them do Activity 5. Tell them to use their notes from Activity 4 to write two new questions and answers. If necessary, play the track again. Invite pairs to role-play their dialogues for the class.

Extend

- Tell students to work in pairs. Say *We've learnt a little about the work of a pastry chef, a waiter and a ship captain. Choose one of these jobs and write an ad about it.* Tell students to review the information about each job in their books and the ad on page 31. They should include in their ads what the work involves, the skills it requires and the number of hours the person will work. Say *Use the new vocabulary and present simple verbs where appropriate.*

Consolidate

- Say *Let's play a game of* Who Am I? Tell students to use the information in their books to write clues about two or three of the jobs they've learnt about. Clues should describe something about the work and what it involves: adventure, risk and so on. Say *But don't say too much. The rest of us must guess what the job is.* Say *Try to use the unit vocabulary and present simple verbs in your descriptions.* Model for students. Say *Here's a clue: I have a passion for delicious, tasty things. I create them with tools almost every day of the week. Who am I?* (a pastry chef)

- When students have written their clues, line the class up in two teams facing each other. One at a time, students read a clue to the person on the other team facing them. If the person identifies the job correctly, his/her team earns a point. Then he/she reads his/her clue. Play until there are no clues left. The team with the most points wins.

Objectives

Students will
- explain ideas about jobs that involve taking risks.
- use new words from the reading text.
- compare and contrast two people with unusual jobs.

Reading Strategy Compare and contrast

Vocabulary Strategy Base words and the suffixes *-er, -or* and *-ist*

Target Vocabulary *advisor, commute, create, photographer, scientist*

Academic Language *compare, contrast*

Content Vocabulary *inspiration, microscopic, planetary*

Resources Online Workbook/Workbook pages 16–17; Worksheet 1.2.4 (Teacher's Resource CD-ROM/ Website); Tracks 028–029 (Audio CD/ Website/CPT); CPT: Reading

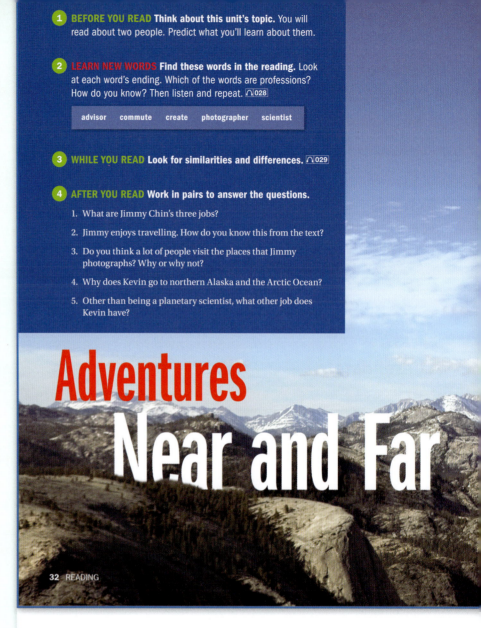

1. **BEFORE YOU READ Think about this unit's topic.** You will read about two people. Predict what you'll learn about them.

2. **LEARN NEW WORDS Find these words in the reading.** Look at each word's ending. Which of the words are professions? How do you know? Then listen and repeat. 🔊028

| advisor | commute | create | photographer | scientist |

3. **WHILE YOU READ Look for similarities and differences.** 🔊029

4. **AFTER YOU READ Work in pairs to answer the questions.**
   1. What are Jimmy Chin's three jobs?
   2. Jimmy enjoys travelling. How do you know this from the text?
   3. Do you think a lot of people visit the places that Jimmy photographs? Why or why not?
   4. Why does Kevin go to northern Alaska and the Arctic Ocean?
   5. Other than being a planetary scientist, what other job does Kevin have?

Adventures
Near and Far

32 READING

Warm Up

- **Activate prior knowledge** Say *Early in the unit we talked about jobs that involve physical activity and danger. What are some of these jobs?* (underwater archaeologist, firefighter, astronaut) *Why do people have jobs that involve taking risks?* (to experience adventure, to help people in need, to learn new things)

- Tell students that people with these jobs learn not to take unnecessary risks. Ask *What would you need to do first before taking one of these jobs?* Explain that people who do these jobs usually have certain basic skills, such as athletic ability or scientific knowledge, and then they undergo years of special training.

These explorers love working in extreme places.

You're more likely to find photographer Jimmy Chin commuting to Mount Everest than to an office. Not only is he a photographer, he's also a professional climber and skier. He takes photographs and videos in some of the most amazing – but dangerous – places on Earth.

Jimmy has climbed and photographed the world's highest mountains in Nepal, Tibet and Pakistan. And he does all of this while carrying heavy cameras. Why does Jimmy do such difficult work in such extreme places? 'Creating films and photographs in situations that few others could experience is my life's inspiration,' he says.

Jimmy isn't the only explorer working in extreme places. Planetary scientist Kevin Hand drills through the ice in northern Alaska and the Arctic Ocean to study microscopic life in the water underneath it. He hopes that studying microscopic life under ice on Earth will help him to find and study life under the ice on Jupiter's moon, Europa.

Not all of Kevin's work is in cold, faraway places, though. He also works with directors as a science advisor for films, such as *Europa Report*. Kevin has even been in a film! He was a featured scientist in the film *Aliens of the Deep*.

Jimmy and Kevin make it clear that work doesn't have to be boring!

Jimmy Chin in Yosemite National Park, California, USA

 Work in pairs. Compare and contrast Jimmy Chin and Kevin Hand.

 Discuss in groups.

1. Jimmy and Kevin take risks doing their work. Would you want a job where you had to take risks? Do you think it's good or bad to take risks? Why?

2. Do you think it's important to explore outer space? Why or why not?

READING **33**

Reading Strategy

Compare and contrast When you compare, you look for the ways two or more people or things are alike. When you contrast, you look for the ways in which they're different. Words that show comparison include *alike, both* and *similar*. Words and phrases that show contrast include *unlike, but* and *different*. Thinking about how things are similar and different as they read can help students improve their focus and, consequently, their comprehension.

Vocabulary Strategy

Base words and the suffixes *-er, -or* and *-ist* Refer to the Vocabulary Strategy lesson on page 69 in this Lesson Planner. You may want to tell students that being able to break up a long word into its parts can help them work out the meaning of an unknown word. For example, recognising the suffix *-er, -or* or *-ist* at the end of a base word should signal to students that the word may be a noun for a person who performs a particular action.

Teaching Tip

Encourage students to make notes on unfamiliar words as they read. Tell them to write down the words. Then ask them to use context clues or clues in any images that accompany the text to make a prediction about what the words mean. Tell students to use a dictionary to verify their predictions and confirm word meanings.

Before You Read

- Tell students to open their books at pages 32–33 and look at the photo. Ask *What can you see? What do you think the man is doing?* (a man hanging on a rope from a mountain; he's probably rock or mountain climbing) Tell students to read Activity 1 instructions. Say *Remember that to predict what the reading will be about, you look at the photo and read the title. Now look, think and make predictions about what you think you'll learn from the text.* When students are ready, invite them to share their predictions.

- **LEARN NEW WORDS** Tell students they're going to learn some new words from the text. Read aloud the instructions for Activity 2 and the words in the box. Ask *Which words are professions?* (advisor, photographer, scientist) *What word parts help you know that?* (*-or, -er* and *-ist*) *What are these word parts called?* (suffixes)

Adventures Near and Far

- **Vocabulary Strategy** Remind students of the lesson they had on *-er*, *-or* and *-ist*. Ask *What are the base words these suffixes are added to?* (*advise*, *photograph* and *science*) *How does knowing the meaning of these suffixes help you work out what* advisor, photographer *and* scientist *mean?* Help students to see that recognising when a suffix has been added to a base word can sometimes help them work out an unfamiliar word's meaning.

- Ask pairs to find all the words in the box in the text and discuss what they think they mean. Then play **Track 028** and ask students to listen and repeat.

While You Read

- Say *Now you're going to hear more information about Jimmy Chin and another man with a job that includes adventure and risk.* Explain to students that many people engage in outdoor sports that involve extreme physical activity and taking risks, but for them it's a hobby, a way to occasionally experience adventure. Say *The people in the text engage in extreme activity for a living. It's their job. Now listen and read. Were your predictions correct?* Play **Track 029** and ask students to listen and follow.

- Say *Now read* Adventures Near and Far *again. This time, look for the ways that Jimmy and Kevin and their jobs are similar and different.* Play **Track 029** again or allow students to read in silence.

After You Read

- Ask student pairs to work together to read and answer the questions. As students work, circulate and give assistance as needed. Give prompts, such as *Think about why Jimmy Chin and Kevin Hand do what they do. Can you find text evidence to support your ideas?* Make sure students understand what *planetary* means and that it describes Kevin's study of the planet Jupiter and its moon Europa.

- Read aloud Activity 5. Say *Remember that when you compare, you describe how people or things are alike, and when you contrast, you describe how they're different.* Tell students that a Venn diagram can help them compare and contrast Jimmy and Kevin and their work. Begin a Venn diagram on the board. Say *The men's jobs are very different. But consider also the environments they work in, or where they are, and what they have to do.* Tell pairs to complete their diagrams and use them to discuss the two men.

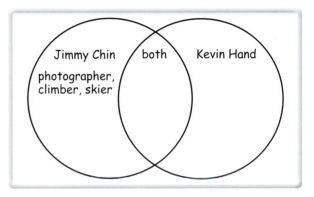

- 6 Put students into small groups to discuss the activity questions. Remind students that people with dangerous professions are not reckless. They are prepared to take risks.

- Say *As you discuss whether it's good or bad to take risks, consider how special training can prepare you to take risks and whether the possible rewards make risks worth taking.* Ask *What are some possible rewards?* For each group, ask one member to act as secretary and write down information from the discussion.

Extend

- Ask *What are some of the professions we learnt about that involve adventure?* (astronaut, underwater archaeologist, ROV operator, cruise ship captain, mountain climber, planetary scientist) List them on the board. Then write *explorer.* Point to the jobs and ask *Which of these jobs involve exploring? Are the people who do these jobs explorers? How would you define* explorer*?* Ask groups to work together to write a definition of the word. Tell groups to complete this sentence frame: *An explorer is someone who _____.*

- **Worksheet** If time allows, you may want to hand out **Worksheet 1.2.4** in class. Students will get additional practice with the new words on page 32 and other Target Vocabulary words from the unit.

Consolidate

- Use the list of jobs on the board. Add other jobs that students have discussed in the unit. Invite students to sit in a circle. Go around the circle, and ask each student to consider which job they might be best suited for and to give a reason why. Model for students. Say *If I weren't a teacher, I think I would like to be an underwater archaeologist because I'm interested in ancient cultures and I love water!* After everyone has had a chance to speak, discuss which were the most popular and least popular jobs and why.

Teaching Tip

Keep track of students' participation during whole-class discussions and group work. Let students know that you expect everyone to speak aloud and participate. Make a note of which students have not spoken aloud. It may be helpful for these students to write down answers to questions before answering. Allow them to read their answers if that's more comfortable for them. This will help them gain confidence with speaking in class.

Answer Key

Comprehension

1. photographer, climber, skier
2. Answers will vary. Example answer: Helping others to experience the amazing places he visits inspires him.
3. No. The places are the highest mountains in the world.
4. To study microscopic life under the Arctic ice.
5. science advisor for films

Formative Assessment

Can students
- explain ideas about jobs that involve taking risks?

  Ask students to explain why some people like jobs that involve taking risks.
- use new words from the reading text?

  Ask *What word means 'to travel back and forth regularly'?* (commute) *What's another word for* design*?* (create)
- compare and contrast two people with unusual jobs?

  Ask students to name one similar thing and one different thing about Jimmy Chin and Kevin Hand.

Workbook For additional practice, assign Workbook pages 16–17.

Online Workbook Reading

Objectives
Students will
- discuss underwater exploration.
- apply the message of the video to their personal lives.

Content Vocabulary *biodiversity, copepod, fissure, pump, sample, species*

Resources Video scene 2.1 (DVD/Website/CPT); Online Workbook; CPT: Video

Materials map of the world or globe

VIDEO ▶

1 **BEFORE YOU WATCH Discuss in pairs.**

1. Look at the photo. What do you think the divers are looking for? List three ideas.

2. Imagine you're diving in this fissure. Describe what you see.

2 **Work in pairs.** You're going to watch *Searching for Life in Iceland's Fissures*. In this video, you'll see scientists enter the water of an underground fissure in Iceland. Predict a problem they might have.

3 **WHILE YOU WATCH Check your prediction from Activity 2. Watch scene 2.1.**

4 **AFTER YOU WATCH Work in pairs.** Answer the questions below.

1. How did Jónína feel the first time she dived in a fissure? Why?

2. What were Jónína and her team the first to do?

3. Why is it risky to dive in the fissure?

4. Why does it seem that there isn't much living in the waters?

5. How do scientists get the material off the walls of the fissures?

6. What do the scientists do with the samples they collect underwater?

7. What are Jónína's two passions?

Jónína and a team member explore Iceland's underwater fissures.

34 VIDEO

Before You Watch

- Tell students to open their books at pages 34–35. Ask *What can you see?* (two divers underwater) *What do you think they're doing?* (exploring) Tell students that the divers are exploring an underwater fissure, which is a deep crack in the ground. Put students into pairs. Then read aloud the first question. Ask pairs to discuss and make their lists.

- Discuss that the divers are most likely collecting samples of the water and the sand to see what's in it. Read the second activity aloud and invite pairs to describe to each other what they imagine they would see in the fissure. Write students' ideas on the board.

- Read aloud Activity 2. Point to Iceland on a map or globe and tell students that it's an island in the North Atlantic Ocean midway between the southern part of Greenland and Norway.

- Ask *What problems do you think the scientists might have?* (cold water, becoming lost, dangerous creatures)

While You Watch

- Say *Now we're going to watch* Searching for Life in Iceland's Fissures. *As you watch, check to see if any of your predictions are correct.* Play **Video scene 2.1**.

- If students have trouble following the video or understanding the text, pause the video and allow them to ask questions. Try replaying the video with and without sound, and ask students to describe and comment on what they see.

- When the video is over, ask students to revisit their predictions. Discuss that they could infer that problems might relate to the heavy equipment the divers had to carry, jumping into a narrow space, or the fact that they were exploring unknown regions.

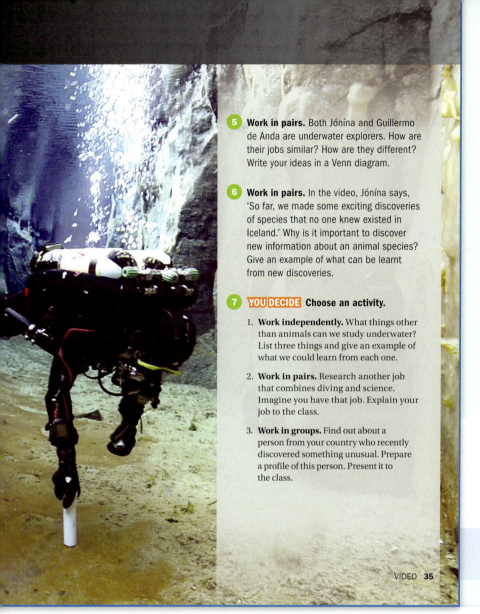

5 **Work in pairs.** Both Jónína and Guillermo de Anda are underwater explorers. How are their jobs similar? How are they different? Write your ideas in a Venn diagram.

6 **Work in pairs.** In the video, Jónína says, 'So far, we made some exciting discoveries of species that no one knew existed in Iceland.' Why is it important to discover new information about an animal species? Give an example of what can be learnt from new discoveries.

7 **YOU DECIDE** **Choose an activity.**

1. **Work independently.** What things other than animals can we study underwater? List three things and give an example of what we could learn from each one.

2. **Work in pairs.** Research another job that combines diving and science. Imagine you have that job. Explain your job to the class.

3. **Work in groups.** Find out about a person from your country who recently discovered something unusual. Prepare a profile of this person. Present it to the class.

VIDEO **35**

After You Watch

• **4** Tell pairs of students to work together to answer the questions. Review them as a class.

• **5** You may want to put students into new pairs. Remind students that a Venn diagram is used to show similarities and differences between two people or things. Begin one on the board to compare and contrast Jónína and Guillermo de Anda. Ask *What goes in the middle, overlapping section?* (how they're the same) Write *underwater explorer* in that part of the diagram.

• Tell pairs to copy and complete the diagram. When they have finished, invite students to come up to the board and complete the diagram. Students' diagrams should include information such as the following: Jónína – biologist, dives in fissures, studies life forms; Guillermo – archaeologist, dives in caves, searches for Mayan artefacts.

• **6** Read aloud Activity 6. Invite pairs of students to discuss. Ask *What might scientists discover by studying the creatures in the fissures?* When students have finished, ask pairs to share their ideas. Discuss why it's important to find out how life survives in extreme temperatures and how it might help scientists to understand how life on Earth began.

• **7** **YOU DECIDE** Read aloud the three options. Students who are interested in science and underwater diving might like options 1 or 2. Ask *What else is there to see and explore underwater?* (plants, mountains, volcanoes, vents, shipwrecks, fossils)

• Say *If you're interested in becoming a news reporter or a writer, you might like option 3.* Say *Perhaps there's a professor you could interview about his or her research, or a bird-watcher or fossil hunter who saw or found something rare. Use your imagination!*

Objective
Students will
• use possessives.

Grammar Possessives: Showing ownership

Academic Language *apostrophe, ownership, possessives*

Content Vocabulary *engineer, porch, programmer*

Resources Online Workbook/Workbook pages 18–19; Track 030 (Audio CD/Website); Worksheet 1.2.5 (Teacher's Resource CD-ROM/Website/CPT); CPT: Grammar 2

GRAMMAR 🎧 030

Possessives: Showing ownership

This **dentist's** job isn't done in an office.
Dr Perkins's job is to get the equipment on the plane.
Pilots' days are very long.

My job is helping ill people. What's **your** job?
The flying dentist thinks **her** job is great. The pilot likes **his** job, too. The job also has **its** advantages.
In **our** job, we help everyone, no matter what **their** problem is.

1 **Read.** Circle the possessives.

(My) name is Dr Smith, and I'm a flight dentist with the Royal Flying Doctor Service of Australia (RFDS). (Its) 63 planes fly every day of the year. (Our) goal is to deliver health services to people in rural areas.

I work with a great team. (Our) days are very long, but no two days are ever the same. One doctor on the team says that he loves (his) job because it's never boring! I don't have an office so I check (patients') teeth in (their) homes. This morning I checked (Ms Lee's) teeth in (her) living room and the Watson (family's) teeth on (their) porch!

2 **Work independently.** Interview classmates to learn about jobs that their family and friends have. Put an X over the job when you find a classmate who knows someone with that job. Play until you cross out five jobs. Then report to the class using possessives.

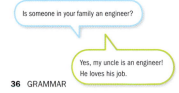

Is someone in your family an engineer?

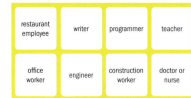

Yes, my uncle is an engineer! He loves his job.

restaurant employee	writer	programmer	teacher
office worker	engineer	construction worker	doctor or nurse

36 GRAMMAR

Warm Up

• **Activate prior knowledge** Hold up a pen or another object that belongs to a student. Say *This is (Jasmine's) pen. It belongs to (Jasmine).* Write *(Jasmine's) pen* on the board. Circle the apostrophe and explain that an apostrophe is a symbol added to the end of a name to show ownership. Say *apostrophe* slowly and ask students to repeat. Then continue holding up different students' things, one at a time, and repeat the phrase *(student's name)'s hat, pencil, book, phone,* and so on.

Present

• Say *We're going to hear and read sentences with possessives, which are words that show ownership.* Read aloud the sentences on the left side of the table. Point out the words in dark print and the 's and s' endings. Say *When you're talking about more than one person or thing, the apostrophe follows the s.*

• Read aloud the sentences on the right side of the table. Say *The words in bold are also possessives.* Repeat the words. Remind students that these words are used to refer to who or what something belongs to without having to repeat the name of the person or thing. Play **Track 030.** Tell students to read silently. Then ask students to read each grammar example aloud.

• Write on the board some examples of possessives. Invite students to alternate reading the phrases in each column one at a time.

Dr Smith's office	his office
the dentist's job	her job
the plane's engine	its engine
the pilots' days	their days

Practise

- Say *Look at the picture with Activity 1. I'm going to read the text first. Listen for the possessive words.* Read the text. Then ask students to read and complete the activity independently. Tell them to refer to the words on the board if they need help recognising the possessives. Review the answers as a class.

Apply ②

- ② Ask students to read the game instructions. Tell them to look over the table of jobs and read the speech bubbles. If necessary, explain that a programmer writes instructions that allow computers to work, and an engineer is someone with specialised knowledge who works with structures, such as bridges and roads, or with mechanical or electrical devices.

- When students have had enough time to interview several classmates, ask them to report their interview results. Say *Report your results in sentences using possessives. For example, James's father is a teacher. His mother works in an office.*

Extend

- Challenge students to make a new table of jobs. Tell them to include a few of the jobs they've learnt about in the unit and to make some of the jobs plural. Say *Play a new game with a partner. Take turns to choose a job and say a sentence about it with a possessive.* Give examples: *A pastry chef's job is interesting. Doctors' jobs are important.* Say *Then tell your partner whether the possessive ends in 's or just '. If you're correct, put an X over the job.*

- Hand out **Worksheet 1.2.5** to give students more practice with possessives.

Consolidate

- Divide the class into small groups. Display the phrases below. Say *Work as a group to write a possessive with an apostrophe for each of the phrases on the board. The first team to finish must come to the board and write each possessive form. If they make any mistakes, the team that finished second will come up and correct the mistakes. If they're wrong, the next team has a chance, and so on.* Tell students that if anyone calls out anything, that student's team will be disqualified.

the careers of the men	the tools of the pastry chefs
the duties of the nurses	the football team of the women
the book of Mateo	the skills of the mountain climber

- Review the answers as a class. (the men's careers, the nurses' duties, Mateo's book, the pastry chefs' tools, the women's football team, the mountain climber's skills)

BE THE EXPERT

Grammar in Depth

Use 's after singular nouns and plural nouns that don't end with an s: *John's shoes, women's football kits*; and after singular nouns ending in s: *my boss's office*.

Use ' (apostrophe alone) after plural nouns ending in s: *boys' clothes*.

Ownership is just one of the meanings of 's. It is also used to express human relationships: *John's cousin, Anne's neighbour*; who or what something is named after: *St. Peter's Square*; time or location: *tomorrow's class*; representations: *John's photo* (as opposed to the photo of John); and physical or mental traits: *Mary's hair*.

Teaching Tip

If time allows, practise reading fluency. Reading aloud helps students practise speaking fluently and quickly, without having to worry about grammar structures and producing new vocabulary. Invite students to read aloud the same sentence more than once. Repeating the same sentences or passages aloud helps students become more familiar and comfortable and will help to increase the speed and accuracy of their reading.

Formative Assessment

Can students
- use possessives?

Ask students to substitute possessives for the words in brackets and rewrite the sentence:

(The job of a dentist) requires special knowledge of (the teeth of people).

(A dentist's job requires special knowledge of people's teeth.)

Workbook For additional practice, assign Workbook pages 18–19.

Online Workbook Grammar 2

WRITING

Objectives

Students will
- recognise elements of descriptive writing.
- recognise the basic parts of a paragraph.
- analyse a model of descriptive writing.
- produce a paragraph describing a daily routine.

Writing Descriptive paragraph

Academic Language *concluding sentence, descriptive paragraph, details, sequence, title, topic sentence*

Content Vocabulary *sanctuary*

Resources Online Workbook/Workbook page 20; Process Writing Worksheets 1–5, Genre Writing Worksheet: Description (Teacher's Resource CD-ROM/Website); CPT: Writing

---

WRITING

A descriptive paragraph should include the following:

Title: Gives an idea of what the paragraph is about
Topic sentence: Is usually the first sentence; says what the paragraph is about
Details: Give more information about the topic sentence
Concluding sentence: Ends the paragraph

1 **Read the model.** Work in pairs to identify the title, topic sentence, details and concluding sentence. Underline each part.

A Typical Work Day

My aunt has a great job at an orangutan sanctuary. She's the daytime babysitter for a five-month-old orangutan called Coco. Coco's mother died, so they need to take care of her 24 hours a day. When my aunt arrives in the morning, she gives Coco milk in her bottle and changes her nappy. She does this several times a day. Then she works as Coco's teacher, teaching her the skills she needs for living in the forest, such as climbing. Coco likes climbing up, but not down! She screams for my aunt's help sometimes. My aunt hugs her when she gets scared. In the early evening, it's Coco's bedtime, and their time together that day is over. My aunt puts Coco to bed and goes home. My aunt says, 'I love Coco, and I love my job!'

2 **Work in pairs.** What is unusual about the orangutan babysitter's job? Would you like to have this job? Why or why not?

3 **Write.** Describe the daily routine of someone you know who has an unusual job. Include a title, a topic sentence, details and a concluding sentence.

Warm Up

- **Revisit** Say *Remember that we talked about routines, or things you do in a specific order, and about using present simple verbs when we describe routines. Let's think about how we might describe a typical, or usual, morning routine for a student.* Write on the board:

> Anika has a morning routine she follows every school day. She gets up at 7.30. She gets dressed. Then she greets her parents. Before she eats breakfast, she feeds her cat. She washes up after breakfast. Next, she washes her face and brushes her teeth. At 8.30 Anika leaves for school. She's never late!

- Ask *What words and phrases help you understand the order of the activities in Anika's routine?* Ask students to come to the board and underline the words and phrases. Then ask *What does Anika do after she feeds the cat?* (eats breakfast) If students answer 'washes up' instead, point out that they need to read carefully and analyse the words that show sequence. Say *A description of a routine will not always use such obvious words as* first, second, next *and* last.

- Put students into pairs. Ask students to work together to make a numbered list of all the activities in Anika's routine. When students have finished, ask *How many separate activities have you got?* (eight) Ask pairs to stand up and read their lists. Leave the paragraph on the board for use later in the lesson.

Present

- Tell students to open their books at page 37. Say *When you write a paragraph describing something, there are certain things you should include.* Review the parts of a paragraph with students. Then say *Let's look at the paragraph about Anika. Check it against the parts of a paragraph listed in your note book. Is any part missing?* Help students to see that there's no title. Ask *What do you think the title should be?* Then ask students to read the sentences that match the other parts of a paragraph.

Read the Model

- Say *Now we're going to look at an example of a descriptive paragraph. First, read the title and look at the photo.* Invite students to predict what the text will be about. Ask *What do you think the paragraph is about?*

- Read the instructions aloud. Say *Work with a partner to identify and underline the parts of the paragraph. Don't underline every detail, just the most important ones. The text is about a typical day at work, so focus on what the person does at the beginning, the middle and the end of the working day. Remember to look for words that signal the order of the activities.*

- When students have finished, review the parts of the text with them. Say *We know the title. What's the topic sentence?* (sentence 1) *What are the most important details?* (the woman babysits a baby orangutan named Coco; she feeds Coco, changes her nappy, teaches her important skills, comforts her and puts her to bed.) *What's the concluding sentence?* (last sentence) *What words and phrases helped you understand the order of the woman's activities?* (*in the morning, then, early evening, day is over*)

- Put the students into pairs and ask them to read the instructions for Activity 2. Before they discuss, tell students to read the text again and think about the woman's job. Ask *Do you know anyone who has a job like this woman's? What does she do that is unusual?*

- **Worksheet** If your students need a reminder of the elements of descriptive writing, you may want to hand out **Genre Writing Worksheet (Description)** and review it together.

Writing Support

Potential routine description problems When describing a routine, it's most important to clearly indicate the order of the activities in the routine. The whole point of describing a routine is to give the reader a clear picture of how something is done or what takes place within a particular period of time on a regular basis, so sequence words and phrases are important.

In addition to the words *first, next, then, finally,* and so on, students can make their writing more interesting by indicating sequence in other ways, such as by using dates, times and words that indicate the passage of time (for example, *after I make my bed, before I walk the dog, later on, when it gets dark,* and so on).

Teaching Tip

Texts that give information often include many details that students may forget. After an initial reading, provide opportunities for revisiting the text and making notes. For example, ask students to re-read the text at the end of the lesson and make notes. At the beginning of the next lesson, tell students to refer to their notes to answer questions about the text.

Workbook For scaffolded Writing support, assign Workbook page 20.

Online Workbook Writing

WRITING

A descriptive paragraph should include the following:

Title: Gives an idea of what the paragraph is about
Topic sentence: Is usually the first sentence; says what the paragraph is about
Details: Give more information about the topic sentence
Concluding sentence: Ends the paragraph

1 **Read the model.** Work in pairs to identify the title, topic sentence, details and concluding sentence. Underline each part.

A Typical Work Day

My aunt has a great job at an orangutan sanctuary. She's the daytime babysitter for a five-month-old orangutan called Coco. Coco's mother died, so they need to take care of her 24 hours a day. When my aunt arrives in the morning, she gives Coco milk in her bottle and changes her nappy. She does this several times a day. Then she works as Coco's teacher, teaching her the skills she needs for living in the forest, such as climbing. Coco likes climbing up, but not down! She screams for my aunt's help sometimes. My aunt hugs her when she gets scared. In the early evening, it's Coco's bedtime, and their time together that day is over. My aunt puts Coco to bed and goes home. My aunt says, 'I love Coco, and I love my job!'

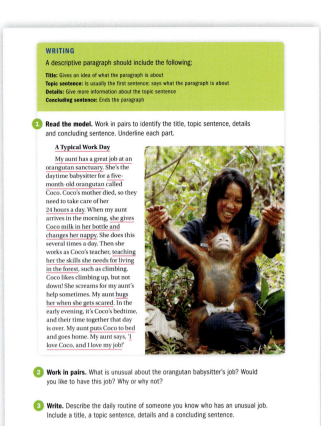

2 **Work in pairs.** What is unusual about the orangutan babysitter's job? Would you like to have this job? Why or why not?

3 **Write.** Describe the daily routine of someone you know who has an unusual job. Include a title, a topic sentence, details and a concluding sentence.

WRITING **37**

• **Worksheets** If your students need a reminder of any of the steps of process writing, you may want to hand out **Process Writing Worksheets 1–5** and review them together.

• **Workbook** Refer students to Workbook page 20 to help them organise and plan their writing.

Write

• After students have finished their pre-writing, tell them to work on their first drafts. If you don't have enough time in the lesson, assign the first draft as homework.

Revise

• After students have finished their first drafts, tell them to review their writing and think about their ideas and organisation. Ask each student to consider the following: *Have they included a topic sentence and a concluding sentence? Is the order of activities clearly indicated? Are the details arranged in a logical way? What seems good? What needs more work?*

Edit and Proofread

• Invite students to consider elements of style, such as sentence variety, parallelism and word choice. Then tell them to proofread for mistakes in grammar, punctuation, capitalisation and spelling. Remind them to make sure they have used present simple verbs when describing the routine and that they have used possessives correctly.

Publish

• Publishing includes handing in pieces of writing to the teacher, sharing work with classmates, adding pieces of work to a class book, displaying pieces of work on a classroom wall or in a hallway, and posting on the Internet.

Plan **3**

• **3** Say *Now you're going to plan your writing. You already know your topic – describing the daily routine of someone with an unusual job. So your next step is pre-writing.* Say *Let's review. What are some ways we do pre-writing?* (brainstorm, freewrite, make lists, use a graphic organiser, use sentence starters)

• Say *Now decide what you want to use for pre-writing.* If you have time in the lesson, allow students to work on this step. If not, assign it as homework. If students have workbooks, remind them to use Workbook page 20 for writing support.

Writing Assessment

Use these guidelines to assess students' writing. You can add other aspects of their writing you'd like to assess at the bottom of the table.

4 = Excellent
3 = Good
2 = Needs improvement
1 = Re-do

	1	2	3	4
Writing Student includes all the parts of a paragraph and uses a variety of details to describe a daily routine.				
Grammar Student uses correct grammar, including present simple verbs and possessives.				
Vocabulary Student uses a variety of word choices, including descriptive language used in this unit.				

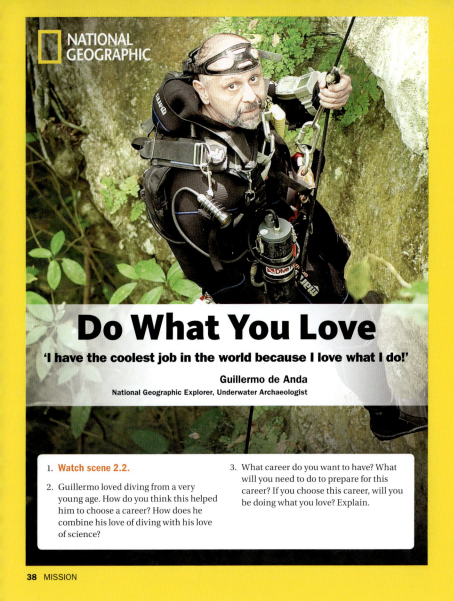

Do What You Love

'I have the coolest job in the world because I love what I do!'

Guillermo de Anda
National Geographic Explorer, Underwater Archaeologist

1. **Watch scene 2.2.**

2. Guillermo loved diving from a very young age. How do you think this helped him to choose a career? How does he combine his love of diving with his love of science?

3. What career do you want to have? What will you need to do to prepare for this career? If you choose this career, will you be doing what you love? Explain.

MISSION

Objective
Students will
• discuss the importance of finding something you love to do.

Resources Video scene 2.2 (DVD/Website); Worksheet 1.2.6 (Teacher's Resource CD-ROM/Website); Online Workbook: Meet the Explorer

BE THE EXPERT

Teaching Tip
Even advanced students may have difficulty understanding spoken English. Modify your speaking pace throughout class. When you are giving instructions or explaining a project, make sure you speak slowly and clearly. Other times, such as when you're modelling speech or a dialogue, it may be more appropriate to speak faster so students can have practice listening to English as it is spoken by native or proficient speakers.

Online Workbook Meet the Explorer

Mission

• Invite students to read aloud the quote by Guillermo de Anda. Say *Guillermo has found the perfect job for him because it combines two things he loves – diving and science. Do you think he was just lucky to find such a job? Do you think someone called him one day and said 'Guillermo, how would you like a job where you could go diving and do archaeology at the same time?'* Discuss with students how Guillermo's job requires years of study and training. He must have thought about what career he'd like from an early age.

• **Activity 1** Say *Now let's watch a video about Guillermo de Anda.* Ask students to focus on Guillermo's ideas about what makes his job the 'coolest job in the world'. Play **Video scene 2.2.**

• **Activity 2** Put students into pairs. Ask them to consider how the knowledge you gain and the experiences you have at an early age can influence your whole life. Say *Remember, in Unit 1 we talked about the importance of exploring your world. The more experiences you have, the more likely you'll be to find something you really love!*

• **Activity 3** Invite students to work individually to answer the Activity 3 questions. Say *Think about your passions. Make a list of the things you like to do. Then think about the jobs we've learnt about, other jobs you've read about, the jobs your relatives do, and the routines involved. Do you see any matches?*

• **Worksheet** Hand out **Worksheet 1.2.6.** Explain that students will use the worksheet to further consider and write about Guillermo de Anda's job and finding a career they love.

Objective

Students will

- choose and complete a project related to unusual jobs or unusual aspects of typical jobs.

Content Vocabulary *comic strip, job fair*

Resources Assessment: Unit 2 Quiz; Workbook pages 21 and 91; Worksheet 1.2.7 (Teacher's Resource CD-ROM/Website); CPT: Make an Impact and Review Games

Materials art materials

Assessment Go to page 255.

Unit Review Assign Worksheet 1.2.7.
Workbook Assign pages 21 and 91.
Online Workbook Now I can

Make an Impact

YOU DECIDE Choose a project.

1 **Write a job advert.**

- Imagine you own a company and you need someone for an unusual job.
- Create a job advert. Write a description of the job. Include information about your company.
- Share your job advert with the class. Is anyone interested in your unusual job? Interview them for the job!

2 **Create a comic strip.**

- Interview a person who has a typical job. Ask this person to mention three or four unusual or unexpected parts of the job.
- Design a comic strip to illustrate the unusual aspects of this person's job.
- Share your comic strip with the class.

3 **Plan a job fair for unusual jobs.**

- Find information about five interesting and unusual careers.
- Make posters showing a typical day for these workers.
- Display the posters in your classroom. Talk to your classmates about what each job involves.

PROJECT **39**

Prepare

- **YOU DECIDE** Ask students to choose a project.

- **Activity 1** Make sure students understand that they have to come up with an idea for a company and an unusual job within that company. For example, a company that sells unique jewellery might need an adventurous person to travel all over the world to find materials to make the jewellery. Say *Remember to review the ad on page 31 and the ad you created in that lesson.*

- **Activity 2** Ask *What ordinary jobs might include some surprising work? Jobs that involve animals or babies might be a place to start. Babies of any kind are always surprising!* Ask *And what about the photo on page 39? I wonder what work that person does when he's not wearing the boot?* Remind students of the game they played where they interviewed classmates about their relatives' jobs.

- **Activity 3** Suggest that students work in a group to plan the job fair and create posters. Explain that a job fair is an event where many companies come together to present information about their jobs to potential employees. Say *Make your posters inspire your classmates to imagine amazing careers for themselves!*

Share

- Schedule time for groups to present their final projects to the class. Allow time for company 'owners' to interview potential 'employees'. After an initial presentation to the class, students may want to refine their projects and display their ads, comic strips, and unusual job posters together at a school job fair.

- **Modify** Help students simplify a project by eliminating an option or step. You might suggest using pictures from old magazines on some posters to cut down on the amount of artwork students need to create.

Track 017 ① **Listen and read.** See Student's Book pages 26–27.

Track 018 ② LEARN NEW WORDS **adventure** / Going to an underwater cave would be an exciting adventure. **archaeologist** / Archaeologists study people and things from long ago. **career** / For a career in archaeology, you must love history. **clue** / We're looking for a clue to solve this puzzle. **consider** / My brother is considering a career as a firefighter. **explore** / You need light to explore a cave. **job** / My uncle has a job as a university professor. **office** / Most offices have a desk, a telephone and a computer. **passion** / Exploring new places is her passion. **profession** / To work in a medical profession, you must go to school for many years. **study** / You can learn a lot about a culture if you study its history. **take a risk** / People take risks when they explore underwater. **train** / Before you train as a diver, you must know how to swim. **work** / Teaching is fun, but it is also a lot of work.

Track 019 ⑤ Do you love history, but don't want a dangerous job? You could work as a historical researcher. You would read a lot and study artefacts that explorers find. It's a good career choice if you love to learn about ancient cultures, but don't love adventure. You could travel in time, without ever leaving your office!

Track 020 ⑤ LEARN NEW WORDS **choice** / Think about what you like doing when making a career choice. **dangerous** / Being a firefighter is a dangerous profession. **researcher** / Researchers look at artefacts to learn about history.

Track 021 SPEAKING STRATEGY See Student's Book page 29.

Track 022 ① **S1**: Hi, Tony. I finished our project about jobs today. I thought it was fun. And you? **S2**: Yeah, it was great. I especially liked learning about baking. I think I'd like to be a pastry chef. I love cake! What do you think? **S1**: A pastry chef? Are you sure? You have to start work really early in the morning. I can't get up that early. Can you? **S2**: Getting up early doesn't bother me. I get up at 5 o'clock every day. What about you? **S1**: Not me! I prefer to get up late, so I think I'd like a job with night-time hours. **S2**: What kind of job can you do at night? **S1**: Lots of jobs! You can work in a restaurant, or in a hospital, or even at an airport. I think working at an airport would be exciting. How about you? **S2**: Hmm. I'm not sure. I think I'd rather bake cakes. In fact, I just made a chocolate cake! I want some. Do you? **S1**: Mmm, yes, please!

Track 023 GRAMMAR See Student's Book page 30.

Track 024 ① **S1**: So you're a pastry chef. That's a pretty cool job. What do pastry chefs do? **S2**: I design and make beautiful desserts. I also teach other people how to make pastries. **S1**: When do you work? **S2**: I work from 4.30 to 11.30 in the morning. **S1**: Do you work every day? **S2**: I work six days a week. **S1**: Where do you work? **S2**: I work in a hotel. **S1**: How do you make fancy pastries? **S2**: I use a lot of different tools. I also ask my colleagues for help when the project is too difficult. **S1**: Who works with you? **S2**: Two other pastry chefs work with me. We share ideas and help each other a lot.

Track 025 ③ Do you want to travel the world and meet new people? If you say, 'Yes, I do', consider a career with Exploration Cruises. Here's how to apply:

First, look at the jobs we need. What can you do? If you find a job that you like, apply for it. If we're interested, we will call you. Then, look at your schedule. Find a time when you can come for an interview. We have offices in most cities. If we're happy with your interview, we'll invite you to come on board one of our ships and show us your skills. With any luck, you'll become the next Exploration Cruises' employee!

Track 026 ③ LEARN NEW WORDS **apply for** / Many people apply for jobs online. **employee** / The employees work on the cruise ship. **interview** / It's important to answer all the questions in an interview. **schedule** / A schedule shows the days and times people work. **skill** / Creativity and imagination are important skills for chefs.

Track 027 ④ **S1**: Thank you so much for doing this interview, Captain Parker. **S2**: It's my pleasure. Thank you for coming on board my cruise ship. **S1**: How many employees do you have on your ship? **S2**: We have about 1,000 employees. It's a big ship! **S1**: Wow! That's a lot! Do you have a very busy schedule? **S2**: Oh, yes. I work every day, and I work long hours. **S1**: What skills do you use as captain? **S2**: Well, I control the ship. I use maps. I also use new technology to help me. I work well with others. **S1**: Do you like your job even though it's busy? **S2**: Oh, yes. I love my job. I work six months at sea. Then I take ten weeks off. **S1**: Sounds great! I think I'd like your job! **S2**: Well, you can apply for my job, but you won't get it!

Track 028 ② LEARN NEW WORDS **advisor** / An advisor helps people to make good decisions. **commute** / She commutes to her job by train. **create** / Artists create works using a lot of different materials. **photographer** / Some photographers take risks to get a good photo. **scientist** / Some scientists want to learn more about outer space.

Track 029 ③ WHILE YOU READ See Student's Book pages 32–33.

Track 030 GRAMMAR See Student's Book page 36.

Track 031 ① **Express Yourself** See Student's Book pages 40–41.

Objectives

Students will
- identify the purpose and features of a travel review.
- connect ideas about unusual places and unusual jobs.

Academic Language *opinion, recommend, recommendation, reviewer, travel review*

Content Vocabulary *embarrassing, holiday*

Resources Workbook pages 22–23/ Online Workbook (Units 1–2 Review); Worksheet 1.2.8 (Teacher's Resource CD-ROM/Website); Track 031 (Audio CD/Website/CPT); CPT: Express Yourself Units 1–2

Express Yourself

Express Yourself

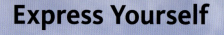

1 Read and listen to the online travel review. 🎧 031

   JGirl, Seoul

GoTravel REVIEWS

GONDOLA TOURS OF VENICE

🧳🧳🧳🧳 210 reviews

'Our gondolier saved my holiday!'

Well, I'm in Venice, Italy, with my family! Venice is incredible! The city is hundreds of years old, and it's built on WATER. People get around on special boats called *gondolas*, and today I had my first gondola ride!

A gondolier controls the gondola using an oar and his own strength. (These gondoliers are REALLY strong.) The gondolier's job is to describe Venice's culture and history as he takes you through the city's canals. Our gondolier was so good at telling stories I almost forgot I was sharing the ride with my parents.

That might sound exciting, and it was, but of course I was with … my dad. And Dad thought it would be funny to wear a striped shirt to match the gondolier's shirt. How *embarrassing*!

Warm Up

- **Preview** Ask students to turn to pages 40–41. Tell students they're going to read a model of a travel review. Ask *What is the purpose of a review?* (to say whether or not you like something) *What is being reviewed here? Who wrote this review?* Point out that 'JGirl' is an online identity, a made-up name that people use to protect their privacy when communicating online.

- Explain to students that a review is a nonfiction text. Reviews are written by real people about real places or things. They include facts and details, as well as the writer's opinions about the subject of the review.

- **1** **Read together** Say *Now we'll listen to and read the online review. Look for ways the writer lets you know what she thought of the gondola tour.* Play **Track 031** once as students listen and read along.

Engage

- **2** **Discuss** Put students into small groups. Say *Now we're ready to talk about the review. Read question 1.* Ask *What's the first thing JGirl says that gives you an idea of what she thinks of the gondola tour?* (last sentence of paragraph 2) *What words does she use to describe her experience? (incredible, exciting, great, beautiful)* Invite groups to discuss question 1.

- Say *Now, let's hear your review of the review!* Invite students to answer question 2. Ask *What other information might be helpful to know?* (how long the tour is, the cost, what if you didn't understand the gondolier's language) Finally, ask *How many of you want to go on a gondola ride in Venice? How many don't?* Ask students to put their hands up. Discuss.

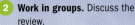

My parents loved looking at the beautiful bridges, churches and palaces along the route. I really enjoyed listening to our gondolier talk about his work. He told us that it takes years of study and practice to get the job. Who knew? He also told us that of all the gondoliers in Venice, only one is a woman! I think I need to change that! It's time to start training for my dream job! Maybe my dad will let me borrow his shirt. ;)

Gondola Tours of Venice gave me a great tour of a beautiful city – and an interesting idea for my future career! I recommend the gondola tour to anyone who's interested in learning about unusual places and unusual jobs ... especially if they're stuck on a boat with their parents!

2 Work in groups. Discuss the review.

1. Does JGirl's review make you want to visit Venice and go on a gondola ride? Why or why not?

2. Do you think the review gives enough information? Is it funny and interesting? What else would you like to know about Venice or about Gondola Tours of Venice?

3 Connect ideas. In Unit 1, you learnt about exploring and unusual places. In Unit 2, you learnt about unusual jobs. What connection can you see between the two units?

Gondolas in Venice, Italy

4 **YOU DECIDE** Choose an activity.

1. Choose a topic:
   - an unusual place
   - an unusual job

2. Choose a way to express yourself:
   - a review
   - an advertisement
   - an interview

3. Present your work.

41

Print features

You may want to point out the travel review's use of such print features as words in all capital letters, exclamation marks, italics, and emoticons. These punctuation marks and features help to convey a writer's feelings or mood, as well as contribute to an informal, conversational tone. Explain that these devices, which should not be used in formal writing, can be overused.

Cumulative Review

Hand out Cumulative Review Worksheet 1.2.8.

Formative Assessment

Can students
- identify the purpose and features of a travel review?

  Ask students to identify the purpose of the Gondola Tours of Venice review.
- connect ideas about unusual places and unusual jobs?

  Ask *How can exploring new places help you decide on a career?*

Workbook Assign pages 22–23.
Online Workbook Units 1–2 Review

Connect

- **3 Critical Thinking** Read the Activity 3 text aloud. Give prompts as necessary: *What's unusual about Venice? What kind of person would like being a gondolier? What combination of skills would that person need?*

- To sum up the discussions, ask *What things might you discover by exploring a new place? Does reading this review make you think of careers you never thought of before? Which ones?* (tour guide, historian, travel writer)

Prepare 4

- **YOU DECIDE** Read the activity options. You may want to assign this activity in advance so that students have more time to work on it in the lesson or at home.

- **4** To help students decide on an activity, ask them to review the unusual places and jobs they read about in Units 1 and 2. Tell them to think about the main purpose of their writing. Ask *Will it be to inform or explain about a place or a job, make people laugh, or express how you feel about something, such as a favourite place?*

Share

- Set aside time for sharing students' work with the class. Before a presentation, remind students to focus on the speaker or presenter and to listen politely. Point out that it's all right for audience members to ask questions, but they should put their hand up and wait to be invited to speak. Tell students that interrupting another speaker is never acceptable.

In This Unit

Theme This unit is about life in the dark.

Content Objectives
Students will
- examine the world at night, living in darkness and nocturnal animals.
- read about creatures that live at the bottom of the ocean and create their own light.
- discuss a marine biologist and his ideas about how to protect ocean life.

Language Objectives
Students will
- talk about night, darkness and nocturnal activities.
- ask for and give help with schoolwork.
- use the present continuous to say what is happening now.
- use *at, on* and *in* to talk about when things happen.
- write about an event using sensory details.

Vocabulary
pages 44–45 *active, dark, darkness, festival, go to sleep, headlight, horizon, light up, north, south, sunrise, sunset*
page 46 *daylight, healthy, streetlight*
page 49 *asleep, awake, east, time zones, west*
page 50 *dawn, fascinate, glow, observe, pattern*
Vocabulary Strategies Compound words; Using a dictionary

Speaking Strategy
Asking for help with schoolwork

Grammar
Grammar 1 Use the present continuous to say what is happening now
Grammar 2 Use *at, on* and *in* to say when things happen

Reading
In the Dark of the Ocean
Reading Strategy Describing words

Video
Scene 3.1: *What Glows Beneath*;
Scene 3.2: Meet David Gruber

Writing
Description of an event

National Geographic
Mission Understand and Protect

Project
- Poster
- Blog entry
- 'Day-and-night' video

Pronunciation
Present continuous: Stress of the verb *be*

Pacing Guides
1.3.1, 1.3.2, 1.3.3

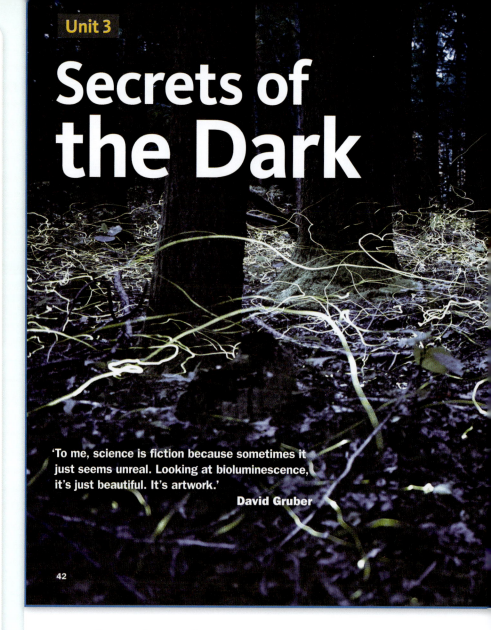

Unit 3

Secrets of the Dark

'To me, science is fiction because sometimes it just seems unreal. Looking at bioluminescence, it's just beautiful. It's artwork.'

David Gruber

42

Introduce the Unit

- **Build background** Ask *What is darkness?* (the absence of light) Say *Some people don't like being in the dark. They think it's uncomfortable, even scary.* Ask *Why do you think that is?* Explain that although people can see in the dark, we can't see colours well in the dark. Ask *What can you see at night that you don't see in the day?*

- Ask students to open their books at pages 42–43. Ask *What do the squiggly lines look like?* (coloured string, worms, tree roots) Invite a student to read the caption. Tell students the photo was taken using a special technique (time-lapse photography) that takes a series of photos over a long period of time and then sped up, so that things appear to happen in a short space of time.

- Ask questions to encourage further discussion of the photo:
   Are there any other ways to describe the photo? How does it make you feel about nature, photography and darkness?

- Ask a student to read Question 1 on page 43 aloud. Write some responses on the board. Explain that the light produced by fireflies

Blue ghost fireflies

Objectives
Students will
- describe and discuss a photo.
- discuss darkness and how some animals create their own light.

Content Vocabulary *comfortable, fireflies*

Resources Worksheet 1.3.1 (Teacher's Resource CD-ROM/Website); CPT: Unit Opener

BE THE EXPERT

About the Photo

This photo of thousands of blue ghost fireflies was taken in a forest in North Carolina, USA. These tiny fireflies are common throughout the south-eastern United States and are called blue ghosts because of the blue and green light they produce. Their uniqueness lies in the fact that their 'blink pattern' is much longer than the common firefly's, and they tend to hover about a foot off the ground. They don't seem to flash as much as glow.

Fireflies emit light to attract mates, defend their territory and warn predators to stay away. In some species, only one gender lights up. In most, however, both genders produce light.

Teaching Tip

Students may not tell you when they don't understand a word or a concept. Before beginning a lesson, preview some of the more challenging concepts or vocabulary. You may want to pair a fluent student with a less fluent one and allow them to communicate briefly in their first language, if necessary, to clarify understanding. During class discussions, walk around the room and check students' understanding by asking individuals to share ideas with you.

TO START

1. In the photo, fireflies create a beautiful light. What other things in nature produce light?

2. Bioluminescent animals use lights to communicate with one another. How do humans use lights to communicate?

3. Where do you feel comfortable in the dark? Why?

43

and other creatures is called *bioluminescence* and is the result of a chemical reaction within their bodies.

- Say *bioluminescent* and tell students to repeat. Say *This is the adjective that describes an animal that produces light.* Then read aloud Question 2. Explain that animals use bioluminescence to attract mates, defend their territory and keep predators away. Ask *How do we use light to communicate?* (for signalling; with lighthouses and flashlights)

- Ask a student to read Question 3 aloud. Ask *Do you ever feel uncomfortable in the dark?* Help students to think about and discuss what it is about darkness that makes some of us uncomfortable.

- Read the quote on page 42 by David Gruber aloud. Then say *Science is about finding out how real things work. How can science be fiction, which is about things that are made-up?*

Extend

- Hand out **Worksheet 1.3.1**. Explain that student pairs will be thinking and writing about the dark and the beauty to be found in science.

Objectives

Students will

- use vocabulary related to sunlight and darkness.
- use new vocabulary to read about and discuss winter in northern Norway.

Target Vocabulary *active, dark, darkness, festival, go to sleep, headlight, horizon, light up, north, south, sunrise, sunset*

Content Vocabulary *Norway, Norwegian, nutrients, sunlight, vitamins*

Resources Worksheet 1.3.2 (Teacher's Resource CD-ROM/Website); Tracks 032–033; (Audio CD/Website/CPT); CPT: Vocabulary

Materials globe of the world *(optional)*

1 What would be difficult about living without sunlight for two months every year? Discuss. Then listen and read. 🎧 032

For most of us, the days are divided into day and night. But for two months each winter in northern Norway, it's **dark** for 20 hours a day. There is no **sunrise** or **sunset** because the sun never gets above the **horizon**.

Would you like to live in **darkness** for this long? It may seem difficult, but many Norwegians love the beautiful colours of these months. To the **south** are the red and gold colours of the horizon. To the **north**, the sky is a magnificent blue. Even the moon and stars look blue. In the towns, streetlights shine like little yellow diamonds.

People do need light to be healthy and happy. Since they don't have much daylight during this time of the year, Norwegians

In the town of Longyearbyen, in northern Norway, there's no sunlight from November to January. However, the sun doesn't set from the end of April to the end of August.

44 VOCABULARY

Warm Up

- **Build background** Say *We're going to read about a place in Norway where people live in darkness for two months every year in winter. Imagine that! Does anyone know why that is?* Explain to students that this annual occurrence, called the Polar Night, happens because of the way Earth is tilted.

- At that time, the Arctic Circle is angled the furthest away from the sun. In other words, the rest of the planet blocks the sun's light. If possible, demonstrate for students the movement of Earth on its axis and the locations of both Norway and the Arctic Circle with a globe of the world.

Present

- **1** Ask students to open their books at pages 44–45. Read the photo caption on page 44. Then ask a student to read aloud the Activity 1 question at the top of the page. Ask *What would it be like to be in darkness for 24 hours a day? What would be missing?* Write students' responses on the board. (sunrise, daylight, the sun, sunlight, warmth)

- Ask *How would life be different without sunlight?* Prompt students with ideas such as the following: getting up every morning in the dark, always having a light on, using a flashlight when you go outside.

- Say *Let's list some things that would be difficult to do without sunlight.* Invite several students to take turns to complete the following sentence:

> I think _____ would be difficult without sunlight.

exercise and eat foods with vitamins A and D, nutrients people normally get from being in the sun. And darkness doesn't stop Norwegians from having a good time. Each winter, people are skiing on hills and skating on ponds that are **lit up**. Some people are dogsledding (with **headlights**, of course!). Others are going to film and music **festivals**. And other people are spending time with friends in cafés and restaurants. Of course, not everyone is so **active** in the dark months. Many people are just **going to sleep** a little earlier until the sun returns in the spring.

2 LEARN NEW WORDS Listen and repeat. 🎧 033

3 Work in pairs. What would you like about living in the dark for two months? What wouldn't you like? Write three things for each. Compare your list with your partner's.

VOCABULARY **45**

Our World in Context

Longyearbyen is one of the world's northernmost towns. It is located on one of the Svalbard Islands, between Norway and the North Pole, in a region of the world called the high Arctic. The town is named after an American, John Munro Longyear, who founded the town and the neighbouring coal mine. Mining remains an important part of the local economy, but today the town is a centre of tourism and research. Snow covers the town from late September until May and, as everywhere in Svalbard, roaming polar bears pose a significant threat to the town's 2,500 inhabitants.

Teaching Tip

When an activity calls for classmates to work in pairs or groups and exchange information, remind students to pay close attention to what their partner or group members are saying. Encourage students to repeat aloud what their partners say, ask their partners to clarify unfamiliar or unclear information and ask follow-up questions. These techniques will help students become active listeners and allow them to learn more about their classmates.

Related Words

glacier

- Play **Track 032** and tell students to listen and read. Then discuss the photo and the reading with students. Ask questions such as the following:

  What do you think is beautiful in the photo?

  Why do we need sunlight to be healthy?

  How do Norwegians enjoy themselves in winter?

- **2 LEARN NEW WORDS** Play **Track 033**. Ask students to listen and repeat. Put students into pairs or small groups and ask them to take turns saying each word. Then assign three or four vocabulary words to each group. Say *Work together to write a new sentence for each of your words.* Model an example. Write *In winter, people in Norway go to film and music festivals.*

- When students have finished, invite a person from each group to read their sentences to the class.

Practise 3 4 5

- **3** Put students into pairs. Say *Think about the reading. Look at the photo again. How do the people of northern Norway experience winter? Now imagine you've been sent to live there for two months without sunlight.* Tell student pairs to read and complete Activity 3 on page 45.

- **4** Tell students to turn to page 46 and read the words and phrases in the word box aloud. Tell them to choose two terms and use them in a sentence. Repeat until all of the words have been used. Ask students to complete Activity 4 independently. Ask a student to come to the front of the class and read the completed paragraph aloud.

Objectives
Students will
- practise using vocabulary related to sunlight and darkness, day and night.
- use a vocabulary strategy to learn new vocabulary.

Target Vocabulary *daylight, healthy, streetlight*

Vocabulary Strategy Compound nouns

Academic Language *observe*

Content Vocabulary *electric lights*

Resources Online Workbook/Workbook pages 24–25; Worksheet 1.3.2 (Teacher's Resource CD-ROM/Website); Tracks 034–035 (Audio CD/Website/CPT); CPT: Vocabulary

Materials drawing materials

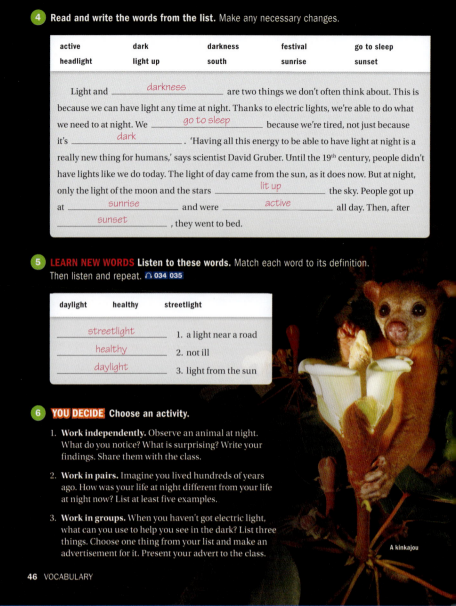

4 Read and write the words from the list. Make any necessary changes.

active	dark	darkness	festival	go to sleep
headlight	light up	south	sunrise	sunset

Light and _____ darkness _____ are two things we don't often think about. This is because we can have light any time at night. Thanks to electric lights, we're able to do what we need to at night. We _____ go to sleep _____ because we're tired, not just because it's _____ dark _____ . 'Having all this energy to be able to have light at night is a really new thing for humans,' says scientist David Gruber. Until the 19th century, people didn't have lights like we do today. The light of day came from the sun, as it does now. But at night, only the light of the moon and the stars _____ lit up _____ the sky. People got up at _____ sunrise _____ and were _____ active _____ all day. Then, after _____ sunset _____ , they went to bed.

5 **LEARN NEW WORDS** Listen to these words. Match each word to its definition. Then listen and repeat. ∩ **034 035**

daylight	healthy	streetlight

_____ streetlight _____	1. a light near a road
_____ healthy _____	2. not ill
_____ daylight _____	3. light from the sun

6 **YOU DECIDE** Choose an activity.

1. **Work independently.** Observe an animal at night. What do you notice? What is surprising? Write your findings. Share them with the class.

2. **Work in pairs.** Imagine you lived hundreds of years ago. How was your life at night different from your life at night now? List at least five examples.

3. **Work in groups.** When you haven't got electric light, what can you use to help you see in the dark? List three things. Choose one thing from your list and make an advertisement for it. Present your advert to the class.

A kinkajou

46 VOCABULARY

- **5** **LEARN NEW WORDS** Read the words in the box. Tell students they've heard and read two of these words before. Challenge pairs of students to find the words on pages 44–45. Then play **Track 034** as students listen. Tell students to pronounce each word and use it in a sentence. Then play **Track 035** and ask students to listen and repeat. Tell students to complete Activity 5 independently.

- **Vocabulary Strategy** Write *streetlight* on the board. Draw a vertical line between *street* and *light*. Point to the board and ask *What two smaller words make up the word* streetlight? Tell students that a word made up of two smaller words is called a compound noun. Say *Recognising the words that make up a compound noun can help you work out what the compound noun means.* Point to *street* and ask *What is a street?* (a road in a city or town with houses on it) Point to *light* and ask *What is a light?* (something that produces light, such as a lamp) Say *Putting those two meanings together, what do you think* streetlight *means?* (a lamp that lights up a street)

- Ask *What other compound words can you see on page 46?* (*daylight, headlight, sunrise, sunset*) Tell pairs to work together to write the meanings of the four words. Remind them to break each word into its two smaller words.

Apply

- **6** **YOU DECIDE** Tell students to look at Activity 6. Say *All of these activities have to do with living in the dark.* Point to the animal in the photo. Tell students it's a kinkajou, a cat-sized animal that lives in the tropical forests of Central and South America. Kinkajous are active at night and sleep in the treetops during the day.

- **Think Aloud** Model thinking about an activity. *The first activity sounds interesting. I like animals, but what animal can I watch at night? Fireflies are out at night, but I'm not sure how much I'd learn by watching them. Owls and bats are not easy to observe. I know! My cat sleeps all day because he's up at night. I'll observe him. I know he can see better at night than I can.*

- Students who choose options 2 and 3 may benefit from doing some research on the Internet. Tell those thinking of option 2 to start by re-reading the paragraph in Activity 4. Suggest that students considering option 3 spend some time looking at product ads in magazines or newspapers.

Extend

- Give students the option of either writing a paragraph explaining what causes the Polar Night or drawing a map of Norway. Maps should include the Norwegian mainland and the Svalbard Islands, as well as labels for Longyearbyen, the Arctic Ocean and the Arctic Circle. Allow students time to research the Polar Night or to consult a globe or map. Then invite them to share their work.

- If time allows, hand out **Worksheet 1.3.2**. Explain that students will use it to practise the new vocabulary items.

Consolidate

- Write the following on the board:
  Night: *dark, darkness, go to sleep, sunset*
  Day: *active, daylight, festival, sunrise*

- Say *Let's play a game called* Night and Day. *You'll make sentences with the new vocabulary items. When I point to you. I'll say either 'You're a night person' or 'You're a day person'. Then you choose a word from the board and say a sentence.* Model by saying *For example, I'm a night person, so I choose sunset. My sentence is 'I love pink and orange sunsets'.*

SPEAKING STRATEGY

Objectives
Students will
- use words and phrases to ask for help with schoolwork.
- use words and phrases to respond to questions asking for help.

Speaking Strategy Asking for help and helping with schoolwork

Academic Language *pronounce, pronunciation*

Resources Online Workbook; Worksheet 1.3.3 (Teacher's Resource CD-ROM/ Website); Tracks 036–037 (Audio CD/ Website/CPT); CPT: Speaking Strategy

Materials large sticky notes *(optional)*, pieces of card

SPEAKING STRATEGY 🎧 036

Asking for help with schoolwork	Helping with schoolwork
What does *nocturnal* mean?	It means *active at night*.
How do you pronounce it?	I'm not sure. I think you say *nock-tur-null*.
How do you spell it?	It's spelt *n-o-c-t-u-r-n-a-l*.

1 **Listen.** How do the speakers ask for help and respond? Write the phrases you hear. 🎧 037

2 **Read and complete the dialogue.**
Possible answers:

Mae: This video about carnivorous plants is really cool.

Hwan: _What does carnivorous_ mean?

Mae: _____ *It means* _____ *things that eat meat.* This one is called a *Nepenthes.*

Hwan: What? _How do you spell that?_ _____

Mae: _____ *I'm not sure.* _____ Let's look it up. *N-e-p-e-n-t-h-e-s.* Another name is *pitcher plant.* It eats arthropods.

Hwan: Arthro ... what? _____ _How do you pronounce that?_

Mae: _____ *I think you say* _____ *ar-throw-pod.* You know, insects, spiders and things like that. Insects see the plant's light and go to it. Then they fall inside and die! That's how the plant eats them.

Hwan: Amazing!

A glowing pitcher plant

3 **Work in pairs.** Talk about the animals on the cards. Help your partner to spell, pronounce and learn more about each animal.

It's a Gila monster.
A *what*? How do you pronounce that?

Tell me about ...imal.

Go to page 157.

SPEAKING **47**

4 **Work in groups.** Think of a situation where you wanted to ask for help with schoolwork but didn't. Why didn't you ask? How can knowing these phrases help you in the future?

Warm Up

- **Activate prior knowledge** Say *Science is full of interesting facts. Think of bioluminescence. It's amazing that some animals can produce their own light. But science words can be hard to say and spell.* Explain to students that a dictionary can help, but sometimes your first reaction is to ask someone for help.

- Ask *How do you ask someone for help when you see or hear a word you don't understand? How do you respond when someone asks you for help?* Discuss students' responses. Then put students into pairs and tell them to act out situations in which they make and answer requests for help. Say *Point to a classroom object or a word in a textbook and ask a classmate for help with the word. Take turns asking and answering questions.*

Present **1**

- Tell students to open their books at page 47. Say *We're going to hear people making and responding to requests for help with schoolwork.* Play **Track 036**. Ask *Do you sometimes have to ask for help like that? When?* Invite students to describe situations in which they ask for help with words in English. Then replay **Track 036**. Say *Let's listen again.*

- Ask pairs of students to practise reading aloud the questions and answers. Say *One partner reads the questions, the other reads the answers. Do them one at a time. Then switch roles.* Ask more fluent pairs to model for the class. Then ask less fluent students to read the sentences. Tell them to do their best and that you don't expect everyone to read everything correctly.

- Say *Listen as one speaker asks for help with schoolwork and the other responds. Write down the questions you hear and the speaker's responses. You'll hear words like the ones at the top of page 47.* Play **Track 037**. Invite students to share what they wrote. Replay the track if necessary.

Practise

- Once students seem comfortable with the speaking strategy, direct them to Activity 2. Ask students what they know about plants that eat insects. Tell them the dialogue is about these plants. Tell students to do the activity independently. Tell several pairs to read their completed dialogues aloud, taking turns as Mae and Hwan. Discuss any new words or phrases students used.

Apply

- Tell students to cut out the cards on page 157. Read the Activity 3 instructions aloud and ask pairs to read the speech bubbles. Point to a pair. Say *(Michele), choose a card and say, 'Tell me about this animal'. (Jorge), read the information about the animal. (Michele), write down the information. Ask for help with spelling, meaning and pronunciation if you need it.* Then explain that pairs will change roles and continue to play until they both have all the information about all the animals.

- **4** Read the activity instructions aloud. Then put students into small groups with new partners. Say *Think about a time when you needed help. What happened as a result of not asking for help?*

Extend

- Divide the class into groups of six. Each group will use one set of animal fact cards from Activity 3. Cover the picture on each card. Attach a piece of paper with a clip or place a sticky note over it. Give each student in the group one card. Say *Take turns to describe your animal, but don't read the name, and don't let the others see it. Group members will put their hands up to answer. Use the phrases you've learnt. For example, if you know the animal, but you're not sure of the name, say, 'I think it's pronounced …' or 'I think it's spelt …'*

- If time allows, hand out **Worksheet 1.3.3**. Explain that students will use the worksheet to practise how to make and respond to requests for help.

Consolidate

- Write these words on cards: *arthropod, carnivorous, hemisphere, kinkajou, nocturnal* and *Norwegian*. Put students into pairs and give each partner two or three cards. Tell partners to use the phrases they've learnt to ask and answer questions about their words.

Strategy in Depth

Here is a list of some other common sentences used to ask for help in the classroom:

> *I don't understand.*
> *Can you help me, please?*
> *Is this right/wrong?*

Another strategy students should learn is asking to repeat:

> *Could/Can you repeat that, please?*
> *Could/Can you say that again, please?*
> *Pardon me? Can you repeat that?*

Encourage students to learn these words and phrases and use them often.

Formative Assessment

Can students

- use words and phrases to ask for help with schoolwork?

  Say *Imagine you don't know what* nocturnal *means or how to spell it.* Ask *How would you ask a classmate for help?*

- use words and phrases to respond to questions asking for help?

  Ask *How would you respond to a classmate who asked you what* nocturnal *means?*

Online Workbook Speaking Strategy

GRAMMAR 1

Objectives

Students will
- identify and use non-action and action verbs.
- use the present continuous to talk about actions.
- use words associated with time zones.

Grammar Present continuous: Saying what is happening now

Target Vocabulary *asleep, awake, east, time zones, west*

Academic Language *action verb, non-action verb*

Pronunciation Present continuous: Stress of the verb *be*

Resources Online Workbook/Workbook pages 26–27; Tracks 038–041, 121–123 (Audio CD/Website/CPT); Pronunciation Answer Key (Teacher's Resource CD-ROM/Website); CPT: Grammar 1 and Pronunciation

Materials a fruit or vegetable, pieces of card

GRAMMAR 🎧038

Present continuous: Saying what is happening now

Non-action verbs	Action verbs
I **like** stories about unusual animals.	While I'**m reading** in bed at night in Mexico, my friend Akiko **is reading** at school in Japan!
Many animals **see** well enough to hunt in the dark.	While some animals **are hunting** in the dark, others **are hiding** or **sleeping**.
It **is** 2.00 a.m. in the jungle, but that doesn't **mean** all the animals **are** asleep.	The monkeys **are sleeping** in trees, but the kinkajous **are looking** for food.

1 Listen. Circle the non-action verbs you hear. Underline the action verbs you hear. 🎧039

bake   (be)   drive   (enjoy)   fly   help
(know)   (like)   (need)   open   search   sleep

2 Read and complete the sentences. Use the *–ing* ending for action verbs.

1. People ___*agree*___ (agree) that it's good to spend time with family.
2. This is difficult for family members who ___*live*___ (live) in different countries.
3. It's difficult because of different time zones. This ___*means*___ (mean) that it might be morning in one place and afternoon in another.
4. For example, Omar in Santiago ___*is eating*___ (eat) breakfast while his cousin Ali in Dubai ___*is coming*___ (come) home from school.
5. So when Ali ___*is thinking*___ (think) about calling Omar, he ___*has*___ (have) to consider the time in Santiago first.

3 Work in pairs. Write what you do at these times. Compare your answers with a partner.

If it's Monday night, I'm studying, but Julia is making dinner.

	Me	
Monday night		
Wednesday during school		
Friday evening		
Saturday afternoon		
Sunday morning		

48 GRAMMAR

Warm Up

- **Pre-teach** Say *Right now I'm talking to you, and you're listening to me. I'm also walking around the room, and maybe you're wiggling your leg or touching something on your desk. But we're all doing some action.* Ask a few students to say what they did before coming to class. Write the present simple form of the verbs students use on the board. (e.g. *eat, ride, play, read, listen, practise*) Say *All of these words describe actions – things you do with your body. They're called action verbs.*

- Point to a student and say *How are you today?* Invite the student to respond. (I'm fine/OK/good.) Pick up a piece of fruit or a vegetable and smell it. Say *This smells (fresh, sweet, spicy).* Hand it to a student and ask *How does it feel?* Let the student respond. (It feels smooth/bumpy/soft.) Write on the board *are, am, smells* and *feels*. Ask *Do these words describe actions?* (not really) *These verbs are called non-action verbs.*

4 **LEARN NEW WORDS** Listen to learn about time zones. Then listen and repeat. 🎧 **040** **041**

World **Time Zones**

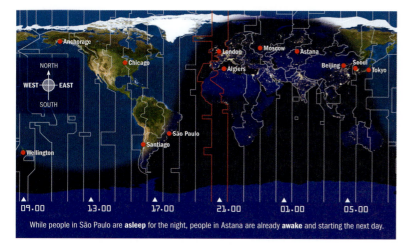

While people in São Paulo are **asleep** for the night, people in Astana are already **awake** and starting the next day.

5 **Work in pairs.** Find these cities and their time zones on the map. How many time zones separate them? Write a sentence about what people might be doing in each city.

1. Seoul / Santiago *There are 13 time zones between Seoul and Santiago. While people in Santiago are coming home from school and work, people in Seoul are asleep.*

2. Anchorage / London _____ *Time zones apart: 9* _____

3. São Paulo / Tokyo _____ *Time zones apart: 12* _____

4. Chicago / London _____ *Time zones apart: 6* _____

6 **Work in groups.** Find the place where you live on the map. Note the time now. Choose three other cities. Say if they are to your east or west and what time it is there. Take turns comparing what you're doing with what people in those cities are probably doing.

GRAMMAR **49**

- Explain to students that they're called non-action verbs because they describe a state of being or a situation, as in *I am a teacher, You are a boy, You look sleepy, The desk feels hard.* If students suggest that *feels* or *smells* involves action, point out the difference between *touch,* which describes an action you perform, and *feels,* which describes the 'state' of the thing you're touching.

Present

- Ask students to open their books at page 48 and look at the table at the top of the page. Say *Let's listen to some sentences with non-action verbs and action verbs.* Play **Track 038** as students listen. Then read aloud each sentence on the left side of the table.

- Explain that although most verbs that relate to the senses – such as *see, taste* and *feel* – are non-action verbs, they can sometimes be used as action verbs.

Grammar in Depth

Non-action verbs are used primarily to describe a state of being or situation as opposed to an action or process. Examples include be, like, seem, prefer, understand, doubt and know. They do not describe actions and typically are not used in the present continuous form, that is, with the -ing ending. For example, you wouldn't say *He's seeming to be nervous* or *I'm knowing your name.*

Pronunciation

Go to Student's Book page 145. Use Audio Tracks 121–123.

Present continuous: Stress of the verb *be* The verb *be* is used both as a main verb (*The cat is cute.*) and as an auxiliary verb in the present continuous (*I am working.*) and other tenses.

Affirmative forms of *be* are unstressed except when at the end of a short answer (*Yes, I am*) or in other less common situations, such as clarifying an answer (*I said I am coming*).

Negative forms, such as in a negative statement (*We aren't leaving*) or a negative question (*Aren't you hungry?*) are stressed.

Teaching Tip

Students who feel valued and supported in class are likely to take an active role in the learning process. Create a classroom atmosphere in which students do not need to be overly concerned about making mistakes. At the beginning of a lesson, explain to students that they're learning new things and that making mistakes is a natural and expected part of learning.

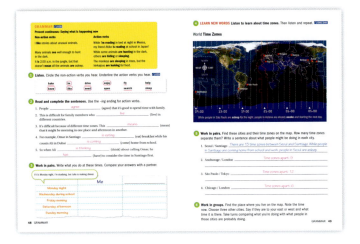

• Say *If I said, 'See the tree over there', what I really mean is 'Look at the tree over there', which describes an action. So, in that case,* see *would be an action verb.* Explain that similarly, *hear* is a non-action verb, but *listen* is an action verb because listening is something you have to actively do. Put up a list of common non-action verbs:

Non-action verbs		
agree	like	sound
be	believe	taste
feel	mean	want
has	need	wish

• Ask students to stand up and model using a non-action verb in a sentence. *(Do you agree with me? Do you like the darkness? That sounds really loud.)*

• Now read aloud the sentences on the right side of the table on page 48. Point out that each verb includes a form of *be* and *-ing*. Explain that this is the present continuous and is it used to show a continuing action. Tell pairs of students to read all of the sentences in the table to each other. Say *Read a sentence to a partner. Then ask, 'Is the verb an action or a non-action verb?' Take turns.*

Practise

• Say *Now we'll listen to some sentences with non-action and action verbs.* Play **Track 039** once and ask students to listen. Play the track again and ask students to complete the activity. Say *Pay attention to each verb you hear. Does it describe an action or state of being that is going on right now? Does it end in -ing?* Review the answers as a class.

• ② Read the instructions for Activity 2 aloud. Say *Let's do the first one together.* Read item 1. Say *I have to fill in the gap with the correct form of the verb* agree. Agree *is a non-action verb, so I won't add a form of* be *and -ing.* Ask students to complete the activity.

• ③ Ask a student to read the activity instructions aloud and the text in the speech bubble. Say *Fill in the 'Me' column of the table with the activity you're usually doing at each time of day shown in the first column.* Explain that students should then write their partner's name at the top of the third column, and add his or her information in each row. When they've finished, ask *How do your activities compare?* Ask students to stand up and to read their completed tables.

Apply

• ④ **LEARN NEW WORDS** Say *Look at the map on page 49. It shows the 24 time zones the world is divided into.* Tell students to count the zones on the map. Explain that moving from left to right, each zone advances the time by one hour. Read aloud the caption. Say *When it's 18.00 in the evening (6.00 p.m.) in São Paulo, it's 02.00 in the morning in Astana.* Play **Track 040** and ask students to listen. Then play **Track 041**. Ask students to listen and repeat.

• ⑤ Read the activity instructions aloud. Put students into pairs. Read the answer to item 1 and tell students to count the time zones on the map between the two cities. Explain that if there are 13 time zones between the two cities, then Seoul is 13 hours ahead of Santiago.

• Circulate as pairs work and provide assistance as necessary. When students have finished, confirm the number of time zones for each item. Ask different students to come to the front and read their sentences to the class.

• ⑥ Put students into small groups. Read the instructions aloud. Ask *What time is it now?* Say *Write it down. Now find our time zone on the map.* Make sure everyone agrees where it is. Appoint a secretary for each group and tell them to write down their group's three cities and the time in each one. Then ask groups to do the activity. Say *Use the vocabulary items as you discuss what the people in your cities are doing.* Circulate to make sure everyone gets a chance to talk.

Extend

- Tell groups to make a table showing their cities, times, directions and activities. Put up the table below as a model. Ask groups to present their tables to the class.

	Your City	Chicago	Algiers	Beijing
Time				
Direction	/			
Activity				

Consolidate

- Choose vocabulary from the following list to write on pieces of card, one to a card: *active, awake, dark, darkness, daylight, east, festival, headlight, healthy, horizon, north, south, streetlight* and *west*. Give each student a card. Take one yourself. Put up the following lists on the board:

Non-action verbs		Action verbs	
agree	like	get	read
be	mean	go to sleep	rise
feel	need	light up	set
has	seem	live	shine

- Divide the class into teams of equal numbers of students. Say *Use the word on your card and a verb from the board to make a sentence.* Tell students they'll get one point for a correct sentence, another point for using an action verb with a form of *be* and ending in *-ing*, and a third point for using both an action and non-action verb in their sentence.

- Model. Say *My word is* streetlight. *I choose the verb* light up. *My sentence is 'The streetlights are lighting up now that it is dark'. I earned three points – one for a correct sentence, one for using the -ing form of an action verb, and one for using a non-action verb.* Ask one student at a time to give his/her sentence. Alternate groups. Say *Let's see which team gets the most points!*

Our World in Context

China is the largest country with only one time zone. It should really have five! It's as if New York, Chicago, Denver and Los Angeles (each in a different time zone in the United States) were all in the same zone. India is the second largest country with only one time zone.

Teaching Tip

Be mindful of the different ways that students learn. Some students learn best when they hear information. Others learn best when they write things down. Still others find that using their bodies by pointing, acting out, or walking and talking helps them learn best. Provide a variety of activities and use different ways of explaining. A mix of activities gives different learners different ways to be involved with the lesson.

Formative Assessment

Can students

- identify and use non-action and action verbs?

  Ask students to identify the action and non-action verbs in this sentence: *Do you agree that many kids are spending too much time on indoor activities?*

- use the present continuous to talk about actions?

  Ask students complete this sentence with the correct *-ing* form of the verb in brackets: *It's not as if we _____ in darkness for 20 hours a day.* (live)

- use words associated with time zones?

  Ask students to fill in the gaps: *When the sun rises in the _____, it's time to be _____ and active!*

Workbook For additional practice, assign Workbook pages 26–27.

Online Workbook Grammar 1

Objectives

Students will
- read about and discuss life in the deep ocean.
- use new words from the reading.
- discuss the ocean and ocean research.

Reading Strategy Describing words

Target Vocabulary *dawn, fascinate, glow, observe, pattern*

Content Vocabulary *disco, marine, neon, recognise*

Vocabulary Strategy Using a dictionary

Resources Online Workbook/Workbook pages 28–29; Tracks 042–043 (Audio CD/Website/CPT); Worksheet 1.3.4 (Teacher's Resource CD-ROM/Website); CPT: Reading

Materials drawing materials, including neon-coloured crayons or markers; set of classroom dictionaries

---

1 **BEFORE YOU READ** Discuss in pairs. What do you know about the ocean and life in the ocean? What do you want to learn?

2 **Look at the text and photos quickly.** Then answer the questions.

   1. Who is this reading about?
   2. What sea animal has got really big eyes?

3 **LEARN NEW WORDS** **Find the words in the text.** Guess their meaning. Then look at the first meaning given for each word in the dictionary. Compare those meanings with your guesses. Then listen and repeat. 🔊042

dawn	fascinate	glow	observe	pattern

4 **WHILE YOU READ** Think about what makes animals in the deep ocean different. 🔊043

5 **AFTER YOU READ** Work in pairs. Tick T for *true* or F for *false*.

   1. David observes life in the ocean when it's dark. Ⓣ Ⓕ

   2. We know a lot about everything that lives in the ocean. Ⓣ Ⓕ

   3. We can see all the glowing colours in the ocean with our eyes. Ⓣ Ⓕ

   4. Only one type of animal glows in the dark through the lens of David's camera. Ⓣ Ⓕ

   5. A lot of animals at the bottom of the ocean make their own light. Ⓣ Ⓕ

   6. The vampire squid has very large eyes to help it see in the dark. Ⓣ Ⓕ

6 **Review.** Look at your answers from Activity 2. Were they correct? What else did you learn about the person and the sea animal?

50 READING

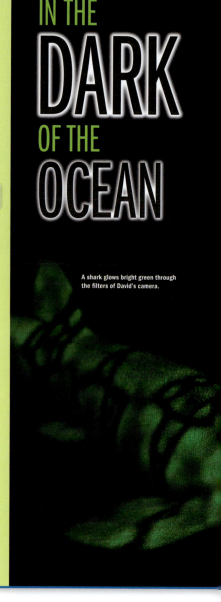

IN THE DARK OF THE OCEAN

A shark glows bright green through the filters of David's camera.

Warm Up

- **Activate prior knowledge** Ask *What's the title of this unit?* (Secrets of the Dark) Write the unit title on the board. Ask *What things have we learnt about that can only be seen in the dark or at night?* (bioluminescence, nocturnal animals) Write the terms under the unit title. Ask students to explain what *bioluminescence* and *nocturnal* mean.

- Discuss how being able to produce their own light and having large eyes to see better are special characteristics, or features, that certain animals have developed over millions of years. These special features allow the animals to live successfully in the dark.

Before You Read   ① ② ③

- ① Ask *What do you know about the ocean? What do you know about things that live in the ocean?* Put students into pairs and ask them to discuss the ocean and ocean life. Ask *What secrets might be hiding there? What do you want to learn about the ocean?*

There are incredible creatures living in the darkness.

In the darkness before dawn, marine biologist David Gruber dives into the ocean to observe the amazing creatures that live there. 'Seventy-one per cent of Earth is ocean, and much of it is dark, with tonnes of life down there that we don't know about,' he says.

David discovered that many sea animals can see colours in the water that we cannot. So he designed a camera that allows him to see the colours just as a fish does. His camera shows a secret world of neon green, red and orange colours on ocean life that glows in the dark.

In this fascinating world, David discovered a special kind of shark that glows bright with green spots. 'When you see all these little bright spots and patterns, it's like flowers and butterflies. Why do they make patterns? It's to attract each other. It's to recognise each other,' he says.

At the bottom of the ocean where there is no light at all, many animals produce their own light. The unusual vampire squid is an example. It can turn itself on or off, just like a lamp. It also has very big eyes to help it see in the dark. In fact, compared to its body size, the vampire squid has the largest eyes of any animal in the world. And this is just one animal: ninety per cent of the animals that live at the bottom of the ocean produce their own light.

It's easy to see why the darkness of the sea fascinates David. 'Marine animals in the dark ocean produce lights to communicate with each other,' says David. 'It's an underwater disco party. We human beings are the last ones to join in!'

A vampire squid

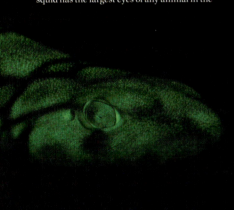

7 **Discuss in groups.**

1. What things about the ocean fascinate you? Why do they fascinate you?

2. It's difficult to study the ocean at night because of the darkness. What are some other difficulties David might have when studying the ocean at night?

3. Do you think it's important to learn about what lives in the ocean? Why or why not?

READING **51**

Reading Strategy

Describing words Describing words make writing clear and help readers visualise what they read. Many of the words used to describe in English are adjectives. Precise, vivid adjectives that appeal to the senses add detail and clarity to writing. For example, ask students to compare the following two sentences, which have the describing words underlined. Ask which one gives them a clearer picture in their minds of the undersea world that David Gruber's camera captures.

His camera shows a world of colours on ocean life that gives off light.

His camera shows an exciting, secret world of neon green, red and orange colours on ocean life that glows in the dark.

Vocabulary Strategy

Using a dictionary When students find more than one entry for a word in the dictionary, tell them to check the part of speech in each entry. For example, *glow* can be a noun or a verb and there's a separate entry for each one. The parts of speech are often abbreviated as *n.* (noun), *v.* (verb), *adj.* (adjective) and *adv.* (adverb), to name a few.

Teaching Tip

Don't let limited vocabulary restrict students when they brainstorm ideas or participate in discussions. If students have an idea but don't know or can't remember the words to express it, ask them to act it out, draw a picture, or use other words to describe it. Then help them remember or learn the English words to describe their ideas.

- **2** Ask students to open their books at pages 50–51. Read the Activity 2 instructions aloud. Say *Read the title. Look at the photos and read the captions. Take a minute to look over the text.* Explain to students that there are strategies they can use when they need to find specific information in a text quickly. Say *One strategy is called scanning. When you scan a text, you look for words that will help you find what you need.*

- Say *The first question asks who the reading is about, so look for a name.* When students are ready to move on, ask *What words might help you answer the second question?* (the name of an animal, the words *big eyes*) Tell students to write down their answers and set them aside to use later.

- **3** **LEARN NEW WORDS** Say *Now you're going to learn some new words.* Read the first two sentences of the instructions aloud. Ask students to find the word *dawn* in the reading (the first line). Say *What context clue can you see that might help you work out what dawn means?* Help students to understand that 'the darkness before dawn' suggests that after dawn it's not dark. Tell students to write what they think *dawn* means.

- Put students into pairs, and tell partners to work together to find the rest of the words in the reading and guess their meanings. Tell them to write down what they think each word means.

- **Vocabulary strategy** Remind students that they can always check or look up an unfamiliar word's meaning in a dictionary. Use the word *pattern* to point out that many words have more than one meaning, and that the first meaning listed in the dictionary is not always the meaning they're looking for.

- Say *The word* pattern *has many meanings.* Write the first couple of definitions on the board and read them for students.

> pattern: 1. a model that can be used as an example
>   to be imitated
>   2. something used as a model for making
>   things, such as clothing
>   3. an arrangement of lines, shapes, or colours

- Help students to understand that the third definition makes the most sense in the reading. Say *Now, look up each of the new words in the dictionary and compare the first definition with the meaning you wrote down. If that definition doesn't seem right, look at the other meanings. Is there another one that better matches the context from the reading?*

- When students have finished comparing definitions, say *Now that you've looked up the words, do you want to change any of your definitions?* Finally, play **Track 042.** Ask students to listen and repeat.

While You Read 4

- **4** Say *Now we're going to listen to* In the Dark of the Ocean *and learn about some of the animals that live in it.* Play **Track 043** and ask students to listen and read.

- Say *Now read again. Look for the words the writer uses to describe animals that live in the deep ocean. Can you picture the animals in your mind? How does the writer help you do this?* Play **Track 043** again or allow students to read in silence.

After You Read 5 6 7

- **5** Put students into pairs. Tell partners to read the activity instructions. If necessary, do the first item with the class. If pairs disagree on an answer, tell them to read the text again and find information that supports their answers. Ask pairs to complete the activity. Review the answers as a class.

- **6** Say *Now that you've read* In the Dark of the Ocean, *look at the answers you wrote to the Activity 2 questions.* Ask *Were your answers correct?* Say *We already knew that David Gruber is a scientist who's interested in light and darkness. What else did you learn about him? Did anyone think the vampire squid would be the animal with the really big eyes?* Invite students to share the answers they wrote and the new information they have learnt.

- **7** Put students into small groups and read the activity questions. Appoint a group member to act as secretary and write down notes from the discussion about each question. Provide ideas (such as the discussion prompts on the next page) if students are struggling with their discussions.

Extend

- Say *David Gruber says there's 'tons of life' in the ocean we don't know about.* Tell students to review the words in the reading used to describe the unusual features of some creatures that live at the bottom of the ocean. Then say *Draw a picture of what you think one creature that hasn't been discovered yet might look like.*

- If time allows, you may want to hand out **Worksheet 1.3.4** so students can practise the new vocabulary words.

Consolidate

- Write the following words on the board: *active, dark, darkness, light up, asleep, awake, fascinate, glow* and *pattern.* Say *Now present your picture of an undiscovered creature to the class. First, name your creature and write a sentence or two about it. Try to use some of the words on the board.* When students have finished displaying their pictures and reading their sentences, ask the class to vote for their favourite creature. Then ask students to come to the front and say why it's their favourite. You might want to display students' drawings in a *Secrets of the Dark* classroom display.

Teaching Tip

Make sure students use new vocabulary when they work in groups. Sometimes, it's possible to answer a question without using a new vocabulary item. In those cases, write sentence starters or frames on the board to remind students to use the new words. Walk around the room to check that students are using new vocabulary items.

Formative Assessment

Can students
- recall information about life in the deep ocean?

  Ask students to describe the animals they read about in *In the Dark of the Ocean*.

- use new words from the reading?

  Ask students to use *fascinate, glow,* or *observe* to say something about David Gruber or his work.

- discuss the ocean and ocean research?

  Ask students to say one thing about the ocean they would like to know more about.

Workbook For additional practice, assign Workbook pages 28–29.

Online Workbook Reading

VIDEO

VIDEO

Objectives

Students will
- discuss David Gruber and his underwater research.
- apply the message of the video to their personal lives.

Content Vocabulary *coral, coral reefs, fluorescence, scuba diving*

Resources Video scene 3.1 (DVD/Website/CPT); Online Workbook; CPT: Video

Materials drawing materials, large pieces of card

Answer Key 4

1. surfing
2. They both take place in the water.
3. He studies in places where there is no natural light.
4. They allow him to see the sea the same way the fish see it.

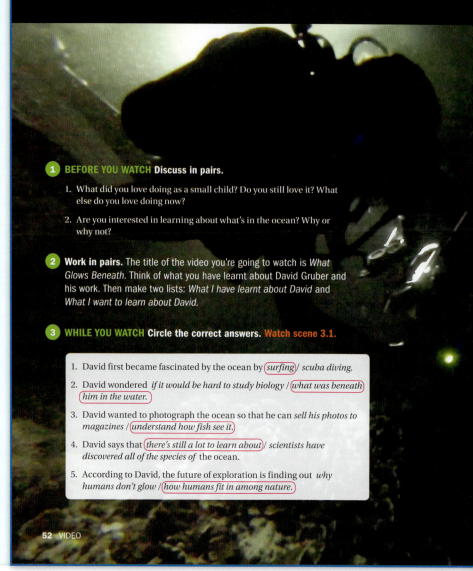

1 BEFORE YOU WATCH Discuss in pairs.

1. What did you love doing as a small child? Do you still love it? What else do you love doing now?

2. Are you interested in learning about what's in the ocean? Why or why not?

2 Work in pairs. The title of the video you're going to watch is *What Glows Beneath.* Think of what you have learnt about David Gruber and his work. Then make two lists: *What I have learnt about David* and *What I want to learn about David.*

3 WHILE YOU WATCH Circle the correct answers. Watch scene 3.1.

1. David first became fascinated by the ocean by *surfing* / *scuba diving*.

2. David wondered *if it would be hard to study biology* / *what was beneath him in the water.*

3. David wanted to photograph the ocean so that he can *sell his photos to magazines* / *understand how fish see it.*

4. David says that *there's still a lot to learn about* / *scientists have discovered all of the species of* the ocean.

5. According to David, the future of exploration is finding out *why humans don't glow* / *how humans fit in among nature.*

52 VIDEO

Before You Watch

- Ask *What did you like to do when you were very young? Did you build things? Did you like to explore? What did you like reading about? Animals? Dinosaurs? Outer space? Do you still like any of these? What's your favourite thing to do now?* Tell students to open their books at pages 52–53. Put students into pairs and ask them to discuss the Activity 1 questions.

- After pairs have talked for several minutes, ask *Did anyone spend time at the sea when they were young? What did you like about it? Did you ever think about what creatures were in the water with you?* Ask pairs to talk about what they'd like to learn about the sea.

- Say *Look at the photo.* Read the caption aloud. Then read Activity 2. Ask *What have we learnt about David Gruber so far?* (He's a marine biologist, he works in the dark at the bottom of the ocean, he studies bioluminescence and sea creatures that glow.) Write students' responses on the board. Then tell pairs to work together to make their lists.

While You Watch

- Say *Now we're going to watch* What Glows Beneath. Draw students' attention to Activity 3. Say *As you watch and listen, circle the correct answers.* Read aloud item 1. Say *David first became fascinated by the ocean by surfing, or scuba diving. Now listen and circle.* Play **Video scene 3.1**. Ask students to work independently. Tell them to write down other interesting information. Say *Keep in mind the lists you made for Activity 2.*

- If students have trouble following the video or understanding the text, pause the video and allow them to ask questions or re-read the text. Try replaying the video with and without sound, and ask students to

④ **AFTER YOU WATCH** Work in pairs to answer the questions.

1. What was David's hobby when he was a teenager?
2. How does this hobby connect to his job?
3. What is special about how David studies the ocean?
4. What do the filters in David's camera allow him to do?

⑤ **Work in pairs.** List three of the sea animals you saw in the video. Describe what they look like. Now think of three sea animals you know about or have seen photos of. How are they different from the animals in the video?

David uses a camera with special filters to explore the dark ocean.

⑥ **YOU DECIDE** Choose an activity.

1. **Work independently.** Imagine that you went scuba diving and saw some of the animals in the video. Write a postcard to a friend or family member, describing what you saw. In your postcard, explain how you were able to see the animals glow.
2. **Work in pairs.** Role-play a conversation between David and a reporter who's asking him about his work. Share your dialogue with the class.
3. **Work in groups.** Prepare a glow-in-the-dark presentation. Each person finds out about a different sea animal that glows in the dark. Draw it or find a photo of it. Write three pieces of information about it. Present your group of animals to the class.

VIDEO **53**

describe and comment on what they can see. When they've completed Activity 3, review the answers as a class.

After You Watch

• ④ Put students into pairs. Remind them to use information from the video to answer the questions. Tell them to review their answers to Activity 3 before they begin.

• ⑤ Read the activity instructions aloud. Think about pairing less fluent students who would benefit by helping each other with the language. Say *Talk about the animals in the video. Then talk about other sea creatures you've seen.* Tell students they can draw pictures if it helps them to describe the animals.

• Say *You may want to use a Venn diagram to help you discuss similarities and differences between how the* animals look and act and where they live. If necessary, begin one on the board. Circulate as students talk to provide assistance.

• ⑥ **YOU DECIDE** Make sure students know what scuba diving is. Explain that's how David does his exploring. Ask students to describe the special suits and equipment divers use and why they use them.

• Put students who choose the second option into pairs. Say *Remember the information you wanted to learn about David. Use what you wrote in your list and information from the video to write interview questions and answers.*

• Put students who choose the third option into small groups. Tell them to discuss who will research which animal. If students choose the same animal, you could replay the video to remind them of different creatures. You could ask someone to list the name of each animal as they watch.

GRAMMAR 2

Objectives

Students will
- use *at*, *on* and *in* to say when things happen.
- differentiate between *at*, *on* and *in*.

Grammar *At*, *on* and *in*: Saying when things happen

Content Vocabulary *market stalls*, *regularly*

Resources Online Workbook/Workbook pages 30–31; Worksheet 1.3.5 (Teacher's Resource CD-ROM/Website); Track 044; (Audio CD/Website/CPT); CPT: Grammar 2

Materials glue or tape, large pieces of card

GRAMMAR ∩ 044

At, on and in: Saying when things happen

at eight o'clock / **at** night / **at** the weekend
on Monday(s) / **on** 1st June / **on** my birthday
in the winter / **in** the morning / **in** 2017 / **in** May

1 **Read.** Complete the paragraph with *at*, *on* or *in*.

My family and I visited Marrakesh, Morocco, __in__ 2015. We went __in__ December. The weather is warm there __in__ the winter. __On__ Monday, our first day, we spent a lot of time in the Jemaa el Fna, the old city square. __At__ lunchtime, we ate at a rooftop café, and __in__ the afternoon, we watched some dancers. __At__ five o'clock __in__ the evening, we watched the day market stalls leave and the night market stalls arrive. __At__ night we enjoyed the storytellers, magicians, musicians and acrobats, as well as the food from the many food stalls. The Jemaa el Fna is incredible both day and night!

The Jemaa el Fna market

2 **Work in pairs.** Talk about places you go to regularly. Use *at*, *on* and *in*.

1. Tuesdays _____ *On Tuesdays, I go to the park after school.* _____
2. night _____
3. afternoon _____
4. March _____
5. weekend _____
6. 8.00 a.m. _____

3 **Work in pairs.** Take turns throwing the cube. Talk about things that happen at different times.

In the summer, we often go to the beach.

Go to page 159.

54 GRAMMAR

Warm Up

- **Activate prior knowledge** Say *I got up this morning at 6.30.* Ask several students *What time did you get up?* Write *at 6.30* on the board. Underline *at*. Say *On Saturday, I usually do my washing.* Write *on Saturday*. Underline *on*. Say *My birthday's in (May).* Write *in (May)*. Underline *in*. Ask several students *What month is your birthday in?*

- Say *In Unit 1, we learned to use* in *and* on *to talk about location:* in Guatemala, in the ocean, on an island. Point to the board and say *We also use* in *and* on, *as well as* at, *to say when things happen.*

Present

- Ask students to open their books at page 54. Play **Track 044**. Ask students to listen and read silently. Then replay **Track 044** while students read aloud along with the audio.

- Say *There are rules for using* at, in *and* on *when we talk about times.* Using the examples at the top of page 54, say *We use* at *with exact times and certain times of the day. We use* on *with the days of the week and specific dates. We use* in *with months, years, seasons and certain times of the day. We say* in the morning, in the afternoon *and* in the evening. *But, there is one exception – we say* at *night.*

- Write these sentence frames on the board:

  I get home from school _____. (exact time)

  I do my homework _____. (time of day)

  I practise / hang out with my friends _____. (day of the week)

  I like to swim / go snowboarding _____. (month or season)

110   UNIT 3

- Point to the board. Say *Talk to a partner about when things happen. Take turns. Use at, in and on.* Tell students that for the third sentence, they should say any activity they do regularly, or usually, on a specific day of the week. For the last sentence, they should name something they do in a particular month or season.

Practise

- Say *Now you're going to read a paragraph about a family trip. You'll fill in each gap with* at, in *or* on. *Let's do the first one together.* Read the sentence aloud: *My family and I visited Marrakesh, Morocco, at? in? or on? 2015.* Say *2015 is a year. Look at the table. What's the correct word?* (in) Ask students to work independently. Review the answers as a class.

- **2** Put students into pairs and ask them to read the instructions and sample answer. Say *Write complete sentences. Then take turns reading your sentences to your partner.* Write some prompts, such as the following: *go to the market, go to the library, practise or play an instrument, visit a relative* and *feed the dog.* Circulate and listen. Invite pairs to stand up and read their sentences to the class.

Apply **3**

- **3** Put students with a new partner. Tell them to cut out and assemble the cube on page 159. Read the instructions and the speech bubble. Say *Roll the cube. Then say a sentence that is true for you, using the word at the top of the cube. You get one point for each correct sentence. Keep track of the time words you both use, such as* evening, summer, December, *and so on. If you repeat a word, you lose a point. Remember to be polite. The person with the most points at the end wins.*

Extend

- Put students into different pairs to play a new version of the game. Demonstrate with a student partner. Roll the cube. Say *The word is* (at). *I'll ask, 'What did you do last night at 8.00?'* Prompt your partner to answer with a complete sentence, including the phrase *at 8.00.* Say *Now it's my partner's turn to roll and ask me a question.* Tell pairs to play until they've each asked and answered questions with all three prepositions.

- Hand out **Worksheet 1.3.5** for further practice with prepositions you use to say when things happen.

Consolidate

- Divide the class into teams of three. Give each team three cards: an *at*, an *in* and an *on* card. Give one to each student on the team. Say *I'll call out an expression of time. You hold up the card with the right word to use with that expression. I'll call the first student who holds up a card. If it's the right one, that team gets a point.* Explain that if students prompt one another, their team loses a point. The team with the most points wins.

Grammar in Depth

Other rules for using the prepositions *in* and *on* include the following:

in

- Use for decades or centuries: *in the 80s, in the 19th century*
- Use with a period of time in the future to say what will happen after that period of time: *in a few weeks, in a couple of months.*

on

- Use for specific days and holidays: *on Tuesday, on Christmas Day, on the first day of Diwali.*

Teaching Tip

When the class begins an activity, listen for students who are doing the activity correctly. The first time you hear a correct sentence, ask the class to pause the activity. Ask the student to stand up and share his or her example or say that student's sentence aloud. Hearing a correct example will help other students who are struggling to begin an activity.

Formative Assessment

Can students

- use *at, on* and *in* to say when things happen?

  Ask students to say what they regularly do after school and when they do it. They can use exact times or times of the day.

- differentiate between *at, on* and *in*?

  Ask students to complete this sentence with *at, on* or *in: David Gruber does most of his ocean research _____ night.*

Workbook For additional practice, assign Workbook pages 30–31.

Online Workbook Grammar 2

Objectives

Students will
- apply elements of descriptive writing.
- use describing words.
- analyse a model of sensory writing.
- produce a paragraph of descriptive writing, including sensory words.

Writing Description of an event

Academic Language *sensory writing*

Content Vocabulary *dragons, dumplings, night-time*

Resources Online Workbook/Workbook page 32; Process Writing Worksheets 1–5, Genre Writing Worksheet: Description (Teacher's Resource CD-ROM/Website); CPT: Writing

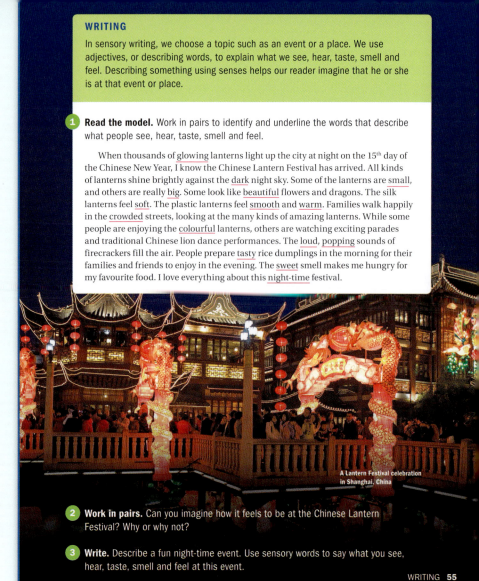

WRITING

In sensory writing, we choose a topic such as an event or a place. We use adjectives, or describing words, to explain what we see, hear, taste, smell and feel. Describing something using senses helps our reader imagine that he or she is at that event or place.

1 **Read the model.** Work in pairs to identify and underline the words that describe what people see, hear, taste, smell and feel.

    When thousands of glowing lanterns light up the city at night on the 15th day of the Chinese New Year, I know the Chinese Lantern Festival has arrived. All kinds of lanterns shine brightly against the dark night sky. Some of the lanterns are small, and others are really big. Some look like beautiful flowers and dragons. The silk lanterns feel soft. The plastic lanterns feel smooth and warm. Families walk happily in the crowded streets, looking at the many kinds of amazing lanterns. While some people are enjoying the colourful lanterns, others are watching exciting parades and traditional Chinese lion dance performances. The loud, popping sounds of firecrackers fill the air. People prepare tasty rice dumplings in the morning for their families and friends to enjoy in the evening. The sweet smell makes me hungry for my favourite food. I love everything about this night-time festival.

A Lantern Festival celebration in Shanghai, China

2 **Work in pairs.** Can you imagine how it feels to be at the Chinese Lantern Festival? Why or why not?

3 **Write.** Describe a fun night-time event. Use sensory words to say what you see, hear, taste, smell and feel at this event.

WRITING **55**

Warm Up

- **Activate prior knowledge** Say *In Unit 1, you wrote a paragraph about a beautiful place. We talked a lot about using describing words to help your readers experience the place in their minds – how the place looked, how it sounded, how it smelt. Sight, sound, smell.* Ask *What do these words relate to?* (the senses) *Who can name all five senses?* (sight, sound, smell, taste, touch).

- Say *Talk to the person next to you. Describe something you're wearing – your shirt, skirt, shoes, a piece of jewellery. Say the colour, the design, how the material feels. Does it make a sound? Is it shiny? Is it rubbery? Take turns.* When students have finished, ask *Did your partner describe the article well? Could you see it in your mind? Are there other words your partner could have used?*

Present

- Say *Open your books at page 55.* Ask a student to read the text in the green box. Then write the words for the five senses. Say *Let's write some describing words for each sense.* Begin the table below and ask students to help you complete it.

sight	colourful, dark, shiny
sound	loud, whispery, screechy
taste	yummy, sweet, sour
touch	soft, rough, smooth
smell	fresh and clean, like flowers, like burnt toast

Read the Model

- Say *Now we're going to look at a model of sensory writing. First, look at the photo and read the caption.* Ask students to predict what they think the text will be about. Ask *What do you think the text will be about?* Invite students' responses.

- Tell students to read the text silently. Say *Read through the text once. Try to imagine being at the festival. What can you see, hear, taste and smell?* Then read the instructions aloud.

- **Model** When students have finished underlining words, model analysing one of the descriptions. Say *Right away, I read the words* thousands of glowing lanterns. *That's a good description.* Ask *Which of the five senses does it relate to?* (sight)

- Ask *Would the phrase* lots of lanterns *work as well?* Help students to understand that the words *thousands* and *glowing* help readers to see in their minds a scene of so many lanterns they would be difficult to count, filling the night sky with a beautiful light. Tell students to review what they have underlined, and discuss how well they think the descriptions worked.

- When students have finished reading, put them into pairs. Tell them to read the text again and do Activity 2 together.

- **Worksheet** If your students need a reminder of the elements of the Descriptive Writing genre, you may want to hand out **Genre Writing Worksheet 7 (Description)** and review it together before proceeding to Activity 3.

Plan

- Say *It's time to plan your own writing. Read the Activity 3 instructions. Your topic is describing a fun night-time event.* Ask *What kind of events occur at night?* Write some helpful student responses on the board. Suggest others, such as family or cultural night-time celebrations, New Year's Eve events, Carnival, the Thai lantern festival of Yi Peng or Christmas Eve.

- Say *Your next step is pre-writing. Let's review. What are some ways we do pre-writing?* (brainstorm, freewrite, make lists, use a graphic organiser, use sentence starters) Say *Now decide what you want to use.* If you have time in class, allow students to work on this step. If not, assign it as homework. If students have Workbooks, remind them to use Workbook page 32 for writing support.

Writing Support

Describing an event Describing an event is different from describing a person or place. There's usually a lot going on during an event that you want the reader to experience. You need to convey a sense of movement and unfolding action by using exact, vivid verbs such as *feasted* instead of *ate*, *battled* instead of *played*, *charged* instead of *ran*, *gawked* instead of *looked at*.

Good organisation will help, too. Students may want to consider putting events in order – either describing their favourite part of the event first and progressing to their least favourite, or starting with their least favourite part and progressing to their favourite.

Teaching Tip

Create a display of descriptive words for each of the five senses. Add new sensory adjectives to it from the Target Vocabulary in each unit. For example, sensory words based on the Unit 3 vocabulary include *dark*, *glowing*, *patterned* and *sleepy*. Encourage students to practise using the words in their descriptive writing.

Related Vocabulary

pagoda

Workbook For scaffolded Writing support, assign Workbook page 32.
Online Workbook Writing

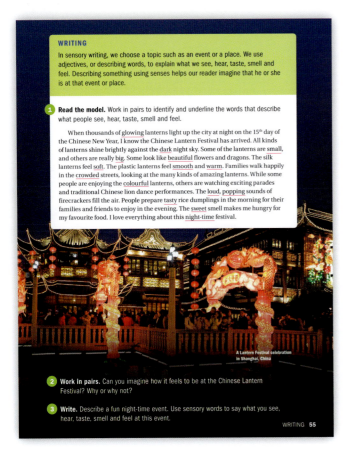

WRITING

In sensory writing, we choose a topic such as an event or a place. We use adjectives, or describing words, to explain what we see, hear, taste, smell and feel. Describing something using senses helps our reader imagine that he or she is at that event or place.

1 **Read the model.** Work in pairs to identify and underline the words that describe what people see, hear, taste, smell and feel.

When thousands of glowing lanterns light up the city at night on the 15th day of the Chinese New Year, I know the Chinese Lantern Festival has arrived. All kinds of lanterns shine brightly against the dark night sky. Some of the lanterns are small, and others are really big. Some look like beautiful flowers and dragons. The silk lanterns feel soft. The plastic lanterns feel smooth and warm. Families walk happily in the crowded streets, looking at the many kinds of amazing lanterns. While some people are enjoying the colourful lanterns, others are watching exciting parades and traditional Chinese lion dance performances. The loud, popping sounds of firecrackers fill the air. People prepare tasty rice dumplings in the morning for their families and friends to enjoy in the evening. The sweet smell makes me hungry for my favourite food. I love everything about this night-time festival.

A Lantern Festival celebration in Shanghai, China

2 **Work in pairs.** Can you imagine how it feels to be at the Chinese Lantern Festival? Why or why not?

3 **Write.** Describe a fun night-time event. Use sensory words to say what you see, hear, taste, smell and feel at this event.

WRITING **55**

Write

- After students have finished their pre-writing, tell them to work on their first drafts.

Revise

- After students have finished their first drafts, ask them to review their writing and think about their ideas and organisation. Tell them to quietly read their drafts aloud to themselves. Tell each student to consider the following: *Is the subject of the description easily identifiable? Does the description develop in a logical way? What seems good? What needs more work?*

Edit and Proofread

- Ask students to consider elements of style, such as sentence variety, parallelism and word choice. Then tell them to proofread for mistakes in grammar, punctuation, capitalisation and spelling.

Publish

- Publishing includes handing in pieces of writing to the teacher, sharing work with classmates, adding pieces to a class book, displaying pieces on a classroom wall or in a hallway, and posting on the Internet.

- **Worksheets** If your students need a reminder of any of the steps of process writing, you may want to hand out **Process Writing Worksheets 1–5** and review them together.

- **Workbook** Refer students to Workbook page 32 to help them organise and plan their writing.

Writing Assessment

Use these guidelines to assess students' writing. You can add other aspects of their writing you'd like to assess at the bottom of the table.

4 = Excellent
3 = Good
2 = Needs improvement
1 = Re-do

	1	2	3	4
Writing Student organises the description in a way that makes sense and uses a variety of describing words and phrases that appeal to all the senses.				
Grammar Student uses non-action and action verbs correctly; student uses *at, in* and *on* correctly.				
Vocabulary Student uses a variety of word choices, including words taught in this unit.				

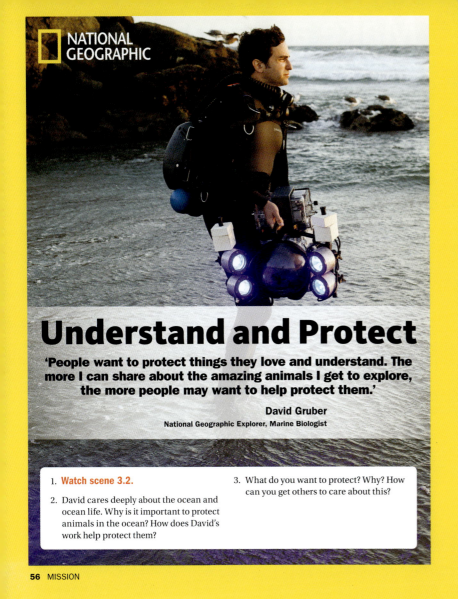

Understand and Protect

'People want to protect things they love and understand. The more I can share about the amazing animals I get to explore, the more people may want to help protect them.'

David Gruber
National Geographic Explorer, Marine Biologist

1. **Watch scene 3.2.**

2. David cares deeply about the ocean and ocean life. Why is it important to protect animals in the ocean? How does David's work help protect them?

3. What do you want to protect? Why? How can you get others to care about this?

Objective

Students will

- discuss the importance of learning about and protecting the world's resources.

Resources Video scene 3.2 (DVD/ Website/CPT); Worksheet 1.3.6 (Teacher's Resource CD-ROM/ Website); Online Workbook: Meet the Explorer; CPT: Mission

BE THE EXPERT

Teaching Tip

It's easy for students to become overwhelmed when listening to long sentences and paragraphs in English. Try to keep listening activities brief so students have time to process and ask questions about what they've heard. Pause longer audio recordings whenever necessary to check for comprehension.

Online Workbook Meet the Explorer

Mission

- Say *Turn to page 56.* Read aloud the Mission. Then ask a student to stand up and read aloud the quote from David Gruber. Ask *What does David mean when he says people want to protect things they love and understand?* Discuss with students how people sometimes think the things they don't know much about or understand are dangerous, so they don't care about protecting them. Ask *What amazing animals do you think David wants to protect?* (the unusual bioluminescent creatures at the bottom of the ocean)

- **Activity 1** Say *Now let's watch a video about David Gruber.* Play **Video scene 3.2**. Tell students to pay attention to David's research at the bottom of the ocean.

- **Activity 2** Put students into pairs. Remind them of David's discoveries about unusual marine animals and how they use bioluminescence in their dark world. Tell them to look back at the reading on page 51. Ask *Does learning about these animals make you want to protect them? What might yet be discovered at the bottom of the ocean?*

- **Activity 3** Ask students to consider the things they care about. Ask *Perhaps there's some animal or habitat you want to protect? Is there something in the world that's endangering the people or things you care about? How can you protect them? Do you have any knowledge or information that might help?*

- **Worksheet** Hand out **Worksheet 1.3.6**. Explain that students will use the worksheet to think and write about David Gruber and his ideas about protecting marine environments.

Objective

Students will

- choose and complete a project related to the extremes of light and darkness.

Content Vocabulary *blog entry, organisms*

Resources
Assessment: Unit 3 Quiz; Workbook pages 33 and 92; Worksheet 1.3.7 (Teacher's Resource CD-ROM/Website); CPT: Make an Impact and Review Games

Materials
art materials, video camera

Assessment Go to page 256.

Unit Review Assign Worksheet 1.3.7

Workbook Assign pages 33 and 92.

Online Workbook Now I can

Make an Impact

YOU DECIDE Choose a project.

1 Design a poster.

- Research animals or plants that glow in the dark. Find out how and why they glow.
- Make a poster to describe three of the glow-in-the-dark organisms you researched. Include photos.
- Present your poster to the class.

2 Write a blog entry.

- Research a place that is light for more than two months a year.
- Pretend that you visit during the light season. Write a blog about your visit. Include photos.
- Publish your blog. Answer questions and respond to your classmates' comments.

3 Make a 'day-and-night' video.

- Choose an interesting place in your region.
- Make a video of that place during the day and during the night. Mention what is the same and what is different.
- Share your video with the class.

Bioluminescent fungi glowing on a tree trunk

PROJECT **57**

Prepare

- **YOU DECIDE** Ask students to choose a project.

- **Activity 1** Ask students to research bioluminescence and biofluorescence. Tell them that along with photos and descriptions of creatures, objects, or products and plants they read about, they should include scientific information they discover in their research. Tell them to title their posters and include a message about the importance of marine research.

- **Activity 2** Explain that just as places on Earth, like northern Norway, are dark for a long time in the winter, they are also light for a similar amount of time in the summer. The Polar Night in winter is balanced by a time called the Midnight Sun in summer.

- Tell students to research various blogs in order to identify the elements you usually find in a blog. Explain that their blog entries can be done on paper to be shared with classmates or shared online via a school website.

- **Activity 3** Help students brainstorm locations that might provide an interesting day and night contrast (*e.g.* a local pond or somewhere that is brightly lit up at night).

Share

- Schedule time for students to present their final projects to the class. Allow time for students to ask questions, provide feedback on the posters and videos, or otherwise comment on their classmates' research.

- **Modify** Help students simplify a project by eliminating one of the options or steps. For example, search for appropriate websites for students to use for their research. Help them locate and print pictures of sea creatures that glow and scenes from places that have midnight sun in summer. Arrange for adult supervision for those students wishing to video a place at night.

Track 032 **1** **Listen and read.** See Student's Book pages 44–45.

Track 033 **2** **LEARN NEW WORDS** **active** / Most people are active during the day. **dark** / We turn on the lights when it gets dark. **darkness** / We couldn't see anything in the darkness of the night. **festival** / Many places celebrate winter with festivals and music. **go to sleep** / It's easy to go to sleep when you're tired. **headlight** / A car's headlights help the driver to see at night. **horizon** / The sun sets on the horizon. **light up** / The sun lights up the sky during the day. **north** / People who live in the far north often have cold winters. **south** / Many birds fly south for the winter. **sunrise** / There was a beautiful sunrise early this morning. **sunset** / The sunset was beautiful this evening.

Track 034 **5** In central Greenland there is no sunset for nearly eight weeks a year, from the end of May until the end of July. There's daylight 24 hours a day. During this time, people can enjoy their favourite outdoor activities in the middle of the night, without even turning on the streetlights! Some people find it difficult to sleep during this time, and losing sleep isn't healthy. However, most people prefer summer to winter, when there are 24 hours of darkness.

Track 035 **5** **LEARN NEW WORDS** **daylight** / There is daylight between sunrise and sunset. **healthy** / To be healthy, you should eat well and exercise. **streetlight** / The streetlights shine brightly at night.

Track 036 **SPEAKING STRATEGY** See Student's Book page 47.

Track 037 **1** **S1**: What are you doing? **S2**: I'm doing research on nocturnal animals. **S1**: Really? What does *nocturnal* mean? **S2**: It means something that sleeps during the day and is active at night. Actually a lot of animals are nocturnal. Look at this kinkajou. **S1**: A kinka – what? How do you pronounce it? **S2**: I think you say *kin-ka-jou*. **S1**: OK, and how do you spell that? **S2**: It's spelled k-i-n-k-a-j-o-u. Kinkajous are nocturnal animals. They live in the forests in Central and South America. They spend most of their time in trees. **S1**: I've never seen one. Have you? **S2**: No. That's probably because we're not nocturnal, and we don't live in trees!

Track 038 **GRAMMAR** See Student's Book page 48.

Track 039 **1** Do you enjoy sleeping? People need sleep, but many people also need to work. Some people are working at night when many of us are sleeping. Think about this. It's 4.00 a.m. While you're sleeping, doctors are helping patients, news reporters are driving to work, and bakers are baking bread.

A lot is happening at night in the natural world, too. We know that many animals and flowers are busy at night. Think about this. It's 11.00 p.m. While owls are flying around and are searching for food, flowers are opening and are filling the air with sweet smells. Insects that like to eat at night are attracted to the smell and go to the flowers to eat.

You may be asleep at night, but much of the world around you is awake!

Track 040 **4** Time zones exist because the world is so big. While the sun is rising on one side of the world, it's setting on the other side. There are 24 time zones across the world. One time zone is usually one hour of time difference. The cities of Anchorage, Alaska, in the United States, and Wellington in New Zealand, have 21 time zones between them. Anchorage is west of Wellington so it's earlier there. Wellington is east of Anchorage, so it's later there. When it's 11.00 p.m. on Sunday in Anchorage, it's 8.00 p.m. on Monday in Wellington. People in Anchorage are asleep, getting ready for Monday. But, at that same moment, people in Wellington have almost finished Monday.

Track 041 **4** **LEARN NEW WORDS** **asleep** / Most people are asleep at midnight. **awake** / Most people are awake at 10 o'clock in the morning. **east** / The sun rises in the east. **time zone** / The world has 24 time zones. **west** / The sun sets in the west.

Track 042 **3** **LEARN NEW WORDS** **dawn** / Dawn is when the day begins. **fascinate** / Fish that make their own light fascinate me. **glow** / We can easily see animals and plants that glow in the dark. **observe** / Scientists observe ocean life with special equipment. **pattern** / Some fish have interesting patterns on their bodies.

Track 043 **4** **WHILE YOU READ** See Student's Book pages 50–51.

Track 044 **GRAMMAR** See Student's Book page 54.

In This Unit

Theme This unit is about interactions between animals and humans.

Content Objectives

Students will

- examine conflicts between humans and wild animals.
- read about animals that are trained to use their special abilities to help people.
- discuss an animal conservationist and her efforts to protect wildlife.

Language Objectives

Students will

- talk about interactions between animals and humans.
- ask for and give reasons.
- use modals to describe obligation and advice.
- use *can, can't, could,* and *couldn't* to describe ability in the present and past.
- write about a relationship between an animal and a human, and edit and proofread their writing.

Vocabulary

pages 60–61 *access, afraid of, behaviour, conflict, disappear, frighten, habitat, interact, learn, need, smart, wild, wildlife*

page 62 *hunt, mistreat, relationship, survival*

page 65 *defend, injured, predator, prey, to rescue*

page 66 *avoid, chemical, domestic, feeling, sniff*

Vocabulary Strategies Prefix *mis-*, Collocations

Speaking Strategy Asking for and giving reasons

Grammar

Grammar 1 Use modals to describe obligation and advice

Grammar 2 Use modals to describe ability in the present and the past

Reading *Four-Legged Heroes*

Reading Strategy Problems and solutions

Video Scene 4.1: *The Elephant Whisperers*; Scene 4.2: Meet Amy Dickman

Writing Description of a relationship between an animal and a human

National Geographic Mission Start Small

Project

- Poster or brochure
- Presentation
- Video interview

Pronunciation *Can* and *can't*

Pacing Guides 1.4.1, 1.4.2, 1.4.3

Unit 4

Living Together

'Let's think about what we can do today to make sure our grandchildren have the option of seeing wildlife in the future.'
Amy Dickman

58

Introduce the Unit

- **Activate prior knowledge** Say *In Unit 1, we talked about wild animals in the city. In this unit, we'll be talking about wild animals in their natural habitats – the places where they are normally found. Where do wild animals live?* Write some animal habitats on the board. (forests, jungles, the sea, grasslands, woods) Ask *Has anyone ever seen a wild animal in its natural habitat? How is this different from seeing it in an animal park or a zoo?*

- Ask students to open their books at pages 58–59. Ask *What animal is that?* (a rhino, a rhinoceros) Read the caption aloud. Explain that the photo was taken at a nature conservancy which is an organisation that protects plants and animals. The one pictured manages thousands of acres of land for the purpose of protecting wild animals. Then read Question 1 aloud. Discuss how the man and the rhino in the picture might be feeling.

- Ask questions to encourage further discussion of the photo:
  Where is Kenya?
  What other kinds of wild animals live in Africa?
  Do you think caring for a young rhino is difficult?

A rhinoceros and its caretaker at a conservancy in Kenya

TO START

1. What's happening in the photo? How do you think the man feels? The animal?

2. What are situations where people and animals live together peacefully? What are situations where they don't get along?

3. Do you think that seeing wild animals where they live is a good idea? Why or why not?

59

Objectives
Students will
- describe and discuss a photo.
- discuss good and bad interactions between people and animals.

Content Vocabulary *conservancy, option, rhinoceros*

Resources Worksheet 1.4.1 (Teacher's Resource CD-ROM/Website); CPT: Unit Opener

BE THE EXPERT

About the Photo

The photo shows an orphaned rhino named Kilifi and his caretaker, Kamara, at the Lewa Wildlife Conservancy in northern Kenya. Kilifi's mother was killed by poachers and Kamara spends hours every day, sometimes in pouring rain, watching over Kilifi and a number of other young rhinos. Today, very few rhinos survive outside national parks and reserves. Kenya's black rhinos, whose population had plummeted to near extinction, are doing well at Lewa, which was named a UNESCO World Heritage Site in 2013.

Rampant poaching and loss of habitat are the two main challenges facing rhinos today. Despite the fact that conservation efforts have led to the doubling of the black rhino population from its low point of 2,480 individuals, total numbers today are still a fraction of the estimated 100,000 that existed in the early part of the 20th century.

Teaching Tip

When introducing students to a new unit, help them make connections between the new content and the content they've learnt in previous units. For example, ask what words from past units might be used to describe the photo in the unit opener. Encourage students to use grammar structures they've learnt in previous units to describe what they see.

Related Vocabulary

poncho, umbrella

- Read aloud Question 2. Say *Pets and their owners usually live together peacefully.* Ask *Can you name any other animal–human relationships that work well?* (people who have guide dogs, therapy animals or farm animals) *Can you think of any examples of when people and animals don't get along?* Prompt students to consider when wild animals, such as foxes, wolves and coyotes kill farm animals or pets, or when people enter the habitats of dangerous wild animals.

- Ask a student to read Question 3 aloud. Begin a two-column table on the board to list why it is or is not a good idea to see wild animals where they live. Invite students to help you add ideas to the table.

- Ask a student to read aloud the quote on page 58 by Amy Dickman. Say *Amy Dickman believes people should have the option to see wildlife where they live.* Ask *Why do you think she says we need to make sure children in the future will be able to do that?*

Extend

- Hand out **Worksheet 1.4.1**. Explain that pairs will be thinking and writing about humans' impact on wildlife.

Objectives

Students will

- use vocabulary related to human–wildlife conflict.
- use new vocabulary to read about and discuss human and animal interactions.

Target Vocabulary *access, afraid of, behaviour, conflict, disappear, frighten, habitat, interact, learn, need, smart, wild, wildlife*

Content Vocabulary *baboon, device, luckily, monitor, protection, steal*

Resources Worksheet 1.4.2 (Teacher's Resource CD-ROM/Website); Tracks 045–046 (Audio CD/Website/ CPT); CPT: Vocabulary

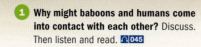

1 Why might baboons and humans come into contact with each other? Discuss. Then listen and read. 045

Human-**wildlife conflict** is a big problem all over the world today, and it's getting bigger. Imagine finding a baboon or two eating breakfast at your table! That would definitely be a conflict between a human, you, and wildlife, the baboons! Because baboons are **wild**, this type of conflict could be dangerous.

In Cape Town, South Africa, humans are **interacting** with baboons more than ever, right in their own neighbourhoods. Because about half of the natural baboon **habitat** and food in this region **disappeared**, baboons needed to find new ways to get food. So they started going into urban areas and stealing the food they need for survival.

A family of baboons at the breakfast table

60 VOCABULARY

Warm Up

- **Build background** Say *We're going to read about a city on the coast of South Africa where contact between baboons and people is creating problems for both species.* Tell students that baboons are among the largest monkeys. They eat many different things, including crops and meat, and they've become serious pests to both farmers and residents of urban areas.

Present

- Ask students to open their books at pages 60–61. Read the photo caption on page 60. Ask *Do you think these baboons are pets?* Invite students to respond. Then ask a student to read aloud the Activity 1 question at the top of page 60. Say *Let's list some reasons why these wild animals might leave their natural habitat and come into places where people live.* You may want to remind students of the urban foxes

in Bristol, England, and how it's easy for them to get food from gardens and rubbish bins.

- **1 TO START** Play **Track 045** and tell students to listen and read. Then discuss the photo and the reading with students. Ask questions such as the following:
  How do you think the baboons got into the house?
  Why do you think they came into the house?
  Is this a good way to see wildlife? Why or why not?

- **2 LEARN NEW WORDS** Play **Track 046**. Ask students to listen and repeat. Put students into pairs or small groups and ask them to take turns saying each word. Tell them to think of a true or false statement for each target word. Tell the class to decide whether each statement is true or false.

- Say *Use each word in a true or false statement. Your classmates will decide whether the statement is true or false. If the statement is false, the student*

Baboons are very **clever** animals. Once they **learn** that they can easily get food from humans, they won't try as hard to hunt for their own food. People who live near baboon habitats have to control this **behaviour** by limiting the baboons' **access** to human food and rubbish.

Both humans and wildlife **need** protection from each other. Luckily, in some places in South Africa, there are people who work as baboon monitors. Their job is to keep baboons away from homes. Because baboons are **afraid of** loud noises, monitors use noise-making devices to **frighten** them away. They might also use paintballs to frighten the baboons.

The monitors don't form relationships with the baboons, but they don't mistreat them either. They simply work to limit conflicts between humans and wildlife.

 LEARN NEW WORDS Listen and repeat. 🎧 046

 Work in pairs. Think about a time when an unwanted animal came into your house. How did you feel? What did you do?

VOCABULARY **61**

Our World in Context

The Republic of South Africa is a country on the southern tip of the continent of Africa. Cape Town, one of its largest cities, is known for its harbour and other geographic landmarks and its rich biodiversity, all of which make it a popular tourist destination. Chacma baboons are part of the area's wildlife and are a protected species. In an effort to keep roaming baboons out of urban areas, the city has undertaken a baboon management plan to keep the baboons safe – and wild. It is illegal to feed them, and touching them and even eating in front of them are strongly prohibited. A number of other guidelines have been issued to cut down on baboon–human conflicts. It is an unfortunate fact that feeding a baboon makes it more aggressive and often leads to it having to be destroyed.

Teaching Tip

Texts that give information often include details that students may forget. After an initial reading, give opportunities for revisiting the text and taking notes. For example, tell students to re-read the text at the end of the lesson and make notes. At the beginning of the next lesson, ask students to refer to their notes to answer questions about the text.

---

who identifies it will restate it to make it true. If the statement is true, a student who agrees with you will repeat the true statement.

- Model an example for students. Say *You don't need to be careful if you interact with a baboon because it's not a wild animal. True or false?* (false) Ask a student to correct the example so that it becomes a true statement. (*Be careful if you interact with a baboon because it's a wild animal.*)

Practise ③ ④

- ③ Say *I've heard of small mammals or snakes getting into people's houses, but it's never happened to me. I'm not sure what I'd do if a large monkey broke into my house!* Invite a student to read Activity 3 on page 61. Put students into pairs and ask them to discuss and then list some of the ways they, or

others, dealt with an unexpected animal break-in. When everyone has finished, invite them to share their stories.

- ④ Tell students to look at Activity 4 on page 62. Say *Now you're going to read about Amy Dickman and her work with big cats, like lions and tigers.* Point to the text and say *Circle the words that make sense in each sentence.*

- Say *The first two words are* wildlife *and* conflicts. Wildlife *refers to animals, and* conflicts *means 'troubles' or 'problems'. Try out each word in the sentence. Which word makes sense?* (conflicts) Tell students to complete the activity independently. Ask different students to stand up and read the completed paragraph aloud.

Objectives

Students will
- practise using vocabulary related to human and animal interactions.
- use a vocabulary strategy to learn new vocabulary.

Target Vocabulary *hunt, mistreat, relationship, survival*

Vocabulary Strategy Prefix *mis-*

Resources Online Workbook/Workbook pages 35; Worksheet 1.4.2 (Teacher's Resource CD-ROM/Website); Tracks 047–048 (Audio CD/Website/CPT); CPT: Vocabulary

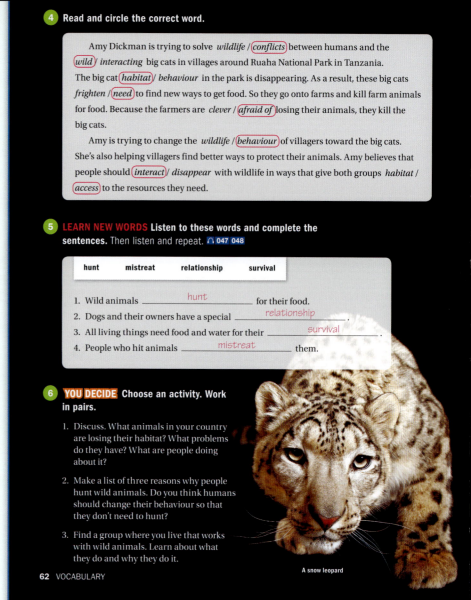

4 Read and circle the correct word.

Amy Dickman is trying to solve *wildlife / (conflicts)* between humans and the *(wild) / interacting* big cats in villages around Ruaha National Park in Tanzania. The big cat *(habitat) / behaviour* in the park is disappearing. As a result, these big cats *frighten / (need)* to find new ways to get food. So they go onto farms and kill farm animals for food. Because the farmers are *clever / (afraid of)* losing their animals, they kill the big cats.

Amy is trying to change the *wildlife / (behaviour)* of villagers toward the big cats. She's also helping villagers find better ways to protect their animals. Amy believes that people should *(interact) / disappear* with wildlife in ways that give both groups *habitat / (access)* to the resources they need.

5 **LEARN NEW WORDS** Listen to these words and complete the sentences. Then listen and repeat. 🎧 047 048

hunt	mistreat	relationship	survival

1. Wild animals _____ hunt _____ for their food.
2. Dogs and their owners have a special _____ relationship _____.
3. All living things need food and water for their _____ survival _____.
4. People who hit animals _____ mistreat _____ them.

6 **YOU DECIDE** Choose an activity. Work in pairs.

1. Discuss. What animals in your country are losing their habitat? What problems do they have? What are people doing about it?

2. Make a list of three reasons why people hunt wild animals. Do you think humans should change their behaviour so that they don't need to hunt?

3. Find a group where you live that works with wild animals. Learn about what they do and why they do it.

A snow leopard

62 VOCABULARY

- **5** **LEARN NEW WORDS** Read aloud the words in the Activity 5 word box. Tell students to listen for these words as they listen to the audio. Play **Track 047**. Ask students to complete the sentences. Then play **Track 048**. Ask students to listen and repeat.

- **Vocabulary Strategy** Write *mistreat* on the board. Circle the prefix *mis-*. Remind students that a prefix is a word part that has meaning. Underline the base word *treat*. Say *I know that when someone treats me well, they're nice to me. We just heard that people sometimes mistreat animals by hitting them.* Ask *Are the people being nice to the animals?* (no) *What do you think the prefix mis- means?* ('bad', 'wrong') *What does mistreat mean?* ('to treat badly') Help students to determine the meanings of the words *misunderstand* and *misuse*.

Apply

- **6** **YOU DECIDE** Ask students to look at Activity 6. Say *All of these activities are about animal and human interactions.* Tell students to read the three activities. Put students who choose the same option into pairs. Help them to focus their thinking with questions such as the following:

> 1. Why are animals losing their habitats?
> 2. What are good/bad reasons that people hunt?
> 3. Are there parks or zoos where you can see wild animals? How do they help those animals?

- Invite students to come to the front of the class and share their thoughts about habitat loss, hunting and organisations that work with wild animals.

Extend

- Tell students to use the Activity 6 questions and answers to conduct interviews with each other. Pairs don't have to agree with each other, but they should share as much information as possible.

- When students have had sufficient time to prepare their interviews, say *First, one partner asks the questions and the other partner reads her or his answers. Then switch roles.* If time permits, allow pairs to present their interviews to the class.

- If time allows, hand out **Worksheet 1.4.2**. Explain that students will use the vocabulary to write about and discuss conflict between humans and baboons.

Consolidate

- Write the following words on the board:

> **Column 1:** *access, behaviour, conflict, habitat, wildlife, relationship, survival*
> **Column 2:** *afraid of, disappear, frighten, interact, learn, need, hunt, mistreat*

- Say *Let's play a game!* Divide the class into two groups. Invite each group to form a line. Tell students that the first person in one line will pick a word from Column 1, and the first person in the other line will pick a word from Column 2. Say *Then the two of you will work together to make up a sentence with both words in it. The same two words can't be used together again.* Give the last pair of students enough time to make up a sentence. Say *Make sure your sentence makes sense.* Then tell partners to take turns reading their sentences.

BE THE EXPERT

Vocabulary Strategy

Prefix *mis-* Explain that not every word that begins with *mis-* will follow the pattern of prefix + base word. To help determine whether or not a group of letters is a prefix, remove the letters from the base word. If a known word remains, then the group of letters is probably a prefix, as in *mistreat*. However, in the case of *misery*, for example, *mis-* is not a prefix.

Note that this technique does not always help in determining a word's meaning. It's also important to consider whether the word that remains after the prefix is removed bears any relationship to the whole word. In the case of *mischief*, for example, the word *chief* remains and has its own meaning. (leader or ruler) That meaning, however, has nothing to do with the meaning of *mischief*.

Other words with the prefix *mis-* include *misbehave, misspelt, misunderstanding,* and *misuse.*

Teaching Tip

Remember to give all students a chance to answer questions and give examples in class. Avoid repeatedly calling on the same students. Sometimes, ask students who do not put up their hands, and be patient with these students if they need extra time to speak.

Formative Assessment

Can students
- use vocabulary related to human–wildlife conflict?

  Ask *Why do baboons sometimes break into people's homes for food?*
- use new vocabulary to discuss human and animal interactions?

  Ask students to describe one good and one bad example of human and animal interaction.

Workbook For additional practice, assign Workbook pages 34–35.
Online Workbook Vocabulary

SPEAKING STRATEGY

Objectives
Students will
- use words and phrases to ask for reasons.
- use words and phrases to give reasons.

Speaking Strategy
Asking for and giving reasons

Content Vocabulary
reserve, trick, tricking

Resources
Online Workbook; Worksheet 1.4.3 (Teacher's Resource CD-ROM/ Website); Tracks 049–050 (Audio CD/ Website/CPT); CPT: Speaking Strategy

Materials
pieces of card

SPEAKING STRATEGY 🎧 049

Asking for reasons	Giving reasons
Why <u>are villagers afraid of wild animals</u>?	Because <u>they're dangerous</u>.
<u>Farmers need to protect their animals from wild animals</u>. Do you know why?	It's because <u>wild animals hunt farm animals for food</u>.
<u>Wild animals are interacting with people more often</u>. Why is that?	Since <u>their habitats are disappearing, they're going where humans live</u>.

1 **Listen.** How do the speakers ask for and give reasons? Write the words and phrases you hear. 🎧 050

2 **Read and complete the dialogue.**   *Possible answers:*

Abdul: Look at this picture of people on an Indian tiger reserve.

Anna: The people are wearing masks. _____ *Why is that?* _____

Abdul: _____ *It's because* _____ they're trying to trick the tigers.

Anna: They're wearing the masks on the *backs* of their heads! _____ *Do you know why?* _____

Abdul: _____ *Since* _____ tigers attack people from behind, they see the mask and think the person is looking at them. That scares them.

Anna: Incredible! But _____ *why* _____ do people go onto the tiger reserve?

Abdul: _____ *Because* _____ they fish there. They also collect honey and wood in the reserves.

Anna: So the people wear masks _____ *because* _____ they believe the masks will protect them from tigers?

Abdul: That's right. In three years, tigers only attacked people who weren't wearing masks!

Anna: Wow! Tigers are clever, though. They might soon learn that people are tricking them.

3 **Work in pairs.** Take a card and read the sentence. Ask your partner for the reason. Your partner will answer the question. Then swap roles.

4 **Work in pairs.** Talk about animals. Talk about three problems, interesting facts or interactions. Your partner will ask for reasons. Respond and then swap roles.

> Why are there baboon monitors in Cape Town?

> Baboons go into urban areas. Monitors help to keep them away from humans.

There are baboon monitors in Cape Town.

Go to page 161.

SPEAKING **63**

Warm Up

- **Activate prior knowledge** Ask *When you ask someone a question to find out the reason for something, what word do you use?* Write *why* on the board. Point to a student and say *I want to know the reason (Kaleefa) is wearing (red) today.* Ask *Why are you wearing (red) today, (Kaleefa)?* Prompt the student to answer. (I like red; because red is my favourite colour; because this shirt was on the top of my clothes pile) Write *because* on the board.

- Put students into pairs or small groups and tell them to open their books at pages 60–61. Tell them to use the reading to ask and answer *why* questions about baboons and people in Cape Town. Say *If you ask, for example, 'Why are baboons dangerous?' your classmate might answer, 'Because they're big, wild animals'.*

Present

- Say *We're going to listen carefully to people asking for and giving reasons.* Play **Track 049.** Ask *What word is used in each question?* (*why*) *What word is used in two of the answers?* (*because*) *What other word did you hear in an answer?* (*since*) Add *since* to the board. Then tell students to turn to page 63. Invite pairs to come to the front of the class and read the questions and answers.

- **1** Say *Now listen to another conversation.* Point to the board. Say *You'll hear these words used in phrases or sentences. Write down the expressions that include these words.* Play **Track 050.** Ask students to share what they have written. Replay the track if necessary.

Practise

- **2** Once students are comfortable with the speaking strategy, start Activity 2. Say *You're going to read about a tiger reserve.* Ask *Does anyone know what an* *animal or nature reserve is?* Explain that it's an area of land where animals and plants are protected. Say *Complete the dialogue by adding words, phrases or sentences that ask for and give reasons.* Tell students to do the activity independently.

- Invite several pairs to read their completed dialogues aloud, taking turns as Abdul and Anna. After a few readings, ask *Did the students use the words and phrases we talked about? What are they?*

Apply

- Ask student pairs to cut out the set of cards on page 161. Read the instructions and the speech bubbles aloud. Say *Place the cards face down. One student in each pair turns over a card, reads the sentence silently, and then turns it into a* why *question to ask his or her partner. The partner answers the question, using* because *or* since. *Then he/she turns over a card, reads it silently and asks for a reason.*

- Say *There's more than one way to ask for a reason.* Read the question in the speech bubble. Then say *You could also say, 'There are baboon monitors in Cape Town. Why is that?' or 'Do you know why?'* Tell partners to play until they've both asked for and given reasons about each card.

- Put students into new pairs. Say *Now that you've practised asking for and giving reasons, talk to your new partner about the facts you've learnt so far in this unit.* Read the activity instructions aloud. Say *Spend a few minutes to think of things to tell your partner.*

Extend

- Invite students to make new game cards with the facts they used in Activity 4. Put students into small groups in order to play a new version of the game. Say *Mix all the cards together. Place them face down in the middle of the group. Take turns to turn over a card, ask for a reason, and put the card back down in the middle of the group. The first person to touch the card and give a good reason gets a point. The person with the most points wins.*

- If time allows, hand out **Worksheet 1.4.3**. Explain that students will use the worksheet to practise asking for and giving reasons.

Consolidate

- Make cards with one of the following vocabulary items on each of them: *access, afraid of, baboons, conflict, frighten, habitat, hunt, interact, learn, leopards, mistreat, need, smart, tigers, wild,* and *wildlife.* Give one to each student. List on the board: *why, Do you know why?, Why is that?, because, It's because* and *since.* Tell students to stand in a circle.

- Say *Make a sentence about some animal or human behaviour. Include the word on your card. Ask the next person in the circle for a reason for the behaviour. He or she responds, then asks the next person a new question. Use the words and phrases on the board.* Give students time to write a few sentences on their cards.

Strategy in Depth

Teaching students how to ask for and give reasons is one step towards acquiring the important skill of recognising expressions of cause and effect in English. When students turn a statement of fact into a *why* question, they're essentially asking for the cause of an effect. When they respond to such a question using *because* or *since*, they're stating the cause.

Using *because* or *since* in this way will help prepare students to learn such expressions of cause and effect as:

Cause: Because baboons' natural habitats are shrinking, they're raiding people's homes for food.

Effect: Baboons' natural habitats are shrinking. As a result, they're raiding people's homes for food.

Formative Assessment

Can students

- use words and phrases to ask for reasons?

  Ask *How would you ask a classmate for the reason people wear masks on the backs of their heads in tiger reserves?*

- use words and phrases to give reasons?

  Ask *How would you respond to a classmate who asked you why people wear masks on the backs of their heads in tiger reserves?*

Online Workbook Speaking Strategy

Objectives

Students will
- identify modals that describe obligation and advice.
- use modals to describe obligation and advice.
- use words associated with endangered sea turtles.

Grammar Modals: Describing obligation and advice

Target Vocabulary *defend, injured, predator, prey, rescue*

Academic Language *advice, modal, obligation*

Content Vocabulary *endangered, extinct, fur, necessary, ranger, recommended*

Resources Online Workbook/Workbook pages 36–37; Tracks 051–055 (Audio CD/Website/CPT); CPT: Grammar 1

Materials crayons or markers, sheets of card cut into strips

GRAMMAR 🔊 051

Modals: Describing obligation and advice

Necessary	We **must** learn more about the fight to save rhinos.
	We **have to** protect rhinos.
Not necessary	We **don't have to** use products made from rhinoceros horn.
Recommended	We **shouldn't** ignore the rhino problem.
	Everyone **should** do something, even if it's a small action.

RHINOCEROS POPULATIONS WORLDWIDE

20,405 — WHITE RHINO
5,055 — BLACK RHINO
3,333 — GREATER ONE-HORNED RHINO
<100 — SUMATRAN RHINO
58–60 — JAVAN RHINO

1 **Listen.** How can we save rhinos? Complete the sentences. Then tick the correct box. 🔊 052

	necessary	not necessary	recommended
1. Rangers _____have to_____ go into the rhino areas and catch the hunters.	☑	☐	☐
2. Rhino monitors _____should_____ know when rhino babies are born.	☐	☐	☑
3. We _____shouldn't_____ use rhino horn in medicine.	☐	☐	☑
4. We _____have to_____ keep some rhinos in protected places to have babies safely.	☑	☐	☐
5. We _____don't have to_____ save rhinos ourselves.	☐	☑	☐

2 **Work in pairs.** Listen again to the passage. Write two additional ways to save rhinos. Say if they are *necessary*, *not necessary* or *recommended*. 🔊 053

1. _____

2. _____

64 GRAMMAR

Warm Up

- **Build background** Write *endangered* on the board. Ask *Can you name some endangered animals?* Students may name some of the big cats, whales, gorillas or turtles. Ask *You've heard the word endangered, and you've probably used it yourself, but do you know what it means?* Note students' responses. Underline *danger* in the word and, if necessary, explain that *endangered* is used to describe a group of animals that is in danger of becoming extinct – of no longer having any living members anywhere in the world.

- Say *The rhinoceros on pages 58 and 59 is part of an endangered group of animals.* Ask *Why do animals become endangered?* (hunting, habitat loss, climate change, the animal is considered a pest) *Do you think people should try to keep animals from becoming endangered?* Invite students to respond. Write *should* on the board. Ask *When do we use the word should?* Help students to understand that one of the ways we use *should* is when we want to suggest that someone does something. For example, when an adult says you should tidy your room or do your homework.

3 **Work in pairs.** Give advice on how people can protect wildlife. Use *must, (don't) have to, should* and *shouldn't*.

> We shouldn't hunt wild animals just for fun.

> You're right. And we must stop hunters that hunt for fur.

4 **LEARN NEW WORDS** Listen to learn about saving sea turtles. Then listen and repeat. 🎧 054 055

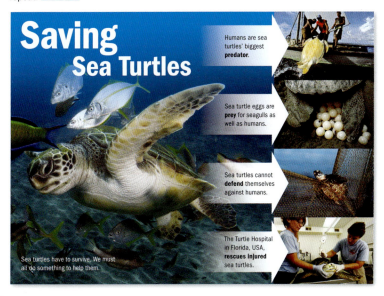

Saving Sea Turtles

Humans are sea turtles' biggest **predator**.

Sea turtle eggs are **prey** for seagulls as well as humans.

Sea turtles cannot **defend** themselves against humans.

The Turtle Hospital in Florida, USA, **rescues injured** sea turtles.

Sea turtles have to survive. We must all do something to help them.

5 **Work independently.** Think of another wild animal that is endangered. Write about why it's endangered. Give advice on how to protect it. Remember to use *must, (don't) have to, should* and *shouldn't*.

_____
_____
_____
_____

6 **Work in groups.** Imagine you work for a group that helps protect sea turtles. What five pieces of advice would you give people on what to do?

> We must help people who sell eggs find other ways to make money.

GRAMMAR **65**

Present

- Ask students to open their books at page 64 and look at the grammar box at the top of the page. Read the title and tell students that modals are words, such as *can, would* and *should,* that are used with a main verb to express certain kinds of ideas. Say *Follow in your books as we listen to sentences with modals.* Play **Track 051**.

- Ask students to focus on the left side of the grammar box. Say *You know that if something is necessary, it's needed for something else to happen, as in 'It's necessary for animals to eat in order to survive'.* Read the first sentence on the right side of the box. Ask *What is necessary?* (to learn more) *Why is it necessary?* (to save rhinos)

- Read the second sentence. Ask *What is necessary?* (to protect rhinos) Explain that this sentence doesn't say why protecting rhinos is necessary, but we understand what is meant. Ask *Why is protecting rhinos necessary?* (to keep them safe, to keep them from becoming endangered or extinct) *In these sentences, what words tell you that something is necessary?* (*must, have to*)

Grammar in Depth

Modals, often called modal auxiliary verbs or helping verbs, complete the meaning of the main verbs they are used with. Modals are used in a variety of situations, such as to ask for permission, to express probability, or to describe an obligation or give advice, which are covered in this unit. Categories of modals include the following:

To express:	Use the modals:
ability	*can, could,* as in *I can play the guitar.*
permission/ polite requests	*can, may, could,* as in *Can I play for you now?*
degrees of certainty or probability	*can, could, may,* or *might,* as in *You might be famous one day!*
prohibition/obligation	*have (got) to, must, can't,* as in *I have to practise now.*
advice and suggestions	*could, should, can,* as in *You should perform more often.*

Point out that *must* and *have (got) to* are both used to talk about obligation. *Must* is more common when we are talking about things the speaker feels or thinks he/she is obliged to do: *I must try to lose weight.*

Have (got) to, is more often used for things that are imposed upon the speaker from outside, as in *We have to be at school for 9.00 a.m.* (There is a rule about this.)

Teaching Tip

To give students additional practice with new vocabulary or grammar structures, ask them to create items or questions similar to the ones they completed in an activity. Tell students to exchange the new items with a partner and complete them.

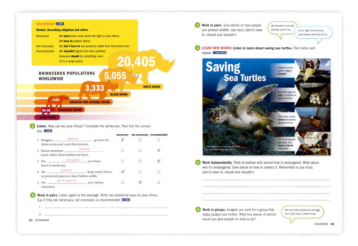

• Work through the example of a modal used when something is not necessary. Explain that many rhinos are killed for their horns, which are carved into objects and also used to make traditional medicines, although there is little scientific proof that these medicines work. Then explain that when something is recommended, it's not considered necessary, just good or useful. Work through these modal examples with students.

Practise 1 2 3

• **Graphic literacy** Read aloud the title of the bar graph below the grammar box. Say *This bar graph shows the population, or number, of each type of rhino alive in the world today.* Ask *How many types of rhino are there?* (five) Tell students that Sumatra and Java are two of the islands that make up the country of Indonesia. Black and white rhinos live in Africa, and one-horned rhinos are found in India. Point out the symbol before the number 100 and tell students it means 'less than'.

• Ask *Which type of rhino is the most endangered?* (the Javan rhino) Ask *How can you see at a glance the size of each population?* (the length of the coloured bars)

• **1** Say *Now we'll hear some ways to protect the remaining rhinos in the world. Then you'll need to complete the sentences and tick the boxes. But first, listen.* Play **Track 052** as students listen. Play the track again and ask students to complete the activity. Say *Pay attention to each modal. Does it express a necessary action or a recommended one? Tick the correct box. If you're not sure, look at the grammar box.* Review the answers as a class.

• **2** Read the activity instructions aloud. Play **Track 053** and put students into pairs to complete the activity. When they've finished, invite pairs of students to read their sentences to the class. Ask *Does everyone agree with the modals the students used and what they mean?*

• **3** Ask one pair to stand up and model the dialogue in the speech bubbles. Then read the activity instructions aloud. Say *Now talk to your partner about how to protect any of the endangered animals you know about. Use the modals you have learnt.* Give students the opportunity to share their advice with the class.

Apply 4 5 6

• **4** **LEARN NEW WORDS** Say *You've learnt about endangered rhinos. Now you'll hear about the plight, or difficult situation, of sea turtles. Look at the photos on page 65.* Read the photo captions aloud. Invite students to share what they know about sea turtles. Play **Track 054** and ask students to listen. Then play **Track 055**. Tell students to listen and repeat.

• **5** Read the activity instructions aloud. Say *Look back through the unit to remember some of the endangered animals we talked about. Other animals also need help – certain whales, penguins and tigers. All endangered animals face some of the same problems. Write about an animal you know something about.* Tell students to work on their own. Say *Before you begin, read the instructions. Review the modals on page 64.*

• **6** Read the Activity 6 instructions aloud. If time permits, replay **Track 054** for students. Put students into small groups. Say *Brainstorm ideas. Listen politely to one another. Appoint someone in the group to write down the group's advice. Use the example in the speech bubble as a model. Remember to include modals.* Circulate to make sure everyone gets a chance to join in the discussion.

Extend

- Copy the table below on the board. Put students into pairs. Say *Choose one of the dangers listed in the table. Write a dialogue between a person who wants to protect sea turtles from that danger and a person who's causing that danger. How would the first person educate the other about how he or she is hurting sea turtles? Include modals. What might that person say in response?* Ask students to role-play their dialogues for the class.

Danger to Sea Turtles	Cause of the Danger
the sale of eggs, meat, shells	people who use these products
fishing nets	the fishing industry
plastic bags and other rubbish	careless people, rubbish-collection companies
habitat loss	people who live near the sea, building companies
oil spills and chemical pollution	various industries

Consolidate

- Say *Think about the animals you've learnt about. Which problems concern you the most?* While students think, write these vocabulary items on the board: *afraid of, behaviour, defend, feed, frighten, habitat, hunt, injured, learn, mistreat, need, rescue, smart, survival, wild* and *wildlife.*

- Say *You've seen bumper stickers on cars – signs that have a message on them, such as* Save the whales! *Well, now you can create your own bumper sticker. Include the new vocabulary in your message.* Give examples: *Keep the 'wild' in wildlife, Don't feed the baboons! Rescue injured sea turtles! Defend the rhinos – they need us!* When students have finished, ask them to stand up one at a time. Say *Stand up and shout your message!*

Our World in Context

Another hazard to sea turtles that is a side effect of coastal development is artificial lighting. Sea turtles need dark beaches to reproduce successfully. Bright, artificial lights discourage nesting females, who are then forced to lay their eggs in undesirable places. Consequently, the hatchlings face more difficulties to survive.

Furthermore, bright shore lights often cause the hatchlings to become disoriented when they are born. Instead of heading for the water, they wander inland where they die of dehydration, are eaten by animals, or are run over by cars. Various programmes are being implemented to reduce the amount of artificial light in critical locations.

Formative Assessment

Can students

- identify modals that describe obligation and advice?

  Ask students to identify which sentence includes a modal with a recommended action:

  Don't buy products made of rhino horn.

  We should help people learn about sea turtles.

- use modals to describe obligation and advice?

  Ask students to complete this sentence with a modal that describes an action that's not necessary:

  People _____ eat turtle eggs. (don't have to)

- use words associated with endangered sea turtles?

  Ask students to complete this sentence frame:

  Sea turtles can't _____ themselves against their biggest _____, humans. (defend, predator)

Workbook For additional practice, assign Workbook pages 36–37

Online Workbook Grammar 1

Objectives

Students will
- read about and discuss animal heroes.
- use new words from the reading.
- make a problem and solution table.

Reading Strategy Problems and solutions

Target Vocabulary *avoid, chemical, domestic, feeling, sniff*

Vocabulary Strategy Collocations

Academic Language *problem, solution*

Content Vocabulary *laboratory, landmine, sunblock, treat*

Resources Online Workbook/Workbook pages 38–39; Tracks 056–057 (Audio CD/Website/CPT); Worksheet 1.4.4 (Teacher's Resource CD-ROM/Website); CPT: Reading

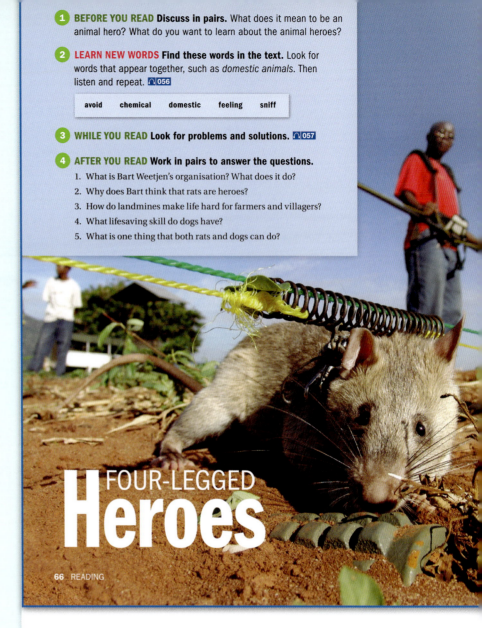

1 BEFORE YOU READ Discuss in pairs. What does it mean to be an animal hero? What do you want to learn about the animal heroes?

2 LEARN NEW WORDS Find these words in the text. Look for words that appear together, such as *domestic animals*. Then listen and repeat. 🎧 056

| avoid | chemical | domestic | feeling | sniff |

3 WHILE YOU READ Look for problems and solutions. 🎧 057

4 AFTER YOU READ Work in pairs to answer the questions.
1. What is Bart Weetjen's organisation? What does it do?
2. Why does Bart think that rats are heroes?
3. How do landmines make life hard for farmers and villagers?
4. What lifesaving skill do dogs have?
5. What is one thing that both rats and dogs can do?

FOUR-LEGGED
Heroes

66 READING

Warm Up

- **Build background** Write the word *hero* on the board. Ask *What does hero mean?* Write students' responses. (a great person, someone who does something brave or dangerous, someone who helps people in need) Ask *Do you know any heroes? What did the person do to be a hero?* Invite students to share their ideas and experiences.

Before You Read

- Ask *Can an animal be a hero?* Invite students to respond. Put students into pairs. Say *Discuss with your partner what you think it means to be an animal hero.* Ask *What would you like to learn about animal heroes?* When pairs have finished talking, ask students to say what they want to learn.

- Tell students to open their books at pages 66–67. Ask a student to read the title of the reading at the bottom of page 66. Then point out the subtitle on page 67. Say *Look at the photos and read*

Animals with Amazing Abilities

Most people have mixed feelings about rats and avoid them if they can. Bart Weetjens thinks that we must treat rats as heroes.

Bart started an organisation called APOPO in Tanzania. Bart's organisation trains African giant pouched rats to sniff the ground in order to find underground landmines left in the area during past wars. Many of these landmines are still active. They often explode, killing and injuring thousands of people each year. Villagers avoid places where the dangerous landmines are. But much of this land could be used as valuable farmland if the mines weren't there. These rats are helping villagers get their land back.

The giant rats are never mistreated. None of them die doing their work. They even have sunblock put on their ears and tails while they work. And when they find a landmine, they get a treat!

While rats aren't usually seen as heroes, some domestic animals, like dogs, often are. There are many stories about dogs that save lives, but dogs have another lifesaving skill that we're still learning about. Just like landmine-sniffing rats, dogs have an amazing sense of smell. They're now being trained to sniff out chemicals from the body that are connected to certain diseases, sometimes even before doctors or laboratory tests can find them!

So, the next time you see a rat or dog, don't be afraid. Remember, these animal heroes can save lives.

A medical dog sniffing for diseases

A giant pouched rat sniffing a landmine

5 **Complete the table.** Write two problems and two solutions.

Problem	Solution
landmines kill people	train rats to find them
tests don't find some diseases	train dogs to sniff out the diseases

6 **Discuss in groups.**

1. Did the reading change your feelings about rats? Dogs? Explain.
2. What other animals do you know about that have helped people or saved lives? How did they help?
3. Imagine you train animals to help people or save lives. What kind of animal would you train? Why? How would it help?

READING **67**

---

the captions. *Look over the text.* Then ask *What do you know about landmines?* Ask *What makes landmines explode? What do you think the reading is about?* Invite students to share their predictions.

- **2** **LEARN NEW WORDS** Say *Before we read about animal heroes, you're going to learn some new words.* Read the instructions for Activity 2 aloud. Then tell students to read the words in the box. Say *When you find the words, see if any others, besides domestic, are paired with another word in a phrase that may sound familiar.* Play **Track 056**. Ask students to listen and repeat.

- **Vocabulary strategy** Tell students that when two or more words are often used together in English, it's helpful to remember them together, almost as if they were one word. Point out, for example, that although *animals* is a common word that is used in lots of different ways and paired with many other words (*farm animals, wild animals, animal habitats*), the word *domestic* is less common, but it's often paired with *animals*.

Reading Strategy

Problems and solutions Texts can be organised in different ways. These organisational structures include describing events in chronological order or comparing and contrasting people, objects or events. Another way is describing problems and then explaining solutions to those problems. Sometimes signal words, such as *problem, solution, solved, fixed, as a result,* and *in order to* are used and can help students identify problems and solutions in a text, but not always. Recognising an obvious problem in a text, such as buried landmines in this unit's reading, should alert students to look for the solution.

Vocabulary Strategy

Collocations A collocation is two or more words that are often used together. These combinations just sound 'right' to native English speakers, who use them all the time. There are several different kinds of collocations, including adverb + adjective (*terribly sorry*), verb + noun (*make a plan*), and adjective + noun (*domestic animals*). Sometimes, it's possible to work out the phrase's meaning by thinking about each word – but not always, as in *terribly sorry*. That's why it's helpful to teach collocations as single blocks, or chunks, of language. Learning and using collocations will help your students improve their fluency in English.

Teaching Tip

To improve reading fluency, encourage students to practise reading aloud in phrases instead of individual words. Play audio recordings and pause after each sentence. Tell students to repeat the sentence exactly as they heard it. Learning to read in phrases helps students become more fluent readers. This will help them recognise common phrase types and apply the familiar pattern to different texts.

FOUR-LEGGED
Heroes

- Say *Remembering the phrase* domestic animals *is helpful in understanding the difference between pets, for instance, and wild animals. Remembering it can also help you work out what* domestic *means when it's paired with another word.*

- Tell students to read the first paragraph of the reading. Ask *Do you see another word from the word box that's part of a phrase that sounds familiar?* Point out *mixed feelings* in the first line. Tell students that it's a phrase they'll often hear in English. Ask *What do you think* mixed feelings *means?* Explain that when you have mixed feelings about something, you have both good and bad feelings about it.

While You Read ③

- ③ Say *Now we're going to listen to* Four-Legged Heroes *and learn some surprising things about a couple of familiar animals.* Play **Track 057** and tell students to listen and read.

- Discuss the reading. Tell students that the rats, while big, are light enough that they don't cause the mines to explode if they walk over them. Say *Now you'll read again.* Remind students that a problem is a situation that causes difficulties for people, and a solution is something that is done to remove the difficulties. Then say *As you read, write down each problem you come across. Then match the solutions to the problems.* Play **Track 057** again or allow students to read in silence.

After You Read

- ④ Put students into pairs. Tell students to read the questions and answer them. If partners disagree on an answer, tell them to read the text again and find information that supports their answers. Tell students to complete the activity. Review the answers as a class.

- ⑤ Say *Look at the notes you made about problems and solutions. Use them to complete the table in Activity 5.* Then draw a blank version of the table from page 67 on the board. Ask different students to come up and add information to the table. Review it as a class.

Problem	Solution
Buried landmines injure and kill people.	Train rats to find the mines.
Tests don't find some human diseases soon enough.	Train dogs to sniff out the chemicals related to the diseases.
Buried mines prevent land from being farmed.	Train rats to find the mines.
Rats can get sunburnt.	Put sunblock on their ears and tails.

- ⑥ Put students into small groups and read the activity questions. Then ask a group member to act as secretary and write down notes from the discussion about each question. Give some ideas if students are struggling. You might mention therapy animals, such as dogs, cats and horses, that provide comfort to the sick and elderly. Another example is service animals, such as dogs, cats, monkeys and pigs, that can be trained to perform certain tasks to help people who are disabled.

Extend

- Tell students to write a letter thanking an animal that helps people for the work it does. Say *Imagine that the person who trains the animal will read your letter to the animal. In your letter, tell the animal what you learnt about it. Say why you want to thank it. Try to use some new vocabulary – and use your imagination!* When they've finished, choose some students to read their letters to the class.

- **Worksheet** If time allows, you may want to hand out **Worksheet 1.4.4** in class. Students will use the worksheet to practise the new vocabulary and increase their vocabulary by recognising related forms of words.

Consolidate

- Put students in groups of four to play a game. Tell groups to work together to write four pieces of information based on the reading. Some of these should be true and some should be false. Alternatively, they can all be true or all false, but they must be complete sentences.

- When groups have finished writing, say *Now you'll play a game of True or False with another group. Group members take turns to read a 'fact' to one student in another group. That student responds by saying 'True' or 'False.' Each correct answer counts as one point. Keep the score. The group that has the most points after all the sentences have been read, wins.* Circulate to settle any disputes that may arise. If time permits, let each winning group play another winning group, to see which group ends up with the highest number of points.

About the Photo

Areas suspected of containing buried landmines are marked off with a rope grid. The mine-sniffing rats are then harnessed and connected to a rope suspended between two handlers. The giant rats sweep up and down the area and indicate the scent of explosives by scratching at the ground. Though large, the rats are light enough in weight that they don't detonate the landmines. Since APOPO was founded in 1997, mine-sniffing rats have helped clear 13,200 mines from minefields in Tanzania, Mozambique, Angola and Cambodia.

Related Vocabulary

harness

Answer Key

Comprehension **4**

1. APOPO. It trains rats to find landmines buried underground.
2. The rats are heroes because they're preventing many deaths and making the land safe to farm again.
3. Many of the mines are still active and can explode and kill people.
4. They're able to smell chemicals from humans' bodies that show the presence of certain diseases.
5. They can use their sense of smell in lifesaving ways humans cannot.

Formative Assessment

Can students

- recall information about animal heroes?

  Ask students to say why the animals in *Four-Legged Heroes* are heroes.

- use new words from the reading?

  Ask students to complete these sentence frames:

  African giant rats locate landmines by _____ the ground. (sniffing)

  Dogs are trained to use their sense of smell to recognise _____ related to certain diseases. (chemicals)

- discuss problems and solutions?

  Ask students to name a problem and solution associated with buried landmines.

Workbook For additional practice, assign Workbook pages 38–39.

Online Workbook Reading

Objectives
Students will
- discuss how humans care for orphaned elephants.
- apply the message of the video to their personal lives.

Content Vocabulary *bush, camp, elephant keepers, whisperer*

Resources Video scene 4.1 (DVD/Website/CPT); Online Workbook; CPT: Video

VIDEO ▶

1 BEFORE YOU WATCH Discuss in pairs.

1. An orphan elephant is a young elephant without a mother. What do you think happened to the orphans' mothers? Give one or two ideas.

2. Why do you think people have to take care of the young orphan elephants?

2 Read and circle. You're going to watch *The Elephant Whisperers.* Use the title to predict what the video is about. Circle the number.

1. Baby elephants in a zoo
2. Elephant and human conflicts
3. People who take care of baby elephants

3 WHILE YOU WATCH Write two words that describe the elephants and two words that describe the humans. Watch scene 4.1.

Elephants:
Possible answers for either:
caring, loving, friendly, playful

Humans:
_____
_____

68 VIDEO

Before You Watch

- Say *We are going to watch a video about some other wild animals cared for by humans. Why do humans sometimes care for wild animals?*

- **1** Tell students to open their books at pages 68–69. Ask a student to read the Activity 1 questions aloud. Put students into pairs and ask them to discuss the questions. When they've finished, invite pairs to share their ideas and write them on the board.

- Invite students to look at the photo on this page. Ask *Who do you think the man is?* (the elephant's keeper) *What does it look like they're doing?* (talking, hugging) *Do you think they like each other?*

- **2** Read the Activity 2 instructions. Write *whisperer* on the board. Underline *whisper* and ask students

what it means. Tell them to act out *to whisper* with a partner. Then circle the *-er* ending. Ask *How does this ending change the meaning of the word?* (It changes the meaning to 'a person who whispers'.)

- Explain that *whisperer,* when used with the name of an animal, such as *horse whisperer* or *elephant whisperer,* means someone who works closely with an animal, and studies its behaviour to try and understand how the animal is feeling. Invite students to do the activity.

While You Watch

- **3** Ask a student to read the Activity 3 instructions. Say *Pay attention as you watch* The Elephant Whisperers. *Write words you think describe the elephants and humans.* Play **Video scene 4.1**.

4 **Work in pairs.** Put the daily events in order, according to the video.

_3_ The keepers feed and play with the elephants.

_4_ The keepers and elephants go back to the camp.

_2_ The keepers and elephants go to the bush.

_1_ The elephant keepers get up at 5.30 a.m.

_5_ The elephants and their keepers go to bed.

5 **AFTER YOU WATCH** Read the sentences. Tick T for _true_ or F for _false_.

1. The elephants are not very friendly. T **F**
2. The elephants are from different places in Kenya. **T** F
3. The elephants want to be alone. T **F**
4. The elephants only like to be with their keepers. T **F**
5. The keepers stay with the elephants at night so that they don't cry. **T** F

6 **Discuss in pairs.**

1. How are elephants and humans alike? Name three similarities.

2. What do you think is fun about being an elephant keeper? What do you think is hard?

7 **YOU DECIDE** Choose an activity.

1. **Work independently.** Imagine you're an elephant keeper. Write a letter to your family explaining a day in your life.

2. **Work in pairs.** Write a job advertisement for an elephant keeper. Describe the job and the type of person needed to do it.

3. **Work in groups.** In the video, you saw workers playing ball with the elephants. Think of at least three other fun ways that humans can interact with elephants. Present your ideas to the class.

VIDEO **69**

Teaching Tip

Keep order in the classroom by helping students stay focused during activities. Review instructions, focusing on one step at a time. Encourage students to ask you to explain directions or suggestions they don't understand. Make sure each student knows what he or she is supposed to do.

Formative Assessment

Can students
• discuss how humans care for orphaned elephants as a result of watching the video?

Ask _How have human actions contributed to the need for elephant keepers?_

• If students have trouble following the video or understanding the text, pause the video and allow them to ask questions or re-read the text. Try replaying the video with and without sound, and invite students to describe and comment on what they see.

• **4** Put students into pairs. Read the directions. Remind students that putting events in order means to show what happens first, next, and so on. Say _Show the order with numbers. The first event is numbered for you._

After You Watch

• **5** Tell students to work independently to decide if the sentences are true or false. When they've finished, share the answers as a class. If students disagree about an answer, replay the video.

• **6** Put students into pairs. Read the discussion questions. Tell students that the words they wrote to describe the elephants and humans will help them in their discussions.

• **7** **YOU DECIDE** Tell students to read the activity options. If students choose to write the letter in option 1, tell them to review Activity 4 and write about a day's activities in the correct order. Say _Remember that you are the elephant keeper, so use the words I and me when explaining what the keeper does._

• For students who choose option 2, say _Remember, the elephant keepers are with the baby elephants all day and all night. What kind of person would be good for that job?_

• If students choose option 3, ask them to discuss what they remember about the boy and the elephants playing with the ball.

Objectives

Students will
- identify modals that describe ability in the present and the past.
- use modals to describe ability in the present and the past.

Grammar Modals: Describing ability in the present and the past

Content Vocabulary *ability, salamanders*

Resources Online Workbook/Workbook pages 40–41; Worksheet 1.4.5 (Teacher's Resource CD-ROM/ Website); Pronunciation Answer Key (Teacher's Resource CD-ROM/ Website); Track 058, Tracks 124–126 (Audio CD/Website/CPT); CPT: Grammar 2 and Pronunciation

---

GRAMMAR 058

Modals: Describing ability in present and past

Many types of wildlife today **can't** cross roads safely.

What **can** we do about it?

We **can** help them by building animal crossings.

In 1987, salamanders **couldn't** safely cross a street in Amherst, Massachusetts, USA.

How **could** they avoid cars?

People built tunnels under the street. This way, the salamanders **could** cross safely.

1 Read. Complete the paragraph with *can, can't, could* or *couldn't.*

Roads _____can_____ be dangerous for both humans and wildlife. Roads go though wildlife habitat, so animals _____can't_____ cross safely. When cars hit animals, people _____can_____ get hurt, too.

This is changing now in many countries. Before 2011, elephants _____couldn't_____ safely cross a road in Kenya. But now they _____can_____ because the government built a tunnel under the road.

On Christmas Island in Australia, cars killed around 500,000 red crabs every year. People thought of ways they _____could_____ help the crabs. They built special bridges over the road. Now the crabs _____can't_____ be harmed because they _____can_____ climb over the bridges to safety.

In Holland, people knew they _____could_____ help their wildlife stay alive. So they worked to create over 600 animal crossings. Now wildlife and people _____can_____ travel where they need to go safely.

2 Work in pairs. Play Noughts and Crosses. Describe your own abilities now and in the past. Mark X or O. Try to get three in a row.

> When I was six, I couldn't teach my dog to do tricks.

can	couldn't	could
could	**wild**	can't
couldn't	can	can't

70 GRAMMAR

Go to page 159.

Warm Up

- **Revise** Say *You've learnt about the modals* must, have to, don't have to, should, *and* shouldn't. Ask *When do we use these modals?* If necessary, remind students that they're used to talk about obligation and advice, such as in *You <u>must</u> tidy your room before Grandma comes.* Remind students that modals are always used with a main verb.

- Say *There are other modals used to express other kinds of ideas. For example, how do you tell someone that you're able to do something?* Write *can* on the board. Point to it. Say *We usually use this word. Here's an example: I can speak two languages.* Ask students *What can you do?*

Present

- Say *Today, you'll learn modals that are used to talk about ability.* Write *ability* on the board. Tell students

the word means 'power or skill to do something'. Say *Able and* ability *are related words. Able is an adjective, or describing word: You are able. Ability is a noun: You have the ability. If you have the ability to do something, you can do it.*

- Tell students to open their books at page 70 and look at the grammar box at the top of the page. Read the title and tell students that they're going to learn the modals *can* and *could,* and their negative forms *can't* and *couldn't.* Say *Follow in your books as we listen to sentences with these modals.* Play **Track 058**.

- Read the sentences on the left-hand side of the grammar box. Say *All of these sentences are set in the present.* Then read the sentences on the right-hand side of the grammar box. Say *These sentences are set in the past. They tell you that the actions took place in the past.*

Practise

- **1** Ask students to look at the photo. Tell them it shows an animal crossing that was built in Canada to allow animals to safely walk over the motorway.

- Read the instructions aloud. Say *Read each sentence carefully. Does it talk about the present or the past? Look for dates or past verb forms. Does the sentence require a positive or negative modal? If you're not sure, try out each modal. Which one makes the most sense?* Tell students to work independently. Review the answers as a class.

Apply **2**

- **2** Put students into pairs and read aloud the activity instructions. Make sure students know how to play *Noughts and Crosses.* Ask pairs to flip a coin to see who will go first. Point out *wild* in the centre of the grid. Tell pairs that either of them can use this square as long as they say a correct sentence with *can, could, can't* or *couldn't.*

- Ask a student to read aloud the sentence in the speech bubble. Ask *Where on the grid would you place your mark?* Make sure students understand they could place their *X* or *O* on either of the two 'couldn't' squares, or in the centre *wild* square. Tell pairs to play the game. If time permits, invite students to play again with a new partner.

Extend

- Tell students to use *can, can't, could,* and *couldn't* to describe abilities related to the following groups: orphaned elephants, chemical-sniffing dogs, African giant rats, sea turtles, and animals that need to cross motorways.

- Say *Imagine you're telling a friend something about these animal groups, either about their abilities or the abilities of people who help them. Use can, can't, could or couldn't.* Give some examples: *Baby sea turtles can't find their way in bright lights. People couldn't let the orphaned elephants die.* Ask students to stand up one at a time to say their sentences.

- Hand out **Worksheet 1.4.5** for further practice with modals describing ability in the present and past.

Consolidate

- Write these topics on pieces of card, one on each card: *baboons, big cats, rhinos, sea turtles* and *baby elephants.* Put students into small groups and give each group one card. Say *This is your animal. Think about it.* Tell the 'big cats' groups that they can think about big cats in general or about specific big cats – lions, tigers, or leopards. As students talk, write the following vocabulary items on the board: *frighten, hunt, rescue, interact, mistreat, learn, defend* and *avoid.*

- Then say *Work together to write as many sentences about your animal as you can, using the verbs from the board and can, can't, could or couldn't.*

Grammar in Depth

Can't is a contraction of *cannot.* You do occasionally come across *cannot,* but *can't* is more common, especially in conversation. *Cannot* tends to be used in more formal situations or in writing.

An alternative to *can/could* that is used in certain situations is *to be able to* as in *The baby turtle wasn't able to find the water in the bright lights.*

Pronunciation

Go to Student's Book page 145. Use Audio Tracks 124–126.

Can and ***can't*** The modal *can* has a strong, stressed form (/kæn/) and a weak, unstressed form (/kən/). Generally, the strong form is only pronounced at the end of short answers (*Yes, I* ***can.***) and in negatives (*I* ***can't*** *do that.*)

This stressed vowel sound in *can't* (/aː/) is important because English speakers do not usually release the /t/, which makes it difficult to hear. The vowel sound is what distinguishes *can* from *can't.*

Formative Assessment

Can students
- identify modals that describe ability in the present and the past?

  Ask students to name the two modals they learnt that describe ability in the present.

  Ask students to name the two modals they learnt that describe ability in the past.

- use modals to describe ability in the present and the past?

  Ask students to use a modal to describe an ability they have now or didn't have in the past.

Workbook For additional practice, assign Workbook pages 40–41.

Online Workbook Grammar 2

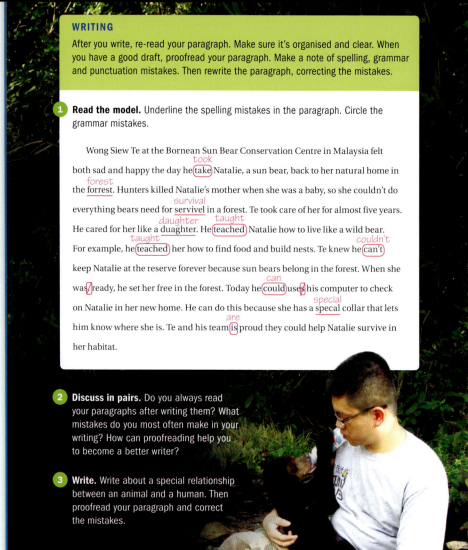

WRITING

Objectives

Students will
- proofread a paragraph describing a relationship.
- produce and proofread a paragraph of descriptive writing.

Writing Description of a relationship between an animal and a human

Academic Language *proofread*

Content Vocabulary *collar, relationship*

Resources Online Workbook/Workbook page 42; Process Writing Worksheets 1–5, Genre Writing Worksheet: Description (Teacher's Resource CD-ROM/Website); CPT: Writing

---

WRITING

After you write, re-read your paragraph. Make sure it's organised and clear. When you have a good draft, proofread your paragraph. Make a note of spelling, grammar and punctuation mistakes. Then rewrite the paragraph, correcting the mistakes.

1 Read the model. Underline the spelling mistakes in the paragraph. Circle the grammar mistakes.

Wong Siew Te at the Bornean Sun Bear Conservation Centre in Malaysia felt both sad and happy the day he ~~take~~ *(took)* Natalie, a sun bear, back to her natural home in the ~~forrest~~ *forest*. Hunters killed Natalie's mother when she was a baby, so she couldn't do everything bears need for ~~servivel~~ *survival* in a forest. Te took care of her for almost five years. He cared for her like a ~~duaghter~~ *daughter*. He ~~teached~~ *taught* Natalie how to live like a wild bear. For example, he ~~teached~~ *taught* her how to find food and build nests. Te knew he ~~can't~~ *couldn't* keep Natalie at the reserve forever because sun bears belong in the forest. When she was ready, he set her free in the forest. Today he could ~~uses~~ *can* his computer to check on Natalie in her new home. He can do this because she has a ~~specal~~ *special* collar that lets him know where she is. Te and his team is *are* proud they could help Natalie survive in her habitat.

2 Discuss in pairs. Do you always read your paragraphs after writing them? What mistakes do you most often make in your writing? How can proofreading help you to become a better writer?

3 Write. Write about a special relationship between an animal and a human. Then proofread your paragraph and correct the mistakes.

Warm Up

- **Activate prior knowledge** Say *You've written paragraphs describing a place, a routine and an event.* Ask *What are some things to remember about writing a description?* Take students' responses. Remind them, if necessary, about using words that appeal to the senses and describing events in an order that makes sense.

- Say *In addition to using words that describe how something looks, sounds, smells, and so on, there are words you can use to describe how someone feels about something.* Explain that when you describe feelings, you're describing emotions. Write *emotions* on the board. Ask *Can you name some emotions that people feel?* Invite students' responses. Ask students to help you create a table, such as the following, on the board:

Emotions (Words That Describe Emotions)	
happiness (happy, glad)	anger (angry, furious)
sadness (sad, unhappy)	fear (afraid, scared, fearful)

Present

- Say *You're going to read about a relationship, or close friendship, between a young man and an animal. But first, we'll talk a little about part of the writing process. Open your books at page 71.* Read aloud the text in the green box. Ask *What is proofreading?* Make sure students understand that proofreading means checking your writing for mistakes in spelling and grammar. Remind them that *grammar* refers to verb forms, singular and plural nouns, and whether a sentence sounds right to your ear.

- Say *Let's practise proofreading.* Put students into pairs and ask them to copy the following sentences. Say *Work with your partner to circle any mistakes in spelling and grammar that you find.*

> My brother and I took bred to the park for the ducks.
> We are sad when we saw a sign that said, 'Don't feed the bird!'

- Ask students to come up to the board and circle the three mistakes. (*bred, are, bird*) Then invite other students to come up and write the correct words on the board. (*bread, were, birds*) Remind the class that *bred* is a spelling mistake. Then explain that *are* is a grammar mistake because the sentences talk about past events, and *are* is a present verb form. Ask *Why is bird a mistake?* (There is more than one bird at the park. You need to add *-s*.)

Read the Model

- Say *Now we're going to read a model paragraph about a relationship. Look at the photo.* Ask *Who is the relationship between?* (a man and a bear) Say *As you read, notice the words the writer uses to describe how he feels. Draw a box around them.* Say *We'll talk about these words before you begin your own writing.*

- Read the activity instructions aloud. Say *Pay attention to the verbs and the modals. Remember which verb forms and modals are used to talk about the past and which ones are used to talk about the present.*

- When students have finished, ask individual students to stand up and identify the mistakes they found. Write each mistake on the board and then invite other students to say why each word is a mistake and how to correct it.

- Put students into pairs to discuss the Activity 2 questions. When pairs have finished talking, ask students to identify the kinds of mistakes they make a lot. List them on the board. Ask the more proficient students to come to the front of the class and share any advice they have on how to avoid certain errors. Finally, say *If you think a word is misspelt but you're not sure how to spell it correctly, you can always look it up in the dictionary. You can also ask the teacher or a classmate for help.*

- **Worksheet** If your students need a reminder of the specifics of proofreading, you may want to hand out **Process Writing Worksheet 4 (Editing and Proofreading)** and review it together.

Writing Support

Proofreading Proofreading means looking for grammar, punctuation and spelling mistakes in your writing. These could be verb tense mistakes, subject–verb agreement errors, sentence fragments, run-on sentences, incorrect singular or plural words and many other types of errors.

Warn students that they shouldn't rely on their computer software to point out or correct errors in their writing. Learning to proofread their own and others' writing and becoming adept at identifying common grammar, spelling, and punctuation errors will help students become better writers. Explain to students that it's usual for a piece of writing to undergo several rounds of proofreading before it is considered good or complete.

Teaching Tip

Students are now halfway through the book. Ask them to review the contents of their portfolios in order to evaluate their writing progress over time.

Workbook For scaffolded Writing support, assign Workbook page 42.
Online Workbook Writing

WRITING

After you write, re-read your paragraph. Make sure it's organised and clear. When you have a good draft, proofread your paragraph. Make a note of spelling, grammar and punctuation mistakes. Then rewrite the paragraph, correcting the mistakes.

1 **Read the model.** Underline the spelling mistakes in the paragraph. Circle the grammar mistakes.

Wong Siew Te at the Bornean Sun Bear Conservation Centre in Malaysia felt both sad and happy the day he *took* take Natalie, a sun bear, back to her natural home in the *forest* forrest. Hunters killed Natalie's mother when she was a baby, so she couldn't do everything bears need for *survival* servivel in a forest. Te took care of her for almost five years. He cared for her like a *daughter* daughter. He *taught* teached Natalie how to live like a wild bear. For example, he *taught* teached her how to find food and build nests. Te knew he *couldn't* can't keep Natalie at the reserve forever because sun bears belong in the forest. When she was ready, he set her free in the forest. Today he *can* could use his computer to check on Natalie in her new home. He can do this because she has a *special* specal collar that lets him know where she is. Te and his team *are* is proud they could help Natalie survive in her habitat.

2 **Discuss in pairs.** Do you always read your paragraphs after writing them? What mistakes do you most often make in your writing? How can proofreading help you to become a better writer?

3 **Write.** Write about a special relationship between an animal and a human. Then proofread your paragraph and correct the mistakes.

WRITING 71

Plan 3

- **3** Say *It's time to plan your own writing. Read the Activity 3 instructions. Your topic is to write about a special relationship between a person and an animal. It can be a relationship you or someone you know has had, or a relationship you've read or heard about.*

- Say *Your next step is pre-writing. What are some of the things we do when we pre-write?* (brainstorm, freewrite, make lists, use a graphic organiser, use sentence starters) If you have time in class, allow students to work on this step. If not, assign it as homework. If students have Workbooks, remind them to use Workbook page 42 for writing support.

- **Worksheets** If your students need a reminder of any of the steps of process writing, you may want to hand out **Process Writing Worksheets 1–5** and review them together.

- **Workbook** Refer students to Workbook page 42 to help them organise and plan their writing.

Write

- After students have finished their pre-writing, ask them to work on their first drafts. If you don't have enough time in class, assign the first draft as homework.

Revise

- After students have finished their first drafts, tell them to check their writing and think about their ideas and organisation. Tell each student to consider the following: *Have I included a topic sentence? Is the order of events clear? Have I included enough details to describe the relationship?* If time permits, they could read their drafts to a classmate for feedback.

Edit and Proofread

- Ask students to consider elements of style, such as sentence variety and word choice. Then tell them to proofread for mistakes in grammar, punctuation, capitalisation and spelling. After they have found and corrected their mistakes, tell them to neatly rewrite the paragraph, making sure to correct the mistakes.

Publish

- Publishing includes handing in pieces of writing to the teacher, sharing work with classmates, adding pieces to a class book, displaying pieces on a classroom wall or in a hallway, and posting on the Internet.

Writing Assessment

Use these guidelines to assess students' writing. You can add other aspects of their writing you'd like to assess at the bottom of the table.

4 = Excellent
3 = Good
2 = Needs improvement
1 = Re-do

	1	2	3	4
Writing Student organises the descriptive paragraph in a way that makes sense. Student uses enough details and words that describe feelings to make the nature of the relationship clear.				
Grammar Student uses modals of obligation/advice and ability correctly.				
Vocabulary Student uses a variety of word choices, including words taught in this unit.				

NATIONAL GEOGRAPHIC

Start Small

'If everyone did something small, it would be huge.'

Amy Dickman
National Geographic Explorer, Animal Conservationist

1. **Watch scene 4.2.**

2. What do you think is the most important thing Amy is doing to help big cats? How does Amy's work help both humans and wildlife?

3. What are some simple things you could do to help protect wildlife? How could it help both humans and animals?

Objective
Students will
- discuss what people can do to protect wildlife.

Resources Video scene 4.2 (DVD/Website/CPT); Worksheet 1.4.6 (Teacher's Resource CD-ROM/Website); Online Workbook: Meet the Explorer; CPT: Mission

BE THE EXPERT

Teaching Tip
Encourage students to be active listeners when they work in pairs or groups. As classmates discuss, encourage them to make notes on what their classmates say, to ask for clarification, or to repeat something that was said. Circulate during pair discussions and occasionally stop and ask students to repeat what their partner has just said.

Online Workbook Meet the Explorer

Mission

- Say *Turn to page 72.* Read aloud the Mission and the quote from Amy Dickman. Ask *How could one person doing one small thing create a huge effect?* Discuss the idea that if enough individuals do something, all of their actions together can have a big impact.

- **Activity 1** Say *Now let's watch a video about Amy Dickman.* Tell students to pay attention to what Amy says about the number of lions left in the wild. Play **Video scene 4.2**.

- **Activity 2** Put students into pairs. Tell them to read the activity questions. Tell them to discuss one question at a time. Ask students to re-read the paragraph about Amy's work on page 62 and replay the video if necessary. After pairs have discussed Amy's work with big cats, tell them to consider this question: *Why does Amy want to protect big cats?*

- **Activity 3** Say *Not everyone can go to Tanzania and work with lions. What can you do here and now? Think about this: How can people help if they don't know there's a problem?* Tell pairs to write one or two sentences about what they can do to protect all wildlife. Say *Try to use must, have to, should, can, or could in your sentences.*

- **Worksheet** Hand out **Worksheet 1.4.6.** Explain that students will use the worksheet to think and write about Amy Dickman and her work with big cats, and about how doing something small can have a big impact.

MISSION **141**

Objective

Students will
- choose and complete a project related to human–wildlife interaction.

Content Vocabulary *brochure, journalist, raise awareness*

Resources Assessment: Unit 4 Quiz and Units 1–4 Mastery Test; Workbook pages 43 and 93; Worksheet 1.4.7 (Teacher's Resource CD-ROM/ Website); CPT: Make an Impact and Review Games

Materials art materials, smart phone or video camera

Assessment Go to pages 257–258.

Unit Review Assign Worksheet 1.4.7
Workbook Assign pages 43 and 93.
Online Workbook Now I can

Make an Impact

YOU DECIDE Choose a project.

1 **Raise awareness for an endangered animal.**
- Research an unusual wild animal that is endangered.
- Make posters or brochures with information about that animal.
- Share the information with your classmates.

2 **Teach others about a human-wildlife conflict.**
- Research a human-wildlife conflict where you live.
- Find out what's being done to solve this issue.
- Make a presentation to your class.

3 **Create a video interview.**
- Role-play an interview between a wild-animal expert and a journalist.
- Talk about the wild animal and the problems it faces.
- Film your interview and share it with the class.

Orphaned koalas with a carer in Queensland, Australia

PROJECT **73**

Prepare

- **YOU DECIDE** Ask students to choose a project.

- **Activity 1** Make sure students know that when you *raise awareness* about something, you inform people about it. Say *We've read about some lesser-known wild animals in this unit. I wonder how many unfamiliar or unusual wild animals are endangered. Amy Dickman reminds us that people tend to conserve what they love and that it's important to let the world know that these animals are in trouble. Your poster or brochure can help educate people about these animals!*

- **Activity 2** If students are not already aware of a problem with wild animals in their area (for example, foxes, monkeys, or an invasive fish or bird), tell them to contact a local nature organisation or newspaper for information.

- **Activity 3** Say *We've learnt a lot about the problems affecting certain wild animals – and you've done a lot of thinking and talking about what can be done about them. Work with a partner to write interview questions.*

Share

- Schedule time for students to present their posters, brochures, research or films. Allow time for the student audience to ask questions and give feedback. Tell students that if they talk to an animal expert in the course of their research, they should feel free to invite the person to come and talk to the class.

- **Modify** Help students simplify a project by eliminating one of the options or steps. For example, you could provide students who choose option 1 with a list of unusual endangered animals to choose from or, for those who do option 2, the names of persons or organisations they can contact.

Track 045 **1** **Listen and read.** See Student's Book pages 60–61.

Track 046 **2** **LEARN NEW WORDS** **access** / Wild animals must have access to food. **afraid of** / Many farmers are afraid of lions harming their animals. **behaviour** / Human actions can affect animal behaviour. **clever** / Baboons are clever animals that know how to get food. **conflict** / Baboons cause conflict when they enter people's homes. **disappear** / If we don't protect animals, they could disappear. **frighten** / Loud noises frighten baboons. **habitat** / Loss of habitat means a loss of food for baboons. **interact** / When you interact with a wild animal, you must be careful. **learn** / People and animals must learn to live together. **need** / Animals and people need food and water. **wild** / Baboons are one type of wild animal. **wildlife** / It's important to protect the wildlife found in nature.

Track 047 **5** Wild snow leopards in Central Asia face two big problems. The first is the loss of their habitat. This causes them to lose their natural food so they hunt animals on farms for food. Local people don't want these leopards to harm the farm animals that they depend on for survival. So, snow leopards need to find a different food source.

The second problem facing the snow leopards is that people use their fur to make things such as handbags and shoes. So hunters look for and catch them. They often mistreat them when they catch them.

The World Wildlife Fund is working to find solutions to these problems. The organisation hopes that education will bring a better relationship between people and leopards.

Track 048 **5** **LEARN NEW WORDS** **hunt** / Wild animals like leopards hunt for their food. **mistreat** / Hunters sometimes mistreat wildlife. **relationship** / People and animals that live together need to have a good relationship. **survival** / The survival of leopards depends on saving their habitat.

Track 049 **SPEAKING STRATEGY** See Student's Book page 63.

Track 050 **1** **S1**: Look at this! Some farmers in Africa are planting chilli peppers around their fields to keep elephants out. **S2**: Really? Why do they want to keep elephants out? **S1**: Since elephants can eat about seventy per cent of their crops, farmers need to protect them. **S2**: Seventy per cent? Wow? But they use chilli peppers. Why is that? **S1**: Because it causes a burning feeling on their skin. And listen to this: it's usually just the male elephants that go onto the farms. **S2**: Really? Do you know why? **S1**: Yes, it's because female elephants stay away from places where humans live. **S2**: Female elephants are cleverer, I guess!

Track 051 **GRAMMAR** See Student's Book page 64.

Track 052 **1** Rhinos are in danger. In 1900, over 500,000 rhinos lived in their natural habitat in Asia and Africa. Now there are fewer than 30,000. Rhinos today are killed mostly for their horns. One organisation, Save the Rhino, is trying to protect rhinos. This is what they do, and what they say we need to do, to stop the killing of rhinos:
1. Catch the hunters. Rangers have to go into the rhino areas and catch the hunters. Rangers must have excellent equipment to catch the hunters.
2. Check rhino numbers. Rhino monitors must often check the numbers of living rhinos. Rhino monitors should know when rhino babies are born.

3. Stop using rhino horn in medicine. We shouldn't use rhino horn in medicine. We should try to find other things to use instead.
4. Protect rhinos in sanctuaries. We have to keep some rhinos in protected places to have their babies safely. We must not allow hunters into the sanctuaries.
5. Teach people about rhinos. We don't have to save rhinos ourselves. We must help people understand why it's important to save rhinos.

Track 053 **GRAMMAR** See **Track 052**.

Track 054 **4** Sea turtles have existed for more than 100 million years, but today they are endangered for several reasons. Sea turtle eggs are prey for seagulls and other animals, but humans are their biggest predator. People collect the eggs to sell them. Humans also eat turtle meat and sell their shells. We should help people find other ways to make money.

Sea turtles also die when they get caught in fishing nets, or when they eat plastic bags thrown in the sea. Fishermen should help turtles that get caught in their nets. We should keep the seas clean.

People are building more houses by the sea, so sea turtle nesting areas are disappearing. We should ask governments to provide protected areas where turtles can lay their eggs. We shouldn't continue to take away sea turtles' habitats.

Sea turtles cannot defend themselves. We must ask governments to make sea turtle protection laws. We must also rescue injured sea turtles. The Turtle Hospital in Florida is one organisation that does this. When the turtles are healthy again, they put them back in the sea. Sea turtles have to survive. We must all do our part to help them.

Track 055 **4** **LEARN NEW WORDS** **defend** / Sea turtles can't defend themselves against fishing nets. **injured** / When sea turtles are injured, they need people to help them. **predator** / An animal that eats other animals is a predator. **prey** / Turtle eggs are prey for birds that eat them. **rescue** / Rangers rescue animals that are hurt in the wild.

Track 056 **2** **LEARN NEW WORDS** **avoid** / We should avoid interacting with wildlife. **chemical** / Chemicals can harm the natural habitat of wildlife. **domestic** / Domestic animals need humans to give them food and water. **feeling** / People have warm feelings when they think of their pets. **sniff** / Some working dogs sniff to find dangerous things.

Track 057 **3** **WHILE YOU READ** See Student's Book pages 66–67.

Track 058 **GRAMMAR** See Student's Book page 70.

Track 059 **1** **Express Yourself** See Student's Book pages 74–75.

Objectives

Students will
- identify the purpose and features of a visual narrative.
- connect ideas about life in the dark and human–animal interactions.

Content Vocabulary *cartoon, comic strip, hardly, oral, paw prints, props, visual*

Resources Workbook pages 44–45/ Online Workbook (Units 3–4 Review); Worksheet 1.4.8 (Teacher's Resource CD-ROM/Website); Track 059 (Audio CD/Website/CPT); CPT: Express Yourself Units 3–4

Present ①

- **Preview** Tell students to turn to pages 74–75. Tell students they're going to read a graphic story – a series of drawings that tells a story and looks like a cartoon or a comic strip. Say *This story doesn't rely on speech bubbles to tell the whole story. The important thing is that the images and the words work together to tell a story that's interesting and fun to read.*

- Invite students to read the title of the story and look at the pictures. Point out that the style of the drawings is to look unfinished and to give the basic idea of the events without a lot of visual detail. Explain to students that the story is based on a real event in Amy Dickman's life. Ask *Who's the woman in the story supposed to be?* (Amy Dickman) *What animal is involved in the story?* (a lion)

- ① **Read together** Say *We're going to listen to and read the story.* Explain to students that, as with any piece of writing, they should read from left to right, and look at all of the pictures on page 74 before moving on to page 75. Point out the drawing of Amy in the third picture on page 74. Tell students that the object in Amy's right hand is a can of liquid that can be sprayed. Say *As you follow the story, look for the ways the artist lets you know that a sound is being made.* Play **Track 059** once as students listen and read. When the story is over, ask *How does the story let you know that Amy wasn't dreaming?*

Practise ②

- ② **Discuss** Put the students into small groups to discuss the story. Read aloud the Activity 2 questions. Say *Remember, the story may look like a cartoon or comic, but the events described really happened!*

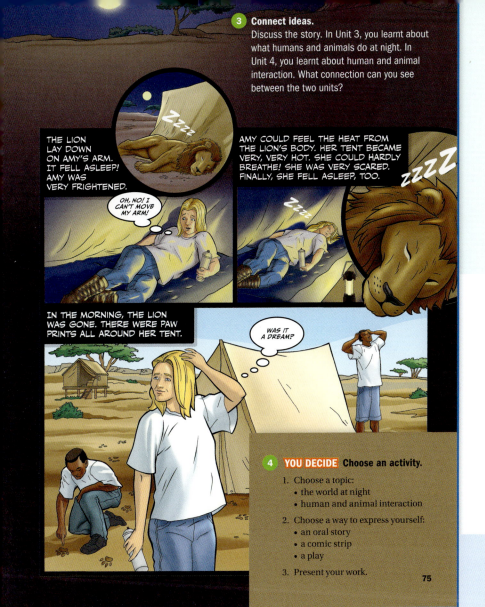

3 Connect ideas.
Discuss the story. In Unit 3, you learnt about what humans and animals do at night. In Unit 4, you learnt about human and animal interaction. What connection can you see between the two units?

THE LION LAY DOWN ON AMY'S ARM. IT FELL ASLEEP! AMY WAS VERY FRIGHTENED.

OH, NO! I CAN'T MOVE MY ARM!

AMY COULD FEEL THE HEAT FROM THE LION'S BODY. HER TENT BECAME VERY, VERY HOT. SHE COULD HARDLY BREATHE! SHE WAS VERY SCARED. FINALLY, SHE FELL ASLEEP, TOO.

IN THE MORNING, THE LION WAS GONE. THERE WERE PAW PRINTS ALL AROUND HER TENT.

WAS IT A DREAM?

4 YOU DECIDE Choose an activity.
1. Choose a topic:
   • the world at night
   • human and animal interaction
2. Choose a way to express yourself:
   • an oral story
   • a comic strip
   • a play
3. Present your work.

75

Genre in Depth

Visual narratives include comic books, graphic novels, graphic stories, and various other genres that tell a story visually. A good visual narrative combines words and images into a seamless story, in which the images are an essential part of the story.

Cumulative Review

Hand out Cumulative Review Worksheet 1.4.8.

Formative Assessment

Can students

• identify the purpose and features of a visual narrative?

Ask students to describe the purpose and main features of 'Sleeping with a Lion'. (It tells a good story based on a real event, using words and drawings.)

• connect ideas about life in the dark and human–animal interactions?

Ask *What do humans need to know when they're in a wild animal's habitat at night?* (Being in the wild at night can be very dangerous; Many animals are better adapted to life at night than humans.)

Workbook Assign pages 44–45.
Online Workbook Units 3–4 Review

Give prompts to help students with their discussions. Ask *What situation put Amy in danger in the first place? Do you think she could have defended herself with a small knife and a can of spray? What should people be aware of when they go into a wild animal habitat?*

Connect 3

• **3 Critical Thinking** Put the students into new groups. Read the Activity 3 text aloud. Give prompts as necessary: *What do most humans do at night? Do you remember what* nocturnal *means? What do nocturnal animals do at night? Who do you think is more comfortable at night in the dark: people or animals?*

Prepare 4

• **YOU DECIDE** Review the activity options. Allow students to choose their own topic. You may want to assign this activity in advance so that students have more time to work on it in class or at home.

• 4 Explain to students that *oral story* means a story you tell from memory or with just a few notes. Say *It will be like telling a story around a campfire. Imagine you're a favourite relative – someone who tells great stories that everyone loves listening to.* Tell those who choose a comic strip to use 'Sleeping with a Lion' as a model. Remind them that they'll need to include drawings. Say *If you decide to write a play to tell a story, you'll need to think about a setting and characters. Who will the actors be and what props will you need?*

Share

• Set aside time for sharing students' work with the class. Remind students to listen politely to the oral stories and plays, and to wait until the story or play is over before asking any questions.

In This Unit

Theme This unit is about clothing, accessories and body decoration.

Content Objectives
Students will
- examine how clothing styles change over time.
- read about the significance of jewellery in certain cultures.
- discuss a geoscientist and his work.

Language Objectives
Students will
- compare modern clothes with the clothes people wore in the past.
- ask for opinions and agree or disagree.
- use the past simple of regular verbs to describe the past.
- use the past simple of irregular verbs to describe the past.
- write a description of a uniform that has changed over time.

Vocabulary
Vocabulary Strategies Base words and the prefix *re-*; Using a dictionary

Speaking Strategy Asking for opinions; agreeing and disagreeing

Grammar
Grammar 1 Use the past simple of regular verbs to say what happened
Grammar 2 Use the past simple of irregular verbs to say what happened

Reading *Jewellery Talks*
Reading Strategy Compare and contrast

Video Scene 5.1: *What to Wear?*; Scene 5.2: Meet Andrés Ruzo

Writing Description of a uniform

National Geographic Mission Learn to Adapt

Project
- Clothing design
- Scavenger hunt
- Presentation

Pronunciation Pronunciation of *-ed* ending

Unit 5

What We Wear

'The right clothes can make life a lot easier and, in some cases, even save your life.'
Andrés Ruzo

76

Introduce the Unit

- **Activate prior knowledge** Say *In Unit 2, we talked about jobs, including some that combine adventure and danger. Think about an astronaut, an underwater archaeologist and a firefighter. What do they have in common?* If necessary, prompt students to see that they all wear special clothing to be safe while they work.

- **TO START** Ask students to open their books at pages 76–77. Invite a student to read the unit title. Ask *Where do you think this picture was taken?* Read the caption aloud. Tell students that Turkmenistan is a country in Asia, and the crater – or large hole – is in a natural gas field, a place where there's a lot of natural gas under the ground.

- Ask questions to encourage further discussion of the photo:
  What does protective mean?
  Why do you think the man wants to explore the crater?
  Would you like to visit this place? Why or why not?

- Ask a student to read aloud the quote on page 76. Then read Question 1 to the class. Ask students to describe the man's clothes

A man in a protective suit, ready to explore the Darvaza Crater, Turkmenistan

TO START

1. Describe the clothes you see in the photo. Do you think these clothes are important at this place? Why or why not?

2. What do you wear to school? On special days? On weekends?

3. What did you buy the last time you went shopping for clothing and accessories? Why did you buy these things?

77

Objectives

Students will

- describe and discuss a photo.
- discuss reasons for wearing different kinds of clothing, the clothes they buy and why they buy them.

Content Vocabulary *crater, fireproof, harness, natural gas field, protective*

Resources Worksheet 1.5.1 (Teacher's Resource CD-ROM/Website); CPT: Unit Opener

BE THE EXPERT

About the Photo

Turkmenistan is in Central Asia, bordered on one side by the Caspian Sea. The Darvaza Crater, called the Door to Hell, is located in the desert in the northern part of the country. The photo shows George Kourounis, a Canadian explorer, at the rim of the crater, which was created over 40 years ago as a result, most people believe, of a drilling accident.

The crater was set on fire to burn off the poisonous gases coming from it, assuming they would eventually burn off, but to this day the crater continues to burn. In 2013, Kourounis descended into the crater, wearing a heat-resistant suit and harness, to look for signs of life. Despite the very high temperatures, bacteria were found living in soil samples collected from the bottom of the crater.

Teaching Tip

Begin each class with a familiar phrase in English. As a class, choose or write a short poem, song lyric or phrase in English. At the start of each lesson, tell students to repeat it aloud. This provides a transition point, signalling to students that it is time to start speaking, thinking and writing in English.

---

and say what the suit is protecting him from. Ask *How do you think his clothes will protect him?*

- Say *The man's suit and equipment are made of fireproof material.* Ask *Do you ever have to wear protective clothing?* If necessary, remind students that they may wear protective clothing in certain kinds of weather, or for certain sports or activities.

- Read aloud Question 2. Ask *Why do people wear different kinds of clothes?* Read aloud Question 3. Begin a T-chart on the board. Record in one column items students have bought recently, and write their reasons for buying them in the other column. Ask *Are the reasons you've given all good reasons for buying clothing?*

Extend

- Tell students to copy the chart and complete it with their own information. Then put students into pairs and ask them to compare information.

- Hand out **Worksheet 1.5.1**. Explain that student pairs will be thinking and writing about clothing.

VOCABULARY

Objective

Students will
- use new vocabulary to read about and discuss different types and styles of clothing.

Target Vocabulary *casual, century, dress up, fashion, formal, heel, jeans, look, practical, suit, sweatshirt, tie, uniform, wear*

Content Vocabulary *fashionable, tear*

Resources Worksheet 1.5.2 (Teacher's Resource CD-ROM/Website); Tracks 060–061 (Audio CD/Website/CPT); CPT: Vocabulary

1 **What clothes do you like to wear?**
Discuss. Then listen and read. 060

At some point, you've probably looked at old photos of people and asked yourself, 'Why did they **wear** *that*? What were they *thinking*?' The people in the photo probably thought that they **looked** great! The truth is, nothing stays the same forever, especially in the world of **fashion**. What's cool today will be ugly before long. What we like to wear changes all the time.

A **century** ago, many men – from businessmen to taxi drivers – wore **suits** to work. Even young boys regularly wore suits and **ties**. Women didn't just wear skirts or dresses when they wanted to **dress up**. They wore them all the time – even if they were just staying at home!

Over time, **casual** clothes replaced **formal** clothes. For example, **jeans** are very popular today. They were first made for workers who needed trousers with strong fabric that didn't **tear** easily. In 1873, tailor Jacob Davis and businessman Levi Strauss created denim trousers they called *overalls* because people wore them over their clothes. Cowboys wore denim jeans and, thanks to the Western films of the 1930s, many people began wearing them. Today, jeans and a **sweatshirt** are practically a **uniform** for teens around the world.

Cowboys helped make jeans popular.

78 VOCABULARY

Warm Up

- **Activate prior knowledge** Say *The man who explored the Darvaza Crater was dressed for an extremely dangerous and unusual activity. But the work people do, even ordinary work, influences the clothes they wear. I'm going to name a job, and I want you to say an item of clothing it makes you think of.* Then say and write words and students' responses, such as the following, on the board: construction worker (hard hat), office worker (suit, tie, dress, skirt), gardener (jeans, old clothes), basketball player (kit).

- After students have brainstormed a list of word associations, ask them to use the words on the board to say sentences. Model an example. Point to (*tie*) and say *Some office workers wear ties to work.*

Present

- Ask students to open their books at pages 78–79. Invite a student to read aloud the Activity 1 question at the top of page 78. Discuss with students the things they like to wear on ordinary days. Write examples on the board. Then point to items and ask the students who named them *Why do you like to wear (shorts/lots of bracelets/a T-shirt)?*

- Say *Let's hear about some people's clothing over the years and the reasons they wore it.* Play **Track 060** and tell students to listen and read. Then discuss the photo and the reading with students. Ask questions such as:

  Do you wear jeans because they don't tear easily?
  Do you think ordinary men in the 18th century wore high-heeled shoes and wigs? Why not?
  What's the most interesting thing you learnt from this reading?

Louis XIV of France

Like clothes, shoes have also changed over time. You may prefer to wear trainers, but in the past both men and women wore shoes with high **heels**. In the early 18th century, King Louis XIV of France started wearing tights with red high-heeled shoes. This was the fashion for nearly a century before men began wearing more **practical** shoes without heels.

Things change. You might think your clothes are fashionable now, but if a hundred years from now people see a photo of you, they might just ask, 'Why did they wear *that*?'

2 **LEARN NEW WORDS** Listen and repeat. ⌂ **061**

3 **Work in pairs.** Think about photos that you've seen of people from long ago. Compare their clothes with what you wear now.

VOCABULARY **79**

About the Photo

The young man in the photo is dressed like a typical cowboy of the American West in the second half of the 19th century. The American cowboy was a ranch worker as well as a figure in American folklore. Skilled riders and ropers, cowboys employed tools and techniques perfected by Spanish vaqueros in Mexico and the south-western United States. They used their ropes, also called lassos or lariats, to catch horses and cattle for branding and herded them from open rangeland to a railway town for shipment to market.

As the agricultural frontier moved west, much of the open range was fenced in, and by 1890 the legendary era of the cowboy was over. Cowboys lived on, though, in fiction and films as the brave, silent and self-reliant loners of the American frontier.

Related Vocabulary

barn, belt buckle, lasso, portrait, saddle, spurs, wig

- **2** **LEARN NEW WORDS** Play **Track 061**. Ask students to listen and repeat. Then put students into pairs to practise the new vocabulary. Tell pairs to take turns to choose words and to ask and answer questions about them. Say *Pick a new vocabulary item and ask your partner a question with the word in it.* Model with a student. Say *What kind of men's fashion was popular in the 18th century?* If necessary, prompt the student to answer *high-heeled shoes.* Say *Then it would be your partner's turn to pick a word and ask you a question with the word in it.*

Practise

- **3** Tell students to look again at the picture of King Louis XIV of France on page 79. Say *King Louis lived 300 years ago, but it's hard to believe men ever*

dressed like that; it's so different from today's fashions. Explain that even though fashions change over the years, you can still find similarities in the clothing people wore years ago and now.

- Put students into pairs and invite one to read Activity 3 on page 79. Ask *Has anyone ever seen a photo of their grandparents or older relatives when they were young?* Say *Close your eyes. Try to picture the photo.* Then ask a few students to come to the front of the class and describe their photo – what the people were wearing and how they looked. Ask pairs to do Activity 3. Say *Think about the clothes. Think about how the people looked. Did they look happy or serious? Formal or casual? Write down what you remember.* When pairs have finished, ask them to share some similarities and differences they noted.

Objectives

Students will

- use new vocabulary to discuss reasons for wearing clothes.
- use a vocabulary strategy to learn new vocabulary.

Target Vocabulary *denim, fabric, replace, tights*

Vocabulary Strategy Base words and the prefix *re-*

Content Vocabulary *geothermal, percentage, poll, sandals*

Resources Online Workbook/Workbook pages 46–47; Worksheet 1.5.2 (Teacher's Resource CD-ROM/Website); Tracks 062–063 (Audio CD/Website/CPT); CPT: Vocabulary

---

4 **Read and write the words from the list.** Make any necessary changes.

dress up	fashion	formal	jeans	look
practical	suit	sweatshirt	uniform	wear

Andrés Ruzo works with geothermal energy, which is produced using heat from the Earth. To do this, Andrés needs to work in very hot places. He _____wears_____ clothing for protection, not _____fashion_____ . He can't always work in _____jeans_____ and a T-shirt. Andrés doesn't wear a _____uniform_____ like a police officer or a pilot does, but he does wear different clothes for different tasks. He needs to wear a special all-in-one _____suit_____ to protect himself in extremely hot, dangerous places. He also wears heavy boots to protect his feet. It might not _____look_____ fashionable, but for Andrés, safety is more important.

Sometimes lighter clothes are safer and more _____practical_____ . On one research trip, Andrés wore shorts and sandals. The water was very hot, and he needed to quickly check the temperature. Sandals were safer than boots because boots can fill with hot water and burn his feet.

Andrés Ruzo testing hot water

5 **LEARN NEW WORDS** Listen to these words. Use them to complete the sentences. Then listen and repeat. 🎧 062 063

denim	fabric	replace	tights

1. Clothes are made of _____fabric_____ .
2. Girls often wear _____tights_____ with a skirt.
3. New fashion can _____replace_____ old fashion.
4. Jeans are made of _____denim_____ .

6 **YOU DECIDE** Choose an activity.

1. **Work independently.** Interview a parent or grandparent. Find out how clothing has changed from when he or she was young. Write a paragraph to say what you learnt.
2. **Work in pairs.** Make a T-chart with the headings *practical* and *not practical*. Then write examples of clothes you wear under each category.
3. **Work in groups.** What percentage of your clothing is chosen for practical reasons? What percentage is for fashion? Take a poll. Compare your results with another group.

80 VOCABULARY

- **4** Ask students to turn to page 80. Point to the photo. Tell students that Andrés Ruzo is a geoscientist. Say *Geoscientists study the Earth and other planets.* Then ask students to read the words in the word box. Tell them to pick a word and use it in a sentence. Then say *Let's read a little about Andrés, what he does, and the clothes he wears when he works.* Read aloud the first two sentences of the Activity 4 text. Make sure students understand the instructions. Then tell them to do the activity independently. When students have finished, ask several to read the completed paragraphs aloud.

- **5** **LEARN NEW WORDS** Read the words in the word box. Tell students to listen for those words as they hear about what people have worn over the centuries to cover their legs. Play **Track 062**. Tell students to complete the activity sentences. Then play **Track 063**. Students should listen and repeat.

- **Vocabulary Strategy** Write *replace* on the board. Circle the prefix *re-*. Remind students that a prefix is a word part that has meaning. Underline the base word *place*. Ask *What does the verb* to place *mean?* ('to put', 'to set in a certain place or position') Explain that the prefix *re-* means 'again' or 'back', as in *re-read* ('to read again') or *recover* ('to get back again').

- Explain that *replace* sometimes means 'to place again', but it has another, more common meaning. Tell students to re-read the third sentence of Activity 5. Ask *Does anyone know what* replace *means in this sentence?* ('to take the place of') Help students think of other words with the prefix *re-*. (*re-do, refill, rethink, rewrite*)

Apply 6

- **6** YOU DECIDE Tell students to look at Activity 6. Explain that the first option is to interview a parent or older relative about how fashion has changed over the person's lifetime and then to write about it. Say *Ask the person what clothing was 'cool' when he or she was young.*

- Point out that the second and third options require students to classify, or sort, their clothes into two categories – practical and not practical. Review the meaning of *practical*. Say *Remember the reasons for the practical clothing Andrés Ruzo wears.*

- **Think aloud** Model thinking about the third option. Say *After I complete my T-chart, I need to add up the number of practical clothes I have got and divide it by the total number of clothes in my chart to get a percentage. I wonder what it will be. I never thought about how many practical clothes I've got. Then I need to poll, or take a survey of, the other members of my group to see what their percentages are.*

Extend

- Tell students to look again at the pictures of the Darvaza Cave explorer, the cowboy, the king, and Andrés Ruzo on pages 77–80. Say *Choose a picture and write a description of the clothing the person in the picture is wearing. Explain why the person is wearing those clothes and whether they are practical or not practical.*

- If time allows, hand out **Worksheet 1.5.2**. Explain that students will use vocabulary items to write about and discuss clothing.

Consolidate

- Write the following clothing words on the board: *baseball cap, denim, dress, high-heeled shoes, jeans, leather shoes, shorts, skirt, trainers, suit, sweatshirt, tie, tights* and *T-shirt*.

- Say *Let's play a game of categories.* Divide the class into two groups. Ask each group to form a line. Tell students that you will say either 'casual' or 'formal' to each student. Say *When it's your turn, depending on the category I give you, pick an item of clothing from the board that fits the category, and use the word in a sentence.* Model for students. Say *My category is 'casual'. My word is denim. My sentence is 'I wear my denim jacket when I go to the mall'.*

Vocabulary Strategy

Base words and the prefix *re-*
The prefix *re-* means 'again' (as in *rebuild*) and 'back' (as in *react*). Students will likely encounter many words with this prefix that include the former meaning, but here are some useful words that relate to the second meaning of 'back':

reject *The small fish was rejected and thrown back into the river.*

repay *I repaid my debt as soon as I was able.*

retrace *If you get lost in the woods, go back and retrace your footsteps.*

revert *While I was away, my new puppy reverted to his untrained state.*

Teaching Tip

Make it a goal to always find time to walk around the class and monitor students and groups as they do activities, have discussions, write or complete projects. Interact with students and give positive reinforcement such as *Well done!* or suggestions such as *Remember to add -ed to words when you write about things that happened in the past.*

Formative Assessment

Can students
- use new vocabulary related to different types and styles of clothing?

  Ask *What might someone wear to a formal event?*

- use new vocabulary to discuss reasons for wearing clothes?

  Ask students to name a practical reason for wearing jeans.

Workbook For additional practice, assign Workbook pages 46–47

Online Workbook Vocabulary

SPEAKING STRATEGY

Objectives
Students will
• ask for opinions.
• agree and disagree.

Speaking Strategy Asking for opinions, agreeing and disagreeing

Content Vocabulary *progress*

Resources Online Workbook; Worksheet 1.5.3 (Teacher's Resource CD-ROM/ Website); Tracks 064–065 (Audio CD/ Website/CPT); CPT: Speaking Strategy

Materials coins for the board game

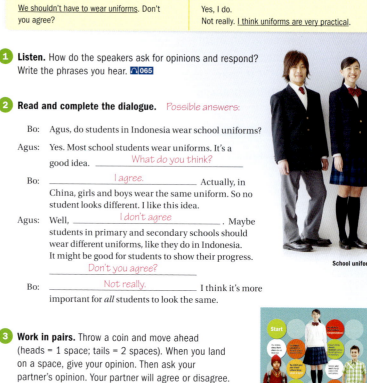

SPEAKING STRATEGY 🎧064

Asking for opinions	Agreeing and disagreeing
I think school uniforms are a good idea. What do you think?	I agree. / I'm not really sure. / I don't agree.
We shouldn't have to wear uniforms. Don't you agree?	Yes, I do. / Not really. I think uniforms are very practical.

1 Listen. How do the speakers ask for opinions and respond? Write the phrases you hear. 🎧065

2 Read and complete the dialogue.   *Possible answers:*

Bo: Agus, do students in Indonesia wear school uniforms?

Agus: Yes. Most school students wear uniforms. It's a good idea. ____*What do you think?*____

Bo: ____*I agree.*____ Actually, in China, girls and boys wear the same uniform. So no student looks different. I like this idea.

Agus: Well, ____*I don't agree*____. Maybe students in primary and secondary schools should wear different uniforms, like they do in Indonesia. It might be good for students to show their progress. ____*Don't you agree?*____

Bo: ____*Not really.*____ I think it's more important for *all* students to look the same.

School uniforms

3 Work in pairs. Throw a coin and move ahead (heads = 1 space; tails = 2 spaces). When you land on a space, give your opinion. Then ask your partner's opinion. Your partner will agree or disagree.

I think our clothes show who we are. What do you think?

I agree.

Go to page 163.

Warm Up

• **Activate prior knowledge** Ask *Can someone tell me what an opinion is?* (what you think or believe about something, how you feel about something)

• Say *We all have opinions about things, and we want people to agree with our opinions, don't we? But do they always?* Ask pairs or small groups to ask one another for their opinions on things such as the latest style in clothing, the best way to protect animal habitats, a new band or hit song, or a book or TV programme. Choose students to come up to the front to act out their dialogues for the class.

Present

• Say *We're going to hear how people talk to one another about their opinions.* Ask students to turn to page 81. Play **Track 064**. Tell students to listen and read. Ask *How do the speakers ask for opinions? What words do they use?* List some of the phrases on the board.

• Point out the different phrases you can use to agree and disagree. Say *If you're not sure what your opinion is, you can respond 'I'm not sure', or if you think you disagree with something but you don't feel strongly about it, you can say 'Not really'.* Then ask students to read aloud the sentences in the strategy box.

• **1** Say *Now listen to a conversation about school uniforms.* Point to the board. Say *Listen for these and other expressions the speakers use to ask about and express their opinions. Write them down.* Play **Track 065**. Ask students to share what they wrote. Replay the track if necessary.

Practise **2**

• **2** Direct students' attention to Activity 2. Say *Here's another conversation about school uniforms. You'll read about different countries' ideas about uniforms and two people's opinions of them.* Ask students to complete the dialogue by asking for an opinion and agreeing or disagreeing.

152 UNIT 5

- You may want to read the dialogue aloud first, without filling in the gaps. Ask students to read their completed dialogues aloud, taking turns as Agus and Bo. Point out that there are several possible ways to fill in the gaps.

Apply

- **3** Put students into pairs and ask them to play the board game on page 163. Give each pair a coin. Invite a student to model throwing a coin and identifying heads or tails. Point out the two possible opinions on some of the game circles. Say *Choose your opinion, express it, and then ask your partner what he or she thinks.* Ask a pair to model the game by reading the speech bubbles aloud. Then say *After your partner agrees or disagrees, it's his or her turn to throw the coin and move along the board. Follow all of the instructions. See who gets to the end first!*

Extend

- Put students into groups of three and tell them to work together to write a short scene from a play in which the three students pictured on the game board are the characters. Explain that in the scene, the three characters should comment on one another's clothing, and ask for opinions on dressing for school. Say *Give each character a name and write words for them to say to one another. Use some of the phrases you learnt. Keep it polite!*

- When groups have finished, ask them to read their scenes aloud. Each student should take the role of one of the characters. Tell them that gender doesn't matter. Girls can read the boys' lines, and boys can read the girls' lines.

- If time allows, hand out **Worksheet 1.5.3**. Explain that students will use the worksheet to practise asking for opinions and agreeing or disagreeing.

Consolidate

- On the board, write several of the opinions from the game board on page 163. Below that, write the following phrases:

What do you think?	I agree.	I don't agree.
Do you agree?	I'm not sure.	Not really.
Don't you agree?	Yes, I do.	No, I don't.

- Tell students to stand in a circle. Explain that you'll begin a conversation by expressing one of the opinions on the board. Say *Then I'll ask a student for his/her opinion. He/She'll say whether he/she agrees or disagrees, and then turn to the next person and ask what he/she thinks. He/She can have the same opinion, or not, but he/she has to use a different phrase to respond.* Explain that any student can also give a reason for his or her opinion, and that when enough has been said about a topic, the next student should choose another topic from the board. Say *Let's see how long we can keep the conversation going!*

Objectives
Students will
- identify the form, meaning and use of the past simple tense.
- use the past simple to say what happened.
- use words associated with body decoration.

Grammar Past simple: Saying what happened

Target Vocabulary *bride, decorate, paint, pierce, tattoo*

Content Vocabulary *henna, herd, knot, prefer, rodeo*

Pronunciation Pronunciation of *-ed* ending

Resources Online Workbook/Workbook pages 48–49; Tracks 066–070, Tracks 127–130 (Audio CD/Website/CPT); Pronunciation Answer Key (Teacher's Resource CD-ROM/Website/CPT); CPT: Grammar 1 and Pronunciation

Materials pieces of card

GRAMMAR 🎧 066

Past simple: Saying what happened

Ancient Greek women **preferred** golden hair to dark hair.

Did Ancient Greek men **like** to wear their hair short? No, they **didn't**.

Ancient Greek women **didn't like** short hair either.

What **did** Ancient Greek women **use** to make their hair shiny? They **used** olive oil.

like ➝ lik**ed**	
prefer ➝ prefer**red**	
brush ➝ brush**ed**	

1 Listen. Circle the correct forms of the verbs you hear. 🎧 067

1. (wanted)   didn't want
2. believed   (didn't believe)
3. (used)   didn't use
4. (attached)   didn't attach
5. (helped)   didn't help
6. (protected)   didn't protect
7. (liked)   didn't like
8. (washed)   didn't wash
9. used   (didn't use)
10. (mixed)   didn't mix
11. (coloured)   didn't colour
12. (loved)   didn't love

An Egyptian woman with long hair

2 Read. Complete the sentences about women's hair in Ancient Greece. Use the correct form of the verbs in brackets.

1. How did women _____like_____ (like) to wear their hair?
   They _____pulled_____ (pull) their hair off their faces and _____tied_____ (tie) it into a knot.

2. How did they _____colour_____ (colour) their hair red?
   They _____combed_____ (comb) a special paint, called *henna*, through their hair.

3. What did they _____use_____ (use) to curl their hair?
   They _____used_____ (use) a metal tool, shaped like a pencil. They _____curled_____ (curl) their hair around it.

4. Did they _____place_____ (place) anything in their hair?
   Yes, they did. They _____placed_____ (place) fresh flowers in their hair.

82 GRAMMAR

Warm Up

- **Build background** Say *When we talk about what happened yesterday, we're talking about the past. The past is everything that happened before right now, which is the present.* Ask *Is what happened this morning the past or the present?* (the past) *Why?* (because it already happened, because it's over) Say *The past covers a lot of time. It includes this morning and it also includes hundreds and millions of years ago!*

- Write the following on the board:

> Over a hundred years ago, cowboys used horses and ropes in their work.
>
> Today, cowboys use horses and ropes in contests called rodeos.

- Read aloud the first sentence on the board. Ask *Is this sentence about the past or the present?* (the past) *How do you know?* (the

3 **LEARN NEW WORDS** Listen to learn about how people decorate their bodies now and how they decorated them long ago. Then listen and repeat. 🎧068 069

People **decorate** their bodies in many ways.

Artists **paint** the hands and feet of Indian **brides** with henna.

In the past, most Maori men covered their faces in **tattoos**. Some still do today.

In some cultures, people **pierce** babies' ears to show that they're girls.

4 **Work in pairs.** Listen again. Answer the questions in complete sentences. 🎧070

1. How did people decorate their bodies long ago?   *Possible answers:*
   They pierced and painted their bodies. They decorated their bodies with tattoos.

2. What did Maori men do to their faces in the past?
   They covered their faces with tattoos.

3. Why did some people paint their bodies instead of getting tattoos?
   They painted their bodies because the paint washed off.

4. What parts of brides' bodies did artists paint with henna?
   They painted their hands and feet.

5. What did people do to their ears 5,000 years ago that they still do today?
   They pierced their ears.

5 **Work in groups.** Think of people you know who have done things to change their hair and bodies. Use the past simple to describe what they did.

GRAMMAR **83**

Grammar in Depth

Below is a review of spelling rules for forming the past simple of regular verbs:

If the verb ends in

- silent *e* → add -d (*traded*)
- a vowel + *y* → add -ed (*played*)
- a consonant + *y* → replace *y* with -ied (*studied*)
- a single vowel and a single consonant (except *x*) → double consonant and add -ed (*begged, jogged*)
- *r* or *l*, has two or more syllables, and the last syllable is stressed → double the *r* or *l* and add -ed (*preferred, controlled*)
- *x* → add -ed, never double *x* (*boxed*)

For all other regular verbs → add -ed

Pronunciation

Go to Student's Book page 146. Use audio Tracks 127–130.

Pronunciation of -*ed* ending The -*ed* ending has three possible pronunciations. It sounds like:

- *ed* (/ɪd/) when the final sound of a word is /t/ or /d/; this adds another syllable to the word.
- *t* (/t/) when the final sound of a word is /f/, /k/, /p/, /s/, /ʃ/ (*sh*), /tʃ/ (*ch*) or /ks/ (*x*).
- *d* (/d/) when the final sound of a word is a vowel or any other consonant.

Students often have difficulty with /t/ or /d/ endings, especially when those endings form a consonant cluster. English speakers may link the endings to a vowel at the beginning of the next word (*believed in* sounds like 'believ-din') If the next word begins with a /t/ or /d/ sound, then the sounds blend and are said only once (*liked to wear* sounds like 'like-to wear').

Students may add a syllable when they see -*ed* after other consonant sounds (e.g. *packed* may be incorrectly pronounced 'pack-ed' (/pæk ɪd/), so it's important for them to know that only /t/ and /d/ allow an extra syllable.

---

words *a hundred years ago*) Read aloud the second sentence. Ask *Is this sentence about the past or the present?* (the present) *How do you know?* (the word *today*) Students may also recognise the present simple verb *use*.

Present

- Point out the difference in the verbs in the sentences on the board. Circle the *d* in *used*. Say *When a verb ends in* d *or* ed, *it's a sign that a sentence is talking about something in the past.* Point to the verb *use*. Remind students that it's a present simple verb and that the present simple is used to talk about a situation that exists now or that happens regularly.

- Add the following two sentences to the board:

> Cowboys used horses and ropes to control large herds of cows.
>
> Cowboys use horses and ropes to show off their skills.

• Read aloud the sentences. Explain to students that even though they don't include words that show time, the verbs in these sentences let you know that the first one talks about the past and the second one talks about the present.

• Ask students to open their books at page 82, and look at the grammar box at the top of the page. Read the title aloud and tell students that past simple verbs are used to say what happened in the past. Say *Follow in your books as we listen to sentences about the Ancient Greeks and their hair.* Play **Track 066**.

• Read aloud the first sentence on the left side of the grammar box. Ask *How does this sentence show that it's talking about the past?* (The word *ancient* refers to the past; the verb ends in *-ed.*) Read the second sentence. Point out that it's a question beginning with *did*. Say *The complete verb in this sentence is* did like. *Like doesn't end in* d, *but* did *is the past form of the verb* do. Tell students that they'll learn more about verbs with special past forms later in the unit.

• Work through the other example sentences with students. Then point to the information on the right side of the grammar box. Tell students that there are certain rules to remember about how to form the past simple. Tell students to point to each line as you go over these three rules for forming the past simple. Say *When a verb ends in e, add -d. When a verb ends in a vowel and a consonant, double the consonant and add -ed. For most other regular verbs, add -ed.*

Practise

• **1** Say *Now we'll hear how Egyptian women from long ago took care of their hair. Pay attention to the verbs. Circle the ones you hear.* Play **Track 067** as students listen. If necessary, play the track a second time.

Ask *Are the verbs past or present forms?* (past) Ask students to explain how they know the verbs are past forms. Review the answers as a class.

• Say *Women today still do some of the things you heard in the audio. Let's make a T-chart of past and present hair care.* Invite students to tell you some of the activities they heard. Ask *What do some of today's women do with their hair that's similar?* Tell students to help you add sentences to the chart. Then ask students to come up to the board and underline the verbs and say whether they're past or present forms.

Past	Present
Women liked long hair.	Some women prefer long hair.
They attached hair or wool to their hair to make it look longer.	They use extra pieces of hair called hair extensions.
They washed their hair with fruit juice.	We wash our hair with shampoo.
They protected their hair with oil.	We wear hats.

• **2** Read the instructions for Activity 2 aloud. Say *Remember, if the verb includes the past form* did, *you use the present simple form for the main part of the verb.* Explain to students that in item 2, the word *henna* refers to a paste made from the leaves of the henna plant. You may want to review the rules for forming past simple regular verbs. Then ask students to do the activity. When they've finished, ask students to read aloud the completed sentences and write the verbs on the board. Review the answers together.

Apply   5

• **3** **LEARN NEW WORDS** Say *Now we'll hear about body decoration through the years.* Ask students to look at the photos on page 83. Ask students to read the captions. Then discuss the photos as a class. Play **Track 068** and ask students to listen. Then play **Track 069**. Tell students to listen and repeat.

- **4** Put students into pairs. Read the activity instructions aloud. Explain to students that they'll listen to the information about body decoration again, then they'll write sentences to answer the activity questions. Say *Work with your partner. Help each other. Remember to use past simple verbs.* Play **Track 070**. Tell students to listen and complete the activity. Invite student pairs to come to the front and take turns to read their sentences.

- **5** Put students into small groups. Read the activity instructions aloud. Say *Take turns discussing the topic. Ask one another questions. Use the past simple.* If students need help getting started, provide discussion prompts, such as *Have you got any family members who coloured their hair? Do you know someone who got a tattoo? Has anyone had their ears pierced?* Circulate to make sure everyone gets a chance to contribute to the discussion.

Extend

- Put students into pairs. Tell them to do their own research on the history of one of the types of body decoration they've heard about: body painting, henna, tattoos or piercing. Ask them to work together to write a short paragraph about what they have learnt and share it with the class.

Consolidate

- Say *I'm going to call out two words, a noun and a verb, and then say either* present simple *or* past simple. *If you hear* present simple, *use the two words in a sentence with the present simple form of the verb. If you hear* past simple, *use the two words in a sentence with the past simple form of the verb.* Model with a student. Call out *(Enrique), fashion–learn–present simple.* (Enrique) responds, for example, with *We learn about different fashions.*

- When students understand what to do, ask them to make sentences with present simple or past simple verbs, using one of the word pairs on the board. You may need to help students with the past form of *wear: wore.*

sweatshirt/look	jeans/replace
uniform/wear	ears/pierce
tattoos/decorate	high heels/dress up
bride/paint	fashion/learn

Our World in Context

New Zealand, the home of the Maori, is a mountainous group of islands in the south-western Pacific Ocean. It has two main islands, North Island and South Island, as well as other smaller ones. Maori are the indigenous Polynesian people of New Zealand and make up about 15 percent of the population. Other New Zealanders, nicknamed Kiwis after the unique flightless bird that has become a symbol of the country, are mostly descended from British settlers who went to the country in the 19th century.

Due to its isolation, New Zealand has developed unique animal and plant life. The bird species of New Zealand are particularly diverse, including alpine parrots and ground-dwelling kiwis.

Formative Assessment

Can students

- identify the form, meaning, and use of the past simple tense?

  Ask What verb form do you use to talk about what happened? What did you do yesterday (after school)?

- use the past simple to say what happened?

  Ask students to complete this sentence with the correct form of *wash*:

  In Ancient Egypt, women _____ their hair with fruit juices. (washed)

- use words associated with body decoration?

  Ask students to answer this question with a complete sentence:

  What did the Maori men of New Zealand do to decorate their bodies?

Workbook For additional practice, assign Workbook pages 48–49

Online Workbook Grammar 1

Objectives

Students will
- read about and discuss jewellery and the reasons people wear it.
- use new words from the reading.
- compare reasons for wearing jewellery.

Reading Strategy Compare and contrast

Vocabulary Strategy Using a dictionary

Target Vocabulary *accessory, bracelet, necklace, outfit, wealth*

Academic Language *compare, contrast, pronounce, pronunciation key, syllable*

Content Vocabulary *husband, jade, marriage, protection, security, tribe*

Resources Online Workbook/Workbook pages 50–51; Tracks 071–072 (Audio CD/Website/CPT); Worksheet 1.5.4 (Teacher's Resource CD-ROM/Website); CPT: Reading

Materials drawing materials, set of classroom dictionaries

---

1 BEFORE YOU READ Discuss in pairs. Look at the photo. What is the woman wearing? Why do you think she's wearing it?

2 LEARN NEW WORDS Find these words in the dictionary. Notice how they're pronounced. Then listen and repeat. 🎧 071

accessory	bracelet	necklace
outfit	wealth	

3 WHILE YOU READ Think about your own habits. What type of jewellery do you wear? Why do you wear it? 🎧 072

Throughout history, people have used accessories to make their outfits look more special. Jewellery was, and still is, in fashion all over the world. Through the years, people have worn jewellery for different reasons: to make themselves look beautiful, to protect them from bad things, and to show how much money they have.

In South Africa, men in the Ndebele tribe often gave their wives jewellery made of metal rings. Ndebele women wore necklaces around their necks and bracelets around their arms. Rings were even worn on their legs. The rings showed wealth. A woman with many rings had a richer husband. In the past, women only took off the rings when their husbands died. Today, Ndebele women still wear the rings, but not all of the time.

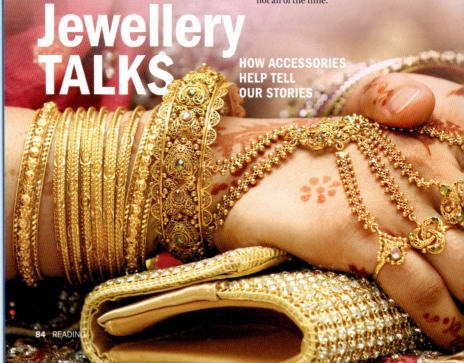

Jewellery TALKS

HOW ACCESSORIES HELP TELL OUR STORIES

84 READING

Warm Up

- **Build background** Write the word *jewellery* on the board. Say *Raise your hand if you're wearing jewellery.* Ask a few students to come to the front and show and describe their jewellery to the class. List some of the items on the board. Ask *Why do people wear jewellery?* Then discuss reasons as a class, such as to dress up, because it's beautiful, it's the latest style, it reminds you of a loved one, to show you're married, for good luck, and so on. To sum up, say *There are lots of different reasons. We're going to read about some other ones, too.*

Before You Read

- Ask students to open their books at pages 84–85. Invite a student to read the title and subtitle of the reading. Explain that *accessories* refers to items such as belts, scarves, sunglasses, bracelets, and so on. Read the subtitle again. Ask *What does that mean? How do our jewellery and accessories tell our stories?*

People in India have been wearing jewellery for more than 5,000 years. In the past, both men and women wore a lot of jewellery. Women wore as many as 50 bracelets at a time! Over time, men stopped wearing so much jewellery, but for women jewellery continues to be very important. In India, jewellery means security. If a family has trouble with money, they can always sell their jewellery. And, as with the Ndebele tribe, jewellery means wealth. Indian women can expect to receive jewellery as gifts for each important life event, such as birth, marriage and becoming a mother. In addition to wearing bracelets and necklaces, Indian women might pierce their nose or wear rings on their toes.

In ancient China, people wore jewellery not just to show wealth but also for protection. They believed that the jade stone used in their jewellery was alive and that it kept bad things away. Many Chinese people today still believe this, and they wear jade bracelets for protection. They only wear the bracelets on their left arms, and they only take them off when necessary.

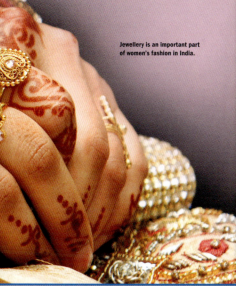

Jewellery is an important part of women's fashion in India.

4 **AFTER YOU READ** **Work in pairs.**
Tick T for *true* or F for *false*.

1. People wear jewellery for a lot of different reasons. (T) (F)
2. Ndebele women buy their own metal rings. (T) (F)
3. Ndebele women today never take off their metal rings. (T) (F)
4. Indian women didn't wear much jewellery in the past. (T) (F)
5. Chinese people still wear jade bracelets for protection. (T) (F)
6. All jewellery today is very different from jewellery long ago. (T) (F)

5 **Work in groups.** Discuss your answers to Activity 3. How many answers were similar? How does your use of jewellery compare with that of the cultures you learnt about in the reading?

6 **Discuss in groups.**

1. Is jewellery important to you? Why or why not? Do you have a favourite piece of jewellery? If so, describe it.
2. Compare and contrast reasons why people wore jewellery long ago with reasons that people wear jewellery today. Use what you already know as well as information from the reading in your answer.
3. Imagine that you design a piece of jewellery. Who is it for? What does it say about that person? What type of jewellery is it? What does it look like?

READING **85**

BE THE EXPERT

Reading Strategy

Compare and contrast Students learnt about comparing and contrasting in Unit 2. Remind them that when you compare, you look for the ways two or more people or things are alike. When you contrast, you look for the ways in which they're different. Words that show comparison include *alike, both* and *similar*. Words that show contrast include *unlike, but* and *different*. Venn diagrams are helpful for students to see how things are the same and different. Comparing and contrasting as they read will help students gain a deeper understanding of a text.

Vocabulary Strategy

Using a dictionary In addition to word definitions, a dictionary also shows how to properly pronounce, or say, a word. In English, there can be several different ways to pronounce a single letter, so it's important for your students to become familiar with how and where dictionaries show pronunciation. Different dictionaries also use different phonetic symbols, so students need to check the pronunciation key, or guide, when using a new dictionary.

In addition, words that are spelt the same can be pronounced differently, depending on which definition of the word is being used. Some common examples include *close* (the adjective, as in *Don't stand too close to the edge*) and *close* (the verb, as in *Close the door*), and *object* (the noun, as in *How many objects do you see?*) and *object* (the verb, as in *I object to your description of my outfit!*) Students need to check the definitions before they decide on the pronunciation they should use.

Teaching Tip

Remind students that making revisions and improvements to their work is part of the learning process. When students give feedback to one another, make sure they use positive language. It's important that students receive feedback in a positive way. Remind them that such feedback is not a personal criticism. These suggestions can make their work even better.

• **1** Help students to make connections between the reasons for wearing jewellery and what people can tell about you from your jewellery. For example, people can tell that you're fashionable, that you like to show off, that you prefer simple things, or that you're married. Ask *What else?* Ask students to share their thoughts. Then put students into pairs and tell them to discuss the Activity 1 questions.

• **2** **LEARN NEW WORDS** Say *Before we read* Jewellery Talks, *you're going to learn some new words.* Point to the words in the box. Say *You know what some of these words mean. But you may not be sure how to pronounce, or say, them. The dictionary will show you.* Tell pairs to look up the words. Say *See if you can work out how to pronounce them.* When students are ready, play **Track 071**. Ask students to listen and repeat.

• **VOCABULARY STRATEGY** Without saying the word, write *history* on the board. Tell pairs to look up the word in a dictionary. Say *The entry word is broken up into syllables or word parts.* Then point out the phonetic spelling that follows it. Say *Accent marks show the syllable to stress when you say the word.* Ask *How many syllables does the word have?* (three)

READING **159**

• Then say *Find the pronunciation key.* Tell students that the pronunciation key explains the different symbols that show the sound each letter stands for. It also includes examples of the sounds shown in the phonetic spelling. Ask a volunteer to pronounce *history.* Tell students that online dictionaries usually include an option to hear the word pronounced correctly.

While You Read 3

• **3** Say *Now we're going to listen to* Jewellery Talks. *As you read, think about your own jewellery and why you wear it.* Play **Track 072** and tell students to read and listen.

• Ask *What was the most interesting or surprising thing you read?* Discuss the reading. Say *I was surprised to learn that people wore rings on their legs and that the ancient Chinese thought jade was a living thing.* Say *Now read again. This time, think about whether the reasons you or people you know wear jewellery are similar to the ones mentioned in the reading.* Play **Track 072** again or allow students to read in silence.

After You Read 4 5 6

• **4** Put students into pairs. Ask partners to read the statements and decide if they're true or false. If partners disagree on an answer, tell them to read the text again and find the information that supports their answers. Ask pairs to complete the activity. Review the answers as a class.

• **5** Put students into small groups. Read the instructions for Activity 5 aloud. Tell group members to compare the kinds of jewellery they or people they know wear and their reasons for wearing it. Make sure students understand that if they don't wear jewellery themselves, they should think about a relative or someone else they know who does, and why they think the person wears it. You may want to appoint someone in each group to act as secretary and take notes.

• Tell students to compare their use of jewellery with that of the cultures they read about in *Jewellery Talks.*

• **6** Ask students to form new groups to discuss the questions in Activity 6. After they've talked about their favourite jewellery, ask group members to help one another make Venn diagrams to discuss the second set of questions. Display a diagram like the one below that students can copy and fill in. Ask group secretaries to share the notes they took to help students.

• After groups have shared their diagrams and ideas, ask them to read and discuss the third set of questions. Ask *Who would you like to give a piece of jewellery to? What would it look like? What would you want it to say about the person? How would it help tell the person's story?*

Extend

- Say *Now think about your ideas for a piece of jewellery and draw it. Below the picture, write a paragraph describing the item. Write something about the person you'd like to give it to.* Ask students to come to the front to present their drawings and paragraphs to the class.

- If time allows, you may want to hand out **Worksheet 1.5.4** in class. Hand out a copy to each student. Students will use the worksheet to practise new vocabulary items.

Consolidate

- Write some items of jewellery and accessories such as the following on the board: *ring, necklace, earrings, scarf, belt, jade bracelet, rope bracelet, pin (brooch), watch* and *hat.*

- Say *Choose an item from the board that you would like for yourself and say why you'd like to have it, when you'd wear it, and what it would say about you.*

Teaching Tip

Reading aloud is a valuable way to practise pronunciation. Listen to students as they read. When you hear them struggling to pronounce a word, take time to review that word with the class. Write the word on the board and model saying it aloud for students. Ask students to repeat the word back to you. Then ask students to re-read the sentence containing the word or words. Monitor students to check that they are pronouncing the word correctly. Tell them to look up the word in a dictionary and help them to use the pronunciation key to say the word correctly.

Formative Assessment

Can students

- discuss jewellery and the reasons people wear it?

  Ask students to give two reasons they or people they know wear jewellery.

- use new words from the reading text?

  Ask students to choose the correct word in brackets to complete the sentence frames:

  To both the Ndebele and the people of India, jewellery is a sign of _____. (wealth, an accessory)

  One reason Chinese people wear jade _____ is to protect them against bad things. (outfits, bracelets)

- compare reasons for wearing jewellery?

  Ask *Can you give a reason why you, or someone you know, wears jewellery that is different from the reasons described in the reading text?*

Workbook For additional practice, assign Workbook page 50–51.

Online Workbook Reading

Objectives

Students will
- discuss clothing that is practical and can keep you safe.
- apply the message of the video to their personal lives.

Content Vocabulary *boat shoes, hard hat, headdress, hike, recycled, shreds, spool, surfaces*

Resources Video scene 5.1 (DVD/Website/CPT); Online Workbook; CPT: Video

BE THE EXPERT

Answer Key

Comprehension

1. dog paws
2. They keep you from slipping on wet surfaces.
3. extreme
4. He needs protection from extreme heat.
5. a tent
6. They used it to make headdresses.

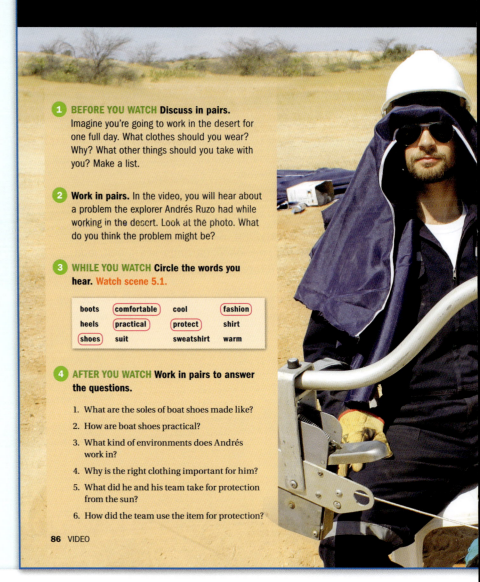

VIDEO ▶

1. **BEFORE YOU WATCH Discuss in pairs.**
Imagine you're going to work in the desert for one full day. What clothes should you wear? Why? What other things should you take with you? Make a list.

2. **Work in pairs.** In the video, you will hear about a problem the explorer Andrés Ruzo had while working in the desert. Look at the photo. What do you think the problem might be?

3. **WHILE YOU WATCH Circle the words you hear. Watch scene 5.1.**

boots	**comfortable**	cool	**fashion**
heels	**practical**	**protect**	shirt
shoes	suit	sweatshirt	warm

4. **AFTER YOU WATCH Work in pairs to answer the questions.**

1. What are the soles of boat shoes made like?
2. How are boat shoes practical?
3. What kind of environments does Andrés work in?
4. Why is the right clothing important for him?
5. What did he and his team take for protection from the sun?
6. How did the team use the item for protection?

86 VIDEO

Before You Watch

- **Revise** Ask students to look at the photo on pages 76–77. Ask *Why is the man wearing a protective suit?* (He's going into a burning crater. The suit will protect him from the heat.) Discuss other kinds of protective clothing people wear.

- **1** Tell students to turn to pages 86–87. Put students into pairs. Ask a student to read Activity 1 aloud. Say *The temperature in some deserts can go as high as 59°C!* Ask *Has anyone ever been in a desert?* If so, ask the student(s) to describe what it felt like. Say *Think of pictures you've seen of people who live in deserts, such as the Sahara Desert in northern Africa. What do they wear?*

- **2** Read Activity 2 aloud. Ask *Why do you think Andrés has that covering on his head?* Say *Before you discuss, let's make a list of what we know or can see*

in the photo. I'll start. Write *desert* and *Andrés* on the board. Ask *What else can you see?* Make a list on the board of students' suggestions. Say *Look at the list and the photo again. What is the problem?*

While You Watch

- **3** Ask a student to read the instructions for Activity 3. Invite different students to read the words. Say *Pay attention as you watch the video because you won't hear all of these words – only some of them.* You may want to pre-teach two words that may not be familiar: *shreds* (small pieces of something torn up, such as paper) and *headdresses* (something worn on the head). Play **Video scene 5.1**.

- If students have trouble following the video, pause it and allow them to ask questions or re-read the text. Try replaying the video with and without sound, and ask students to describe what they see.

Andrés found a practical solution to his problem.

5 **Work in pairs.** At the end of the video, you're asked, 'What clothes are you wearing now? Why are you wearing them?' Answer these questions.

6 **Discuss in groups.** In the video, Andrés says, 'I work in some pretty extreme environments, and I assure you, sometimes the right clothing can save your life.' List three other jobs where workers wear special clothes to protect them.

7 **YOU DECIDE** **Choose an activity.**

1. **Work independently.** Imagine you're going to hike in the Amazon rain forest. Make a list of the clothes and accessories that you'll need to be safe and comfortable. Explain why you need each item on your list.

2. **Work in pairs.** In the video, Andrés found a practical solution to his problem. Think of a time you had a problem and found a solution. Discuss it with your partner. Can your partner think of a different way for you to solve the same problem?

3. **Work in groups.** When he's not working, Andrés wears clothes that both look good and are practical. Find five photos showing practical clothing that also looks good. Show the photos to the class and explain why you chose them.

VIDEO 87

After You Watch

- 4 Put students into pairs. Tell them to write the answers to the questions. Review the answers as a class. If students disagree about an answer, replay the video. Ask *What were the headdresses made from? Do you think the solution was a good one? Why or why not?* Invite students to share their thoughts.

- 5 Say *You may not have thought a lot about why you wear the things you do before now. Are you beginning to think a little differently about your clothes?* Ask pairs to discuss and answer the activity questions.

- 6 Put students into groups. Read aloud Activity 6. When groups have finished, ask them to call out the jobs on their lists. Write them on the board. Challenge students to think of categories they could name to classify the jobs. Say *The categories could be about the level of danger involved in the job, whether the jobs involve science or not, whether the jobs are found in every community, and so on.*

- 7 **YOU DECIDE** Tell students to read the activity options. If students choose the list of rainforest items in option 1, remind them that the rainforest is a very different environment than the desert. Say *Write some features of the rain forest first to help you make your list.*

- Suggest to students considering option 2 that they think about a problem they might have had during an outdoor activity, working on a school project, or repairing something that broke suddenly. Maybe they ran out of a material or ingredient they needed and had to come up with a substitute. Say *Impress us with your problem-solving skills!*

- The third option might be good for students who are interested in fashion or fashion design. Say *Remember, the clothing has to be practical, not just fashionable.*

Objective

Students will
- use the past simple of irregular verbs to describe what happened.

Grammar Past simple: Saying what happened

Academic Language *irregular verbs, regular verbs*

Content Vocabulary *herbs, hood, patient, plague*

Resources Online Workbook/Workbook pages 52–53; Worksheet 1.5.5 (Teacher's Resource CD-ROM/Website); Track 073 (Audio CD/Website/CPT); CPT: Grammar 2

GRAMMAR 🎧 073

Past simple: Saying what happened

Long ago the plague **made** people very ill.

Doctors **had** to help people with the plague.

Doctors **wore** special protective suits. This way, they **didn't** get ill.

Doctors also **put** on red glasses. They **thought** the colour red would protect them.

1 **Read.** Complete the sentences with the past simple form of the verbs in brackets. For help, go to page 148.

Doctors _____began_____ (begin) wearing protective suits in England in the mid-1300s. They _____thought_____ (think) these suits _____kept_____ (keep) them safe from a sickness called the *plague*. So they _____wore_____ (wear) birdlike masks and long leather coats. The coats _____went_____ (go) all the way to the ground. Doctors always _____brought_____ (bring) a cane to their patients' houses. That way, they _____didn't have_____ (not have) to use their hands to touch the patient.

In the 1940s, people _____made_____ (make) a new kind of protective suit. The suit _____didn't leave_____ (not leave) any part of the body uncovered. The rubber fabric _____gave_____ (give) people good protection. People _____got_____ (get) into the suit from the front. Then they _____put_____ (put) on long gloves, boots and a hood. The suit _____had_____ (have) a special machine to help them breathe.

A protective suit

2 **Work in pairs.** Throw the cube. Ask a question about the past using the words on the cube. Your partner answers the question.

What did you wear to the concert?

I wore a blue dress with black shoes.

Go to page 173.

(cube faces: what / wear, how / make, who / see)

Warm Up

- **Activate prior knowledge** Say *You've learnt about using past simple verbs to say what happened. You also learnt some rules for verbs that form the past simple by adding -d or -ed to the base form of the verb.* Explain that verbs that form the past this way are called regular verbs. Tell students that there are other verbs that form the past differently.

Present

- Explain that verbs that have special past forms are called irregular verbs. Say *Many of the past forms of these verbs are familiar, such as did, as in* What <u>did</u> ancient Greek women use to wash their hair? Display some common irregular verbs. Ask students to read them aloud. Point out that *put* is the same in the present and the past. Demonstrate by placing a book on a desk and saying *A moment ago, I <u>put</u> the*

book on the desk. Point to a different location and say *Yesterday, I <u>put</u> the book there.*

Present		Past	Present		Past
do	→	did	put	→	put
have	→	had	think	→	thought
make	→	made	wear	→	wore

- Ask student pairs to use the verbs on the board in sentences. One partner uses the present form, the other uses the past form of the same verb. Suggest topics such as the following for their sentences: what they have/had for lunch, when they do/did their homework and what they make/made for a snack.

- Ask students to open their books at page 88. Say *We're going to be reading sentences about a terrible sickness called the plague that killed millions of people. Follow in your books as we listen.* Play **Track 073**.

- Ask students to tell you the present simple form of the verbs in dark print.

Practise

- **1** Ask students to look at the illustration of the plague doctor in a protective suit. Explain that doctors wore these suits to keep from touching a sick person with their bare skin. They also believed the plague could be carried through the air, so they put sweet-smelling plants called herbs into the beak of the mask to keep from breathing in the air around a sick person.

- Read the Activity 1 instructions aloud. Say *We've gone over the past forms of some of the verbs in these sentences. Do as many as you can. If you don't know the past form, you can find it on page 148 of your books.* Ask students to work independently.

Apply **2**

- **2** Put students into pairs. Ask them to cut out and assemble the game cube on page 173. Then read aloud the activity instructions. Ask a pair to read aloud the dialogue in the speech bubbles. Point out the use of *wear* instead of *wore* with *did* in the question. Say *If you're not sure of a past form, check page 148.* Ask pairs to come to the front and to perform their dialogues for the class.

Extend

- Tell partners to continue the game with a new cube. Tell them to cross out the verbs on their cubes and choose six of the following twelve verbs to replace them.

> what / bring <u>or</u> give   when / sleep <u>or</u> have
> why / get <u>or</u> think   where / leave <u>or</u> find
> who / teach <u>or</u> put   how / feel <u>or</u> stop

- Give an example. Say *For 'how / stop', you could say, 'How did you stop laughing?' Your partner could answer, 'I stopped laughing by holding my breath.'*

- Hand out **Worksheet 1.5.5** for further practice with the past simple of irregular verbs.

Consolidate

- Write these vocabulary words on pieces of card, one to a card: *fashion, heels, jeans, suit, sweatshirt, tie, uniform, fabric, tights, bride, tattoos, accessory, bracelet, necklace, outfit* and *wealth.* Give each student a card. Divide the class into two teams. Then write these verbs on the board: *bring, feel, find, get, give, keep, leave* and *put.*

- Say *When I point to you, use the word on your card and the past simple form of a verb on the board in a sentence. If the sentence is correct, your team scores one point. For example, my word is* fabric. *My sentence is 'I found the best fabric for my new dress'.*

Grammar in Depth

Some verbs have two past forms – one regular, one irregular. The irregular form is the more commonly used form in British English, so students should be encouraged to use it. These verbs include

burn	→	burned/burnt
dream	→	dreamed/dreamt
learn	→	learned/learnt
smell	→	smelled/smelt
spell	→	spelled/spelt

Emphasise that irregular verb forms follow no rules and must be memorised. Remind students to use the base form of a main verb when it's used with *did* in questions and negative statements. Mention to students that *did* is also used for emphasis in statements such as *I <u>did</u> hand in my homework!*

Teaching Tip

Make sure students save any Consolidate activity cards that have vocabulary items on them. They can write definitions on the other side and use them to practise the words, to use as flash cards with a partner, or to make up their own games.

Formative Assessment

Can students

- use the past simple of irregular verbs to describe what happened?

  Ask students to answer this question with the correct past simple verb form:

  What did doctors wear long ago when they took care of people with the plague?

Workbook For additional practice, assign Workbook pages 52–53.

Online Workbook Grammar 2

WRITING

Objectives

Students will
- consider how to publish a model of descriptive writing.
- produce, proofread and publish an essay describing how a uniform changed over time.

Writing Descriptive writing

Academic Language *essay, non-fiction, submit*

Resources Online Workbook/Workbook page 54; Process Writing Worksheets 1–5, Genre Writing Worksheet: Description (Teacher's Resource CD-ROM/Website); CPT: Writing

WRITING

The last step in writing is publishing. After you write, review and proofread your work, you're ready to publish. When you publish, you let other people read your work.

1 Read the model. Do you think this essay is ready to be published? Why or why not? Discuss in pairs.

Before 1870, there were no football uniforms. Players wore their own clothes, which made it hard to know which team they were on. The first football uniform had long, loose shorts. Players wore striped, formal shirts with collars and buttons. The entire uniform was made of a heavy fabric, such as wool. Players then put on leather football boots that went up over their ankles.

Football uniforms have changed many times through the years. Today, football uniforms are very different. The shorts are shorter, and the whole uniform is made out of light fabric. This keeps football players cool as they run. Instead of boots, football players wear soft leather shoes. Each team now has its own colours. For example, players on the Brazilian football team wear bright yellow and green shirts, blue shorts and white socks. But these uniforms will change, too. After all, sports teams need uniforms that are practical but also in fashion!

English football players wearing uniforms, 1888

2 Discuss in pairs. Who do you think would find this essay interesting? Where should the author publish this essay?

3 Write. Research another uniform that has changed over time. Write an essay about the changes. Proofread your work. Then publish it by sharing it with your classmates.

WRITING **89**

Warm Up

- **Revise** Say *In the last unit, you practised proofreading a piece of writing.* Ask *What is proofreading?* (checking writing for mistakes in spelling and grammar) *What do you do after proofreading your own writing?* Remind students that, after proofreading, you make a new copy correcting the mistakes you made. Ask *Then what? After working hard on your writing, and after reviewing and proofreading it, you want other people to read it, don't you? What do we call this last step?* (publishing)

Present

- Say *Open your books at page 89.* Ask a student to read aloud the text in the green box. Ask *How can other people read or hear your work?*

- After students respond, say *That's right, but there are lots of different ways to publish writing.* Ask *Can you think of some others?* Write students' responses, such as the following, on the board.

E-mail it to friends or relatives.	Record an audio version of it.
Print it in the school newspaper.	Make an online video of you reading it.
Send it to a magazine.	Make it a poster with pictures or photos.
Send it to a teens' website.	Turn it into a play or film and perform or show it.

- Talk about the different options. Tell students that when you send a piece of writing to a magazine or website, you *submit* it. Then a person or a group reviews it, and decides whether to publish it in the magazine or on the website.

Read the Model

- Say *Now we're going to read a model of an essay.* Explain that an essay is a short piece of non-fiction writing about a single subject that usually has more than one paragraph. Tell students that there are many types of essays, but the one they're going to read is an essay that describes something. Say *Look at the photos. Read the caption.* Ask *What do you predict the subject of this essay will be?* (football, football players over the years) Discuss students' predictions.

- Read the activity instructions aloud. Say *As you read, keep in mind the parts of any good piece of descriptive writing: title, topic sentence, details, concluding sentence.* Ask students to read the model.

- When students have finished, put them into pairs to discuss their ideas on whether the essay is ready to be published. Say *Re-read the essay with your partner. Then discuss whether it's ready to be published.* Ask *Are all the parts there? What's missing? Could anything have been done better?*

- After they've discussed, ask pairs to share their ideas. If necessary, point out that the essay's two paragraphs are well organised and there are no spelling or grammar errors, but it needs a title. Ask *What's the topic sentence?* Help students to see that the topic sentence is actually at the beginning of the second paragraph. Ask *Where should it be?* (the beginning of the first paragraph)

- Put students into pairs. Read aloud the Activity 2 questions. Explain to students that when thinking about how to publish their writing, they need to consider the audience – the people who will read it. Say *You need to work out which group of people will be most interested in reading what you wrote.* Ask *Would you submit an essay about the history of school uniforms to a science magazine?* Invite pairs to share their ideas.

- **Worksheet** If your students need a reminder of the specifics of publishing, you may want to hand out **Process Writing Worksheet 5 (Publishing)** and review it together.

 **WRITING**

The last step in writing is publishing. After you write, review and proofread your work, you're ready to publish. When you publish, you let other people read your work.

1 **Read the model.** Do you think this essay is ready to be published? Why or why not? Discuss in pairs.

Before 1870, there were no football uniforms. Players wore their own clothes, which made it hard to know which team they were on. The first football uniform had long, loose shorts. Players wore striped, formal shirts with collars and buttons. The entire uniform was made of a heavy fabric, such as wool. Players then put on leather football boots that went up over their ankles.

Football uniforms have changed many times through the years. Today, football uniforms are very different. The shorts are shorter, and the whole uniform is made out of light fabric. This keeps football players cool as they run. Instead of boots, football players wear soft leather shoes. Each team now has its own colours. For example, players on the Brazilian football team wear bright yellow and green shirts, blue shorts and white socks. But these uniforms will change, too. After all, sports teams need uniforms that are practical but also in fashion!

English football players wearing uniforms, 1888

2 **Discuss in pairs.** Who do you think would find this essay interesting? Where should the author publish this essay?

3 **Write.** Research another uniform that has changed over time. Write an essay about the changes. Proofread your work. Then publish it by sharing it with your classmates.

WRITING **89**

Plan **3**

- **3** Say *Read the instructions for Activity 3.* Then say *Your topic is to write about another uniform that has changed over time. Let's list some people who wear uniforms.* Ask students to call out people who wear uniforms. Say *Make your choice. Then research how much the uniform has changed.*

- Say *Your next step is pre-writing. Let's review. What are some ways we do pre-writing?* (brainstorm, freewrite, make lists, use a graphic organiser, use sentence starters) Say *Now decide which technique you want to use for pre-writing.* If you have time in class, allow students to work on this step. If not, assign it as

homework. If students have Workbooks, remind them to use Workbook page 54 for writing support.

- **Worksheets** If students need a reminder of any of the steps of process writing, hand out **Process Writing Worksheets 1–5** and review them together.

- **Workbook** Refer students to Workbook page 54 to help them organise and plan their writing.

Write

- After students have finished pre-writing, tell them to work on first drafts. If you don't have enough time in the lesson, assign the first draft as homework.

Revise

- After students have finished their first drafts, tell them to review their writing and think about their ideas and organisation. Ask each student to consider the following: *Did I include a topic sentence? Is the information organised in a logical way? Did I include enough details to describe how the uniforms changed? What seems good? What needs more work?*

Edit and Proofread

- Ask students to consider elements of style, such as sentence variety, parallelism and word choice. Then tell them to proofread for mistakes in grammar, punctuation, capitalisation and spelling. After they have found and corrected their mistakes, ask them to neatly rewrite their paragraph, making sure to correct the mistakes.

Publish

- Remind students that they can share an essay with classmates either by reading it aloud, adding it to a class book, displaying it on a classroom wall or in a hallway, or posting it on the school website.

Writing Assessment

Use these guidelines to assess students' writing. You can add other aspects of their writing you'd like to assess at the bottom of the table.

4 = Excellent
3 = Good
2 = Needs improvement
1 = Re-do

	1	2	3	4
Writing Student organises the essay in a way that makes sense and uses enough descriptive detail so readers can visualise the different uniforms.				
Grammar Student uses regular and irregular past simple verbs correctly.				
Vocabulary Student uses a variety of word choices, including words taught in this unit.				

NATIONAL GEOGRAPHIC

Learn to Adapt

'Adaptation is key to survival. Whether it's wearing a coat on a cold day or finding new sources of green energy – our ability to adapt to life's challenges allows us to thrive.'

Andrés Ruzo
National Geographic Explorer, Geoscientist

1. **Watch scene 5.2.**

2. How does the environment you're in affect your clothing choices? Give examples.

3. Andrés says it's important to adapt, or change our behaviour, to respond to what's happening around us. Give examples of a time when you did this, and a time when you didn't. What happened in each situation?

Objective
Students will
• discuss how people need to adapt to changing situations.

Resources Video scene 5.2 (DVD/Website/CPT); Worksheet 1.5.6 (Teacher's Resource CD-ROM/Website); Online Workbook: Meet the Explorer; CPT: Mission

BE THE EXPERT

Teaching Tip

During pair or group work, make sure students get to work with many different classmates. Rotate students, pairing them with partners of different strengths and fluency levels. After groups or pairs of students have completed an activity, ask them to form new groups or pairs and repeat the activity. This gives students another opportunity to practise and also helps them get to know their classmates.

Online Workbook Meet the Explorer

Mission

• Say *Turn to page 90.* Read the Mission aloud. Explain that when you adapt, you change your ideas or behaviour in response to a new situation. Then read the quote from Andrés Ruzo. Explain that 'green energy' refers to energy that comes from sources such as the sun, the wind and geothermal energy. These are sources that won't run out like oil and coal will. Ask *How might finding new sources of green energy be important for our survival?* Discuss with students how we need to find new sources of energy to replace oil and gas, which will run out one day and which are also harmful to the environment.

• **Activity 1** Say *Now let's watch another video about Andrés Ruzo.* Tell students to pay attention to what Andrés says about the kind of clothes he likes to wear and why. Play **Video scene 5.2**.

• **Activity 2** Say *Andrés works in hot, sometimes dangerous environments. He wears clothes that are practical for the conditions he works in.* Read the Activity 2 task. Invite students to share their thoughts.

• **Activity 3** Ask a student to stand up and read the Activity 3 task. Make sure students understand what they have to do. If students need help getting started, say *Think about an item of clothing most people wear, for example, boots or hats.* Put students into pairs and ask them to share their ideas. Say *Try to use the correct past simple forms when talking about the past.*

• **Worksheet** Hand out **Worksheet 1.5.6**. Explain that students will use the worksheet to think and write about Andrés Ruzo and his ideas about clothing, survival and the environment.

Objective

Students will

- choose and complete a project related to clothing.

Content Vocabulary *gallery*

Resources
Assessment: Unit 5 Quiz; Workbook pages 55 and 94; Worksheet 1.5.7 (Teacher's Resource CD-ROM/Website); CPT: Make an Impact and Review Games

Materials
art materials, camera

Assessment
Go to page 259.

Unit Review Assign Worksheet 1.5.7

Workbook Assign pages 55 and 94.

Online Workbook Now I can

Make an Impact

YOU DECIDE Choose a project.

1 Be a clothing designer.

- Design an accessory or article of clothing that will look good and protect you.
- Draw a picture of it. Write an explanation to say why it looks good and is practical.
- Present your design to the class.

2 Plan and conduct a clothing scavenger hunt.

- As a group, prepare a list of clothing items and accessories.
- Look around your home, your school or local clothes shops. Take photos of the most interesting examples of each of the items on your list.
- Create a photo gallery to share your group's best photos. Describe the items and why you liked them.

3 Prepare a history presentation.

- Research an article of clothing or accessory not presented in this unit. Find out how it has changed over the years.
- Create a poster or computer presentation about the item you chose. Use photos to show how the item has changed.
- Share your presentation with the class.

PROJECT **91**

Prepare

- **YOU DECIDE** Ask students to choose a project.

- **Activity 1** Ask students to look at the photo on page 91. Ask *What do you think the person is dressed for? Do you think the outfit is practical?* Say *Remember that you thought about a design for a piece of jewellery to give to someone. Now you have the chance to design an article of clothing or an accessory. This time, the item has to be both attractive and protective! That's a challenge.*

- **Activity 2** Put students into groups to make up a list of clothing and accessories for the scavenger hunt. Say *The items can be ordinary or unusual, but the ones you choose to photograph should be interesting!* Explain that a gallery is a place or a space set aside to display works of art. Say *After you take your photos, you'll have to decide which ones are artistic enough to be in a photo gallery!*

- **Activity 3** Say *This could be hard because you can't use anything that was pictured or talked about in this unit.* You might suggest that students talk to older relatives to see if they can suggest or find an older version of something people still wear today. Say *Remember you have to research and prepare a presentation on how the item has changed.*

Share

- Schedule time for students to present their designs, photographs and research. Allow time for students to ask questions, and provide feedback on their classmates' work.

- **Modify** Help students simplify a project by eliminating one of the options or steps. For example, you could limit the scavenger hunt to the school and students' homes, or provide students with a list of clothing items to research.

Track 060 **1** **Listen and read.** See Student's Book pages 78–79.

Track 061 **2** LEARN NEW WORDS **casual** / Shorts and T-shirts are casual clothes. **century** / In the last century, the way we dress has changed. **dress up** / You might dress up to go to a party. **fashion** / Fashion has changed through the years. **formal** / People used to wear formal clothes all the time. **heel** / Today, some women wear shoes with very high heels. **jeans** / People of all ages like jeans. **look** / He looks great in those clothes. **practical** / Boots are practical in the snow. **suit** / Many people have to wear suits to work. **sweatshirt** / A sweatshirt keeps your arms and body warm. **tie** / Years ago, boys wore ties all of the time. **uniform** / Some students don't like their school uniforms. **wear** / Today, a lot of people wear comfortable clothes.

Track 062 **5** More than 4,000 years ago, men covered their legs with animal skins to keep them warm. Over time, fabric replaced animal skins as a leg covering. In the 1500s, in Europe, men's clothing became very short. The tops of their legs showed, so they wore tights to cover them. Originally, women didn't wear tights because they wore long skirts to keep their legs warm. Today, women often wear tights with skirts and dresses whenever they get dressed up. But many of us prefer to cover our legs in denim by wearing jeans.

Track 063 **5** LEARN NEW WORDS **denim** / Jeans are made of denim. **fabric** / Clothes are made from many different fabrics. **replace** / Old things are usually replaced by more modern ones. **tights** / In the 1500s, men wore tights.

Track 064 SPEAKING STRATEGY See Student's Book page 81.

Track 065 **1** **S1**: I like our school uniforms. I don't have to think about what to wear every day. What do you think? **S2**: I don't agree. It's hard to look cool in a uniform. We can't show who we really are. Don't you agree? **S1**: I'm not really sure. Yes, it's hard to look cool. But, uniforms help bring us together. No one looks different, so we feel part of the same group. **S2**: That's true, but uniforms create work for teachers. They have to spend time checking that everyone is wearing their uniform. **S1**: Yes, I agree. I guess there are good things and bad things about wearing school uniforms.

Track 066 GRAMMAR See Student's Book page 82.

Track 067 **1** Clothes are not the only way we can show the world who we are. We can also do this with our hair. Women in Ancient Egypt are famous for spending a lot of time to look beautiful. They wanted their hair to look good and be clean. They didn't believe that short hair looked good. To help their hair grow, they used oil from plants and nuts on their hair. They also attached human hair or sheep's wool to their hair. This helped it look thicker and longer.

Taking care of their hair was also important.
They protected it from the hot sun with oils. Because they liked their hair to be clean, they washed it often. They didn't use soap. Instead, they mixed juices from fruit with water to use as shampoo. They coloured their hair, too. They loved blue, green and gold colours.

Track 068 **3** People from ancient cultures didn't just want their hair or clothes to look special; they actually changed the way their bodies looked. In fact, they decorated their bodies in many ways that we still do today.

You have probably seen people with tattoos. The art of tattooing is nothing new. In New Zealand, Maori men covered their faces in tattoos for centuries. The tattoos showed how important they were. Although many Maori men stopped doing this, some still do.

Many people long ago preferred to paint their bodies instead of getting tattoos. This is because the paint washed off with water. This was true of brides in Pakistan, Northern India, Africa and the Middle East. Before their wedding, they invited family and friends to a party with dancing and games. Then artists painted beautiful designs with henna on their hands and feet. These traditions continue today.

People pierced parts of their bodies for much of history. In fact, pierced ears have been found on a mummy from 5,000 years ago. Ear piercing is still popular today. In some cultures, people pierce a baby girl's ears right after birth. This way, others will know she's a girl.

Track 069 **3** LEARN NEW WORDS **bride** / Some Indian brides have a party the night before their wedding. **decorate** / People decorate their bodies in many ways. **paint** / Artists paint the hands and feet of brides in Northern India. **pierce** / Many people pierce their ears. **tattoo** / Maori men covered their faces with tattoos.

Track 070 **4** See **Track 068**.

Track 071 **2** LEARN NEW WORDS **accessory** / Hats and sunglasses are accessories. **bracelet** / People wear bracelets on their arms. **necklace** / People wear necklaces around their necks. **outfit** / Jeans and a sweatshirt make a practical outfit. **wealth** / Jewellery can show a person's wealth.

Track 072 **3** WHILE YOU READ See Student's Book pages 84–85.

Track 073 GRAMMAR See Student's Book page 88.

In This Unit

Theme This unit is about mash-ups, or things created by combining elements from two or more sources.

Content Objectives

Students will

- examine different kinds of mash-ups.
- read about a photographer and a painter who created art with food.
- discuss a filmmaker and music producer and his search for what's unique.

Language Objectives

Students will

- talk about mash-ups.
- clarify a point.
- use adjectives to compare two or more things.
- use countable and uncountable nouns to talk about amounts.
- write a paragraph of exemplification about animal mash-ups.

Vocabulary

pages 94–95 *audio, cool, DJ, edit, fan, include, mix, opinion, perform, record, recording, song, traditional, video*

page 96 *combine, download, electronic, hit*

page 99 *create, hate, hybrid, love, version*

page 100 *imagine, imitate, modern, original, weird*

Vocabulary Strategies Multiple-meaning words, Context clues

Speaking Strategy Clarifying a point

Grammar

Grammar 1 Use adjectives to compare two or more things

Grammar 2 Use countable and uncountable nouns to talk about amounts.

Reading *A Feast for the Eyes*
Reading Strategy Visualise

Video Scene 6.1: *What's in a Mash-up?*; Scene 6.2: *Meet Josh Ponte*

Writing Paragraph of exemplification about an animal mash-up

National Geographic Mission
Be Unique

Project
- Food art
- Comic strip
- Hybrid sport

Pronunciation Linking: Consonant + vowel sounds

Pacing Guides 1.6.1, 1.6.2, 1.6.3

Unit 6

Mix and Mash

Introduce the Unit

- **TO START Activate prior knowledge** Say *Children love to mix and match. That's why they love playing with building blocks and using their imaginations.* Ask *What memories have you got of creating something with pieces of different things?* Ask students to share their experiences.

- If students don't bring up the point themselves, help them to see that people mix and match naturally. Little children do it when they play, and some adults do it when they mix old and new clothes to create a new look. Say *Put your hand up if you know what* mash-up *means.* Discuss what mash-ups are and then ask *Why do you think people make mash-ups?*

- **TO START** Ask students to open their books at pages 92–93. Read the unit title aloud. Say *This whole unit is about mash-ups.* Ask *Have you seen this mash-up before?* Tell students this image is a mash-up of a famous Japanese work of art and the character Cookie Monster from *Sesame Street*.

'Different is OK.'
Josh Ponte

Sea is for Cookie, a mash-up created from *The Great Wave off Kanagawa* and a television character called Cookie Monster

TO START

1. What are the different parts of this image?

2. What do you think of this image?

3. Think of two things that you could put together to make something different and new. What are they? What can you make?

93

UNIT OPENER

Objectives

Students will

• describe and discuss a photo.

• discuss a mash-up of a work of art.

Content Vocabulary *analyse, devour, image, swamped, throwaway, tsunami*

Resources Worksheet 1.6.1 (Teacher's Resource CD-ROM/Website); CPT: Unit Opener

BE THE EXPERT

About the Picture

The Great Wave off Kanagawa (also known as *Under the Wave off Kanagawa* and *The Great Wave*), by the Japanese artist Katsushika Hokusai, is one of the most famous works of art in the world. It's a woodblock print, produced by a complex process involving a number of skilled artisans, in which a sketch made on very thin paper is pasted face down onto a block of wood. The paper is made transparent with oil or carefully peeled off, and the outline of the drawing is then carved into the wood. It takes several more steps before the final work is complete. The digitally created mash-up with Cookie Monster from *Sesame Street* was created by an artist on the Internet website Reddit.

Teaching Tip

When students activate prior knowledge about a topic, they think about what they already know and relate the topic to their personal experiences. Help students activate prior knowledge when introducing a new topic to the class. Ask them questions that get them to describe their experiences and impressions of the topic.

Related Vocabulary

foam, Mount Fuji, spray

• Ask questions to encourage discussion of the photo:

What's about to happen to the boats and people under the wave? (the boats will be swamped, the people will probably drown)

What is a huge wave like that called? (a tsunami)

What is the similarity between the wave and Cookie Monster? (They both devour things, or swallow them up quickly.)

• Read aloud the quote and Question 1 to the class. Invite students to discuss the different parts of the image. Read aloud Question 2 and invite students to discuss. Ask *Do you think the image is funny, silly, clever or disrespectful? Is it art?* After the discussion, ask students to explain why they like or do not like the image.

• Read aloud Activity 3. Then ask *What's your idea for a mash-up?* Invite students to respond and share any mash-ups they've created.

Extend

• Ask groups to consider whether mash-ups have any real value or whether they're just 'throwaway art'. Hand out **Worksheet 1.6.1**. Explain that student pairs will be thinking and writing about mash-ups.

Objective

Students will

- use new vocabulary to read about and discuss music mash-ups and two bands known for their mash-up styles.

Target Vocabulary *audio, cool, DJ, edit, fan, include, mix, opinion, perform, record, recording, song, traditional, video*

Content Vocabulary *kimono, performer, rap, techniques*

Resources Worksheet 1.6.2 (Teacher's Resource CD-ROM/Website); Tracks 074–075 (Audio CD/Website/CPT); CPT: Vocabulary

Materials a laptop or some other means of playing music

1 **What types of music do you like?**
Discuss. Then listen and repeat. 🎧 074

Mixing different styles of music creates a unique sound called a *mash-up*. Musicians have been creating mash-ups for more than 50 years. Many combine sounds from just two **songs**, but some might **include** parts from as many as 25 songs!

Many mash-up artists are **DJs** who use electronic equipment to mix together songs that already exist. These DJs decide what songs to use and how to mix them. Then they **record** their mash-ups. Next the DJs **edit** their **recordings** to make sure they sound as **cool** as possible.

DJs aren't the only ones that create musical mash-ups: bands do, too. One band that does this is the WagakkiBand from Japan. This band mixes the sounds of **traditional** Japanese instruments with rock music. The song they **performed** in their first **video** was a big hit. More than 30 million people saw the video on the Internet. People from all over the world downloaded the song from this video.

94 VOCABULARY

Warm Up

- **Build background** Say *We talked about art mash-ups; now we'll focus on musical mash-ups.* Ask *Does anyone know what a DJ is?* Ask students to share what they know about DJs and what they do. If necessary, explain that some DJs play pre-recorded music on a radio station or at a wedding or a party. Others are artists and performers who use special techniques to create a particular style of dance music.

Present

- **1** Ask students to open their books at pages 94–95. Invite a student to read aloud the Activity 1 question. Ask *What kind of music do you like? Put your hand up if I name it.* Say *Pop, rock, hip-hop, Latin, dance music, jazz.* Write the genres on the board. Ask *What am I missing? Name it.* If students are unfamiliar with several of the genres, or if they don't know or

recognise the names, use a computer to play short samples of different styles for the class. Identify each genre by name.

- Keep a tally on the board of the number of students who like each type of music. Say *You can like more than one type.* Work out the most popular types. Discuss with students how and when they listen to music.

- Tell students to look at the photo of WagakkiBand. Ask *Does anyone know this band? How about Gokh-Bi System?* There are videos of each band online. You may want to play examples of both bands' music before students read. Play **Track 074** as students listen and read. Then discuss the photo and the reading with students. Ask questions such as the following:

  What do DJs do to create a mash-up? (mix, use electronic equipment to combine different songs)

Another mash-up band is Gokh-Bi System from Dakar, Senegal. This band mixes rap with ancient West African music in a style called 'ancient-meets-urban'. The band performs with other famous singers and artists. **Fans** come from all over to hear them play.

People have different **opinions** of mash-up music. Some people prefer more traditional music styles. Others think that a mix of sounds is cooler than just one type of music. But no matter what you think of them, mash-ups provide an **audio** experience you won't forget!

2 **LEARN NEW WORDS** Listen and repeat. 🎧 075

3 **Work in pairs.** Why do you think some musicians mix modern and traditional music? Do you think it's a good idea to do this? Why or why not?

WagakkiBand with traditional and modern instruments

VOCABULARY **95**

Our World in Context

In addition to the usual guitar, bass and drums you expect to hear in a rock band, traditional Japanese instruments are also an integral part of WagakkiBand's music. These are the *koto*, a 13-string instrument similar to a harp; a *shakuhachi*, a wind instrument that looks like a recorder but is more like a flute; a *shamisen*, a three-string instrument; and *wadaiko*, which are traditional Japanese drums.

Teaching Tip

At times, students may become overly active and talkative in the classroom. To help students develop good listening skills, wait until they are quiet before you speak. Hold one hand in the air and tell students to put their hands up along with you until everyone is looking at you and the room is quiet. Then lower your hand and begin speaking. Continue to use this signal when you need students to stop talking and pay attention.

What instruments in the photo can you name? (electric bass and guitar, drum) You may also want to share the names of the traditional instruments from Our World in Context with students.

What do you think of the clothes the people in the photo are wearing? Tell students that the outfits are also a mash-up – of modern and traditional clothing. Point out that one of the musicians is wearing a kimono, a traditional Japanese robe-like garment.

- **2** **LEARN NEW WORDS** Play **Track 075**. Ask students to listen and repeat. Then put students into pairs or small groups and tell them to take turns saying each word. Allocate three or four words to each pair or group. *Work together to write a new sentence for each of your words. Show that you know what it means.* Model an example. Write on the board *When you record a song, you play it in a way that it can be saved in some form.* When they've finished, ask students to read their sentences aloud.

Practise

- Ask *Do you, your parents, or your grandparents listen to traditional music? Do you enjoy it? Does the music include any special instruments?* Tell students to describe traditional music with which they're familiar. Ask *Can you imagine this music mixed with pop, rock, or hip hop? Have you already heard such a mash-up? Did you like it or not?* Invite students to respond.

- **3** Put students into pairs. Read aloud Activity 3 on page 95. Tell pairs to discuss ideas about why bands mix modern and traditional music. When students have finished, ask them to share their ideas and whether they think these mash-ups are a good idea.

VOCABULARY

Objectives
Students will
- use new vocabulary to discuss Josh Ponte's trip to Gabon.
- use a vocabulary strategy to learn new vocabulary.

Target Vocabulary *combine, download, electronic, hit*

Content Vocabulary *astonishing, crew, producer, tango*

Vocabulary Strategy

Resources Online Workbook/Workbook pages 56–57; Worksheet 1.6.2 (Teacher's Resource CD-ROM/ Website); Tracks 076–077 (Audio CD/ Website/CPT); CPT: Vocabulary

Materials map of the world or globe, pieces of card, set of classroom dictionaries

---

4 **Read and write the words from the list.** Make any necessary changes.

cool	edit	fan	include	mix
opinion	performing	record	recording	traditional

Filmmaker and music producer Josh Ponte travelled to communities in Gabon to _____ **record** _____ a film. He focused on _____ **traditional** _____ Gabonese music and dance. The journey was difficult for Josh. 'It was nuts,' he said. Josh had that _____ **opinion** _____ because on the trip he and his crew had excellent equipment, but no water and little food. In the end, Josh made more than 100 hours of _____ **recordings** _____ . These _____ **included** _____ music, interviews and people _____ **performing** _____ traditional dances. Josh then _____ **edited** _____ the videos to create a very _____ **cool** _____ film called *Gabon: The Last Dance*. 'I hope to show where Gabon is today, in a changing world, with this astonishing music at its heart,' said Josh.

Josh Ponte filming Gabonese musicians

5 **LEARN NEW WORDS** Listen to these words and match them to their definitions. Then listen and repeat. 🔊 076 077

combine	download	electronic	hit

_____ **combine** _____   1. put two or more things together

_____ **hit** _____   2. something successful (such as a song or a film)

_____ **download** _____   3. put something onto a computer

_____ **electronic** _____   4. using electricity to produce something

6 **YOU DECIDE** **Choose an activity.**

1. **Work independently.** Interview three classmates. Find out their favourite musicians and whether any of them mix different styles of music. Report your findings to the class.

2. **Work in pairs.** Research the bands mentioned in the lesson and listen to their music. Which band's music did you like best? Which did you like least? Discuss your responses.

3. **Work in groups.** What are some traditional instruments in your country? What musical instrument from your country do you think would be good to mix with modern music? Share your ideas with the class.

96 VOCABULARY

- **4** Ask students to turn to page 96. Point to the photo. Tell students that Josh Ponte is a filmmaker who's helping to preserve, or save, traditional Gabonese music. Point out the West African country of Gabon on a map or globe.

- Tell students to read the words in the word box. Then say *Let's read a little about Josh Ponte.* Read aloud the first sentence of the Activity 4 text. Ask *What word from the box best fits the context of this sentence?* Model for students.

- **Think aloud** Say *It might be edit, but I think you would edit in a studio after a film has been made. Include and perform don't make sense. I'm pretty sure you can record a film, just like you can record music. I'll read the sentence with record and see if it makes sense.*

- Make sure students understand that they'll have to change the form of some of the words to fit the sentences in the paragraph. When students have finished, ask several to come up to the front of the class and read the completed paragraph aloud. Review the answers as a class.

- **5 LEARN NEW WORDS** Read the words in the word box. Say *You saw these words on page 94. Listen for them as you hear about a band that plays a new style of tango music.* Play **Track 076**. Ask students to complete the activity. Play **Track 077**. Tell students to listen and repeat.

- **Vocabulary Strategy** Point to the word *hit* and read the definition aloud. Ask *Does anyone know another meaning of* hit? (to strike) Tell students that *hit* is a multiple-meaning word. Ask *Can you think of other words that have more than one meaning?* (cool, fan, mix) Write the following on the board:

> The instructions say to <u>mix</u> water and flour in a bowl.
>
> DJs <u>mix</u> recordings to create new music.

- Read the two sentences aloud. Say *Check the meanings of* mix *in the dictionary. When you look up a word, you must read through all of the definitions to find the meaning that fits with the context of what you're reading.*

Apply ⑥

- **6 YOU DECIDE** Tell students to look at Activity 6. For those students who want to do interviews, say *Write down your interview questions and make sure you ask each classmate the same ones. Remember to take notes on your classmates' responses so you can report them to the class.*

- Tell pairs who pick the second option that they can research WagakkiBand, Gokh-Bi System, or Bajofondo. Make sure students who pick the third option have some familiarity with traditional instruments. Set aside time for students to share their work.

Extend

- Put students into pairs and ask them to write a sales pitch to persuade Josh Ponte to record their band. Say *Your band does mash-ups of traditional and modern music. Tell Josh that you want to preserve traditional music. What will you say to convince him?* Invite pairs to share their pitches.

- If time allows, hand out **Worksheet 1.6.2**. Students will use new vocabulary to write about and discuss musical mash-ups.

Consolidate

- Write these words on pieces of card, one to a card: *audio, cool, DJ, fan, hit, electronic, mash-up, opinion, recording, song* and *video*. Then write these words on the board: *combine, create, download, edit, include, mix, perform,* and *record*. Tell students to stand in a circle. Say *Let's play a game. We'll go around the circle. When it's your turn, use the word on your card in a sentence. Then try to mix the word on your card and a word from the board in a sentence!*

Vocabulary Strategy

Words with multiple meanings *Polysemy* is the association of one word with two or more distinct meanings. According to some estimates, more than 40 percent of English words have more than one meaning. If there is more than one definition in a dictionary, each one is numbered. When students find more than one entry or meaning for a word in the dictionary, tell them to check the parts of speech (usually abbreviated as *n., v., adj., adv., prep.*). The part of speech can be a clue to choosing the right definition.

Make sure students understand that the first meaning listed in the dictionary is not always the best meaning. If a definition doesn't seem right, they need to read each of the other definitions, try them out, and find the one that best matches the context of what they're reading or writing.

Formative Assessment

Can students

- use new vocabulary related to music mash-ups and two bands known for their mash-up styles?

Ask *How do DJs create mash-ups?*

Students should use at least two of the following words in their answers: *mix, combine, audio, edit, song, record, recording, electronic.*

- use new vocabulary to discuss Josh Ponte's trip to Gabon?

Ask students to use the words *record* and *traditional* in a sentence explaining why Josh Ponte went to Gabon.

Workbook For additional practice, assign Workbook pages 56–57.

Online Workbook Vocabulary

VOCABULARY PRACTICE **177**

SPEAKING STRATEGY

Objectives
Students will
- make points.
- use phrases to help clarify points.

Speaking Strategy Clarifying a point

Academic Language *clarifying, fiction, non-fiction, point, science fiction*

Content Vocabulary *bizarre, borrow, carnivorous, dwellers, liger*

Pronunciation Linking: Consonant + vowel sounds

Resources Online Workbook; Worksheet 1.6.3 (Teacher's Resource CD-ROM/Website); Tracks 078–079, Tracks 131–133 (Audio CD/Website/CPT); Pronunciation Answer Key (Teacher's Resource CD-ROM/Website); CPT: Speaking Strategy and Pronunciation

Materials drawing materials

SPEAKING STRATEGY ∩ 078
Clarifying a point

Point	Clarification
I really like fiction.	I mean, <u>I love reading made-up stories</u>.
I enjoy reading non-fiction books.	In other words, <u>I like books that teach me something new</u>.
I'm reading a book of myths.	That is, <u>I'm reading a story that's fiction but that many people believe is true</u>.

1 **Listen.** How do the speakers clarify their points? Write the phrases you hear. ∩ 079

A liger

2 **Read and complete the dialogue.**

Luisa: Rob, I'm reading a bizarre book. *Possible answers*
_____ I mean _____, it's really strange.

Rob: Really? What's it about?

Luisa: Well, the author combines a romance novel with science fiction.
_____ In other words _____, the story mixes a love story with strange things that don't exist!

Rob: Wow! Are there monsters from outer space in the story?

Luisa: No, they're all ocean dwellers. _____ That is _____, they live in the sea. Like angry sharks and evil, carnivorous jellyfish. _____ In other words _____, the jellyfish eat meat ... and by meat, I mean people!

Rob: Is it required reading? _____ I mean _____, are you reading it for school?

Luisa: No, the books I read for school are never this strange!

Rob: Good! Let me borrow it when you've finished.

3 **Work in groups.** Cut out the cards and put them in a pile. Take turns choosing two cards. Make a mash-up of the two items. Draw and describe your idea. Get a point for each successful mash-up. If you can't make one, lose a turn.

> I'm making a 'biscar'. In other words, I'm mixing a biscuit with a car. The car has got four giant biscuits as wheels!

car   biscuit

4 **Work in pairs.** Choose a book or film you both like. Then create a mash-up with another type of story. Tell your new story idea to another pair, clarifying your points.

Go to page 165.

SPEAKING **97**

Warm Up

- **Activate prior knowledge** Point to a student and ask *(Marcia), have you ever used a new word when talking to a friend and he/she looked at you in a funny way, like he/she didn't understand what you said?* Invite the student to respond. Ask *So, (Marcia), what would you do to make your friend understand?* Prompt the student to say that she might use simpler words to explain what she meant. Model an example if necessary.

Present **1**

- Say *When you say something in a simpler or clearer way, it's called clarifying.* Write *clarifying* on the board and ask students to repeat the word. Explain that it's a form of the verb *clarify*, or 'make clear'.

- Ask students to open their books at page 97. Read aloud the speaking strategy title. Ask three students to stand and read the points on the left side of the

- table, one at a time. Tell them to remain standing. Then tell students to look at the right side of the box. Tell them that *clarification* is the noun form of *clarify*. Then say to the standing students *Repeat your point and then follow it with the clarification.*

- Say *Let's listen to other people making points and clarifying them.* Play **Track 078**. Then write *I mean, In other words,* and *That is* on the board. Explain that these phrases are a signal that you're going to repeat what you said in a simpler way. Tell students that the underlined words in the table are the easier words used to clarify. Ask *What is fiction?* (made-up stories) *What is non-fiction?* (writing that is factual or tells of real events) *What's a myth?* (a fiction story that was originally told to explain a belief or natural event)

- **1** Point to the photo of a liger. Say *Now listen to a conversation about animals which are a mixture of two animals or 'hybrids'.* Gesture to the board. Say *Listen for these phrases. Write them down when you hear them.* Play **Track 079**. Review the answers together.

Practise

- Direct students to Activity 2. Say *Here's another conversation. Read each person's words first. Then use the clarifying phrases we've heard and talked about to fill in the gaps.* Invite students to come to the front of the class and read their completed dialogues aloud, taking turns as Luisa and Rob. Point out that there's no one correct phrase to use.

Apply

- Tell students to cut out the cards on page 165 in the Student's Books. Put students into groups and hand out drawing materials, if necessary. Read the Activity 9 instructions aloud. Tell each group to use one set of cards. Then ask a student to read the speech bubble. Say *You must name your mash-up, clarify it and then draw it!* Students review the instructions. Then say *Ready? Begin. Play until everyone gets three points.* When students have finished, tell each group to display the best mash-ups.

- Put students into pairs. Read the instructions. Give students examples to clarify what an appropriate mash-up would be, such as a science fiction story that is also a folktale, or a comedy mashed up with a war story. Say *Decide on your mash-up. Then share your story idea with another pair. Clarify your points.*

Extend

- Write the sentences below on the board. Put students into pairs. Say *Take turns clarifying the sentences to each other.*

> A T-shirt and shorts are like a uniform at my school.
>
> People are sea turtles' biggest predators.
>
> My parents' favourite music is totally uncool!
>
> WagakkiBand is an interesting musical mash-up.

- If time allows, hand out **Worksheet 1.6.3**. Explain that students will use the worksheet to practise clarifying and asking for clarification.

Consolidate

- Write the following on the board:

> | | | | |
> |---|---|---|---|
> | Bajofondo | DJs | Gokh-Bi System | hybrids |
> | mash-ups | mixing | traditional music | WagakkiBand |

- Put students into small groups. Tell students to take turns to make a point that includes a word, phrase or name on the board and then clarify it, using the phrases they've learnt. Appoint a captain for each group. Say *Put your hand up when you're ready. The captain will call your name. Everyone needs to take a turn. Help one another and point out mistakes politely.* Circulate and observe group interactions.

Strategy in Depth

Phrases to check understanding and clarify meaning are important examples of functional language for your students to learn, particularly for classroom communication and test-taking. Tell students that being aware of body language and facial expressions will help them recognise that clarification is needed (*e.g.* 'I can see from your face that I haven't explained myself well'.).

Other phrases to help students clarify include the following:

> *What I mean is …*
> *To put it another way …*
> *To put it differently …*
> *What I'm trying to say is …*
> *What I wanted to say was …*
> *To clarify …*

Pronunciation

Go to Student's Book page 146. Use Audio Tracks 131–133.

Linking: Consonant + vowel sounds Students of many language backgrounds have difficulty saying final consonant sounds. Often, they drop the sound(s) altogether, making it difficult for listeners to understand them. Or they overemphasise the final consonant sound and pause too much between words in a sentence, which makes it difficult for listeners to follow what they are saying. Teaching students to link a final consonant to a vowel can help them speak more naturally. Explain that students should think of the consonant sound as the first sound of the next word.

Who i<u>s i</u>t?	=	Who i zit?
I gi<u>ve u</u>p.	=	I gi vup.
body o<u>f a</u> lion	=	body o va lion

Formative Assessment

Can students

- make a point?

  Say *Imagine you're with a friend. Make a point about mash-ups in general or one kind of mash-up in particular.*

- use phrases to help clarify a point?

  Say *You can tell your friend doesn't understand what you mean. How would you clarify your point?*

SPEAKING STRATEGY **179**

Objectives

Students will

- use adjectives to compare two or more things.
- use words associated with hybrid sports.

Grammar Adjectives: Comparing two or more things

Target Vocabulary create, hate, hybrid, love, version

Academic Language comparative, modify, syllable

Content Vocabulary boxing, bucket, cheaper, disc, expensive, golf, handball, hockey, metal, regular, rugby, snowboarding, volcano

Resources Online Workbook/Workbook pages 58–59; Tracks 080–083 (Audio CD/Website/CPT); CPT: Grammar 1

Materials pieces of card, photos of sports mentioned in the lesson *(optional)*

GRAMMAR 🔊 080

Adjectives: Comparing two or more things

Underwater hockey is a **newer** version of field hockey.
Underwater hockey is **more difficult than** field hockey.
Chess boxing is **less tiring than** boxing.
Chess boxing is **noisier than** regular chess.
The rules of boxing are **simpler / more simple than** those of chess boxing.
Ice football isn't **as popular as** traditional football.
Some fans like ice football **better than** traditional football.

hard → harder	simple → simpler
(*but* fun → more fun)	or more simple
noisy → noisier	difficult → more difficult

Bossaball is played on a blow-up court with trampolines.

1 **Listen.** Tick the words you hear. Then write the comparative form of each ticked word. 🔊 081

☐ fast _____

☑ unusual ___more unusual than___

☑ easy _____easier_____

☐ exciting _____

☑ active ___more active___

☑ hard _____harder_____

☐ cool _____

☑ enjoyable ___more enjoyable___

☑ fun ___as fun as___

☑ good _____better_____

2 **Read.** Complete the sentences with the correct comparative form.

1. Kronum is _____newer than_____ (+/new) bossaball, but it's _____as unusual as_____ (=/unusual) bossaball.

2. It's _____more difficult_____ (+/difficult) to play than bossaball because it's a mix of football, basketball, handball and rugby.

3. The special kronum ball is _____smaller than_____ (+/small) a football.

4. Kronum isn't played all over the world yet, so it's _____less popular than_____ (–/popular) bossaball.

3 **Work in pairs.** Make a list of your five favourite sports. Then share your list with your partner. Make comparisons between those sports.

> Football is more exciting than baseball.

98 GRAMMAR

Warm Up

- **Activate prior knowledge** Say *You know that adjectives are words we use to describe things. They modify, or tell us more about, nouns and pronouns.* Write these two sentences on the board: *The old musician performed traditional songs. He was talented and funny, with a beautiful, deep voice.*

- Point to the underlined words and say *The adjectives in these sentences tell us what kind of songs the musician played* (traditional). *They describe some of his characteristics* (old, talented, funny), *and they appeal to our sense of hearing* (beautiful, deep). *With these words and a little help from your imagination, you can almost see and hear the musician in your mind.*

Present

- Say *We also use adjectives to compare two things.* Cut out two circles – one large red one and one larger blue one. Hold up the red one and say *The red circle is big.* Hold up the other one next to it

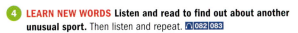

4 LEARN NEW WORDS Listen and read to find out about another **unusual sport.** Then listen and repeat. 🎧 082 083

Do you **hate** how expensive it is to play golf? Try disc golf instead – it's a cheaper **version** of golf. Disc golf is a **hybrid** sport. People **created** it using ideas from golf and disc-throwing. Now it's very popular. Many players **love** it!

5 Work in pairs. Read about the hybrid sport volcano boarding. Circle the correct words.

1. Daryn Webb (created)/ *loved* volcano boarding because he wanted something more exciting than sandboarding.

2. Volcano boarding is a newer *version* /(hybrid) sport than sandboarding.

3. Volcano boarding is a more dangerous (version)/ *hybrid* of sandboarding.

4. Some people (love)/ *hate* volcano boarding because it's more fun and more extreme than many other hybrid sports.

5. Other people *love* /(hate) this sport because the ride down is noisier and less comfortable than sandboarding.

6 Work in groups. Compare the hybrid sports you read about (and any others you know) to traditional sports.

> Football tennis seems fun. It's a hybrid of football and tennis. It's more fun to watch than regular tennis.

GRAMMAR **99**

BE THE EXPERT

Grammar in Depth

In comparatives with *more/less*, the focus is on how the two parts of the comparison are different. In comparative sentences with *as ... as ...*, the focus is on how the two parts of the comparison are similar or equal. The negative (*not as ... as ...*) implies a difference between the two parts.

Here are some rules for forming comparatives:

- With adjectives of three or more syllables, always use *more/less*.
- One-syllable adjectives use *-er*. Double the consonant in one-syllable adjectives that follow the consonant-vowel-consonant format, as in *big* → *bigger*. With one-syllable adjectives ending in a consonant and *e*, just add *r*, as in *nice* → *nicer*.
- With adjectives of two syllables ending in *y*, both forms are possible, but remember to change *y* to *i* if using the *-er* form.

Teaching Tip

When practising new grammar structures, write an example sentence on the board. Remind students to compare their work to the example as they speak or write. As you review their work, point out similarities between it and the example. If something needs to be corrected, help students to use the example to make corrections.

---

and ask *What would you say to compare the sizes of the two circles?* If necessary, prompt students to answer *The blue circle is bigger than the red circle.* Write the following sentences on the board:

The red circle is <u>big</u>.	The blue circle is <u>bigger than</u> the red circle.
The musician played a <u>fast</u> song.	Then he played a <u>faster</u> song.
David Beckham was a <u>talented</u> player.	Is Cristiano Ronaldo <u>more talented</u>?

- Ask individual students to stand up and to read aloud each pair of sentences. Ask each student *What's being compared?* (circles, songs, people/football players) Point to the adjectives on the right side of the board and say *These are all ways we can compare two things with adjectives. Because we're comparing, these are called comparative forms.*

adjectives, such as simple.

- Say *Look at* difficult. *Pronounce the three syllables to yourself. This is an easy rule to remember! When an adjective has three or more syllables, you always use the words more or less to form the comparative.*

Practise ① ② ③

- Point to the photo on page 98. Read the caption. Say *Bossaball is a combination of several things, including music!* Make sure students understand what a trampoline is and how you can bounce on it. Say *Before we hear about bossaball, let's do a review.* Write the following on the board and go over it with the class. Then call students to come to the board and replace the underlined phrases in the examples with different comparatives. Provide some adjectives if necessary (e.g. *easy, serious, athletic, quick, lively*).

To show **difference**, use *more ... than, less ... than*, or *(hard)-er than*. Bossaball is **more fun than** football.	To show **equality**, use *as ... as*. Bossaball players are **as active as** football players.

- ① Read the Activity 1 instructions. Tell students to tick the adjectives they hear in their *non*-comparative forms. Then write the comparative phrases they hear. Say *Just like verbs, some adjectives have irregular forms. You're going to hear one. It's the adjective* good. *See if you recognise the comparative form.* Then play **Track 081** while students listen. If necessary, play the track a second time. Review the answers as a class. Tell students that besides *good/better,* another common irregular adjective and its comparative form is *bad/worse.*

- ② Say *Now you'll read about another mash-up sport called kronum.* Read the Activity 2 instructions. Point out the symbols and words in brackets. Say *The word is the adjective you'll use. A plus sign means you use the word* more *or an -er form, and a minus sign means you use the word* less. Ask *What do you think the equals sign after the second gap in item 1 means?* (equality, use *as unusual as*) Ask students to do the activity. Review the answers together.

- ③ Tell students to read the Activity 3 instructions and make their lists. Then put students into pairs. Say *Take turns making comparisons. And remember to be helpful and polite!* Circulate as students work and provide assistance where necessary.

- Tell students to turn to the person next to them. Say *Take turns comparing things.* Give examples: *My hair is longer than your hair. Your pencil is smaller than mine. A tablet is bigger than a mobile phone. Your backpack is cooler than mine.*

- Ask students to open their books at page 98 and look at the grammar box. Read the heading. Say *These sentences are about sports.* You may want to show pictures of the named sports or invite students to say what they know about different kinds of hockey and boxing. Then say *Follow in your books as we listen.* Play **Track 080**.

- Say *I never knew there were such sports. Did you?* Ask students to stand up and read each pair of sentences. Ask them to say what's being compared in each one. Point out the oblique in the fifth sentence. Tell students that it means that either comparative form is correct.

- Say *Let's talk about the different forms of comparative adjectives.* Tell students to focus on the table at the bottom of the grammar box. Say *We use different forms depending on how the adjective is spelt and how many syllables it has.* Remind students that a syllable is a word part with one vowel sound. Go over the number of syllables in *hard, fun, noisy, simple,* and *difficult.* Say *Look at* hard/harder. *You add -er to the end of many one-syllable adjectives to form the comparative.* Explain that not every one-syllable adjective follows this rule. Point out *fun.* Tell students that they just have to memorise some comparative forms.

- Say *Look at* noisy/noisier. *When a two-syllable adjective ends in a consonant(s) and* y, *you change the* y *to* i *and add -er to form the comparative. However, you can also use the words* more *or* less *with two-syllable adjectives ending in* y, *as well as with other two-syllable*

Apply

- **4** **LEARN NEW WORDS** Point to the photo on page 99. Ask *What's the girl tossing?* Students may say it's a Frisbee. Tell them it's more properly called a disc or a flying disc, and that a disc is any flat, circular object. Say *Let's listen and learn some new words.* Play **Track 082**. Then play **Track 083**. Tell students to listen and repeat.

- **5** Put students into pairs. Ask *What's a hybrid sport?* (a combination/mix/mash-up of two or more sports) Say *That's correct, but* hybrid *can also be used to describe combinations of other things. There are hybrid plants and hybrid cows, for example.* Read the activity instructions aloud. Say *Use your understanding of the new words to make correct sentences.* Ask students to stand up and read the completed sentences. Ask *Why do you think volcano boarding might be dangerous?*

- **6** Put students into small groups. Read the activity instructions aloud. Say *Make a list of all of the hybrid sports we've read and heard about. Add others you may know. Then talk to one another.* Read the speech bubble as an example. Say *Describe a hybrid sport. Say what you think about it. Use comparatives.* Circulate to make sure everyone gets a chance to contribute to the discussion.

Extend

- Put students into pairs. Ask them to research one of the hybrid sports they talked about and then work together to write a short paragraph about the history of the sport – who invented it, where it was developed, and what the rules for playing it are. When pairs have finished, tell to them share their research with the class.

Consolidate

- Write these topics on pieces of card, one to a card: *art mash-up, music mash-up, sport mash-up, WagakkiBand, hybrid animals,* and *Wild Card: mash-up of your choice.* Make enough cards to give one to each student. Say *Think about your topic. Think of examples of it or facts about it.* While students think, write these vocabulary items on the board:

Group 1		Group 2	
mix	hybrid	love	cool
combine	version	hate	fan
create		opinion	

- Say *Write sentences about your topic, using a word from Group 1 in each sentence.* Give students a few minutes to write. Then tell them to stand in a circle. Say *When it's your turn, say a sentence to the person next to you. That person responds with a sentence that includes a word from Group 2. A third student then says a new sentence with a Group 1 word, and so on around the circle.* Repeat until all the topics on the cards have been used. Tell students that they can change the form of the words in both groups. Answer any questions students may have.

Teaching Tip

Be careful not to jump in too early or provide an answer if a student struggles with an activity. It's a natural response to want to help, but a challenge is sometimes necessary for learning something new. Adults and students alike often try harder when they're faced with something that is not easy. Students also gain confidence when they succeed at a challenging task.

Formative Assessment

Can students

- use adjectives to compare two or more things?

  Ask students to use a comparative adjective to compare a hybrid sport to another sport.

- use words associated with hybrid sports?

  Ask students to complete this sentence frame with the correct word in brackets:

  It seems there's a new _____ sport created every year! (version, <u>hybrid</u>)

Workbook For additional practice, assign Workbook pages 58–59.

Online Workbook Grammar 1

Objectives
Students will
- read about and discuss examples of food art.
- use new words from the reading.
- visualise artwork.

Reading Strategy Visualise

Target Vocabulary *imagine, imitate, modern, original, weird*

Vocabulary Strategy Context clues

Academic Language *represent, visualise*

Content Vocabulary *feast, landscape, portrait, scolded, stalk*

Resources Online Workbook/Workbook pages 60–61; Worksheet 1.6.4 (Teacher's Resource CD-ROM/ Website); Tracks 084–085 (Audio CD/ Website/CPT); CPT: Reading

Materials art materials, coloured pencils, pieces of fruit or vegetables in different shapes and colours *(optional)*

A Feast
FOR THE
Eyes

Using food to create art

We've all seen art created from paint, clay, metal and stone. But British photographer and artist Carl Warner goes to the supermarket to buy his art supplies. Carl creates what he calls *foodscapes*. He combines different types of food to imitate real landscapes. Then he photographs them. One of his foodscapes, *Carts and Balloons*, is a countryside scene. In this foodscape a few leafy green stalks of broccoli are a forest. A few pieces of bread

1 BEFORE YOU READ Discuss in pairs. Describe the most unusual piece of art you've seen. What did you like about it? What didn't you like about it?

2 LEARN NEW WORDS Find these words in the reading. What do you think they mean? Notice examples that give their meaning. Then listen and repeat. 🎧 084

| imagine | imitate | modern | original | weird |

3 WHILE YOU READ Try to visualise, or see a picture in your mind, the artwork being described. 🎧 085

4 AFTER YOU READ Work in pairs to answer the questions.

1. What's a foodscape?
2. How did Carl create the landscape you see above?
3. Why does Carl create foodscapes?
4. Who asked Giuseppe Arcimboldo to paint his portrait?
5. Why did Giuseppe call the portrait *Vertumnus*?

100 READING

Warm Up

- **Build background** Say *Were you ever scolded by your parents because you were playing with your food?* Talk about how some young children push food around on their plates, or even make designs or faces with it, when they don't want to eat. Then ask *Has anyone ever seen pictures or other objects made with food?* Tell students to share what they know about food art. Then say *Let's think about food, especially uncooked food and foods with different shapes and colours. Name some.*

- Start a table like the one shown below. Ask students to help you fill in examples for each category.

Food	Colour	Shape
tomatoes	red	round
banana	yellow	long and curved
broccoli	green	treelike

Celery Island by Carl Warner

are used to make a cart. There are some berries in the cart and some potatoes as rocks. Some yellow sweetcorn and a few cucumbers are the fields. Hot-air balloons, made from bunches of bananas and other fruit, float in the sky. Some clouds of white bread float in the sky, too. It might seem a little weird to create art out of food, but Carl hopes that his work will get children excited about eating healthy foods.

Combining food and art is not a modern idea. Giuseppe Arcimboldo, a 16th-century Italian painter, also combined different types of food to create original art. In 1590, Emperor Rudolf II asked Giuseppe to paint his portrait. The result was really unusual! Called *Vertumnus*, after the Roman god of fruit, the painting shows a face made of fruit, vegetables and flowers. Giuseppe painted one pea pod for each top eyelid, two baby onions for each bottom eyelid, one grape for each eye, a pear for the nose, an apple for one cheek and a peach for the other. Can you imagine what the emperor's face looked like? Luckily, the emperor was happy with this unusual portrait!

 Work in pairs. You read about two pieces of food art in the reading: the foodscape *Carts and Balloons* and the portrait *Vertumnus*. Choose one of the pieces to draw. Draw your pictures individually, and then compare your work. How are the pictures similar? How are they different?

 Discuss in groups.

1. Imagine you're creating a piece of food art. What picture do you make? What foods do you use to make it?

2. What problems do you think food artists have when they work? Name two or three.

3. Imagine you're an artist. What everyday things (other than food) could you use to create art? What would you create with those things?

4. Do you think combining food and art is a good idea? Why or why not?

READING **101**

• As you fill in the table, challenge students to think of things the shape of a food reminds them of. If you've brought in any food, hold it up for students to see. Ask *What does a stalk of broccoli or celery look like?* (tree, bush) *A potato or a red bean?* (rock, pebble) *What about a pear, a carrot or a loaf of bread?* Add descriptions to the table. When students' imaginations are engaged, tell them to make a quick drawing of something familiar made out of food.

Before You Read ① ②

• Ask students to open their books at pages 100–101. Invite a student to read the title and subtitle of the reading. Say *Look at the picture and read the caption. What foods can you see?* Ask students to come up to the front of the class and identify different foods they can see in the picture. Then ask what they think of the picture. When students have answered, ask *What do you think the reading will be about?* (pictures made with food) Tell students to close their books.

The image shows a reproduction of the student book pages 100–101, titled "A Feast for the Eyes / Using food to create art" with a landscape image made of food, activity boxes for Before You Read, Learn New Words, While You Read, After You Read, Work in pairs, and Discuss in groups.

- Point out the following sentence part on page 101: *It might seem a little weird to create art out of food.* Say *These words say that creating art out of food seems weird. Knowing that making a painting with food is not the usual way to create art helps you understand that weird probably means 'strange' or 'unusual'.*

While You Read

- Say *Now we're going to listen to A Feast for the Eyes. As you read the descriptions of the artwork, visualise the two pictures. In other words, try to see them in your mind.* Play **Track 085** and tell students to follow.

- Ask *What was the most interesting or surprising thing you read?* Discuss the reading. Ask *Do you think creating art with food is a good way to get children more interested in eating fruits and vegetables?* Play **Track 085** again or allow students to read in silence.

After You Read

- **4** Put students into pairs. Ask pairs to read and answer the questions. If they disagree on an answer, tell them to read the text again and find information that supports their answer. Review the answers as a class.

- Find the two works of art described in *A Feast for the Eyes* online and let students look at them. Discuss with the class whether what they visualised in their minds as they read the descriptions of the two pictures matches the original art. Ask *Does what you visualised match the originals quite well? A little bit? Not at all?*

- **5** Ask pairs to read the instructions for Activity 5. Tell them to re-read the descriptions of the artworks in the reading. Then invite students to make their choice. Make sure pairs understand that they each have to draw the same picture. Give students time to draw. Then tell partners to compare and discuss. Ask *What did you both draw that was the same? What's most different about your versions?*

- **6** Put students into small groups to discuss the Activity 6 questions. Appoint group secretaries to keep the discussions moving and take notes on the group's important points or ideas. Say *Anyone can ask speakers to clarify their points if they don't understand something.* When students have finished, ask different groups to come to the front of the class and share their ideas on one of the four discussion topics.

- **1** Say *That picture is quite unusual, isn't it?* Ask *What's the most unusual piece of art you've ever seen?* Put students into pairs to discuss the question. Provide prompts, if necessary. Ask *Was it a painting, photograph, or sculpture? A tattoo, maybe? Is it in your home or in a museum? Did you see it in a book or on a TV programme?* Finally, say *Tell your partner what you liked or didn't like about it.*

- **2** LEARN NEW WORDS Read aloud the words in the Activity 2 box. Say *One way to work out the meaning of an unfamiliar word is to look at the words around it. They might be clues to the word's meaning.* Ask *What's this strategy called?* (using context clues) *Let's do the first word together.* Tell students to find *imagine* at the end of the reading.

- **Think aloud** Say *Looking around the word* imagine, *I see it's part of a question asking what the emperor's face looked like. In the sentences before this one, there's a description of a painting of the face made with fruits and vegetables. But there's no photo of the painting, so I can only picture it in my mind. I think that's what* imagine *means—to form a picture of something in your mind.*

- Ask students to use context clues to infer the meanings of the other words in the box. Go over the words with students. Finally, play **Track 084**. Tell students to listen and repeat.

- **Vocabulary Strategy** Explain to students that one type of context clue is an example included in a text to represent an idea. Say, for instance, *Disc golf is not the definition of* hybrid sport, *but it is an example of one. It represents the idea of what a hybrid sport is.* Ask *What example can you find in the reading that might represent the idea of* weird?

Extend

- Ask students to choose one of the four topics listed below based on Activity 6 and write their own ideas about it, taking into consideration their group discussion as well as what they heard about their classmates' ideas. Say *Write a paragraph that identifies the topic and describes or summarises your ideas about it.*

Topics
1. Describe a food picture you would like to create. Draw a rough sketch of it.

2. Explain the two biggest problems faced by food artists.

3. Describe a piece of art you would like to create out of everyday things, not including food.

4. Explain why combining food and art is or isn't a good idea.

- **Worksheet** If time allows, you may want to hand out **Worksheet 1.6.4** in class. Students will use the worksheet to practise the new vocabulary items.

Consolidate

- Review the five new vocabulary items: *imagine, imitate, modern, original* and *weird.* Then ask the questions below one at a time. Say *Put your hand up to answer a question. I'll ask you to stand up and give your answer.* Try to get an answer from every student in the class.

---

1. <u>Imagine</u> a new kind of mash-up. What would it be?
2. Of all the different kinds of mash-ups and artwork we've learnt about so far, which one would you most like to <u>imitate</u>? Why?
3. What's the most <u>modern</u> or <u>original</u> idea you've learnt about in the unit so far? Explain.
4. What's the <u>weirdest</u> thing you've learnt about in the unit so far? Explain.

BE THE EXPERT

Teaching Tip

Make reasonable accommodations for students' different learning styles. Remember that some students who are not verbally fluent may be better able to express themselves through different means, such as art or movement. Give those students a chance to show their abilities. For example, if a student prefers not to speak, let him or her demonstrate a response or share a drawing without speaking.

Answer Key

Comprehension

1. A landscape made out of food
2. He combined different foods to look like a landscape of islands. Then he photographed it.
3. To get children excited about eating healthy foods.
4. Emperor Rudolf II
5. He named it after the Roman god of fruit.

Formative Assessment

Can students
- discuss examples of food art?

  Ask students to describe how Carl Warner creates his foodscapes.
- use new words from the reading?

  Ask students to choose the correct words in brackets to fill in the gaps:

  I think _____ (a modern, an <u>original</u>) piece of art is better than a copy, even if it's _____. (<u>weird</u>, cool)
- visualise artwork?

  Ask students to describe how their visualisations of *Cart and Balloons* or *Vertumnus* compared to the original.

Workbook For additional practice, assign Workbook pages 60–61.

Online Workbook Reading

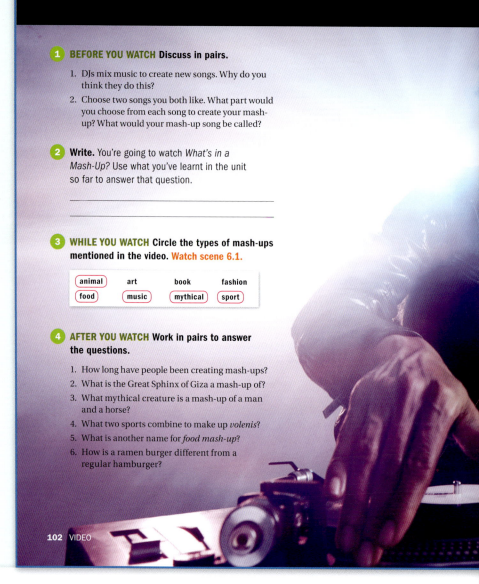

VIDEO

Objectives
Students will
- discuss old and new mash-ups.
- apply the message of the video to their personal lives.

Content Vocabulary *dubstep, fusion, Great Sphinx of Giza*

Resources Video scene 6.1 (DVD/Website/CPT); Online Workbook; CPT: Video

---

1 BEFORE YOU WATCH Discuss in pairs.

1. DJs mix music to create new songs. Why do you think they do this?
2. Choose two songs you both like. What part would you choose from each song to create your mash-up? What would your mash-up song be called?

2 Write. You're going to watch *What's in a Mash-Up?* Use what you've learnt in the unit so far to answer that question.

_____

_____

3 WHILE YOU WATCH Circle the types of mash-ups mentioned in the video. Watch scene 6.1.

animal	art	book	fashion
food	music	mythical	sport

4 AFTER YOU WATCH Work in pairs to answer the questions.

1. How long have people been creating mash-ups?
2. What is the Great Sphinx of Giza a mash-up of?
3. What mythical creature is a mash-up of a man and a horse?
4. What two sports combine to make up *volenis*?
5. What is another name for *food mash-up*?
6. How is a ramen burger different from a regular hamburger?

102 VIDEO

BEFORE YOU WATCH

- **Revise:** Ask *How do DJs create mash-ups?* (They mix sounds from different songs to make a new recording.) Tell students to open their books at pages 102–103 and look at the photo. Say *This DJ is mixing.* Ask *Can anyone name the equipment in the photo?* Point to the headphones the DJ is wearing, the turntable and record and the mixer.

- Ask *Does anyone know what the DJ is doing with his right hand on the turntable?* (scratching) Explain that *scratching* means moving a record back and forth on a turntable to produce a scratchy kind of sound. If possible, let students listen to scratching sound effects. You can find examples online.

- **1** Put students into pairs. Read aloud the Activity 1 questions and ask pairs to discuss. When they've finished, tell pairs to share the name of their mash-up song and the songs they would use to create it.

- **2** Read Activity 2 aloud. Tell students to write their answers. Make sure they understand they're writing an answer to the question *What's in a mash-up?* Ask students to stand up and share their answers. Ask the class to come to a consensus on what the best answer is.

While You Watch

- **3** Draw students' attention to Activity 3. Read the instructions aloud. Then invite students to read the words in the box. Say *This video is about different kinds of mash-ups. Circle each kind you hear about. Now let's watch.* Play **Video scene 6.1**. Ask students to stand up and say what they circled.

- If students have trouble following the video or understanding the text, pause the video and allow them to ask questions. Try replaying the video with and without sound, and ask students to describe and comment on what they see.

188 UNIT 6

5 **Work in pairs.** Of all the mash-ups you've learnt about so far, which is the most interesting? The least interesting? Explain your answers.

6 **Discuss in groups.**

1. At the end of the video, you're asked, 'What would you mash up?' Discuss your answers to this question.
2. Give another example of a mash-up from history. Describe it and its individual parts.
3. What do you think might be difficult in creating a mash-up? Consider art, food and music mash-ups in your answer.

A DJ can create a mash-up by mixing music.

7 **YOU DECIDE** **Choose an activity.**

1. **Work independently.** Imagine you're a centaur. How does it help you? What's difficult about it? Write a paragraph to explain.
2. **Work in pairs.** Think of a mash-up you know. Create an advertisement for it. Describe what it's made of and what's special about it. Present your advert to the class.
3. **Work in groups.** In the video, you saw a historical mash-up, the Great Sphinx of Giza. Use the Internet to learn more about the Great Sphinx. Present the information to the class.

VIDEO **103**

Teaching Tip

Dividing up tasks is a good way for groups to complete projects and assignments more efficiently. Remind students to take a different task each time they work in groups. Check to be certain that the same student isn't always given a speaking or writing task.

Answer Key

Comprehension 4

1. Since ancient times
2. A lion's body and a human's head
3. A centaur
4. Volleyball and tennis
5. Fusion food
6. Instead of a bun, the meat is put between ramen noodles.

Formative Assessment

Can students
• discuss old and new mash-ups?

Ask *Do you think more recent mash-ups, such as hybrid sports, DJ mash-ups, or musical mash-ups will last for a long time? Explain your answer.*

Online Workbook Video

AFTER YOU WATCH

• 4 Put students into pairs. Tell them to write answers to the questions. Review the answers as a class. If students disagree about an answer, replay the video.

• 5 Read aloud the Activity 5 questions. Tell students they can take a few minutes to look in their books to refresh their memories about all the mash-ups they've read and heard about. Reply the video if necessary. Say *You were probably already familiar with some kinds of mash-ups, even though you may not have known that's what they're called. But what mash-ups really surprised you?* Invite pairs to discuss.

• 6 Put students into groups. Read aloud the Activity 6 topics. Say *We've talked a little about what mash-ups you might like to create, but the video has probably given you some new ideas.* Appoint a secretary for each group to manage the discussion.

• 7 **YOU DECIDE** Say *If you're interested in Greek myths and have a good imagination, option 1 is for you! Use lots of adjectives to describe your life, and use comparatives to show what's easier and harder for you than for other people.*

• Remind students that ads are meant to make someone want to try or buy something. Ask *How will your ad get people's attention?* Say *Think about using photos, drawings or other graphics in your ad.*

• Explain that the third option might be good for students who are interested in research and ancient history. Tell students they'll need to find out such information as when the Sphinx was built, who built it, what materials were used, what its purpose was, how big it is, what it looked like when it was first built, and how it has changed over the centuries.

GRAMMAR 2

Objective
Students will
- use countable and uncountable nouns to talk about amounts.

Grammar Countable and uncountable nouns: Talking about amounts

Academic Language *countable nouns, uncountable nouns*

Content Vocabulary *barbecue, cucumber, kimchi, mango, nachos, salsa, sweets, taco, tortilla*

Resources Online Workbook/Workbook pages 62–63; Worksheet 1.6.5 (Teacher's Resource CD-ROM/ Website); Track 086 (Audio CD/ Website/CPT); CPT: Grammar 2

GRAMMAR ∩ 086

Countable and uncountable nouns: Talking about amounts

Countable nouns	Uncountable nouns
A few / Some / A lot of / Many meals are a mix of food from different cultures.	**A little / Some / A lot of / Much** fruit is used in food from different cultures.
How many chefs **combine** foods from different cultures?	**How much** cheese **is** on a Japanese-Italian pizza?
Two / A few / Some / A lot of / Many chefs **combine** foods from different cultures.	**A little / Some / A lot of** cheese.
Restaurants usually have **a couple of / three / too many** special dishes.	Dessert sushi sometimes has **a piece of / some / too much** fruit in it.

1 **Work in pairs.** Choose the correct word or phrase to complete the sentences.

Maiza: We had _____some_____ (a few / some) delicious KoMex food last night.

Gabi: KoMex? In other words, Korean and Mexican food combined? Did they have Korean tacos?

Maiza: Yes, and _____a few_____ (much / a few) different kinds. I like beef tacos. Their tacos had _____a lot of_____ (a lot of / a few) Korean barbecue beef and _____a couple of_____ (a couple of / much) cucumber slices on fresh corn tortillas. Oh, and _____some_____ (some / many) great sauce, too.

Gabi: Mmm. Sounds good. How _____many_____ (much / many) tacos did you eat?

Maiza: Not too _____many_____ (many / much). I only had _____one_____ (one / a little) taco, but I had _____a lot of_____ (much / a lot of) nachos. They had Korean meat and mango salsa.

Gabi: Sounds great! And did you try _____some_____ (a couple of / some) kimchi rice?

Maiza: I only ate _____a little_____ (a few / a little). I was full!

KoMex food

2 **Work in groups.** Throw the cubes. Ask and answer questions about how people in the country eat or drink the item on the cube.

How much rice do you think people in Japan eat?

I think they eat a lot of rice.

104 GRAMMAR

Go to page 167.

Warm Up

- **Revise** Say *We're going to read about food mash-ups.* Ask *Does anyone remember another term for food mash-ups from the video?* (fusion food) Tell students that *fusion* is another word that means 'a combination of different things'.

- Say *When you combine different kinds of food – for example, when you cook – you have to think about amounts: a cup of rice, a teaspoon of salt, some cheese, a little sauce.*

Present

- Say *Nouns are naming words. Book, class, hunger, taco and sauce are all nouns, but they fall into different categories. The two categories are countable nouns and uncountable nouns.* Point out that you can count tacos ('I'll have one taco/two tacos'), but you can't count sauce. Ask *Instead of a saying a number, what could*

you say if you only wanted a small amount of sauce? (I'll have some sauce.) Say *Taco is a countable noun and sauce is an uncountable noun.*

- List some nouns on the board (e.g. *book, apple, shirt, fun, food* and *rice*). Ask students to suggest others. Ask if each is a countable or uncountable noun. Point out that you can say *a book* or *three apples*, but you can't say *a fun* or *three rices*. Say *You can't use a, an, or numbers before uncountable nouns.*

- Ask students to open their books at page 104. Read aloud the grammar skill heading. Say *As I play the track, notice the phrases for amounts that you use with countable and uncountable nouns.* Play **Track 086**.

- Then go through all of the sentences in the grammar box. Point out that you use *a few* and *many* with uncountable nouns and *a little* and *much* with uncountable nouns. Ask *What words can you use with both countable and uncountable nouns?* (*some, a lot of*)

- Write the table below. Leave it on the board for students to refer to during the lesson.

With countable nouns, use	With uncountable nouns, use
• numbers • *a couple of* • *a few* • *many / too many / how many?*	• *a little* • *much / too much / how much?*

Practise

- Ask *Has anyone ever had KoMex food? Who can guess what it's a fusion of?* (Korean and Mexican food) Put students into pairs to do the activity. Say *Look at the examples on page 104 or on the board if you need help.* Review the answers as a class. Then tell pairs to read the dialogue, taking turns as Maiza and Gabi.

Apply 2

- 2 Put the students into small groups. Tell students to cut out and assemble the game cubes on page 167. Ask *Which kinds of food are countable nouns?* (fish, vegetables, sweets) *Which are uncountable nouns?* (rice, tea, meat) Read the game instructions aloud. Ask students to read the example dialogue. Then say *Take turns rolling the cubes. Begin the conversation!* Observe the groups and provide help as needed.

Extend

- Put students into pairs. Display these containers: *a lunch box, a backpack, a shopping trolley,* and *an overnight bag.* Say *Work with your partner. Fill one of the containers on the board with different amounts of countable and uncountable nouns. Use numbers, words and phrases for amounts. How many things can you fit?* When they have finished, tell pairs to share their lists.

- Hand out **Worksheet 1.6.5** for further practice using countable and uncountable nouns with amounts.

Consolidate

- Say *Let's play a game of* Countable or Uncountable. Display the two word groups that follow. Ask students to stand in a circle. Say *When it's your turn, I'll say a word from Group 1. You say whether it's a countable or an unncountable noun. Then the next person chooses an appropriate word or phrase from Group 2 to use with that noun.* Provide an example: *milk* ⟶ *uncountable* ⟶ *a little milk.* Say *Let's see how long you can keep it up!*
Group 1: books, chicken, T-shirt, women, clothing, fun, eggs, milk, information, rain, butter, jobs
Group 2: a couple of, three, too much, lots of, one, some, a little, a few, seven, too many, a lot of, ten

Grammar in Depth

Point out that countable and uncountable nouns can be a tricky topic because certain aspects of uncountable nouns can actually be counted. For example, while you can't count *bread* in English, you can count *pieces, slices,* or *loaves* of bread. Other countable words to use with uncountable nouns to express amount include *a bottle, a cup, a glass, a plate, a spoonful,* and so on.

My brother ate three slices (countable) *of banana bread* (uncountable)*!*
This recipe calls for two cups (countable) *of sugar* (uncountable).

Teaching Tip

When students are asked a question, they should be given enough time to form an answer. Waiting time is an extremely important element of classroom discourse. Students are thinking in a new language and some may need as long as a minute to form an answer before speaking.

Formative Assessment

Can students
- use countable and uncountable nouns to talk about amounts?

Ask students to complete the dialogue with the correct words in brackets.

Gabi: _____ ice cream did you eat?
(*How much*, How many)

Maiza: *I was so full, I only ate* _____.
(a few, *a little*)

Workbook For additional practice, assign Workbook pages 62–63.
Online Workbook Grammar 2

Objectives

Students will
- identify elements of exemplification writing.
- use expressions that introduce examples.
- analyse a model of exemplification writing.
- describe an animal mash-up and produce a paragraph of exemplification.

Writing Paragraph of exemplification about an animal mash-up

Academic Language *example, exemplification*

Content Vocabulary *breeding, fins, scales*

Resources Online Workbook/Workbook page 64; Process Writing Worksheets 1–5, Genre Writing Worksheet: Exemplification (Teacher's Resource CD-ROM/Website); CPT: Writing

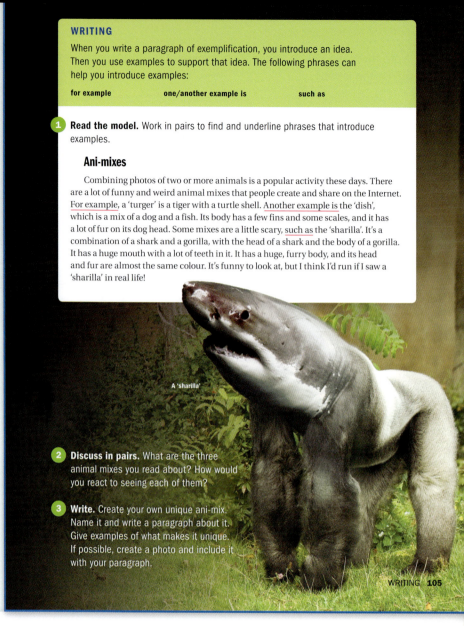

WRITING

When you write a paragraph of exemplification, you introduce an idea. Then you use examples to support that idea. The following phrases can help you introduce examples:

for example   one/another example is   such as

1 **Read the model.** Work in pairs to find and underline phrases that introduce examples.

Ani-mixes

Combining photos of two or more animals is a popular activity these days. There are a lot of funny and weird animal mixes that people create and share on the Internet. For example, a 'turger' is a tiger with a turtle shell. Another example is the 'dish', which is a mix of a dog and a fish. Its body has a few fins and some scales, and it has a lot of fur on its dog head. Some mixes are a little scary, such as the 'sharilla'. It's a combination of a shark and a gorilla, with the head of a shark and the body of a gorilla. It has a huge mouth with a lot of teeth in it. It has a huge, furry body, and its head and fur are almost the same colour. It's funny to look at, but I think I'd run if I saw a 'sharilla' in real life!

A 'sharilla'

2 **Discuss in pairs.** What are the three animal mixes you read about? How would you react to seeing each of them?

3 **Write.** Create your own unique ani-mix. Name it and write a paragraph about it. Give examples of what makes it unique. If possible, create a photo and include it with your paragraph.

WRITING **105**

Warm Up

- **Revise** Ask students to open their books at the reading on pages 100–101. Ask them to find the sentence on page 100 that begins 'He combines different types of food'. Ask a student to stand up and read that sentence and the two that follow it. Then ask the class *What is* Cart and Balloons *an example of?* (a foodscape) *How do you know?* (the phrase 'one of his foodscapes')

- Help students to see that the writer names one of Carl Warner's works of art as an example of a foodscape. He then goes on to describe it. Ask *Would you understand what a foodscape was if the writer didn't include an example of one?* Say *The writer of* A Feast for the Eyes *uses the phrase 'one of his foodscapes' to introduce an example.* Ask *Can you think of another phrase that's often used to introduce an example?* (*for example*)

Present

- Say *Turn to page 105.* Read aloud the text in the green box. Then say *In the reading, the example of* Cart and Balloons *is included to support the idea of what a foodscape is.* Write the following on the board:

  > Fusion food combines food from different countries.
  > _____.
  >
  > I read about a new hybrid sport every day.
  > _____.

- Tell students to copy the sentences. Then ask student pairs to work together to write supporting sentences with examples. Say *Write a sentence with an example to support each sentence on the board. Use a phrase from the top of page 105 in each sentence.* Point out to students that, unlike the other three phrases, *such as* cannot be used to begin a sentence. Review students' sentences as a class.

Read the Model

- Say *Now we're going to read a model of exemplification writing – writing that presents an idea and then includes examples to support that idea.* Ask students to read the title of the writing and look at the photo. Ask *What do you think a sharilla is?* (a combination of a shark and a gorilla) Say *That's a weird-looking animal!*

- Ask *Based on the title and the picture, what do you predict the writing will be about?* Accept students' responses. Then put the students into pairs and read aloud the Activity 1 instructions. Ask students to read the model. Tell pairs to work together to underline the phrases that introduce examples. When they've finished, review what students have underlined as a class.

- Put students into new pairs. Read aloud the Activity 2 discussion questions. When students have finished their discussions, ask questions such as *Do you agree that the sharilla looks scary? What word would you use to describe each of the three animal mixes you read about?* Finally, say *I'm sure you're anxious to create your own animal mix! Well, now you have the chance to do just that.*

- **Worksheet** If your students need a reminder of the elements of exemplification writing, you may want to hand out **Genre Writing Worksheet: Exemplification** and review it together.

Writing Support

The purpose of exemplification writing is to explain and support a main idea by using examples. When they write their exemplification paragraphs, students must be sure to clearly state the idea they're supporting. In addition to describing their animal-mix creations, students are also being asked to give examples of why they're unique. That idea must be clearly expressed with a statement, such as *My ani-mix is weirder than anything else on Earth. For example … , My ani-mix is so adorable, you'll want one. It has a lot of cute features, such as … ,* or *My ani-mix's huge size makes it too dangerous to create. Another example of its scary features is …*

Teaching Tip

To help students understand what they read, tell them to pay special attention to the first sentence of a paragraph. Writers often put a main idea at the beginning of a piece of writing. They include details that support the main idea, such as facts, descriptions, or examples in the sentences that follow.

Workbook For scaffolded writing support, assign Workbook page 64.

Online Workbook Writing

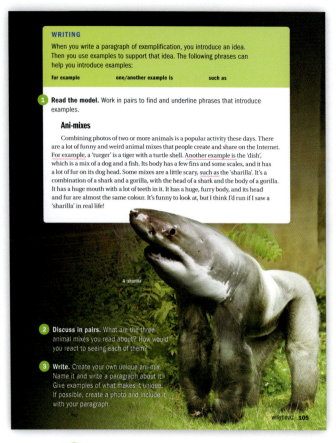

WRITING

When you write a paragraph of exemplification, you introduce an idea. Then you use examples to support that idea. The following phrases can help you introduce examples:

for example   one/another example is   such as

1 **Read the model.** Work in pairs to find and underline phrases that introduce examples.

Ani-mixes

Combining photos of two or more animals is a popular activity these days. There are a lot of funny and weird animal mixes that people create and share on the Internet. For example, a 'turger' is a tiger with a turtle shell. Another example is the 'dish', which is a mix of a dog and a fish. Its body has a few fins and some scales, and it has a lot of fur on its dog head. Some mixes are a little scary, such as the 'sharilla'. It's a combination of a shark and a gorilla, with the head of a shark and the body of a gorilla. It has a huge mouth with a lot of teeth in it. It has a huge, furry body, and its head and fur are almost the same colour. It's funny to look at, but I think I'd run if I saw a 'sharilla' in real life!

A 'sharilla'

2 **Discuss in pairs.** What are the three animal mixes you read about? How would you react to seeing each of them?

3 **Write.** Create your own unique ani-mix. Name it and write a paragraph about it. Give examples of what makes it unique. If possible, create a photo and include it with your paragraph.

WRITING 105

Plan **3**

- **3** Say *It's time to plan your own writing.* Read the Activity 3 instructions. Then say *Your topic is to imagine and describe your own ani-mix and give examples of what makes it unique.*

- Say *Your next step is pre-writing. Let's review. What are some ways we do pre-writing?* (brainstorm, free-write, make lists, use a graphic organiser, use sentence starters) Say *Now decide what you want to use for pre-writing.* If you have time in class, allow students to work on this step. If not, assign it as homework. If students have Workbooks, remind them to use Workbook page 64 for writing support.

- **Worksheets** If your students need a reminder of any of the steps of process writing, you may want to hand out **Process Writing Worksheets 1–5** and review them together.

- **Workbook** Refer students to Workbook page 64 to help them organise and plan their writing.

Write

- After students have finished their pre-writing, tell them to work on their first drafts. If you haven't got enough time in class, assign the first draft as homework.

Revise

- After students have finished their first drafts, tell them to review their writing and think about their ideas and organisation. Ask each student to consider the following: *Did I include a topic sentence? Is the information organised in a logical way? Did I include enough details to allow readers to visualise my ani-mix? Did I include examples and comparatives to support why it's unique? What seems good? What needs more work?* If time permits, they could read their drafts to a classmate for feedback.

Edit and Proofread

- Invite students to consider elements of style, such as sentence variety, parallelism and word choice. Then tell them to proofread for mistakes in grammar, punctuation, capitalisation and spelling. Remind them to make sure they used appropriate phrases to introduce examples.

Publish

- Publishing includes handing in pieces of writing to the teacher, sharing work with classmates, adding pieces to a class book, displaying pieces on a classroom wall or in a hallway, and posting on the Internet.

Writing Assessment

Use these guidelines to assess students' writing. You can add other aspects of their writing you'd like to assess at the bottom of the table.

4 = Excellent
3 = Good
2 = Needs improvement
1 = Re-do

	1	2	3	4
Writing Student organises the paragraph in a way that makes sense; uses enough descriptive detail and examples so readers can visualise the ani-mix; uses appropriate phrases to introduce examples.				
Grammar Student uses correct comparatives and expresses amounts of countable and uncountable nouns correctly.				
Vocabulary Student uses a variety of word choices, including words taught in this unit.				

NATIONAL GEOGRAPHIC

Be Unique

'Look where everyone is looking, then turn 180 degrees and walk. You'll often find that's where the gems are.'

Josh Ponte
National Geographic Explorer, Musical Explorer/Filmmaker

1. **Watch scene 6.2.**

2. When people learnt that Josh planned to quit his job and work in Gabon, many of them thought he was taking a big risk. Do you agree? Why or why not?

3. Think of a time when you did something really different from what everyone else was doing. What did you do? Was it easy or difficult? Were you glad you did it? Why or why not?

Objective
Students will
- discuss the value of striving to be unique.

Content Vocabulary *precious, remote, risk, risky, sonic*

Resources Video scene 6.2 (DVD/Website/CPT); Worksheet 1.6.6 (Teacher's Resource CD-ROM/Website); Online Workbook: Meet the Explorer; CPT: Mission

BE THE EXPERT

Related Vocabulary
lens, magnifying glass

Online Workbook Meet the Explorer

Mission

- Say *Turn to page 106.* Read aloud the Mission. Say *To be unique means to be different or to be one of a kind.* Tell students that Josh Ponte believes people should make an effort to be unique. Ask a student to stand up and read aloud the quote. Then ask *What are you doing when you turn 180 degrees and walk? Can someone demonstrate for us?* Show students that if you're facing in one direction and turn 180 degrees and walk, you're going in the opposite direction.

- Ask *What are gems?* (jewels, precious things) *What do you think Josh's quote means?* (by going in a different direction and looking closely at what's around you, you might discover something special)

- **Activity 1** Say *We read a little about how Josh went to Gabon to research the traditional music of the country. Now let's watch a video about what he found and heard there.* Tell students to listen carefully to the singing and to how Josh describes how the people sing along with one another. Play **Video scene 6.2**.

- **Activity 2** Read the activity text. Ask *What might be risky about going to Gabon?* Remind students that Josh's journey was difficult and he and his crew had little food and water. Ask *What do you think Josh would say about the risk?*

- **Activity 3** Ask a student to stand up and read the activity text. Ask *What are your experiences with being different from everyone else?* Invite students to share experiences and discuss. Ask *What did you learn from your experience?*

- **Worksheet** Hand out **Worksheet 1.6.6**. Explain that students will use the worksheet to think and write about Josh Ponte and the value of being unique.

MISSION **195**

Objective

Students will
- choose and complete a project related to mash-ups.

Content Vocabulary *comic strip*

Resources Assessment: Unit 6 Quiz; Workbook pages 65 and 95; Worksheet 1.6.7 (Teacher's Resource CD-ROM/Website); CPT: Make an Impact and Review Games

Materials art materials, camera

Assessment Go to page 260.

Unit Review Assign Worksheet 1.6.7

Workbook Assign pages 65 and 95.

Online Workbook Now I can

Make an Impact

YOU DECIDE Choose a project.

1 **Make and explain food art.**
- Decide what to create and what food to use.
- Photograph each step as you create your art.
- Share your photographs with the class. Explain how you made your artwork.

2 **Create a mash-up comic strip.**
- Choose any two types of stories to mix for your mash-up. For example, mix a fairy tale and science fiction.
- Write the story in six to eight panels. Draw pictures in each panel.
- Share your story with the class.

3 **Invent a hybrid sport.**
- Choose two or three sports you like. Think of how to combine them.
- Write rules for your sport.
- Explain your sport. If possible, demonstrate it for the class.

Prepare

- **YOU DECIDE** Ask students to choose a project.

- **Activity 1** Tell students to turn to page 107. Remind students that some of them made a rough sketch of a piece of food art for the Reading lesson. Say *You can use that idea if you wish.* Tell students who choose this activity to revisit *A Feast for the Eyes* and re-read how Carl Warner creates his foodscapes and the descriptions of the two examples of food art. Say *You have to create the art, photograph the process and explain to the class how you made it.*

- **Activity 2** Say *Remember that you came up with an idea for a mash-up of a story or film you like and another kind of story. Now you can turn that mash-up into a comic strip!* Suggest that students research classic comic strips online.

- **Activity 3** Point to the illustration of the sport. Ask *What does this look like a combination of?* (volleyball and bowling) *What sports do you think would be fun to combine? Make a list of sports you know, and think about how you might combine aspects of two or three of them.* Explain that students have to make up rules for their hybrid sport. Say *You're going to have to play the game, so the rules must make sense!* This might be a good group project.

Share

- Schedule time for students to present their projects. Allow time for students to ask questions and provide feedback. If possible, arrange a place where students can play their sports.

- **Modify** Help students simplify a project by eliminating an option or step. For example, you might give students guidelines for their game rules, perhaps limiting them to a certain number of rules.

Track 074 **1** **Listen and read.** See Student's Book pages 94–95.

Track 075 **2** LEARN NEW WORDS **audio** / If you can't hear, check your audio equipment. **cool** / Mash-ups can create sounds that are unusual, but really cool. **DJ** / People like to dance to the music that DJs play. **edit** / Musicians edit their music to make it sound better. **fan** / Popular bands have thousands of fans. **include** / Rock bands always include a guitar player. **mix** / Some bands like to mix different styles of music. **opinion** / People have different opinions of rock music. **perform** / It's exciting to watch bands perform on stage. **record** / Some bands record the music at their concerts. **recording** / It can take a long time to make a recording of one song. **song** / Musicians make songs by creating music and writing words. **traditional** / A culture's traditional instruments make its music unique. **video** / Many people watch music videos on the Internet.

Track 076 **5** Bands all over the world combine musical styles. The Argentine band Bajofondo is famous for mixing electronic music with traditional Argentine tango music. This creates a new style called electrotango. Bajofondo's electrotango style has produced many hits. Many of their fans download their music and go to their concerts. In fact, their first concert in Buenos Aires attracted 200,000 fans!

Track 077 **5** LEARN NEW WORDS **combine** / Mash-up musicians combine sounds from different songs. **download** / It's easy to download music on a computer. **electronic** / A lot of people today like the sound of electronic music. **hit** / The band's first song was a hit.

Track 078 SPEAKING STRATEGY See Student's Book page 97.

Track 079 **1** **S1:** Hey, Sandra. Look at this book I'm reading. The pictures of the creatures are amazing! They're hybrids of two animals! That is, they are the offspring of two different species. **S2:** Oh, yes, that's right. Look at this 'tiger'. It's a lion/tiger hybrid. In other words, its dad is a lion and its mum is a tiger! **S1:** Yes. And look at this 'grolar bear' or 'pizzly'. It's a hybrid of two bears. I mean, one of its parents was a grizzly bear, and the other was a polar bear. I think things like this will happen more often. **S2:** What do you mean? **S1:** I mean, because of global warming, polar bears are more likely to come into contact with their cousins, the grizzly bear. **S2:** I'm not sure if it's a good thing. That is, it's only happening because of things like global warming and loss of habitat, which I guess is the fault of us humans. **S1:** Hmm. I hadn't thought of it like that.

Track 080 GRAMMAR See Student's Book page 98.

Track 081 **1** Filip Eyckmans visited Brazil and saw how soccer, volleyball, dance and music all came together on its beaches. He created a sport that mixed all of these together: bossaball.

Bossaball is more unusual than some other sports because it's played on a huge blow-up court with a trampoline in it. It's easier to plan a game because it can be played indoors or outdoors. Players say they're more active playing bossaball than regular volleyball. It's harder, but more enjoyable.

Music is usually played during games. Fans say that bossaball is as much fun as a party. They say it's better than watching other sports because of the music.

Track 082 **4** A hybrid sport mixes two or more sports to create a new sport. Hybrid sports aren't often as popular as the original sports they come from. But they can still be really fun to play!

Most players love golf because they play it outdoors. But some players hate how expensive it can be to play. Disc golf is a hybrid sport that is a less expensive version of golf.

Disc golf is more popular than other hybrid sports. It's played in more than 40 countries. In the game, players try to throw a disc into a metal bucket. Not all discs are the same size. Some are bigger than others, which makes it harder to get them in the bucket.

Track 083 **4** LEARN NEW WORDS **create** / People create new games using ideas from other sports. **hate** / Some people hate hybrid sports. **hybrid** / Disc golf is a hybrid sport. **love** / Many people love to watch sports on TV. **version** / Street soccer is a simple version of traditional soccer.

Track 084 **2** LEARN NEW WORDS **imagine** / Artists imagine their work before they create it. **imitate** / Art often imitates things in nature. **modern** / Some people like modern art more than ancient art. **original** / Artists make original art from many kinds of materials. **weird** / Some people think that using food for art is weird.

Track 085 **3** WHILE YOU READ See Student's Book pages 100–101.

Track 086 GRAMMAR See Student's Book page 104.

Track 087 **1** **Express Yourself** See Student's Book pages 108–109.

Objectives
Students will
- identify the purpose and features of a fashion magazine article.
- connect ideas about clothing and mash-ups.

Academic Language *magazine*

Content Vocabulary *cogwheel, era, gadgets, goggles, industrial, layout, model, prosperous, tubes*

Resources Workbook pages 66–67/ Online Workbook (Units 5–6 Review); Worksheet 1.6.8 (Teacher's Resource CD-ROM/Website); Track 087 (Audio CD/Website/CPT); CPT: Express Yourself Units 5–6

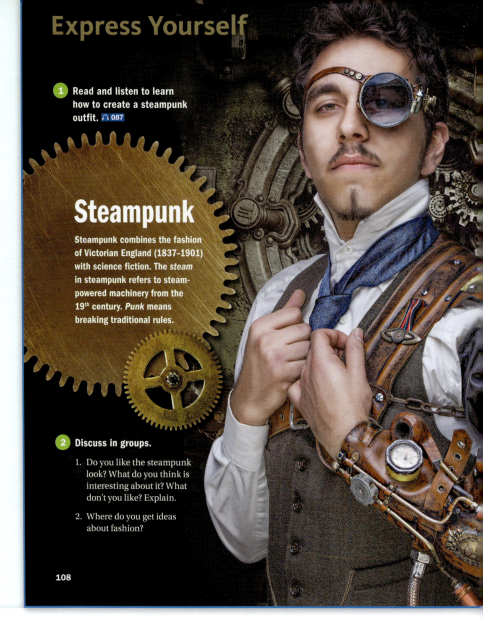

Express Yourself

1 Read and listen to learn how to create a steampunk outfit. 🎧 087

Steampunk

Steampunk combines the fashion of Victorian England (1837–1901) with science fiction. The *steam* in steampunk refers to steam-powered machinery from the 19th century. *Punk* means breaking traditional rules.

2 Discuss in groups.

1. Do you like the steampunk look? What do you think is interesting about it? What don't you like? Explain.

2. Where do you get ideas about fashion?

108

Present **1**

- **Preview** Write *steampunk* on the board. Ask *Does anyone know what steampunk is?* Invite students to share what they know. Then explain that steampunk is a style characterised by a mash-up of industrial machinery from the 1900s and more modern gadgets and devices. Say *Clothing is a big part of steampunk, and we're going to be looking at and reading an article about the steampunk style.*

- Ask students to open their books at pages 108–109. Discuss the photo. Point to the cogwheels and explain that they're used in machinery. Tell students to focus on the layout, or design of the article. Ask *What's different about how the text is laid out?* Point out that the text is integrated with the cogwheels and follows their placement across the pages.

- **1** **Read together** Explain that the purpose of a fashion magazine is to display the latest fashions, usually for a specific audience. These magazines are highly visual, and contain interesting photos and graphics with attractive models in exaggerated clothing and dramatic poses. Ask *What does it look like he's dressed for?* (adventure, exploration, a science experiment) *What do his outfit and his expression say about him?*

- Play **Track 087** as students listen and read. Then, ask *What's the main purpose of the article?* (to explain how to put together a steampunk outfit) *What are the steps to follow to create the look?* (pick a character, find old-fashioned clothes, get the right accessories)

Practise **2**

- **2** **Discuss** Put the students into small groups. Provide prompts if necessary to stimulate discussion. Ask *Have you ever dressed that way? Would you like to? Where would you wear clothing like that? Do you*

Get steampunked. Here's how:

Plan Think about the character you want. Do you want to be a pilot? Or maybe a sailor? How about a scientist or a soldier? Choosing a character will help you select the best clothing and accessories.

Create Now think about what you'll wear: old-fashioned trousers and a jacket, or maybe a beautiful dress. Be creative! Make changes you want, to create something unique. For example, Victorian-era women wore high-heeled boots, but you might prefer flat shoes. Your clothing can be in any colour, though many fans of steampunk prefer dark colours.

Steampunk it! Now for the important part – accessories! If you have an outfit that looks Victorian but doesn't have accessories, it's not steampunk! Steampunk accessories can include goggles, machine parts, old watches, leather belts or interesting hats. Remember to choose accessories that match your character.

3 Connect ideas. In Unit 5, you learnt about fashion. In Unit 6, you learnt about combining things to make something new. What connection can you see between the two units?

4 YOU DECIDE Choose an activity.
1. Choose a topic:
   - fashion
   - mash-ups
2. Choose a way to express yourself:
   - a magazine article
   - a fashion show
   - a video
3. Present your work.

109

try to dress in a certain style? What or who is the inspiration for your style?

Connect

- **3 Critical Thinking** Remind students of the big ideas they talked about in Unit 5 – how clothing has changed over the years and why people wear the clothes they do. Then read the Activity 3 text aloud. Invite students to share their ideas. Say *Isn't it interesting that what's old often becomes new again, although perhaps in a mashed-up way!* Ask *In what way is fashion always a mash-up?* (Our clothes are often a mix of what's practical and what looks good.)

Prepare

- **YOU DECIDE** Review Activity 4. Allow students to choose their own topics. You may want to assign this activity in advance so students have more time in class or at home to review each step.

- **4** Say *This lesson focused on fashion, but remember all the different kinds of mash-ups you have learnt about. Which kind inspired you the most? Write an article about it, or write an article about the history of clothing or the role fashion plays in your life.*

- Tell students who choose to present a fashion show that they can work in groups. Say *You'll need a theme and a supply of clothing your relatives or friends are willing to let you borrow!* For those who choose the video option, ask *What will you film? A fashion show at a local shopping centre, a hybrid sports match, a scene from a steampunk story?*

Share

- Set aside time for sharing students' work with the class. Remind students to listen politely to all of the presentations and to wait until they're over before asking any questions.

Express Yourself **199**

In This Unit

Theme This unit looks at uses of technology.

Content Objectives

Students will
- identify and describe uses of new technology.
- identify and describe unusual mobile apps.
- read about creative teens and their inventions.

Language Objectives

Students will
- talk about the uses of technology.
- make and respond to requests.
- use superlatives to talk about extremes.
- use *will* and *going to* to talk about the future.
- write a product review.

Vocabulary

pages 112–113 *app, chat, connect, gadget, game, Internet, look up, mobile, search, send, share, smartphone, useful, Wi-Fi*

page 114 *incredible, possible, tablet, text*

page 117 *battery, camera, keyboard, microphone, screen*

page 118 *borrow, find, function, invent*

Vocabulary Strategies Suffix *-ible*, Identify parts of speech

Speaking Strategy Making and responding to requests

Grammar

Grammar 1 Use superlatives to talk about extremes

Grammar 2 Use *will* and *going to* to talk about the future

Reading *Thinking Outside the Box*

Reading Strategy Identify main idea and details

Video Scene 7.1: *From Gadgets to Apps,* Scene 7.2: Meet Manu Prakash

Writing Product review

National Geographic Mission Always Keep Learning

Project
- Presentation
- Robot design
- Outdated gadget museum

Pronunciation The two-vowel rule

Pacing Guides 1.7.1, 1.7.2, 1.7.3

Unit 7

Cool Apps and Gadgets

A rider using special LED lights on his bicycle wheels for safety, Hong Kong

110

Introduce the Unit

- **Build background** Say *The title of this unit is* Cool Apps and Gadgets. Hold up a smartphone (or a photo of one) with apps displayed on the screen. Ask *Have you got one of these? What do you use it for?* Ask students to stand up and share ways in which they use smartphones. Make a list on the board of their answers.

- Hold up the smartphone again and say *Let's think about how much time we spend using this.* Create a table on the board with the following categories: I haven't got one; One hour/day; Two hours/day; Three hours/day; Four or more hours/day.

- Say each time period and ask students to put up their hands if it corresponds to their use. Then put a tick for each student in the appropriate category. Add up the final number of replies and say *We spend a lot of time using technology. Think of other electronic or technological items.* Ask *How much time do you spend using them?* Repeat the activity and ask students to answer for all technology use.

- **TO START** Say *Open your books at pages 110–111.* Read the photo caption aloud. Then ask questions for discussion:

'The biggest thing we're trying to do is to make people curious.'
Manu Prakash

TO START

1. Look at the photograph. Why do you think the rider added lights to his bicycle?

2. What electronics are important to you? Which ones do you use every day? Which would you like that you haven't got now?

3. How do you think the electronics you use now will change in the future?

111

Objectives

Students will
- describe and discuss a photo.
- discuss technology use and how technology changes.

Resources Worksheet 1.7.1 (Teacher's Resource CD-ROM/Website); CPT: Unit Opener

Materials a smartphone with apps (or a photo of one)

BE THE EXPERT

About the Photo

The bicycle in the photo features Revolights, which are LED lights that attach to a bike's wheels. Revolights provide additional safety to riders by illuminating both the ground and what is straight ahead and above. This makes it easier for the cyclist to spot obstacles and road signs. Revolights work as both a headlight and a brake light, so a cyclist is always visible to motorists on the road.

Teaching Tip

Keep an organised classroom. Make sure that students know where to find classroom materials such as scissors, pencils and dictionaries. Explain that students can borrow items as long as they put them away properly when they've finished. (Although they may seem old enough to know how to do this, students might be careless about things or they might not be aware of your preferences.) Avoid talking down to students about organisation, as they may feel insulted. Instead, put a dictionary away upside-down or leave several pencils lying on a desk beside a pencil jar. Then, jokingly ask *Does this look right to you? Do you think I like having the pencils here?*

Related Vocabulary

LED lights, skyline, visible

How do you think the lights on this bicycle work? Why are they useful? Would you want these for your bike? Why or why not?

- Ask a student to read Manu Prakash's quote aloud. Say *Manu Prakash is a scientist who wants to get people interested in science.* Tell students to turn to page 124 and look at Manu's photo. Ask *What do you think he's holding? Is it making you curious?*

- Ask a student to read Question 1 aloud and put students into pairs to discuss the photo. Then share information from the About the Photo section. For Question 2, tell students to include any relevant information from the discussion on smartphones. If necessary, encourage them to make a sketch to share their ideas. For a variation on Question 3, put students into groups and assign each a different electronic device. After students have finished, ask each group to share their ideas with the class.

Extend

- Hand out **Worksheet 1.7.1**. Put students into pairs. Explain that each pair will be writing about and discussing their use of technology.

VOCABULARY

Objectives

Students will

- talk about the uses of technology.
- use new vocabulary to read about and discuss the ways and amount of time people use technology.

Target Vocabulary *app, chat, connect, gadget, game, Internet, look up, mobile, search, send, share, smartphone, useful, Wi-Fi*

Content Vocabulary *public space*

Pronunciation The two-vowel rule

Resources Pronunciation Answer Key (Teacher's Resource CD-ROM/Website); Tracks 088–089, Tracks 134–135 (Audio CD/Website/CPT); CPT: Vocabulary and Pronunciation

Materials a smartphone with apps (or a photo of one)

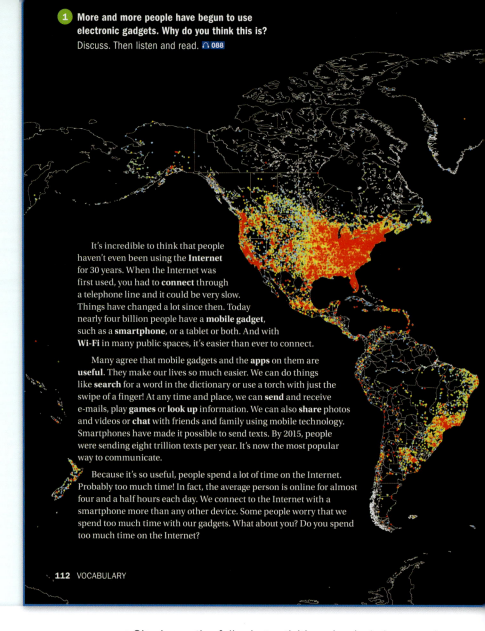

1 More and more people have begun to use electronic gadgets. Why do you think this is? Discuss. Then listen and read. 🎧 088

It's incredible to think that people haven't even been using the **Internet** for 30 years. When the Internet was first used, you had to **connect** through a telephone line and it could be very slow. Things have changed a lot since then. Today nearly four billion people have a **mobile gadget**, such as a **smartphone**, or a tablet or both. And with **Wi-Fi** in many public spaces, it's easier than ever to connect.

Many agree that mobile gadgets and the **apps** on them are **useful**. They make our lives so much easier. We can do things like **search** for a word in the dictionary or use a torch with just the swipe of a finger! At any time and place, we can **send** and receive e-mails, play **games** or **look up** information. We can also **share** photos and videos or **chat** with friends and family using mobile technology. Smartphones have made it possible to send texts. By 2015, people were sending eight trillion texts per year. It's now the most popular way to communicate.

Because it's so useful, people spend a lot of time on the Internet. Probably too much time! In fact, the average person is online for almost four and a half hours each day. We connect to the Internet with a smartphone more than any other device. Some people worry that we spend too much time with our gadgets. What about you? Do you spend too much time on the Internet?

112 VOCABULARY

Warm Up

- **Revisit** Say *In our last lesson, we talked about how much time we spend using smartphones and other types of technology.* If necessary, hold up a smartphone or a photo of a smartphone to help students remember the discussion. Ask *How many people said they used a smartphone for one hour each day?* Tell students to put up their hands and write the number on the board. Repeat this for the other time blocks from the previous lesson. Again, write the students' answers on the board.

- Say *We talked about this type of technology as being only one type of technology. But it is a very useful type of technology.* Tell students to take out a sheet of paper and a pencil. Say *Listen as I name different activities. Write the activity down if you use technology in any way while doing it.*

- Slowly say the following activities aloud: *do homework, read a book, make plans with friends, exercise, play games, tidy your room, talk with friends, get dressed, go shopping, prepare a snack* and *go for a walk.*

- When you have finished, ask students to compare their lists in pairs. Invite pairs to discuss how they use technology for each activity. For example, they might use a fitness band when they go for a walk or they might read a book on an e-reader.

Present

- Ask students to open their books on pages 112–113. Say *We've talked about how often we use technology and how we use it. But technology use isn't the same all around the world. Look at the world map.* Point to the different colours shown on the map. Say *This map shows the use of the Internet around the world.* Point to the key and ask *What does red mean?* (high rate

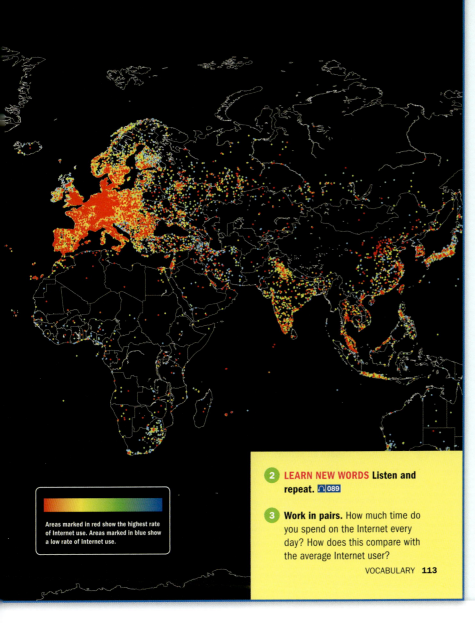

Areas marked in red show the highest rate of Internet use. Areas marked in blue show a low rate of Internet use.

2 LEARN NEW WORDS Listen and repeat. 🎧 089

3 Work in pairs. How much time do you spend on the Internet every day? How does this compare with the average Internet user?

VOCABULARY **113**

Pronunciation

Go to Student's Book page 147. Use Audio Tracks 134 and 135.

The two-vowel rule All consonants and vowels in English have various pronunciations, but vowels are much more difficult for students. There are five written vowels (letters), but there are different possible vowel sounds for each letter or letter combination. The two-vowel rule has exceptions, but it is a good guide for students as it will allow them to feel more confident as they guess the pronunciation of any new words they encounter. They will also begin to see patterns of spelling in the exceptions.

You may want to point out that this rule applies when the vowels are in the same syllable. For example, in *ex-er-cise*, the first *e* is not pronounced with a long *e* sound, but the *i* is pronounced with the long vowel sound.

of Internet use) Then ask *Which continents have a lot of Internet use?* (North America, Europe) Say *Find our region. How do we compare with these places?* Discuss your region's Internet use as a class.

- **1** Play **Track 088.** and ask students to listen and read. Discuss the reading with students. Ask them to answer the following questions:

  How long have people used the Internet? (less than 30 years)

  What has made it easier for us to connect to the Internet? (Wi-Fi)

  Can you give examples of the useful apps mentioned in the reading? (dictionary, flashlight)

  How much time do people spend online each day, on average? (4½ hours)

  How do most people connect to the Internet? (with a smartphone)

- **2** **LEARN NEW WORDS** Play **Track 089**. Tell students to listen and repeat. Then ask students to work in pairs to practise pronouncing the words together.

- Play **Track 089** a second time, this time pausing after each word. Invite a student to make a sentence about his or her own Internet use using the word. Repeat this for all of the new vocabulary.

VOCABULARY **203**

Objectives

Students will
- practise using vocabulary related to technology use.
- use a vocabulary strategy to learn new words.

Target Vocabulary *incredible, possible, tablet, text*

Vocabulary Strategy Suffix *-ible*

Academic Language *explain, research*

Content Vocabulary *biophysicist, chemistry, disease, power*

Resources Online Workbook/Workbook pages 68–69; Graphic Organiser: Sunshine organiser (Teacher's Resource CD-ROM/Website); Worksheet 1.7.2 (Teacher's Resource CD-ROM/Website); Tracks 090–091 (Audio CD/Website/CPT); CPT: Vocabulary

Materials timer *(optional)*

---

4 **Read and circle the correct word.**

Biophysicist Manu Prakash (connected)/ sent to science as a child. He and his brother would spend time in an empty chemistry lab making their own fireworks or electronics. Today, Manu works to make sure that everyone has access to science. He says, 'You can have a kid walking around with a (smartphone)/ Wi-Fi who doesn't know that the human body is made of cells.'

Manu wants to (share)/ look up his love of science with others. So he helped create a computer powered by water and a low-cost chemistry set. Another amazing Wi-Fi /(gadget) Manu created is the *Foldscope*, a paper microscope. People can make it themselves by folding a special piece of paper. It's small and cheap. The Foldscope is very (useful)/ chat for doctors who work in rural areas. They can use them to test for about 20 different diseases. Manu wants children to use them, too. Instead of just (looking up)/ sending all their information on the Internet, children can 'walk around with a microscope in their hands' to learn about the world around them.

Manu Prakash sharing his Foldscope with a young girl

5 **LEARN NEW WORDS** Listen to these words and match them to the clues. Then listen and repeat. 090 091

incredible	possible	tablet	text

tablet	1. It's like a smartphone but bigger.
incredible	2. Something so amazing, we think it can't be true.
possible	3. This means that something might happen.
text	4. We send and receive this with our mobile gadgets.

6 **YOU DECIDE** Choose an activity.

1. **Work independently.** Think of a tool that can be changed so that it's cheaper and easier to use. Why would changing it be useful? Write a paragraph to explain your idea.

2. **Work in pairs.** What would you like an app to help you do at home? List three things and explain how an app could help.

3. **Work in groups.** Research a new app or gadget that a lot of people don't know about. Explain what it does and how it helps people. Present your research to the class.

114 VOCABULARY

Practise ③ ④ ⑤

- ③ To give students a visual of how they compare with the average, draw a timeline on the board. In the centre, draw a star and label it *4½ hours a day*. Write the names of students who use the Internet more to the right of the star. Write the names of students who use the Internet less to the left. After completing the timeline, ask *Is it good or bad to spend this much time on the Internet?* Discuss.

- ④ Ask students to open their books at page 114 and read the instructions aloud for Activity 4. Then tell students to scan the text for unfamiliar words. Clarify meanings as necessary. Students complete the activity independently. When students have finished, ask *Would you like to have a Foldscope? What would you do with it?*

- ⑤ **LEARN NEW WORDS** Play **Track 090** once and ask students to listen. Say *Listen again. This time, match the words from the box with the correct clues.* Play **Track 090** again and tell students to write the correct words. Review the answers as a class. Finally, play **Track 091** and ask students to repeat each word and sentence.

- **Vocabulary strategy** Write the words *incredible* and *possible* on the board. Ask *What is the same about these words?* (suffix *-ible*) Say *When a word ends in -ible, it means 'able to' or 'capable of'.* Underline the suffix *-ible*. Say *Sometimes we see words that end in -able. This suffix has the same meaning as -ible.* Give examples, such as *wearable* and *valuable*. Say *Many words that take the -able suffix can also appear without it, such as* wear *and* value. *But when the -ible suffix is removed, the word cannot stand alone.* Circle *incred* and *poss* and say *Without -ible, these word parts have no meaning.*

Apply 6

- 6 YOU DECIDE Read aloud each of the three activity options. Then put students into pairs or groups if they choose the second or third options. Tell students who choose the first option to include a drawing of how they could modify an object to make it cheaper and easier to carry. Point out that students can be creative – their ideas don't need to be based in reality.

- To extend the second option, tell students to conduct research to see if apps already exist that do what they suggested in the activity.

- Help students to use terms such as *new apps* or *unusual apps* to do an Internet search for the third option. If possible, tell students to download the app and demonstrate how it works.

Extend

- Put students into pairs. Give each pair a copy of the sunshine graphic organiser. Say *Let's review the text on pages 112 and 113. Think of information you could categorise under each of the question words. Let's do one together.* Draw a sunshine organiser on the board and write the word *how* on one of the points. Say *We need to ask a question using the word* how, *such as* How do most people access the Internet? *Let's scan the reading to find the answer.*

- Say *Now, review the reading in pairs. Think of questions you could ask for each question word and write the correct answers.* When students have finished, tell them to suggest one question-and-answer set for each space on the organiser.

- If time allows, hand out **Worksheet 1.7.2.** Explain that students will talk and write about technology and its use.

Consolidate

- Say *You are going to hear me read four sentences. I want you to decide whether they are true or false.* Say the following sentences aloud twice:

1. We have only been using the Internet for 20 years. (F)
2. The apps we have on our smartphones can be very useful. (T)
3. E-mail is the most popular way to communicate. (F)
4. I use the Internet less than the average person. (Answers will vary.)

- Review the answers and ask students to provide correct information for false answers.

BE THE EXPERT

Vocabulary Strategy

Suffix *-ible* In English, the suffixes *-ible* and *-able* typically have the same meaning: 'capable of' or 'able to'. The suffix *-able* can be added onto a word to create an adjective (e.g. *laughable, likeable*). The suffix *-ible* also creates an adjective (e.g. *possible, incredible*). Students may get confused about when to add *-ible* and when to add *-able*. Give examples of words with both endings. Then cross out the suffixes. Point out that without the suffix *-able,* a meaningful word still exists (*laugh, like*), but words with the suffix *-ible* often cannot stand alone (*poss, incred*). If necessary, provide students with additional words that end in *-ible,* such as *responsible* and *horrible*.

Formative Assessment

Can students
- talk about the uses of technology?

  Ask *What is the most popular way to communicate? What do you use to communicate this way?*
- use new vocabulary to read about and discuss the ways and amount of time people use technology?

  Ask students to use the words *app, connect, smartphone* and *useful* in sentences that describes their own Internet use.

Workbook For additional practice, assign Workbook pages 68–69.

Online Workbook Vocabulary

SPEAKING STRATEGY

Objectives
Students will
- use new phrases to make requests.
- use new phrases to respond to requests.

Speaking Strategy Making and responding to requests

Academic Language *request, respond*

Content Vocabulary *calculator, pocket, translator*

Resources Online Workbook; Worksheet 1.7.3 (Teacher's Resource CD-ROM/ Website); Tracks 092–093 (Audio CD/ Website/CPT); CPT: Speaking Strategy

---

SPEAKING STRATEGY 🎧 092

Making requests	Responding to requests
May I borrow your <u>tablet</u>?	Of course. Here you are!
Can you lend me your <u>smartphone</u>?	Sure. Here you go.
Please let me use your <u>dictionary</u>.	Sorry. I need it myself.
	I'm sorry. I'm using it <u>at the moment</u>.
	I'm not allowed to lend it out. Sorry!

1 **Listen.** How do the speakers make and respond to requests? Write the phrases you hear. 🎧 093

2 **Read and complete the dialogue.** *Possible answers:*

Jun: I forgot my electronic translator.
_____ May I borrow _____ yours?

Chin-Sun: I haven't got one. I just use an app to translate words. Look!

Jun: That's cool. _____ Can I borrow _____ your phone for a few minutes?

Chin-Sun: _____ Sure _____. Here you go. Oh wait, I need the calculator app for my maths homework.

Jun: No problem. I've got a calculator in my bag.

Chin-Sun: Please _____ let me use it _____.

Jun: _____ Of course _____. Here you are!

Chin-Sun: Thanks. Wow! This calculator is better than my calculator app!

Jun: Yeah, it *is* good.

Chin-Sun: _____ Can you lend me _____ this calculator for the weekend?

Jun: _____ I'm sorry. I'm using it _____ this weekend. I've got a big maths test on Monday.

3 **Work as a class.** Choose a card: A, B, C or D. Request the items on your card from your classmates. Respond to their requests. Answer *yes* if the item requested is on your card and *no* if it is not.

STUDENT A
video game	translator	pen	skateboard	watch

Could you lend me your video game?

Sorry. I'm using it at the moment.

Go to page 169.

4 **Work in groups.** Place five things from your pockets or school bags on your desk. Take turns asking to borrow those items and responding.

SPEAKING **115**

Warm Up

- **Set the stage** Pretend to be disorganised as you begin the class. To one student, say *Excuse me, could I borrow your pen?* Then approach another student and say *Excuse me, I need to know the date. Can you lend me your smartphone?* Continue by asking several other students to borrow or use something.

- Ask *What have I been doing?* (asking for things) Say *Sometimes, when you need something and you haven't got it, you can ask a friend or classmate to lend it to you. Today, we're going to learn how to ask for things and how to respond when other people ask us for something.*

Present **1**

- Ask students to open their books at page 115. Say *Listen to the sentences in the yellow box.* Play **Track 092**. Explain to students that the first two expressions in the second column are ways to agree

to let someone borrow something and the remaining expressions are different ways to say 'no'.

- Ask several students if you can borrow things they are using or are unlikely to have. For example, ask *Can I borrow your (pencil)?* or *Please let me use your (skateboard).* Ask students to respond with different phrases to tell you that you cannot use the items.

- **1** Say *Listen to the conversation between two friends. One friend is requesting three different things. Write the phrases she uses to make the requests.* Play **Track 093** once and ask students to write the appropriate phrases.

- Say *Now we'll listen again. How does Manuel respond to each request? Write the phrases you hear.* Play **Track 093** a second time and tell students to focus on writing the responses they hear. When they have finished, ask *How many times does Manuel say 'no'?* (two) *How many times does he say 'yes'?* (one)

Present

- Ask students to look at Activity 2. Say *Let's read the conversation between Chin-Sun and Jun.* Students complete the activity independently. Students check their answers in pairs. Ask a pair to come to the front of the class and read the dialogue aloud.

Apply

- Ask students to turn to page 169 and tell them to remove the page. Say *Look at each of the objects. Choose a card, A, B, C or D and cut it out. These are the objects that you want to borrow.*

- **Model** Hold up card *A* and say *I want to borrow one of these things.* Approach a student and say *(Juan), use card B.* Then turn to the class and say *I'm going to ask (Juan) if I can borrow one of the items on my card. If he has it on his card, he must say yes. If not, he must find a way to say no.* Turn back to the student and say *(Juan), please let me use your video game.* Guide the student to agree to let you use it. Repeat, asking for a different item. This time, guide the student to say why you can't use it. Tell all students to select a card. Then ask students to stand up and walk around the room, making and responding to requests for items on their cards. Walk around while they work to make sure that they're asking and answering appropriately.

- Put students into groups of three and ask them to place any five items in front of them. Ask students to take turns making requests and responding to the requests made to them.

Extend

- Ask students to choose an item that belongs to them. Divide the class into two teams and tell each team to stand in a row facing one another. Tell students to take turns requesting items from the student directly opposite them.

- Students may choose to lend their items or they may choose to give a reason why they can't. Once students complete a request, tell each student to take one step to the right and do the activity again with a new partner. The students at the far right of each row should move to the far left of the row. Ask students to continue the game until they return to their original partners.

- If time allows, hand out **Worksheet 1.7.3**. Explain that students will use the worksheet to practise making and responding to requests.

Consolidate

- Put students into pairs to write a short dialogue in which one friend makes an unreasonable request of another friend. For example, *Please lend me one million pounds* or *May I borrow your parents' car, please?* Encourage students to find creative ways to respond.

- Ask as many pairs as possible to share their dialogues with the class. You may want to invite the class to vote on the most creative dialogues.

Strategy in Depth

In school, students will need to borrow items from teachers and classmates. Remind students that *may* and *please* are words they can use to be extremely polite. They should use these words when speaking to a teacher or in formal situations. However, between friends, *Can I borrow your ...?* and *Can you lend me ...?* are more acceptable.

Students will also be asked to lend items out. Sometimes, it's not OK for students to lend their items. For example, a parent may not give permission for the item to be lent or the students may need the item. Explain that it's much more polite to give a reason why the item can't be lent than to simply say no without providing a reason.

Teaching Tip

Make sure to create authentic communicative situations whenever you're practising a new skill or strategy. Instead of telling students to repeat a word or phrase over and over, provide an authentic context for doing so. For example, play a memory game in which you show students a group of items and let them study them. Then take the items away and invite students to ask questions based on their memories.

Formative Assessment

Can students
- use new phrases to make requests.

  Hold up a classroom item and invite students to ask to borrow it.

- use new phrases to respond to requests.

  Ask questions such as *May I borrow your smartphone? Can you lend me your scissors?* Ask students to respond appropriately.

Online Workbook Speaking Strategy

GRAMMAR 1

Objectives
Students will
• use superlatives to talk about extremes.
• identify and describe unusual mobile apps.

Grammar Use superlatives to talk about extremes

Target Vocabulary *battery, camera, keyboard, microphone, screen*

Academic Vocabulary *agree, disagree, superlative*

Content Vocabulary *amazing, blow, charge, extreme, feature, graphics, melon, popular, sound (good/bad), type*

Resources Online Workbook/Workbook pages 70–71; Graphic Organiser: Three-column table (Teacher's Resource CD-ROM/Website); Tracks 094–097 (Audio CD/Website/CPT); CPT: Grammar 1

Materials glue, large pieces of strong card, old magazines, scissors

GRAMMAR 🎧094

Superlatives: Talking about extremes

The newest version of this game is going to be amazing.

This puzzle app isn't **the most difficult** one I've got.

This new word game isn't **the most fun** game I've played, but it isn't **the least fun** either.

This action game is **the best**. It has incredible graphics.

The worst game is the card game. It's so boring!

1 **Listen.** Circle all the superlatives you hear. 🎧095

(the scariest)	the loudest	the most powerful	(the highest)
the cleverest	(the most difficult)	(the most awful)	(the coolest)
the least boring	(the best)	(the most fun)	(the least expensive)

2 **Work in pairs.** Complete the sentences with the superlative of the words in brackets.

Today, music games are some of ____the most popular____ (+/popular) games on the Internet. In one game, you can create your own hits in ____the easiest____ (+/easy) way possible. ____The most exciting____ (+/exciting) thing is that you can create original songs or mash-ups of famous songs. Don't worry! Even ____the least musical____ (–/musical) person can create amazing songs. ____The best____ (+/good) feature of the game is that you can sing with the music you create! The game makes even ____the worst____ (–/bad) singer sound great! ____The most important____ (+/important) thing to remember is to share your hits with your friends.

3 **Work in pairs.** Talk about the best and worst video games. Why do you like them? Use superlatives.

> The most interesting games make you solve puzzles.

116 GRAMMAR

Warm Up

• **Revise** Say *In Unit 6, we learnt to compare two people or things.* Hold up two things for comparison, such as two books or two pencils. Ask students to compare the items using phrases such as *This book is bigger than that one; The red pencil is as long as the yellow pencil.* Continue until students have compared at least five pairs of items.

• Say *Now let's compare people.* Ask two students to come to the front of the class and compare the length of their hair. For example, say *(Julia's) hair is long. Is (Sylvia's) hair shorter/longer than (Julia's)?* Ask students to respond and then say *That's right! (Sylvia's) hair is shorter/longer than (Julia's).* Then invite another student to the front of the class. This student should have the longest hair. Gesture toward this student's hair and say *(Veronica's) hair is the longest.*

• Write the following sentences on the board, underlining the comparative phrases.

4 LEARN NEW WORDS Listen to learn about some pretty unusual apps.
Then listen and repeat. 🎧 096 097

There's an app for that!?!

Your smartphone's **microphone** can tell you if a melon is ready to eat.

Blow into your phone's microphone to create steam on the **screen**. Then you can write in the steam with your finger.

Safely walk as you type into your phone's **keyboard**. The phone's **camera** shows what's in front of you. Be careful: this app uses up your phone's **battery** very quickly!

5 Work in pairs. Complete the sentences using the words in the box. Then say whether you agree or disagree, and why.

> I don't agree with number 5. I record things I need to remember every day.

battery	camera	keyboard	microphone	screen

1. A smartphone _____camera_____ is the quickest and the easiest way to take pictures.

2. Finding a place to charge your phone's _____battery_____ is always easy.

3. Typing on a smartphone's small _____keyboard_____ is the most difficult thing about sending texts.

4. One of the best things about a mobile gadget is that, if you want to, you can see friends on the _____screen_____ while you're talking to them.

5. One of the least-used features on a mobile gadget is the _____microphone_____ .

6 Discuss in groups. Which apps are the most useful, the most difficult and the most fun? Which are the least useful, the least difficult and the least fun?

GRAMMAR **117**

Grammar in Depth

Students learnt to compare two things or people (or groups of things/people) in Unit 6. Superlatives compare one thing in a group of at least three to the rest of the group.

All superlatives have the word *the* before the adjective. Although there are exceptions to these rules, most superlatives are formed according to the following guidelines:

- Adjectives with three or more syllables always follow *the most/the least*: *the most exciting*.
- Adjectives with two syllables that end in *y* take an *-est* ending: *the easiest, the prettiest*.
- Other adjectives with two syllables may follow *the most/the least*: *the most famous*.
- Adjectives with one syllable take an *-est* ending: *the largest, the fastest*. When these adjectives follow the consonant + vowel + consonant format, the last consonant needs to be doubled (e.g. *the biggest*).

It's not common to change a word that takes *-est* into *the least* … If, for example, a speaker wants to express the idea of *the least big*, he or she would simply choose the opposite: *the smallest*. However, words that take *most* also take *least*.

> Julia's hair is <u>long</u>.
>
> Sylvia's hair is <u>longer than</u> Julia's.
>
> Veronica's hair is <u>the longest</u>.

- Repeat the activity, comparing another group of students in a different way. Then say *When we learnt to compare in Unit 6, we focused on comparing two things or groups of things. In this unit, we are comparing more than two things.*

Present

- Ask students to open their books at pages 116–117 and draw students' attention to the grammar box. Say *Today, we're learning to use superlatives. When we use superlatives, we compare several things and identify the most extreme – the tallest, fastest or most interesting – thing in the group.* Play **Track 094** and ask students to listen. Say *Notice the words and word parts used to express superlatives.* Tell students to underline the superlative constructions in the grammar box.

GRAMMAR 1 **209**

- **Explain** Say *When we form superlatives, we always start with the word* the. *This indicates that we are identifying a specific thing – the one thing that stands out in the group. Superlatives have different forms. With some superlatives, you add -est to the end of the adjective.* Re-read the first example and give additional examples such as *fastest, coolest* and *shortest.*

- Say *Most adjectives with one syllable take the -est ending. An adjective with two syllables might take an -est ending, too, especially when it ends in* y. Give the examples *easiest* and *scariest.* Then say *Other two-syllable adjectives do not take -est but instead follow the words* most *or* least. Give examples such as *most boring* and *least common.*

- Point to the second example in the box and say *When adjectives have three or more syllables, such as* difficult *or* interesting, *they do not take an -est ending. They always follow the words* the most *or* the least.

- Explain that there are exceptions to the rules for forming superlatives. Re-read the third sentence, emphasising the phrases *the most fun* and *the least fun.* Explain the meanings of *most* and *least.* Give additional examples of adjectives used with these words: *the least interesting, the least common,* etc. Finally, explain that the adjectives *good* and *bad* also have irregular superlative forms: *the best* and *the worst.* Re-read the last two examples.

Practise

- Say *In this activity, you're going to hear two friends talking about video games. Before we listen, let's look at the words in the box.* Read each of the superlatives in the word box aloud and ask students to provide the root word of words with -*est* endings. Point out the spelling change for adjectives ending in *y* by emphasising the spelling of the first superlative in the box, *scariest.*

210 UNIT 7

- Play **Track 095** once and ask students to circle the superlatives that they hear. Put students into pairs and ask them to compare their answers. Then play **Track 095** again and tell students to check their answers.

- **2** Read the instructions aloud. Before students begin, explain that the plus sign (+) indicates *more,* so students should use *the most* + adjective or the -*est* ending. The minus sign (–) indicates *less,* so students should use *the least* + adjective or *the worst.*

- Tell students to complete the activity in pairs. Walk around as they work to check that they're using the correct forms. When they have finished, ask a student to come up to the front and read the completed paragraph aloud.

- **3** Before students begin this activity, work as a class to brainstorm a list of adjectives that could be used to describe video games. Then review the number of syllables for each of the adjectives on your list to determine how to form the superlative of each.

Apply

- **4** **LEARN NEW WORDS** Say *We've talked about how useful smartphones are. We've also talked about different smartphone apps, such as translators, calculators and video games. Now we're going to be looking at some very unusual apps. What is the most unusual app you have ever heard of?* Invite several students to share their ideas. If students have got their smartphones with them and have the apps installed on their phones, allow them to demonstrate the app for the class.

- Hold up your book to show page 117 and point to the photos. (Students' books should be closed.) Ask *What do you think each of these apps does?* Ask students to predict each app's function using only the photos.

- Say *Let's read and listen to learn about the apps shown here. Check to see if your predictions are correct.* Ask students to open their books at page 117. Play **Track 096** and tell students to listen to the descriptions of all three apps. Then ask students to stand up and read each of the summaries aloud. Ask *Would any of these apps be useful to you or fun? Which ones?* Invite several students to give their reactions.

- Play **Track 097** and ask students to repeat the words and sentences they hear. Review the meaning of each new word. Then put students into pairs and ask them to use the new words in sentences describing different apps or gadgets.

- **5 Model** Read the instructions aloud. Review the meanings of the words in the box. Ask students to scan the sentences for key words to help them identify each correct answer. Model doing this by reading the first sentence aloud and saying *I see the phrase take pictures. If I want to take pictures, I need to use a camera.* Tell students to write the word *camera* in the first gap. Allow time for students to complete the activity in pairs.

- Once students have completed the activity, ask a student to read the model aloud. Then ask students to take turns reading aloud the sentences and saying whether they agree with them and why. After students have discussed all five sentences, review their answers as a class.

- **6** Give students a three-column table graphic organiser and tell them to write *useful, difficult* and *fun* as headings in each of the columns. Then tell them to fold the table to create a top half and a bottom half. Ask students to list apps that are useful, difficult or fun in the top half of their tables. Tell them to list apps that are not useful, difficult or fun in the bottom half. Encourage students to think of at least one or two apps for each category.

- Once students have listed the apps, put them into groups of three. Then invite students to discuss the apps using superlative forms. Ask groups to share their responses with the class.

Extend

- Write the following list of adjectives on the board: *pretty, tall, strange, fun, good, boring, interesting, exciting, intelligent* and *bad*.

- Put students into groups. Give each group a piece of strong card, scissors, glue and a stack of old magazines. Say *You're going to make a collage to show superlatives. Look through these magazines and find ten photos that show superlatives for the adjectives on the board – the prettiest dog, the tallest building and so on. Cut the photos out and paste them onto the card. Then write a sentence for each one using a superlative.*

- Walk around while students work to check their sentences. Remind students that one-syllable adjectives usually take *-est* and many multi-syllable adjectives take *the most/least*. Review the irregular forms of *good* and *bad*.

- When students have finished, collect and display their posters.

Consolidate

- Say *Let's have a contest.* As a class, think of positive traits, such as *friendly, intelligent, funny* and *likely to succeed.* Write the list on the board.

- Say *For each of these categories, let's vote on a classmate. For example, I might vote for (Lin) as the funniest student in the class.* Tell students to write a sentence using a superlative to vote for a classmate for each category. If time allows, ask students to read their sentences aloud.

Our World in Context

Activity 4 is titled *There's an app for that!?!* The answer is almost always going to be *yes.* With 1.5 million mobile apps available in the year 2015 and many more being developed, it's likely that there's an app for just about any activity you can think of!

Teaching Tip

When students are faced with memorising information, help them identify study skills that work for their learning styles. For example, visual learners might benefit from creating diagrams or illustrated flashcards. Auditory learners might benefit most from creating a podcast of the correct forms and then listening and repeating them. Kinaesthetic learners, or those who learn by doing, benefit from creating hands-on activities or providing physical responses.

Formative Assessment

Can students

- use superlatives to talk about extremes?

  Ask students to describe three of their classes with superlatives.

- identify and describe unusual mobile apps?

  Ask *Which app from the reading uses a microphone? Which app uses a camera and the phone's battery?*

Workbook For additional practice, assign Workbook pages 70–71.

Online Workbook Grammar 1

Objectives

Students will

- read about creative teens and their inventions.
- identify and use new words from the reading.
- identify the main idea and details of the reading.

Reading Strategy Identify main idea and details

Vocabulary Strategy Identify parts of speech

Target Vocabulary *borrow, find, function, invent*

Academic Language *describe, detail*

Content Vocabulary *console, controller, get around, have an impact on, material, owner, remarkable, solve*

Resources Online Workbook/Workbook pages 72–73; Worksheet 1.7.4 (Teacher's Resource CD-ROM/ Website); Tracks 098–099 (Audio CD/ Website/CPT); CPT: Reading

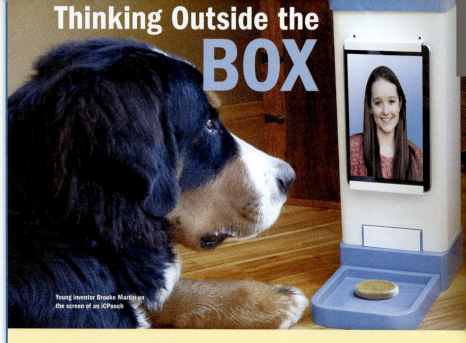

Thinking Outside the BOX

Young inventor Brooke Martin on the screen of an iCPooch

1 BEFORE YOU READ **Discuss in pairs.** Look at the photo. Describe what you think the gadget does.

2 LEARN NEW WORDS **Find these words in the reading.** What do you think they mean? Think about what type of word each one is. Then listen and repeat. 🎧098

borrow	find
function	invent

3 WHILE YOU READ **Look for the main idea and details that support it.** 🎧099

4 AFTER YOU READ **Work in pairs.** Tick T for *true* statements or F for *false*.

1. All you need for Bot2Karot is a smartphone app. **T** (F)
2. Bot2Karot helps people take care of their gardens. (T) **F**
3. Brooke Martin was sixteen when she invented iCPooch. **T** (F)
4. The only thing you can do with iCPooch is look at your dog. **T** (F)
5. Robert Saunt likes playing video games. (T) **F**
6. Robert's gadget will be good for the environment. (T) **F**

118 READING

Warm Up

- **Build background** Say *Today, we're going to read a text called Thinking Outside the Box.* Write the title on the board and say *When we think outside the box, we come up with creative and original ideas 'outside' of our usual thought patterns.*

- Say *Sometimes thinking outside the box can help us solve problems.* Describe a problem that you've been having in your class or invent a problematic scenario. Say *For example, in our class (students have been coming to lessons late).* Then say *Try thinking outside the box. You're going to work in small groups to think about creative solutions to our problem.*

- If you're discussing an existing problem, describe what you've already done to try to solve it and then encourage students to think of new ideas that are different from what you've already tried.

- Put students into small groups. Tell them to take a few minutes to discuss the problem and come up with possible solutions. Invite groups to stand up and share their ideas.

Creative teens can make a difference!

If you think young people can't have an impact on the world, think again. Over the years, teens have invented remarkable things that solve problems and have changed the ways people do things. And they're going to continue to invent things in the future.

Take 14-year-old Eliott Sarrey from France, for example. He invented Bot2Karot, a gardening robot that can take care of a small vegetable garden. The robot is controlled by an app on a smartphone. It helps people grow and take care of vegetables. It also saves water and energy, and makes gardening easy for people who are very busy or have difficulty getting around.

Brooke Martin is an animal lover who missed her dog when she was away. She also knew that her dog suffered from stress when its owners left. So Brooke invented iCPooch® when she was just 12 years old. The iCPooch lets pet owners check on their pets from anywhere in the world using a tablet or a smartphone. This award-winning gadget also allows owners to use their smartphone camera to video chat with their pets. It has another function, too. Owners can quickly and easily give their pet a treat by touching the *drop treat* button on their screen. Dogs and owners must be pretty grateful to Brooke for this invention!

Fourteen-year-old inventor Robert Saunt was tired of buying or borrowing different video-game controllers for each game console. So he invented a controller called *Game Blox*. It can be used with four of the most popular game consoles. His invention will save players a lot of money and space, and it will save 330 million kg. (727 million lb.) of materials every year. Players will also be able to listen to music while they play video games with Robert's gadget.

Youngsters all over the world find ways to solve problems every day. Who knows? Maybe the next time you have a problem, you'll come up with the next amazing idea!

---

5 Discuss your answers to Activity 3 in small groups. Then complete the following:

Main idea
Teens are creative and can invent interesting things.

Detail 1
Eliott Sarrey invented a gardening robot.

Detail 2
Brooke Martin invented iCPooch.

Detail 3
Robert Saunt invented a game controller that can be used with different game consoles.

6 Discuss in groups.

1. Which of these three inventions do you think is the most useful? Why? Which do you think is the least useful? Why?
2. What do you think is the greatest invention of all time? Who invented it? Why is it so great?
3. Brooke worried about her dog when she was on holiday. Think of two other ways she could check on her dog while she's away.

READING **119**

Strategy in Depth

Identify main idea and details Explain to students that when they read a non-fiction text, they must try to identify the main idea. The main idea is the point of the reading: it's what the author wants the reader to know after reading the text. The main idea is usually stated explicitly, often at the beginning of a text. A text will always include supporting information for the main idea. This supporting information includes details, examples and reasons. When reading a text, students should ask themselves the following questions: *What is the author's point? How does the author support this point?*

Vocabulary Strategy

Identify parts of speech As students acquire a larger vocabulary, it's important that they are able to identify a word's part of speech – that is, whether it's a noun, a verb, an adjective and so on. If students know the meaning of a word in one part of speech (e.g. the verb *to find*), then they will more easily identify the meaning of the word when used as a different part of speech (e.g. *This discovery was an important find.*) Knowing that the same word can serve different functions can help students acquire a wide range of vocabulary more quickly. Remind students that when they look a word up in the dictionary, they should always take note of the different parts of speech it could be.

Before You Read

- Ask students to open their books at pages 118–119. Say *We have just talked about what thinking outside the box means.* Read the instructions aloud and tell each pair to study the photo before discussing what the item does. Say *As you do this activity, think about what is creative or unusual about what you see in the photo.*

- **LEARN NEW WORDS** Say *We're going to learn new words that will help you understand the reading.* Say each new word aloud and ask students to repeat. Then say *Let's see how these words are used in the reading.* Tell students to scan the reading and find the words. After a moment, ask students to read the sentences containing each of the new words aloud.

- Play **Track 098**. Ask students to listen and repeat each word and sentence.

• **Play Track 099** and ask students to follow. When they have finished, ask *What is the main idea?* (Creative teens can make a difference.) *Where do we see the main idea?* (in the subtitle/at the beginning of the text)

After You Read

• **4** Put students into pairs and ask them to take turns reading the true and false statements aloud. Then invite them to review the text to find the correct answers. When they have finished, ask students to re-read each sentence to the class and provide the answer. Tell students to correct the false statements, showing where in the text they found the correct information.

• **5** Say *We've already discussed the main idea of the text – that teens are creative and can invent interesting things. Write the main idea in the space provided.* Pause to allow students to do this. Then say *An author always supports the main idea with details or examples. There is space here for three details. Work in groups to re-read the text and identify three details that support this main idea. Write your answers in the spaces provided.*

• When students have finished, invite the groups to discuss their answers and then share them with the class. Students' answers should include the name of each creative teen and a brief description of his or her invention and its impact.

• **6** Put students into different groups to discuss the questions in Activity 6. For the first question, tell each group to provide their answers and give reasons (from the reading or from their own experiences) as to why the inventions are or aren't useful.

• You may choose to assign the second question as a homework assignment. Ask students to research the greatest invention they can think of and provide information to support their claim that it's the best. Students can write a journal entry to summarise their ideas and research. During the next class, ask students to share their work in small groups.

• For question 3, encourage students to think of an app or gadget that could help Brooke and other pet owners who want to check on their pets when they're away.

• **Vocabulary strategy** Say *In English, there are several different types of words. These are called* parts of speech. *Most of the new vocabulary that we learn are one of four parts of speech:* nouns, verbs, adjectives and adverbs. *Review what each of these terms means.* If you wish, you may want to teach students other parts of speech (e.g. pronouns, prepositions, conjunctions, interjections). Then say *When we learn a new word, it's important to remember its part of speech. This will help us identify the meaning of a new word in context. It will also help us use the word correctly in a sentence.*

• Write the word *function* on the board. Then write the following sentences:

> *The function of this gadget is to help people communicate with their pets.*
> *This gadget functions as a communication tool between people and their pets.*

• Say *In these examples, the word* function *is used as both a noun and a verb. We've already heard the word* function *being used as a noun to mean 'job' or 'purpose.' Knowing this, look at the second sentence. What does* function *mean when used as a verb?* (to work, to have a purpose) Say *When we know a word, it's easier to identify its meaning when it's used as a different part of speech.*

While You Read

• **3** Read the instructions aloud. Say *The main idea of the text is the point that the author is trying to make: it's what the text is about. An author usually presents the main idea towards the beginning of a text. Then the author uses details and examples to support the main idea.*

Extend

- Put students into groups to create an advertisement for one of the gadgets mentioned in the reading. Students should further research the gadget and its inventor and include additional information in their adverts.

- Students can act out their adverts in class or they can record their adverts in an audio or video file and share it on a class website.

- **Worksheet** If time allows, hand out **Worksheet 1.7.4** in class. Remind students to review the new words presented on page 118. Ask students to complete the worksheet independently and then compare their answers with a partner's.

Consolidate

- Write the names of each creative teen on the board: Eliott Sarrey, Brooke Martin, Robert Saunt. Ask students to copy the students' names on a sheet of paper.

- Slowly, give facts about each teen aloud. Say the facts in random order. Tell students to write the information under the name of the teen being described. For example, say *invented a game controller* (Robert) or *wanted to help gardeners* (Eliott). Continue until you have reviewed ten facts from the reading. Then review correct answers as a class.

About the Photo

The photo shows Brooke Martin, inventor of the iCPooch®, on the screen of a smartphone that's installed in the iCPooch device. Brooke first presented her idea at a start-up event where she was one of 40 people to pitch an idea. The other 39 were adults and Brooke was 12! Nevertheless, Brooke's idea won the contest and she and her dad worked on building the prototype in their garage. They later built a business and manufacturing team and took the iCPooch to market.

Formative Assessment

Can students

- read about creative teens and their inventions?

  Ask *What is the Bot2Karot and who invented it?*

- identify and use new words from the reading?

  Ask students to use the words *function* and *invent* to talk about one of the teen inventors.

- identify the main idea and details of the reading?

  Ask *What is the main idea of the reading? What are three details that support it?*

Workbook For additional practice, assign Workbook pages 72–73.

Online Workbook Reading

Objectives

Students will
- identify how technology has changed the gadgets we use for different activities.
- apply the message of the video to their own lives.

Academic Language *chart, predict, role-play, timeline*

Content Vocabulary *convenient, depend on, develop, directions, heavy, instant, pendulum clock, pocket, portable, professional*

Resources Video scene 7.1 (DVD/ Website/CPT); Online Workbook; CPT: Video

VIDEO ▶

1 BEFORE YOU WATCH Discuss in pairs. Before smartphones and other new electronic gadgets, how did people tell time? Take photos? Listen to music?

2 Read and circle. You're going to watch *From Gadgets to Apps*. From the title, predict the main idea of the video. Circle the letter.

a. Gadgets are more important than their apps.
b. Useful apps are replacing gadgets.
c. We will use different gadgets and apps in the future.

3 WHILE YOU WATCH Complete the table. Watch scene 7.1.

Function	Today	What people first used for this function	The problem with the original gadget
tell time	clock app	pendulum clock	hard to carry around
listen to music	music app	record player	hard to carry around
take a photo	camera app	big, heavy, box camera	You needed a professional photographer.

4 AFTER YOU WATCH Match the two parts of the sentences.

_d_	1. The digital age	a. were easy to use but only made one copy of a photo.
_b_	2. Watches in the 1950s	b. were small and portable but had only one use.
_e_	3. Before there were instant cameras, people	c. were smaller than before, but they still couldn't fit in our pockets.
_a_	4. Instant cameras	d. actually began in the 1950s.
_c_	5. In the 1950s, gadgets for listening to music	e. depended on professional photographers.

120 VIDEO

Before You Watch

- Ask students to open their books at pages 120–121 and point to the photos. Say *Look at these items. Do you know what they are?* Invite students to identify the items they can and say what they're used for. Then ask a student to stand up and read the question aloud. Tell students to discuss it in pairs. Tell them to match any of the photos to the activities mentioned in the question. Extend the activity by asking how people used to learn new words, get directions and get the news.

- Read the instructions aloud and ask a student to stand up and read each of the answer options. Ask students to circle their predictions and then compare their response with a partner's.

While You Watch

- Point to the table on page 120 and say *Look at the table. There are four columns. The first column is*

the function or an activity that people do. In the second column, we see the names of apps that people use to do this activity today. As you watch, you're going to fill in the last two columns. In the third column, write the name of a gadget that people used to use to do the activity. In the last column, write a problem with that gadget that explains why it was replaced.

- Play **Video scene 7.1** and tell students to fill in the third column. Play it again and tell them to fill in the fourth column. Review students' answers as a class.

After You Watch

- Before students begin, tell them to cover up the right-hand column of the matching activity. For each item on the left, ask students to recall what was said in the video. Model by reading the first item aloud: *The digital age.* Say *The digital age refers to the age of high technology. In the video, it said that the digital age began in the 1950s.* After students have thought about

5 **Work in pairs.** In the video, you heard, 'Your phone might have an app for giving you directions to a friend's house, but you can't ride it there.' Think of three apps you like. What things can they do? What can't they do? Discuss.

6 **Discuss in groups.**

1. At the end of the video, you're asked, 'What other gadgets do you use? Why are they useful? Will there ever be apps for them?' Answer these questions.
2. What old-fashioned item or gadget is still used in your home? Why is it useful?

7 **YOU DECIDE** **Choose an activity.**

1. **Work independently.** Find out about the lives of people in your country one hundred years ago. How did they communicate? Travel from place to place? Take photos? Get information? Share what you learn with the class.

2. **Work in pairs.** Role-play a historical figure and a teenager of today. The teen must show and explain how a certain gadget works. The historical figure must react and ask questions appropriate for his/her time period.

3. **Work in groups.** Choose an activity that you do on your smartphone, such as listening to music or taking photos. Use the Internet to find out about how this activity was done at different times in the past. Make a timeline to show how the activity has changed.

VIDEO **121**

These old-fashioned things have all been replaced by smartphone apps.

Teaching Tip

Students may rely on the Internet to do most of the research assigned in this book's activities, but encourage them to look for information elsewhere. Guide students to use your school or community library to conduct research, especially when studying things about the past. Point out the value of primary sources, such as historical documents or interviews with older community members.

Formative Assessment

Can students
- identify how technology has changed what gadgets we use for different activities?

Ask students to name three objects that have been replaced by modern electronic gadgets.

Online Workbook Video

each item, tell them to uncover the right-hand column and do the matching activity. If necessary, play **Video scene 7.1** again. Review correct answers as a class.

- **5** Explain that students should analyse three of their favourite apps and identify how they're helpful, but they should also identify things that the app isn't able to do. Model by saying *I really like the app for my bank. I am able to move money around in my bank accounts. But I can't borrow money with the app. I have to go to the bank if I want to do that.*

- After students discuss their apps in pairs, ask several students to share their ideas with the class. Finally, discuss as a class whether the app will ever have the ability to do the activity it cannot do currently.

- **6** Read the questions aloud. Point out that the gadgets don't necessarily need to be electronic gadgets. Give students examples of other tools they might use, such as rulers or dictionaries.

- For the second question, tell students to describe the gadget and say how old it is. Encourage students to ask their parents or other family members why they're keeping the gadget. They should report to the class.

- **7** **YOU DECIDE** Read the activity options aloud to students. Tell students to use books and online resources, as well as information from older family and community members.

- Tell students who choose the second option to first identify the period from which the historical figure comes. Encourage pairs to choose different time periods. Tell students to draft the dialogue and rehearse it. Allow time for students to perform the sketch in class.

- To provide structure for the third option, provide a timeline with a series of years, such as *1700, 1800, 1900, 1920, 1970, 2000.*

VIDEO **217**

Objective

Students will
- use *will* and *going to* to talk about the future.

Grammar *Will* and *going to:* Talking about the future

Academic Language *prediction*

Content Vocabulary *attach, company, recognise, swallow, water, wearable*

Resources Online Workbook/Workbook pages 74–75; Worksheet 1.7.5 (Teacher's Resource CD-ROM/ Website); Tracks 100–101 (Audio CD/ Website/CPT); CPT: Grammar 2

Materials a weather forecast, coins for the board game, pieces of card

---

GRAMMAR 🎧 100

Will and *going to:* Talking about the future

Possible	Most likely
We **will have** little machines in our heads that can connect to gadgets.	Everything at home **is going to connect** to a gadget.
People **won't talk** to each other on smartphones anymore.	People **aren't going to use** phones with keyboards anymore.
Will people **need** to have so many gadgets?	**How are** our gadgets **going to help** us every day?
No, they **won't**. One gadget **will be** all you need.	They**'re going to help** us do chores, like watering the garden.

1 Listen and write the future forms. 🎧 101

1. _aren't going to_ have to
2. _will_ attach
3. _will_ recognise
4. _will_ connect
5. _will_ swallow
6. _will_ take
7. _will_ send
8. _going to_ be

A wearable password

2 Work in pairs. Complete the sentences about the future of Internet communication.

1. How is the Internet _going to change_ (change) in the future?
2. We _won't / aren't going to have to_ (not have to) search the Internet for what we want.
3. It _will / is going to know_ (know) what we want before we do.
4. All companies are _going to study_ (study) what people do on the Internet even more than they do now.
5. The companies _will / are going to tell_ (tell) us what they think we need.

3 Work in pairs. Throw a coin and move ahead (heads = 1 space; tails = 2 spaces). When you land on a space, make a prediction about the topic.

We're going to have computers in our bodies.

Go to page 171.

122 GRAMMAR

Warm Up

- **Pre-teach** Print out and display a weather report or show students a video of a television weather forecast for the next five days. Say *Let's look at the weather over the next few days. Today, it's going to be (sunny). What about tomorrow?* Write the following sentence on the board, underlining the words *going to*: Tomorrow, it's going to (rain).

- Say *Since it's going to be (sunny) today, I'm going to go to the park. Tomorrow, it's going to (rain). I think I will stay home and watch a film.* Ask *What are you going to do today? tomorrow?* Invite students to respond.

Present

- **Explain** Ask students to open their books at page 122. Say *In this lesson, we're going to talk about the future.* Point to the box at the top of page 122. Say *Notice that there are two columns. The column on the left describes things that are possible. We often use the verb* will *to talk about things that may possibly happen but aren't definitely planned. We also use* will *to make predictions.*

- Say *Now look at the second column. When we use the words* going to, *we are talking about definite plans or things that are very likely to happen.*

- Play **Track 100**. Point out that the sentences on the left may happen but aren't definite. The sentences on the right talk about things that are more likely to happen.

Practise ① ②

- **①** Say *A password is a special word you use to keep information safe when you use a computer.* Play **Track 101** and pause after the instructions. Say *Remember, if you hear* will, *that means the action is possible; if you hear* going to, *the action is more likely.*

- Continue playing **Track 101**. Tell students to write the appropriate answers. Then play **Track 101** again, this time pausing after each verb on the list to check the correct answers as a class.

- **2** Put students into pairs. Invite a student to stand up and read the instructions aloud. Then draw students' attention to the words in brackets. Tell students to review the examples in the yellow grammar box to determine if they should use *will* or *going to*. When they have finished, ask students to read each sentence aloud.

Apply **3**

- **3** Read the instructions aloud. Tell students to remove the game board from page 171 and scan the words. Point to the term *Smart homes.* Explain that a *smart home* has gadgets that make life easier. For example, a smart home might have features that automatically control temperature, lighting and music using an app.

- Before they begin, ask students to think of predictions for each category. It may help students to write their ideas down.

- Point to the first square on the game board: *Apps.* Say *I predict that in the future, all apps will be free.* Then ask *Am I sure about this prediction?* (no) Say *It's possible but not definite. As you play, listen to see if your partner is sure about his or her predictions.*

- Allow time for students to play the game. Walk around the room as students play to listen to their predictions. When they finish, invite those students whose predictions you found particularly interesting to share their ideas with the whole class.

Extend

- Think of 8–10 activities or events that are relevant to your students and write each one on a separate piece of card. Events can include *a school dance, the weekend, a maths test, an audition for a school play, my next birthday,* and so on. Create enough sets of cards so that each group of students has the same set.

- Put students into groups of three or four and give each group a set of cards. Tell students to take turns to draw a card and talk about the event they read. Students should say one sentence with *will* and one sentence with *going to*.

- Tell students to take turns selecting cards and talking about the events. Listen to students' discussions and ask for additional information using questions with *will* and *going to*.

- Hand out **Worksheet 1.7.5** to provide additional practice with *will* and *going to*.

Consolidate

- Say *Imagine what our school will be like in ten years. Write four predictions – two that are possible and two that are more definite.*

- Put students into pairs and give them several minutes to write their ideas. Then ask students to share their ideas with the class. List students' responses on the board.

Grammar in Depth

Both *will* and *going to* are used to talk about the future. *Going to* is used to express definite plans and intentions. *Will* is used to talk about the future when no plans were made before the statement was made. For example: *That looks delicious! I'll try one! Will* is also used to talk about future facts. For example: *The building will be finished next year. I will turn 15 in July.* Both *going to* and *will* can be used for predictions, although predictions with *going to* are usually based on evidence. For example: *I've got 1,000 more points than you! I'm going to win this game!*

Formative Assessment

Can students
- use *will* and *going to* to talk about the future?

Ask students to say a sentence about what's possible and what's most likely to be true about gadgets in the future.

Workbook For additional practice, assign Workbook pages 74–75.

Online Workbook Grammar 2

WRITING

Objectives

Students will
- identify elements of a product review.
- analyse a model product review.
- write a product review.

Academic Language *adjective, opinion, paragraph, product review*

Content Vocabulary *attach, cartridge, message, scent, smell, stick out*

Resources Online Workbook/Workbook page 76; Process Writing Worksheets 1–5; Genre Writing Worksheet: Review; Graphic Organiser: T-chart (Teacher's Resource CD-ROM/ Website); CPT: Writing

---

WRITING

When we write a product review, we describe a product. We give examples of what's good and what's bad about it. We can use adjectives to help the reader understand our opinions.

1 **Read the model.** Work in pairs to find the good and bad points about the product. Underline the good points. Circle the bad points.

Do you like the smell of cakes baking? Fresh flowers? Well, it's now possible to experience these great smells electronically. You just need a cool new gadget for sending smells, scent pellets, and an app on your smartphone or tablet.

This product is amazing because it lets you share smells with people anywhere in the world. Sharing smells can help us connect to an idea or an experience better than just looking at a photo or reading a text. Think about it: you're making biscuits. You take a photo of the biscuits using the app. Then you tag the photo with certain smells, like chocolate or butter. You can combine tags to create more than 300,000 different smells! I love how the product lets you be creative in mixing different scents. I also like the idea of receiving smells. So if my friends are camping and I'm not there, at least I can smell the burning campfire!

This product is incredible, but there are some things about it that I don't like. First, the gadget is big and not very mobile. It would be great to receive smells wherever I go. The company is working on this problem. They're creating bracelets and smartphone cases that will let users receive smells, but these products aren't available yet. The product is also pretty expensive! It may be a while before a lot of people have them, so there won't be many people to share smells with. All in all, I give this product three out of five stars!

2 **Discuss in pairs.** Would you like to try this product? Why or why not?

3 **Write.** Write a paragraph to review a product that you have used. Give examples of what you like and don't like about it. Use adjectives to help your readers understand your opinion.

People can send scents by tagging photos, and receive them using this tabletop device.

WRITING **123**

Warm Up

- **Build Background** Say *Throughout this unit, we've learnt about different apps and gadgets, but we haven't tried any of them. Let's think about apps that we use on smartphones or tablets.* Ask students to name some of the apps that they use on their smartphones. Then tell them to choose one they like to use.

- Say *I like to use the dictionary app on my phone. I use it whenever I want to learn a new word.* Write *dictionary app* on the board. Then say *There are things I really like about this app. I like that it's quick and that I can hear the pronunciation of a new word.* Draw a T-chart under the name of the app and write what you like.

Like	Don't like
· quick · can hear pronunciation	· adverts are annoying · only one meaning

- Continue by saying *The dictionary app is useful, but it's not perfect. It has too many ads, which can be annoying. And for each word, it gives only the most popular meaning. That's not always helpful.* Write what you don't like in the second column.

- Tell students to choose an app they have named and write two things they like about it and two things they don't like. Invite several students to come to the front of the class and share their responses.

Present

- **Explain** Ask students to open their books at page 123. Draw their attention to the green box at the top of the page. Read the text aloud. Say *We're going to write a review. In a review, we describe a product. We also identify good and bad things about the product.* Point to the T-chart on the board. Say *If I write a review of this app, I would first describe it by explaining how it works. Then I would give information about what I like and information about what I don't like.*

- Re-read the last sentence from the green box. Say *It says to use adjectives in a review. Remember, adjectives are describing words. What adjectives did I use to describe the app?* (*quick, annoying*)

Read the Model

- Say *In a moment, we're going to read a model of a product review. First, let's look at the photo of the product.* Point to the photo and read the caption. Ask *What do you think is attached to this tablet? What function do you think it has?*

- Read the instructions aloud. Say *I'm going to read the paragraph aloud. Listen and notice the good points that the writer mentions. Underline them.* Read the paragraph aloud. Then say *Now I'm going to read it again. This time, circle everything that the writer says is bad about the product.* When you've finished, review students' answers.

- Tell students to discuss the question in pairs, using examples from the model to explain why they would or wouldn't like to try the product. Remind students that they can include their own reasons for wanting (or not wanting) to try the product.

- After pairs have finished discussing the question, ask those who want to try the product to put up their hands. Ask them to give reasons. Repeat by asking students who aren't interested in the product to put up their hands and explain their responses.

- **Worksheet** If your students need a reminder of the elements of a review, you may want to hand out **Genre Writing Worksheet: Review** and review it together.

1 **Read the model.** Work in pairs to find the good and bad points about the product. Underline the good points. Circle the bad points.

Do you like the smell of cakes baking? Fresh flowers? Well, it's now possible to experience these great smells electronically. You just need a cool new gadget for sending smells, scent pellets, and an app on your smartphone or tablet.

This product is amazing because it lets you share smells with people anywhere in the world. Sharing smells can help us connect to an idea or an experience better than just looking at a photo or reading a text. Think about it: you're making biscuits. You take a photo of the biscuits using the app. Then you tag the photo with certain smells, like chocolate or butter. You can combine tags to create more than 300,000 different smells! I love how the product lets you be creative in mixing different scents. I also like the idea of receiving smells. So if my friends are camping and I'm not there, at least I can smell the burning campfire!

This product is incredible, but there are some things about it that I don't like. First, the gadget is big and not very mobile. It would be great to receive smells wherever I go. The company is working on this problem. They're creating bracelets and smartphone cases that will let users receive smells, but these products aren't available yet. The product is also pretty expensive. It may be a while before a lot of people have them, so there won't be many people to share smells with. All in all, I give this product three out of five stars!

2 **Discuss in pairs.** Would you like to try this product? Why or why not?

3 **Write.** Write a paragraph to review a product that you have used. Give examples of what you like and don't like about it. Use adjectives to help your readers understand your opinion.

People can send scents by tagging photos, and receive them using this tabletop device.

WRITING **123**

Plan **3**

- **3** Say *Now you're going to write a review about a product of your choice.* Although the instructions don't specify that students write about technological gadgets, encourage them to do so in order to get sufficient practice of the unit's vocabulary and grammar.

- Give each student a copy of the T-chart graphic organiser. Say *Write Good above the left column and Bad above the right. Then write as many details as possible in each column. Remember to include adjectives, or describing words, in your chart.* Refer students to the T-chart you made in the Warm Up activity. Encourage students to identify at least two

good points and two bad points for their products.

- Walk around the room to check students' work as they complete their pre-writing T-charts. Offer suggestions for appropriate adjectives that students could use to describe the product they choose.

- **Worksheets** If your students need a reminder of any of the steps of process writing, hand out **Process Writing Worksheets 1–5** and review them together.

- **Workbook** Refer students to Workbook page 76 to help them organise and plan their writing.

Write

- After students have finished their pre-writing, tell them to work on their first drafts. If you haven't got enough time for students to complete the first draft in class, assign it as homework.

Revise

- After students have finished their first drafts, tell them to review their writing for clarity and organisation. Ask students to consider the following: *Did I use adjectives to describe the product? Did I mention good points and bad points about the product? Did I include examples? Are my opinions clear and easy to understand? Is my writing organised? What needs more work?*

Edit and Proofread

- Invite students to consider elements of style, such as sentence variety, parallelism and word choice. Then ask them to proofread for mistakes in grammar, punctuation, capitalisation and spelling.

Publish

- Publishing includes handing in pieces of writing to the teacher, sharing work with classmates, adding pieces to a class book, displaying pieces on a classroom wall or in a hallway, and posting on the Internet.

Writing Assessment

Use these guidelines to assess students' writing. You can add other aspects of their writing you'd like to assess at the bottom of the table.

4 = Excellent
3 = Good
2 = Needs improvement
1 = Re-do

	1	2	3	4
Writing Student's ideas are clear and well organised; used adjectives to describe what is good and bad about the product				
Grammar Student uses *will* and *going to* to talk about the future.				
Vocabulary Student uses a variety of word choices, including words used in this unit.				

NATIONAL GEOGRAPHIC

Always Keep Learning

'It's valuable to know what you don't know, and there's so much we don't know.'

Manu Prakash
National Geographic Explorer, Biophysicist

1. **Watch scene 7.2.**

2. Manu made a microscope that was cheap and easy to carry. How could this microscope be useful to a student like you? What could you learn if you had access to a microscope wherever you were?

3. Name something that you're interested in but don't know a lot about. What would you like to learn about it? How could you learn this information?

124 MISSION

Objectives
Students will
- identify how portable technology could change how they learn.
- discuss ways to learn new information about a topic that interests them.

Content Vocabulary *biophysicist, cheap, valuable*

Resources Video scene 7.2 (DVD/ Website/CPT); Worksheet 1.7.6 (Teacher's Resource CD-ROM/ Website); Online Workbook: Meet the Explorer; CPT: Mission

Online Workbook Meet the Explorer

Mission

- Ask students to open their books at page 124. Say *In this unit, we've looked at many different types of technology and how we use them.* Draw students' attention to the mission and read it aloud. Ask *How do you think technology will help us to always keep learning?*

- Point to the photo of Manu Prakash. Say *Manu is a biophysicist. A biophysicist is a scientist who uses physics to solve biological problems.* Ask a student to stand up and read Manu Prakash's quote. Ask *Do you agree with Manu? Is there a lot that you don't know?* Ask several students to respond with examples.

- **Activity 1** Say *Let's watch a video about Manu Prakash.* Play **Video scene 7.2**. Tell students to focus on how Manu's work brings science to children around the world.

- **Activity 2** Read the questions aloud. Ask *Have you used a microscope? Why did you use it?* Students may respond that they have used a microscope in science lessons to study microorganisms. Gesture to indicate students' surroundings and say *There are many microscopic things in this room. What could we view using a Foldscope? What might it teach us about our classroom?* Invite students to respond. Then ask them to discuss the question further, referencing other places where they spend time.

- **Activity 3** After students have discussed this question in small groups, encourage them to go home and research the topic they mentioned, using the method(s) they named. During the next lesson, ask students to describe what and how they learnt about the topic and whether it was interesting or enjoyable.

- **Worksheet** Hand out **Worksheet 1.7.6**. Explain that students will use the worksheet to further discuss learning and technology.

Objective

Students will
- choose and complete a project related to technology.

Academic Language *arrange, explain, label, plan, presentation*

Content Vocabulary *outdated, popular, task*

Resources Assessment: Unit 7 Quiz; Workbook pages 77 and 96; Worksheet 1.7.7 (Teacher's Resource CD-ROM/Website); CPT: Make an Impact and Review Games

Materials pieces of card, poster board, audiovisual equipment for student presentations

Assessment Go to page 261.

Unit Review Assign Worksheet 1.7.7

Workbook Assign pages 77 and 96.

Online Workbook Now I can

Make an Impact

YOU DECIDE Choose a project.

1 **Plan and give a presentation about the future.**
- Take photos of five things in your house that you think we won't use or that will be very different ten years from now.
- Prepare a presentation about what will replace these things or how they'll change and why.
- Present your ideas to the class.

2 **Design a robot.**
- Think about a task you don't like doing. Design a robot to do that task.
- Draw and label a picture of your robot.
- Present your robot to the class. Explain how it will work.

3 **Create an 'outdated gadget museum'.**
- Collect five or six items that were useful in the past but have been replaced by smartphones.
- Arrange the items in a 'museum'. Write descriptions of the items, including when they were invented and when they became less popular.
- Display your museum in class. Answer your classmates' questions about each item.

This solar-powered 'tree' uses energy from the sun to charge the batteries of different mobile gadgets.

PROJECT **125**

Prepare

- **YOU DECIDE** Ask students to choose a project.

- **Activity 1** Students may choose to present the information using a poster or a computer-based slideshow. Tell students to include their photos in their presentations. Students could look for prototype designs or draw their own futuristic design to show how each product should change. Finally, compare and contrast students' ideas on the same items in a class discussion.

- **Activity 2** Tell students to research different types of robots that are already being developed. Encourage students to be creative in their design. Hand out poster board to students so they can create a drawing that's large enough for others to see. Display the posters in class and allow others to study them and ask questions of the designer.

- **Activity 3** Ask students to watch **Video scene 7.1** again to get ideas for their museum. If students haven't got outdated gadgets in their own homes, tell them to ask other family members or find outdated gadgets at school. Give students one piece of card to write information on for each item they choose.

Share

- Schedule time for students to give their final presentations to the class. If necessary, bring in a projector to show students' presentations.

- **Modify** Students who choose Project 1 might prefer to present their information in a blog linked to a class website. Challenge students who choose Project 2 to create a digital rendering of their robot, adding animation if they know how. If possible, ask students who choose Project 3 to create their 'museum' in a hallway display case at school.

Track 088 (1)   **Listen and read.** See Student's Book pages 112–113.

Track 089 (2)   **LEARN NEW WORDS**   **app** / There are many different apps for learning or playing. **chat** / Families can keep in touch by chatting on their computers. **connect** / We can easily connect with friends on our computers. **gadget** / Electronic gadgets help us do many different things. **game** / Teenagers download a lot of games on their computers. **Internet** / It's easy to look up information on the Internet. **look up** / Smartphones make it easy to look up answers to your questions. **mobile** / We can take our mobile gadgets wherever we go. **search** / People search for information on their computers. **send** / I send e-mails to my friends to see how they're doing. **share** / People share digital photos with friends and family. **smartphone** / A smartphone is a phone with a computer. **useful** / Electronic gadgets are useful at school, home and work. **Wi-Fi** / Many places have free Wi-Fi so we can connect to the Internet.

Track 090 (5)   Did you forget to water your mum's flowers again? Or feed your fish? Don't worry! It might sound incredible but now we can take care of things in our homes even when we're not there! Using apps on our tablets or smartphones, we can feed our fish from school, turn off our TVs from a shopping centre and lock our doors without a key! Amazing, isn't it? It's even possible to watch our homes when we're on holiday with an app that sends a text if anything goes wrong. National Geographic Explorer Amber Case, who studies how people use electronics, believes our gadgets should make our lives easier and safer. And that's exactly what mobile apps do!

Track 091 (5)   **LEARN NEW WORDS**   **incredible** / What we can do with a smartphone is incredible. **possible** / It's possible to do a lot of things on our mobile gadgets. **tablet** / A tablet is like a small computer that you can carry around. **text** / Sending texts is the most popular way to communicate.

Track 092 **SPEAKING STRATEGY**   See Student's Book page 115.

Track 093 (1)   **S1**: Oh, no! My smartphone just stopped working. Manuel, can I borrow your charger? **S2**: I'm sorry. I haven't got it with me. **S1**: That's a shame. I wanted to download a cool game that sends birds to other planets. **S2**: I know that game. I downloaded it yesterday. **S1**: Cool! I really want to play it. Uh…Manuel, can you lend me your smartphone? **S2**: No, I'm afraid my dad's going to call me soon. But my tablet has that app, too. **S1**: Great! Please let me use it. **S2**: Sure. Here you go. There's just one thing, Luisa. **S1**: What is it? **S2**: Just don't beat my high score on the game!

Track 094 **GRAMMAR**   See Student's Book page 116.

Track 095 (1)   **S1**: Come and look at this, Lily! This puzzle video game I'm playing is the scariest game I've ever played. **S2**: A puzzle game? What's scary about that? **S1**: Well, while I go through the puzzle, I'm being chased by the most awful monster! I'm at the highest level, so it's also the most difficult to play. **S2**: Well, if anybody can do it, you can – you're the best gamer I know. **S1**: Aw, thanks, Lily. Hey, listen. Check out the game's audio. **S2**: Wow, Greg, this is the coolest game audio I've ever heard. **S1**: I know! This game's the most fun of all my games. Surprisingly, it's also the least expensive.

Track 096 (4)   Have you ever heard the saying, 'There's an app for that'? Well, it's true. So far, people have downloaded about 268 billion apps. Some of them are really useful, while others are kind of, well, unusual!

Do you ever have trouble telling if a melon is ready to eat? Well, don't worry! There's an app that can test a watermelon's ripeness using your smartphone's microphone! Just hold the phone on top of the melon and knock on it. And if that's not the weirdest use of a microphone you've ever heard of, how about blowing into the microphone to make your screen look steamy. Then you can write or draw in the steam and send your picture to your friends.

There's also an app for people who like to send texts as they walk. Using the camera in your smartphone, this app shows you what is in front of you. It's the safest way to walk and type on the keyboard. Use this app and you won't fall into a fountain or walk into traffic. The worst thing about this app, though, is that it uses up your phone's battery very, very quickly.

Track 097 (4)   **LEARN NEW WORDS**   **battery** / All mobile gadgets need a battery to work. **camera** / Many people take photos with the cameras on their smartphones. **keyboard** / A phone's keyboard is much smaller than a computer's. **microphone** / You can record sounds using a phone's microphone. **screen** / To open an app, you touch the phone's screen.

Track 098 (2)   **LEARN NEW WORDS**   **borrow** / If you forget your phone, you might need to borrow a friend's phone. **find** / You can find film times by searching the Internet. **function** / Many game consoles have more than one function. **invent** / People invent new and amazing gadgets all the time.

Track 099 (3)   **WHILE YOU READ**   See Student's Book pages 118–119.

Track 100 **GRAMMAR**   See Student's Book page 122.

Track 101 (1)   Have you got a lot of different passwords? Have you ever forgotten one? Well, don't worry. Soon you aren't going to have to remember your password anymore.

Imagine wearing your password! A wearable electronic gadget will attach to your body like a sticker. It will recognise information about your body that's unique. Then, it will connect to all of your other gadgets through Wi-Fi. The unique information about your body works as a password to let you access different sites.

If you don't want to wear your password, you'll swallow it! You'll take a password pill every day and it will send information to your gadgets through your stomach! Now that's amazing! In the future, the way we access websites is going to be very different.

In This Unit

Theme This unit looks at the past and at why it's important to understand the past.

Content Objectives
Students will
- identify and describe how humans evolved.
- identify characteristics of life in the distant past.
- identify and describe the history of popular games.
- read about how life for children has changed over the years.

Language Objectives
Students will
- talk about the distant past.
- use new phrases to check for understanding.
- use the present perfect to describe a past action that still continues.
- use *there + be* to talk about existence.
- write a classification paragraph about local festivals.

Vocabulary
pages 128–129 *adult, ancestor, believe, bone, civilisation, continue, diet, discover, origin, site, skeleton, skull, species*
page 130 *advanced, back, descendant, helpful*
page 133 *advice, chess, king, piece, queen*
page 134 *age, chore, culture, education, teenager*
Vocabulary Strategies Suffix *-ful*; Definitions and examples

Speaking Strategy Talking about likes and dislikes

Grammar
Grammar 1 Use the present perfect to describe a past action that still continues
Grammar 2 Use *there + be* to talk about existence

Reading *Growing Up: Then and Now*
Reading Strategy Identify cause and effect

Video Scene 8.1: *A Journey Back in Time*; Scene 8.2: Meet Alberto Nava Blank

Writing Classification paragraph

National Geographic Mission Understand the Past

Project
- Mancala game
- Biographical poster
- Sketch

Pronunciation The schwa (/ə/) sound

Pacing Guides 1.8.1, 1.8.2, 1.8.3

126

Into the Past

Introduce the Unit

- **Build background** Say *In the last unit, we were looking towards the future and how technology might change our lives. In this unit, we're going to explore the past and how life has changed over time.*

- Write the following timeline on the board:

65 million years ago		10,000 years ago	
	2 million years ago		500 years ago

- Say *Write what you think was happening on Earth during each time period.* Discuss students' ideas. Do not tell them whether they are correct or incorrect. Rather, tell students to keep their notes and confirm their answers as they progress through the unit.

- Say *Open your books at pages 126 and 127.* Read the photo caption aloud. Then ask questions for discussion:

  What else do you think these divers found?
  How do you think the skull got into the flooded cave?
  What can researchers learn from this skull?

'It's human nature to explore and learn about ourselves by searching for clues of the past.'
Alberto Nava Blank

In the Hoyo Negro cenote in Mexico, divers Alberto Nava Blank and Susan Bird find the skull of Naia, a teenage girl who lived approximately 13,000 years ago.

TO START

1. Look at the photo. How are the divers going 'into the past'?

2. Why do you think researchers try to understand the past?

3. Are you interested in learning about people who lived before you? Why or why not?

127

- Ask a student to read aloud the quote on page 127. Explain that *human nature* refers to the things that all humans tend to do. Ask *Do you agree? Is learning about the past important to you?* Invite several students to respond and then give your own answers to the questions.

- Ask a student to stand up and read Questions 1 and 2 aloud, and then put students into pairs to answer them. Tell students to include examples of research they have learnt about in school or elsewhere. Discuss students' responses as a class.

- Ask a different student to stand up and read Question 3 aloud. Then partners discuss the question, ask *Can you name some interesting people who lived before you?* Give a list of familiar historical figures and ask students to explain why they might be interesting to learn about.

Extend

- Hand out **Worksheet 1.8.1**. Put students into pairs. Explain that pairs will be writing about and discussing the importance of learning about the past.

Objectives
Students will
- describe and discuss a photo.
- discuss reasons for exploring the past.

Content Vocabulary *approximately, clue, diver, human nature, skull, teenage*

Resources Worksheet 1.8.1 (Teacher's Resource CD-ROM/Website); CPT: Unit Opener

BE THE EXPERT

About the Photo

This photo was taken in the Hoyo Negro cenote, about 20 km (12 mi.) north of Tulum, Mexico. The Hoyo Negro, which translates as 'black hole', is so named because there is no opening to the surface and the vast cave is extremely dark. Researchers believe that Naia may have fallen into the cave before it filled with water. The discovery of Naia's skeleton may be important in understanding the theory that early ancestors crossed the Bering Strait from Asia and migrated south through the Americas. In addition to this human skeleton, remains of many animals have been found in the area.

Teaching Tip

Some students might answer negatively in order to to try to avoid participating in an activity or discussion. If a student simply answers *no* to a question such as *Do you like…?* or *Are you interested in …?*, make sure you ask follow-up questions that require the student to explain his or her reasoning. This will engage the student in the conversation, and may also encourage him or her to answer more thoughtfully next time.

Related Vocabulary

flooded, scuba dive

VOCABULARY

Objectives

Students will

- identify and use vocabulary related to human ancestors.
- use new vocabulary to read about and discuss how humans evolved.

Target Vocabulary *adult, ancestor, believe, bone, civilisation, continue, diet, discover, origin, site, skeleton, skull, species*

Content Vocabulary *brain, connection, development, distance, jaw, seed*

Resources Worksheet 1.8.2 (Teacher's Resource CD-ROM/ Website); Graphic Organiser: Word Web (Teacher's Resource CD-ROM/ Website); Tracks 102–103 (Audio CD/ Website/CPT); CPT: Vocabulary

1 **Look at the pictures from Nasca in Peru. What can archaeology tell us about the past?** Discuss. Then listen and read. 🎧 102

For centuries, archaeologists and anthropologists have searched for information about the **origins** of the mysterious lines drawn in the desert sands of southern Peru. There are approximately 300 different figures – called geoglyphs – and 70 designs showing different **species** of animals and plants.

Scientists **believe** that these geoglyphs were created by the Nasca people, an ancient civilization living near the modern town of Nasca. The Nasca people lived from about 200 BCE and survived for almost eight centuries, living along river valleys and cultivating crops such as cotton and important foods for their **diet**, like beans and corn. Indeed, some scientists think that some of the geoglyphs date back even earlier and were made by the **ancestors** of the Nasca people – the Paracas people who date back to approximately 800 BCE.

In addition to the Nasca lines, archaeologists **discovered** an impressive village **site** called Cahuachi with an adobe pyramid, large temples, plazas, and staircases and corridors. They also found smaller items like pottery, textiles and some traces of gold.

128 VOCABULARY

Warm Up

- **Build background** Say *Today, we're going to read about our human ancestors.* Write the word *ancestors* on the board. Say *Our ancestors are people who lived before us. For example, my grandmother and grandfather are my ancestors.*

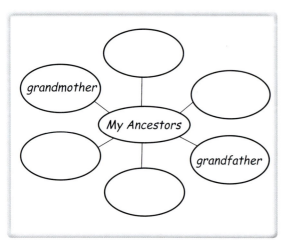

- Give each student a copy of the word web organiser and tell students to write the words *my ancestors* in the centre. Ask *How many of your ancestors do you know? Write their titles in each of the spaces.* Give students several minutes to complete the word web. Walk around to check their work.

- Say *We've looked at our own ancestors: the people in our family. But our ancestors have ancestors, and their ancestors have ancestors, and so on. So ... when did people like us begin to exist? Today, we'll look at this question.*

Present 1 2

- Ask students to open their books at pages 128–129. Say *These photos show the remains of the Nasca people who lived in modern-day Peru.* Point to the photo of the Nasca geoglyph and ask students to scan the text for a date of when the Nasca people lived. Ask students to scan the text again for the date of the Paracus people. Read aloud the instructions for

In the same area, scientists excavated the **bones** of **adults** and children and even entire **skeletons**.

In some cases, the **skulls** were shaped differently and made longer; scientists believe this was done by binding an infant's skull between two pieces of wood. It is thought that this practice showed who belonged to the upper classes in Nasca society.

Since 1994, the area has been designated a UNESCO World Heritage Site. This means it is protected, and future generations will **continue** to learn about the **civilization** and, importantly, enjoy the mysteries of the Nasca.

2 **LEARN NEW WORDS** Listen and repeat. 🎧103

3 **Work in pairs.** Why do you think it's important to understand our ancestors? Name at least two reasons.

VOCABULARY **129**

Our World in Context

The reading mentions two groups of human ancestors: the Paracas people, who lived from 800 BCE to 200 BCE, and the Nasca, who lived in Peru between 100 BCE and 800 CE when their civilisation finally collapsed. The Nasca lived in a very dry area and relied on irrigation to grow their crops which mostly consisted of beans, corn, cotton, squash and sweet potato. They also ate fish, so had a varied diet.

They mostly lived in small villages but had a large capital city called Ventilla. The city had a complex system of underground aqueducts and cisterns to make sure the city had a constant water supply in such a dry climate. Some of the aqueducts are still in use today!

The Nasca made objects from pottery, wove textiles and worked gold to very high standards. Examples of their workmanship still survive because objects were buried with their dead, who were mummified.

It is thought that the Nasca civilisation finally died out because of the effects of El Niño, which brought widespread flooding to the Nasca valleys. The Nasca felled many trees, to make way for agriculture, and created the problem of soil erosion. This made the flooding all the more devastating.

Activity 1. Say *Look at the photos. What do they tell us about the Nasca people?*

- **1** Play **Track 102** and tell students to listen and read. Discuss the reading with students. Ask them to answer the following questions:

  What does the text tell us about what the Nasca people ate? (beans and corn)

  What have archaeologists discovered about Nasca villages? (They were impressive and complex with large buildings such as pyramids, temples, piazzas and buildings with staircases and corridors.)

  Do you think they were rich? Why? (The buildings were substantial and archaeologists have found traces of gold.)

  What is strange about the skulls scientists have found? (some had a longer shape)

  How do scientists explain this? (They think that small children's heads were bound between two pieces

of wood to show that they belonged to the upper classes of Nasca society.)

- **2** **LEARN NEW WORDS** Play **Track 103**. Ask students to listen and repeat. Then ask students to work in pairs to practise pronouncing the words together.

- Play **Track 103** a second time, this time pausing after each word. Repeat the word aloud and then ask a student to use the word in a different sentence about early humans. Model the first word by saying *Adults do different jobs now than they did a long time ago.*

VOCABULARY

Objectives
Students will
- practise using vocabulary related to human ancestors.
- use a vocabulary strategy to learn new words.

Target Vocabulary *advanced, back, descendant, helpful*

Vocabulary Strategy Suffix *-ful*

Content Vocabulary *ancient, appearance, cenote, habit, incredible*

Resources Online Workbook/Workbook pages 78–79; Tracks 104–105 (Audio CD/Website/CPT); CPT: Vocabulary

Materials timer *(optional)*

---

4 **Read and write the words from the list.** Make any necessary changes.

adult	ancestor	believe	bone	civilization
discover	origin	site	skull	species

Alberto Nava Blank

Alberto Nava Blank is an underwater cave explorer. In 2007, Alberto and his team ____discovered____ the skeleton of a young girl in the Hoyo Negro cenote in Mexico's Yucatán Peninsula. 'The moment we entered the ____site____, we knew it was an incredible place,' says Alberto. They named the girl Naia. Her skeleton had all of the most important ____bones____, including the ____skull____ with some teeth still in it. Scientists don't think that Naia was an ____adult____. They ____believe____ she was about 13 when she died around 13,000 years ago. They think that her ____ancestors____ came from an ancient ____civilization____ that lived in north-east Asia.

5 **LEARN NEW WORDS** Listen to these words and complete the sentences. Then listen and repeat. 🎧 **104 105**

Ötzi at age 45

advanced	back	descendant	helpful

1. Our ancestors go ____back____ millions of years.
2. They used less-____advanced____ tools than we do today.
3. Scientists have found 19 of Ötzi's ____descendants____.
4. Fossils are ____helpful____ in understanding the past.

6 **YOU DECIDE** Choose an activity.

1. **Work independently.** Find out about an archaeological discovery in your country. What was discovered? What does it tell you about life long ago? Write a paragraph to tell what you learned.
2. **Work in pairs.** Research Ötzi to learn more about his appearance, habits, habitat and diet. Create a poster profile of the Ice Man.
3. **Work in groups.** Research the discovery of a different primitive species. Where was it discovered? Who discovered it? What did scientists learn? Present the information to the class.

130 VOCABULARY

Practise

- **3** Read the question aloud and say *You've thought about your own ancestors – the people in your family who came before you.* Ask *Why is it important to know about them?* Listen to several students' responses and then ask them to discuss the question in Activity 3 in pairs.

- Ask students to turn to page 130. Point to the photo at the top of the page and say *This is Alberto Nava Blank, the diver we saw in the photo on pages 126 and 127.*

- **4** Ask a student to stand up and read aloud the instruction for Activity 4. Then invite another student to read the words in the box aloud. Draw students' attention to the reading on pages 128–129. Ask them to check the meaning of the words in the box and to see how they might be used in the context of the reading passage. After students have checked the meaning of each word, give them time to complete the activity individually.

- **5** **LEARN NEW WORDS** Play **Track 104** once and ask students to listen. Then tell them to complete the sentences. Then play

Track 104 again and ask them to check their work. Review the answers as a class.

- Play **Track 105** and ask students to repeat each word and sentence. Then tell students to look for each word on pages 128–129.

- **Vocabulary Strategy** Write the word *helpful* on the board and underline the suffix *-ful*. Say *The word* helpful *has the suffix or ending,* -ful. *This suffix means 'full of' or 'characteristic of'. So, someone or something that's* helpful *is characterised by the ability or desire to help.* Write the words *peace, thank* and *wonder* on the board. Say *Add the suffix* -ful *to each of these words.* Allow time for students to write *peaceful, thankful* and *wonderful.* Ask students if they're familiar with the words and then discuss their meanings.

Apply 6

- **6** YOU DECIDE Read aloud the three activity options. Then put students into pairs or groups if they choose Options 2 or 3.

- Guide students who choose the first option to go to the website of a national museum – or even contact museum staff – to learn about local discoveries.

- Encourage students to draw and label an image of Ötzi using information from Activity 5 (**Track 105**) and their research.

- Students who choose the third option might choose a different species of human ancestor not mentioned in the reading or an animal species.

Extend

- Put students into groups of three and ask them to create a guessing game by writing five clues for the new vocabulary items. Students should choose words and then develop clues. Give several examples, such as *This is the bone inside of my head* (skull).

- After students have written down their clues, put each group with another group and tell them to take turns reading their clues aloud. Group members have two chances to guess the correct word. To challenge them, set a timer for three minutes and see if students can correctly guess all of the words in that time.

- If time allows, hand out **Worksheet 1.8.2**. Students will use vocabulary items to talk and write about human ancestors.

Consolidate

- Write the following words on the board: *beginning, bones, culture, find, place* and *think.* Say *The words on the board are synonyms for words we learnt in today's lesson. Synonyms are words that have very similar meanings. Match each word to the vocabulary item that is its synonym.*

- As you review students' answers, ask them to say a short sentence using the vocabulary item, and then to repeat the sentence using the synonym.

SPEAKING STRATEGY

Objective
Students will
- use new phrases to talk about likes and dislikes.

Speaking Strategy Talking about likes and dislikes

Academic Language *mark*

Content Vocabulary *acceptable, experience*

Resources Online Workbook; Worksheet 1.8.3; Graphic Organiser: Three-column table (Teacher's Resource CD-ROM/Website); Tracks 106–107 (Audio CD/Website/CPT); CPT: Speaking Strategy

Materials a paper bag; clip art or photos representing different classes, chores, sports, food or leisure-time activities (one image per student)

SPEAKING STRATEGY 🎧 106

Talking about likes and dislikes

I'm really into <u>history</u>. <u>History</u> is amazing.
I don't mind <u>studying history</u>. It's OK. / It's not bad.
I don't like <u>tests</u> at all. <u>Tests</u> are awful.

1 **Listen.** How do the speakers talk about likes and dislikes? Write the phrases you hear. 🎧 107

2 **Read and complete the dialogue.**
Possible answers:

Julio: I really don't want to study. _____ I don't like _____ history at all!

To me, history is _____ awful _____ .

Carla: Really? _____ I don't mind _____ history. I mean, it's really interesting.

Julio: You're wrong!

Carla: No. What's boring is reading about it. You have to experience history. Trust me! _____ It's not bad. _____

Julio: What do you mean 'experience' it?

Carla: Well, for example, I studied in Peru and learnt about the history of the Incas. I even saw a mummy of a teenage Inca girl. She was really well preserved in a museum. You could see her face, her hair … she was even still wearing clothes! It was _____ amazing _____ .

Julio: Hmm. Maybe I need to visit Peru to get excited about history.

Carla: Yes, you'll be _____ really into _____ ancient civilizations after you spend some time there.

3 **Work in pairs.** Play Noughts and Crosses. Discuss things you like and dislike. Mark X or O. Try to get three in a row.

I'm really into singing.

I'm really into ... (X)	I don't mind ...	I don't like ... at all.
... is OK, but ... is awful.	**wild**	... is OK.
... is amazing.	... is not bad.	... is awful.

4 **Discuss in pairs.** When is it acceptable to use the phrases above to talk about likes and dislikes? When is it not acceptable? What can you say instead of words like *amazing* and *awful* in more formal situations?

Kabuki performers

Go to page 173.

Warm Up

- **Build background** Write the following words on the board: *maths, ice cream, sports* and *cleaning*. Say *Write these words on a sheet of paper. Circle the things you like. Underline the things you don't like. If you don't care either way, don't add any marks.*

- After students have completed the task, point to the first item on the list. Choose a student and ask *(Lee), do you like maths?* Students may answer *yes* or *no*, but try to encourage full sentences, such as *No, I don't like maths.* Repeat this process, asking three or four students about each item.

Present **1**

- Ask students to open their books at page 131. Say *Listen as you read the sentences in the yellow box.* Play **Track 106**. Explain to students that the phrases *I don't mind, It's OK* and *It's not bad* are used to show that the speaker doesn't feel strongly about the topic.

- Refer students back to their notes from the Warm Up activity and say *(Lee), use one of the phrases from the box to tell us how you feel about maths.* Then ask *What about ice cream? Do you like ice cream?* Tell the student to answer using a different phrase from the box. Continue, asking several students to talk about their likes and dislikes.

- **1** Say *We're going to hear a conversation about Kabuki. Kabuki is a form of Japanese theatre. Listen to learn how each speaker feels about Kabuki.* Play **Track 107** once and ask students to listen to the dialogue. Then, play the track again and tell students to write the phrases used to express likes and dislikes.

Practise **2**

- **2** Draw students' attention to Activity 2. Say *Let's read the conversation between Julio and Carla. Use the new phrases to complete their conversation. Then check your answers with a partner.* Allow time for students to complete the activity independently. Put students into pairs and tell them to check their answers. Then, ask a pair to read the dialogue aloud.

Apply

- Ask students to open their books at page 173 and tell them to remove the noughts and crosses board. Hold up the board and point to each section as you read the text aloud. Point to the square at the top-centre of the board and say *I don't mind exercising.* Explain that this means you don't strongly like or dislike it. Say *My sentence is correct and true, so I'll mark an X here.*

- Tell students to complete the activity in pairs. When they finish, ask them to repeat the game on another card, making sure to choose different squares whenever possible.

- Ask students to stay in the same pairs and use a thesaurus to look for more formal ways to say *amazing* or *awful*. Once pairs have finished discussing the question, tell them to work with another pair to summarise their ideas. Ask several groups to share their ideas with the class.

Extend

- Give each student a copy of the three-column table. Ask them to choose any six topics and write them in the left-hand column. Then ask students to use the new words and phrases to say how they feel about each topic.

- Once they have finished, tell students to find a partner with whom they don't normally work. They should take turns interviewing each other and writing their answers, as in the following example:

	Me	Julio
scary films	I'm really into scary films.	Scary films are awful.
basketball	Basketball is OK.	Basketball is amazing.

- When students have finished, ask them to identify what they have in common with their partners.

- If time allows, hand out **Worksheet 1.8.3**. Explain that students will use the worksheet to practise expressing likes and dislikes.

Consolidate

- Find photos or clip art representing things that are relevant to students, such as different subjects, chores, sports, food or leisure-time activities. Make sure you choose images of things that students may not like, such as cleaning or doing homework. Place all images inside a paper bag.

- Walk around the room and invite students to take an image from the bag. Ask *Do you like (watching TV)?* Tell the student to respond by expressing a like or dislike. Repeat this until each student has had a turn.

Strategy in Depth

Learning to express likes and dislikes is something that students learn very early on in English lessons. The phrases presented in this lesson allow students to go beyond simply saying *I like* and *I don't like.*

Additional helpful phrases for expressing likes and dislikes include:

I love …
… is my favourite.
… doesn't bother me.
I'm not into …

About the Photo

The photo on page 131 shows two traditional Kabuki performers. Kabuki started in Japan about 400 years ago and is characterised by its combination of music, dance, mime, high drama, elaborate costumes and make-up. Kabuki means 'song-dance-skill' in modern Japanese and the traditions of Kabuki are highly valued.

By the 18th century, Kabuki was considered an established art form. Traditionally, performances lasted all day, with members of the audience staying for as long as they wanted to. Today, a performance typically lasts for about four hours.

Many Kabuki actors come from long ancestries of Kabuki players with the skills being passed from father to son in each generation.

Formative Assessment

Can students
- use new phrases to talk about likes and dislikes?

  Ask *What are you really into? Can you tell me something you can't stand?*

Online Workbook Speaking Strategy

Objectives

Students will
- use the present perfect to describe a past action that still continues.
- identify and use new words related to the history of chess.

Grammar Present perfect: Describing a past action that still continues

Target Vocabulary *advice, chess, king, piece, queen*

Academic Vocabulary *complete, describe, find out about*

Content Vocabulary *card game, checkmate, powerful, solitaire*

Resources Online Workbook/Workbook pages 80–81; Graphic Organiser: Three-column table (Teacher's Resource CD-ROM/Website); Tracks 108–111 (Audio CD/Website/CPT); CPT: Grammar 1

Materials *sticky notes (optional); chess piece (optional)*

GRAMMAR ∩ 108

Present perfect: Describing a past action that still continues

Games **have** always **been** a popular activity.

People **have enjoyed** games **for** thousands of years.

People **haven't played** board games as much **since** video games became popular.

Why has this game **become** so popular?

Have many games **changed** over time? **Yes**, they **have**.

1 **Listen.** Are the actions completed or continuing? Tick the correct column. ∩ 109

	Completed	Continuing
play		✓
say		✓
begin	✓	
enjoy		✓
go	✓	
take	✓	

People have played mancala for thousands of years.

2 **Work in pairs.** Complete the sentences. Use the present perfect forms of the verbs in brackets, and *for* or *since* where appropriate.

1. People _____have played_____ (play) mancala _____for_____ thousands of years.

2. Players _____have enjoyed_____ (enjoy) different versions of mancala _____since_____ ancient times.

3. _____Since_____ the 1980s, players _____have used_____ (use) computers to play mancala.

4. Players _____have created_____ (create) about two hundred different mancala games.

5. Many players _____haven't played_____ (not play) mancala with seeds or stones _____since_____ computers became popular.

3 **Discuss in groups.** What's your favourite game? Why? Who has played it with you? How often have you played it? How many times have you won?

> My favourite board game is Scrabble™. My dad and I have played it every week since I got it.

132 GRAMMAR

Warm Up

- **Pre-teach** Say *In today's lesson, we're going to learn to talk about things that we've done over a period of time.* Make a three-column table on the board and label the columns *Activity, Since* and *For.*

Activity	Since	For
teaching	2010	8 years
playing piano		

- Say *Think of two activities that you do. For example, I teach. I also (play the piano).* Write these activities in the first column of the table. Then say *I began teaching in (2010). So I'll say that I have taught since (2010).* Emphasise the present perfect form as you speak. Write the correct year in the *Since* column. Then point to the *For* column and say *I began teaching in (2010). It's now (2018). How many years have I taught?* Elicit (eight) years. Then say *That's right, I have taught for (eight) years.*

4 **LEARN NEW WORDS** **Listen to learn about the history of chess.**
Then listen and repeat. 🎧 110 111

> The queen became the most powerful chess **piece** on the board in the 1500s.

> You can checkmate him in four moves!

King Ferdinand and **Queen** Isabella of Spain played **chess**. Isabella gave Ferdinand **advice** on how to win the game.

5 **Work independently.** Complete the sentences using the words in the box. Make any necessary changes.

advice	chess	piece	queen

1. People have played ____chess____ for about 1,400 years.
2. It's played on a board with 32 ____pieces____ .
3. In a chess game, no one should give a player ____advice____ on how to move.
4. The ____queen____ is a very powerful piece in chess.

6 **Work in groups.** Find out about other popular games. Discuss them using the present perfect.

> People in China have played Go for hundreds of years.

GRAMMAR **133**

Again, emphasise the present perfect form and write the correct duration in the *For* column. Repeat this with the second activity on your table.

- Give students a copy of the three-column graphic organiser and tell them to complete the first row with *Activity, Since* and *For*. Say *Think of two activities that you do. Write them in the first column. In the second column, write the month or year you began this activity. Finally, write how many months or years you've been doing the activity in the third column.*

- Allow time for students to complete their tables. Then invite several students to name their activities, the date they began each and the duration. Restate their sentences using the present perfect. For example, say *(Michiko) has (made comic books) since (2013). (She) has (made them) for (five years).*

Grammar in Depth

The present perfect is used for the following reasons:

- to talk about something that began in the past and continues in the present (usually with *for* or *since*)
- to talk about something that happened at an unspecified moment in the past (e.g. *I have been to this restaurant before.*)
- to talk about something that happened very recently (usually with *just*) (e.g. *We've only just begun.*)

Depending on students' native language, some may have trouble using *for* and *since* with the present perfect. In some languages, the equivalent of these words might be used with a different tense (e.g. In German, they're used with the present tense; in some varieties of Spanish, *since* might be used with the present tense). If you're familiar with the structure of students' native language, highlight the distinction for them.

Teaching Tip

Help students to make personal connections by providing in-class experiences that relate to the content being presented. For example, bring in playing cards, mancala and chess sets and allow time for students to play these games in groups. Then, ask students to summarise what they did using the present perfect.

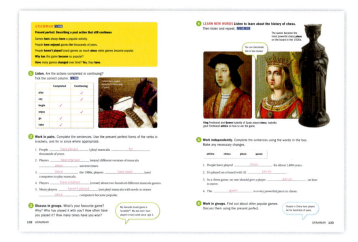

Present

- Ask students to open their books at page 132 and tell students to look at the grammar box. Say *Let's listen to learn about how long people have been playing games.* Play **Track 108** and tell students to listen. Say *Notice that each sentence has a form of the verb* have *and a past participle, such as* been *or* played. Tell students to underline the past participles they can see in the grammar box.

- **Explain** Say *When we want to talk about something that began in the past and still continues, we use a verb tense called the present perfect. We form this tense by using* has *or* have *and a past participle. When we use this tense, only the form of* have *changes. The past participle doesn't change. Often, we form a past participle by adding an -ed ending.* Point out the examples *enjoyed, played* and *changed* in the grammar box. Then say *Sometimes, past participles don't follow this rule.* Point out *been* and *become* and say *Turn to page 148 of your books.* Once students have found the page, say *Here is a list of verbs with their past participles. The verbs in this list do not follow the -ed rule.* You may want to give students a sticky note to bookmark this page. Explain that they may need to refer to it throughout the lesson.

- Ask students to review their tables from the Warm Up activity. Point out the words *since* and *for* and say *We use* since *before a date to say when something started. We use* for *before a period of time to say how long something has been going on.* Tell students to write sentences about the information on their table using the present perfect with *for* and *since.* Walk around the room as they work to give help and check their work. When they have finished, ask students to share their completed sentences.

Practise

- Ask a student to stand up and read the Activity 1 instructions aloud. Say *As you listen, focus on the verbs or action words. If they are in the past simple, that means that a completed action is being described. If you hear the present perfect –* have *or* has *followed by a past participle – the action is still continuing.* Play **Track 109** once and tell students to listen for the verbs they can see in the table. Then play **Track 109** again and tell students to tick the correct column for each verb. Play the track a third time, this time pausing after each sentence to check students' answers.

- Read aloud the Activity 2 instructions. Ask students to scan the activity to determine if sentences contain a specific date or period of time. If necessary, review the difference between *for* and *since* before students begin.

- Tell students to complete the activity in pairs. Walk around as they work, making sure that students are using the correct form of *have* and that they have correctly formed the past participle. Review their answers as a class.

- Before students begin this activity, work as a class to brainstorm a list of popular games – both classic and modern. Then read aloud the instructions. Ask a student to read the model. Ask *What present perfect form do you see?* (have played) Remind students that they need to use the present perfect in their discussions.

Apply

- **LEARN NEW WORDS** Say *We learnt about the game mancala. Now we're going to listen to some information about the game of chess.* Show students a real chess piece. (optional) Ask *Who plays chess?* Ask a student who plays to say who he or she has played with and for how long.

- Play **Track 110** and ask students to listen to the conversation. Then ask a student to read aloud the summary of the information on page 133. Ask comprehension questions such as the following:

  Who were Ferdinand and Isabella?
  What were they doing when Christopher Columbus came to talk to them?
  How did Isabella help King Ferdinand?

- After the discussion, play **Track 111** and tell students to repeat the words and sentences they hear. Review the meaning of each new word as a class.

- **5** Read the instructions aloud. Review the meanings of the words in the box. Then allow time for students to complete the activity independently. When they have finished, ask students to check their answers in small groups.

- **6** Put students into small groups for this discussion. Read aloud the instructions. Refer students to the games that were brainstormed for Activity 3. You may want to tell students to guess the information if they don't know it, and then research the correct information for homework.

Extend

- Invite students to work in pairs to create a game board with twelve squares. Each square should have an activity that students would be likely to do, such as *study English*. Once students have finished making the game boards, collect them and redistribute them to different pairs.

- Tell pairs to take turns asking questions, starting with the first activity. For example, if it says *study English,* Student A asks *How long have you studied English?* Student B should give a response using the present perfect. The student who has been doing the activity longer wins the square and writes his or her initials on it. If one student hasn't done an activity and his/her partner has, then the partner gets the square after making a sentence in the present perfect. If neither student has done an activity, they should move to the next square.

- Once students have discussed each activity, tell them to count the number of squares with each set of initials. The student with the most squares wins.

Consolidate

- Write the following sentences on the board:

> I began playing backgammon in 2000.
>
> People began playing mancala before 1400 BCE.
>
> People began playing backgammon 5,000 years ago.

- Say *Each of these sentences uses the past simple form of* begin (began). *Rewrite the sentences using the present perfect. Use both* for *and* since *in your answers.*

- Allow time for students to rewrite the sentences. Then, ask students to come to the front of the class and share answers for each sentence. Try to get an answer with *for* and an answer with *since* for each sentence.

Objectives

Students will
- read about how life for children has changed over the years.
- identify and use new words from the reading.
- identify the cause and effect relationship of events in the reading.

Reading Strategy Identify cause and effect

Vocabulary Strategy Definitions and examples

Target Vocabulary *age, chore, culture, education, teenager*

Academic Language *cause, chart, definition, effect, example, interview*

Content Vocabulary *cent, complain, enjoyment, factory, get married/marry, grow up, hang out, improve, peer, penny*

Pronunciation The schwa (/ə/) sound

Resources Online Workbook/ Workbook pages 82–83; Worksheet 1.8.4 (Teacher's Resource CD-ROM/Website); Graphic Organiser: T-Chart (Teacher's Resource CD-ROM/Website); Tracks 112–113, 136–139 (Audio CD/Website/CPT); Pronunciation Answer Key (Teacher's Resource CD-ROM/Website); CPT: Reading and Pronunciation

Growing Up: **THEN AND NOW**

How children's lives have changed over the years

1 **BEFORE YOU READ Discuss in pairs.** Look at the girl in the photo. How do you think her life was different from yours?

2 **LEARN NEW WORDS Find these words in the reading.** What do you think they mean? Look for their definitions or examples in the text. Then listen and repeat. 🎧 112

age	chore	education	teenager

3 **WHILE YOU READ Think about cause and effect.** 🎧 113

4 **AFTER YOU READ Work in pairs to answer the questions.**

1. What culture thought that education was very important?
2. Why couldn't some parents teach their children at home?
3. At what age did people start getting married?
4. How often did children work in factories?
5. At what age did children begin working in factories?
6. What did children do with the money they earned?

5 **Complete the table.**

Cause	Effect
They married and had babies when they were very young. / They had to help at home or on the farm.	Most children didn't go to school from 500–1500.
Aztecs believed that education was important.	All Aztec children went to school.
Children didn't have to help on the farms anymore. / They could get money to help their families.	Children began working in factories in cities.

6 **Work in groups.**

1. What would be the hardest thing for you if you were growing up in the past? Why?
2. Interview an older person about his or her life as a teenager. How was it the same as your life now? How was it different?
3. Why do you think the lives of children around the world have improved from long ago? Give three reasons. Do you think it's worse in any way today? Explain.

134 READING

Warm Up

- **Set the stage** Say *In this unit, we've been exploring the past. Today we're going to learn about children's lives in the past. I'm going to tell you about my (grandmother's) life. Listen to the story.* Tell the class what you know about the childhood of an ancestor. If you don't know a story, use the following: *My grandmother grew up on a farm. She only went to school for eight years. She was a good student, but she had to leave school when she was 13. Her parents needed her to work on the farm full time. She also helped in the house with cooking and cleaning. After dinner, the work was done. She played games, read or listened to the radio for fun.*

- When you have finished, ask students to respond to your story. Ask *What did my (grandmother) have to do? What did she do for fun? How was her life different from yours? How was it the same? What would you have liked about her life? What would you dislike?* Discuss these questions as a class.

What's a day in your life like today? You probably go to school and do your homework. At home, you do a few simple chores, like doing the washing up or making your bed. You might complain about not having enough free time to relax.

In the past, children your age probably had a little more to complain about. Throughout much of history, many didn't go to school because they had to help all day at home or on the farm. Their parents taught them what they knew, but very few adults could read or write. The Aztec people, who lived from 1200 to 1473 in present-day Mexico, were unique. The Aztecs believed that education, or learning, was important. Every child went to school, although boys and girls learnt different things.

In addition to going to school, Aztec children were expected to help with chores at home. Girls learnt to weave at the age of about four, and they learnt to cook at the age of about 12. Boys, on the other hand, learnt occupational skills.

By the 19ᵗʰ century, many people began moving into cities to find jobs. In cities, there was no longer a need to have children work on the farm. So they began working in factories instead. In England, many children worked long hours six days a week. And they earned very little money in return. Children started working from a very young age, sometimes at only five or six years old. They gave all of their money to their parents to help pay for the family's needs.

Today, most children go to school. Sometimes teenagers work part-time jobs to earn money. But many use that money for enjoyment, not to help their families. Think about it! Even if you work and go to school, you still have time to relax or spend time with your friends. Next to children from the past, most children nowadays have it pretty easy!

A girl working in a factory, 1908

Before You Read

- Ask students to open their books at pages 134–135. Read the instructions to Activity 1 aloud and ask students to study the photo before discussing the question in pairs. Ask students to think of at least three ways the child's life was different from their own. Discuss their ideas as a class.

- **2** **LEARN NEW WORDS** Say *We're going to look at some new words that will help you understand the reading.* Say the first word aloud: *age.* Invite students to repeat the word. Then tell them to scan the text to look for the word. Repeat this for all of the words.

Strategy in Depth

Identify cause and effect Identifying cause and effect can help students better connect to a text because it helps them understand the relationship between and among events. Point out to students that one cause can have multiple effects and one effect may have multiple causes. After Activity 3, review some of the examples they gave with this in mind and ask students if they can think of additional causes or effects. Words that signal cause include *since* and *because*. Words that signal effect include *so* and *as a result*.

Vocabulary Strategy

Definitions and examples When students learn new vocabulary items using context, it's helpful for them to situate the words' meanings within that context. Sometimes students need to make inferences about a word's meaning, but some words may appear with a definition or examples that clearly state the meaning. Advise students to look for special punctuation that might also signal a definition, such as en-dashes, colons, commas and brackets. If students see phrases such as *for example* or *for instance* near the new vocabulary item, they may find examples that give that word's meaning.

Related Vocabulary

spool, textile, thread

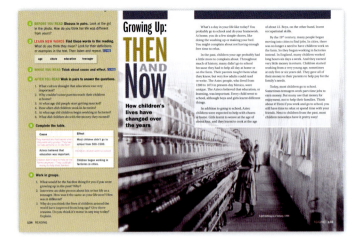

- **Vocabulary strategy** Say *When we find new words in a reading, we know that the context can help us understand a word's meaning. But sometimes, a word is defined in the reading, either with a direct definition or with examples.* Write the words *chore* and *education* on the board. Say *Look for the word* chore *in the reading.* Once students find it, read the sentence aloud, emphasising the phrase *like doing the washing up or making your bed.* Say *These are examples of chores. Based on these examples, what is a* chore? (a household task) Repeat with the word *education* and its definition (learning).

- **2** **LEARN NEW WORDS** Play **Track 112**. Ask students to listen and repeat each word and sentence. Then put students into pairs and tell them to take turns using the new words to make sentences about themselves.

While You Read **3**

- **3** Read the instructions aloud. Say *You've heard about my (grandmother's) childhood. Now we're going to hear what life was like for some children in the past. As you read, think about what caused the events described in the story. Think about what effect the events had on children and families at that time.* Play **Track 113** and tell students to follow in their books. Encourage students to take notes on causes and effects.

After You Read **4** **5** **6**

- **4** Put students into pairs and ask them to read the questions, asking for clarification if necessary. Then tell them to work together to find answers to the questions using evidence from the text. When students have finished, review their answers as a class.

- **5** Give students a copy of the T-chart graphic organiser and ask them to copy the information from the table on page 134, making sure to label the columns *Cause* and *Effect*. Say *As we read, we thought about cause and effect. This is helpful for understanding the relationship between events and information in the story.*

- **Model** Show students how to complete the table by modelling the first item. Read aloud the effect in the first row: *Most children didn't go to school from 500–1500.* Say *This is in the* Effect *column, so we need to think about the cause – why didn't most children go to school?* Point to the second paragraph and ask a student to re-read it, stopping him or her after the word *farm.* Then continue by saying *The text says that children didn't go to school because they had to help all day at home or on the farm. Let's write this under* Cause. Write the response on the board and tell students to copy it into their own tables.

Cause	Effect
Children had to help all day at home or on the farm.	Most children didn't go to school from 500–1500.

- Tell students to complete the rest of the table independently. Allow time for students to review their answers in small groups.

- **6** In groups, ask students to read the questions aloud. You may want to assign Question 2 in advance of this lesson and let students discuss what they have learnt in groups. Or you can ask students to discuss Questions 1 and 3 and then complete Question 2 for homework. They can discuss their findings during the following lesson's Warm Up.

Extend

- Put students into pairs to perform a sketch. In the sketch, a modern teen has travelled back in time to learn about teenage life long ago. Ask pairs to select a time period and context as the setting for their sketch. Encourage students to find appropriate props or costumes if desired.

- Allow time for students to write and rehearse their sketch. One student should role-play a teen from the selected time period and the other should play a modern teen. Students should develop a dialogue about work, family and leisure time.

- Ask students to perform their sketches in class. If time does not allow, tell them to make videos in their free time and post them on a class website.

- **Worksheet** If time allows, hand out **Worksheet 1.8.4** in class. Remind students to review the new words presented on page 134. Tell students to complete the worksheet independently and then compare their answers with a partner's.

Consolidate

- Say *Today we practised the strategy of identifying cause and effect. To review the strategy, let's apply it to our own lives.*

- Give students another copy of the T-chart graphic organiser. Fill it in with four or five sentences that students could relate to, as follows:

Cause	Effect
I left my lunch money at home.	_____
_____	I got wet.
_____	I got an A.
I copied my friend's homework.	_____

- Give students several moments to complete their tables. Then review their tables as a class, discussing several possible causes or effects for each event.

Pronunciation

Turn to Student's Book page 147. Use Audio Tracks 136–139.

The schwa (/ə/) sound The schwa sound is a relaxed unstressed *uh* sound made with a slight separation of the mouth. The main things you may want to share with your students include the following:

- The schwa is the most common vowel sound in the English language.
- Any of the five vowel letters (*a, e, i, o, u*) can be pronounced as a schwa. Many two-vowel combinations are also pronounced as a schwa.
- The schwa sound is almost always used in an unstressed syllable or word.

Answer Key

Comprehension **4**

1. Aztec
2. Because they couldn't read or write themselves
3. At the age of about four
4. Six days a week
5. At age five or six
6. They gave it to their parents.

Formative Assessment

Can students

- read about how life for children has changed over the years?

  Ask *What is one difference between your life and that of an Aztec child?*

- identify and use new words from the reading?

  Ask students to use *chore* and *teenager* in a sentence.

- identify the cause-and-effect relationship of events in the reading?

  Ask *What caused children to begin working in factories?*

Workbook For additional practice, assign Workbook pages 82–83.

Online Workbook Reading

VIDEO

Objective
Students will
• identify and describe changes on Earth over millions of years.

Academic Language *prediction, timeline*

Content Vocabulary *border, boundary, early, partial, snapshot*

Resources Video scene 8.1 (DVD/Website/CPT); Online Workbook; CPT: Video

Material snapshots

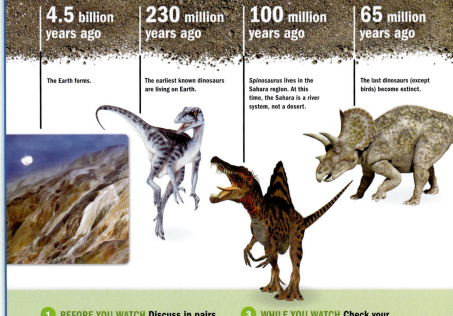

VIDEO ▶

| 4.5 billion years ago | 230 million years ago | 100 million years ago | 65 million years ago |

The Earth forms.

The earliest known dinosaurs are living on Earth.

Spinosaurus lives in the Sahara region. At this time, the Sahara is a river system, not a desert.

The last dinosaurs (except birds) become extinct.

1 BEFORE YOU WATCH Discuss in pairs. Earlier in the unit, you learnt about one civilization – the Nasca people. But Earth has existed for much longer than our ancestors. What do you know about life on Earth before humans?

2 Work in pairs. You are going to watch *A Journey Back in Time*. The explorer Nizar Ibrahim makes a discovery about life before humans. Look at the photo of Nizar (the last photo on the timeline). What do you think he discovered?

3 WHILE YOU WATCH Check your predictions from Activity 2. Watch scene 8.1.

4 AFTER YOU WATCH Work in pairs to answer the questions.

1. Today the Sahara Desert is full of sand. What was it like 100 million years ago?
2. What was Nizar looking for?
3. Where did he work? Why did people think he was foolish to work there?
4. He found part of a skeleton. What type of creature did it belong to?
5. During the time of dinosaurs, what important group was **not** on Earth?

136 VIDEO

Before You Watch

• Ask students to open their books at pages 136–137. Say *Scan the timeline. What do you think we'll learn about in the video?* Listen to several predictions. Then put students into pairs and tell them to read and discuss the question. Point out that while students can refer to the timeline, they should focus on their own background knowledge.

• Hold up your book and point to the last photo in the timeline on page 137. Say *This is Nizar Ibrahim, a National Geographic explorer. Where is he?* (in the desert) *What is he doing?* (digging) Read the instructions for Activity 2 aloud and ask students to answer the question in pairs. Then ask a pair to come to the front of the class and share their ideas with the class.

While You Watch

• Say *I'm going to play the video now. As you watch, think about your answers from Activity 1. What did you say about life on Earth before humans? Review your answers. Listen to see if you were correct as you watch.* Play **Video scene 8.1**. Then invite students to talk about how well their own predictions match what they learnt about in the video.

After You Watch

• Tell students to scan the questions and ask about anything they might not understand. Then tell them to work with a partner to answer the questions. When they have finished, play **Video scene 8.1** again and ask pairs to check their answers.

2.5 million years ago
Our human ancestors begin using stone tools, a sign of advanced intelligence.

5,000 years ago
Ötzi, the Ice Man, lived in the Alps. He used tools such as axes and knives.

2,300 years ago
The Nasca people created the mysterious 'Nasca lines' in Peru.

Present-day
Modern humans have the tools and technology to study and understand the past.

5 Discuss in pairs.

1. Look at the timeline. How many years separate the last dinosaurs the present day? What do you think happened during this period?

2. Nizar says that holding dinosaur fossils is like holding 'a snapshot in time'. What would be exciting about holding something so old?

6 YOU DECIDE Choose an activity.

1. **Work independently.** Nizar describes the Sahara as 'a magical place, both beautiful and frightening, peaceful and cruel'. Think of another place that is beautiful and peaceful, but can still be frightening. Describe this place to the class. If possible, share a photo.

2. **Work in pairs.** In the video, Nizar imagines the world when dinosaurs lived. Discuss how you imagine the world at this time. Draw a picture and share it with the class.

3. **Work in groups.** Create a short story or comic book about life during the time of the dinosaurs. Share your work with the class.

VIDEO **137**

Teaching Tip

When teaching with a graphic organiser, such as the timeline on this page, always take a moment to explain its organisation and purpose. Point out that a timeline shows an order of events from earliest to latest, in order from left to right. Remind students of the organiser's function and purpose each time you use it.

Answer Key

Comprehension 4

1. It was a huge river system.
2. He was looking for fossils.
3. In the area between Morocco and Algeria; because they thought he would never find anything there.
4. *Spinosaurus*
5. Humans

Formative Assessment

Can students
- identify and describe changes on Earth over millions of years?

  Ask *What was different about Earth 65 million years ago?*

Online Workbook Video

- **5** Before students begin Activity 5, review the timeline as a class. Beginning on the left, ask students to read each caption and study each photo. As you review, ask comprehension or critical-thinking questions, such as the following:

  How does Earth look different today from 4.5 billion years ago?

  What is the Sahara today? What was it millions of years ago? How do you think this change was possible?

  Look at the tools. How do they compare with tools we use today?

- After discussing the timeline, put the class into pairs to discuss the questions. After students have shared their ideas on the first question, ask *Would it have been possible for humans and dinosaurs to live together? Why or why not?*

- For Question 2, explain that the word *snapshot* refers to something (usually a photo) that gives quick information about something. Explain that photos show information about a specific time and place. Ask *What else can be called 'a snapshot'? How is holding a dinosaur fossil like looking at a snapshot?*

- **6** YOU DECIDE Read the activity options aloud to students. Allow students who choose the first option to draw and describe their own magical place if they prefer.

- Pairs who choose option 2 should work from their own imaginations. After they have presented their ideas to the class, encourage them to look for historical references online to check for accuracy.

- You may want to give a list of dinosaur names in English to help students with their comic strips. Encourage groups to take on different roles – writer, illustrator, editor and so on.

Objective
Students will
• use *there + be* to talk about existence.

Grammar *There + be*: Expressing existence at different points of time

Academic Language *detail, dialogue, existence, express*

Content Vocabulary *celebration*

Resources Online Workbook/Workbook pages 84–85; Worksheet 1.8.5 (Teacher's Resource CD-ROM/Website); Track 114 (Audio CD/Website/CPT); CPT: Grammar 2

Materials variety of classroom objects

GRAMMAR 🎧 114

There + to be: Expressing existence at different points of time

There have always **been** sun celebrations around the world.	**There has been** a Festival of the Sun in Peru for centuries.
However, **there wasn't** a Festival of the Sun in Peru between 1535 and 1944.	**There weren't** any other traditional Incan festivals at that time either.
Now **there's** a Festival of the Sun every year.	**There are** a lot of different foods to try.
Are there going to be traditional musicians?	Yes, **there are going to be** dancers, too.
Will there be a lot of people?	I think **there will be**. It's very popular.

1 **Read and complete the dialogue.** Use *there* + the correct form of *to be*.

Juan: Andrea, you're from Peru, aren't you? _____*Are there*_____ a lot of fun things to do during your country's Festival of the Sun?

An Inti Raymi celebration

Andrea: Yes, _____*there are*_____. The festival is called *Inti Raymi*. It's a week long, and _____*there are*_____ live concerts and shows. In fact, _____*there's*_____ only one festival in South America that's bigger!

Juan: Really? It sounds amazing!

Andrea: Oh, it is. Last year _____*there were*_____ about 150,000 people in the town of Cuzco watching the ceremony. _____*There were*_____ 500 actors in the ceremony. They really brought the past to life.

Juan: Cool! Does the history of this festival go back a long time?

Andrea: Oh, yes! _____*There have been*_____ Inti Raymi celebrations since the 1400s.

Juan: _____*Will there be*_____ a festival next year?

Andrea: Yes, _____*there will be*_____. It's held every year.

2 **Work in pairs.** Think of a festival you have been to. Describe the festival with as many details as possible. Use *there* with the correct form of *to be*.

3 **Work in groups.** Choose a celebration you all know about. Turn over a card. Try to be the first to slap the card and make a sentence about that celebration.

There will be …

Go to page 175.

Warm Up

• **Build background** Place a variety of classroom objects on a table at the front of the room. Make sure to use single items (*e.g.* a pencil sharpener) as well as groups of the same item (*e.g.* three books). Ask *What's on the table?* Model by holding up an item and saying *There's (a pencil sharpener).*

• Invite students to name the objects on the table using *There is* or *There are*. After each item has been identified, tell students to close their eyes. Take one of the items away and hide it. Then tell students to open their eyes again. Ask *What's different now?* Restate by saying *That's right. There were three books on the table. Now there are only two.* Write the sentences on the board.

• Say *In today's lesson, we'll use these patterns to talk about the past, the present and the future.*

Present

• Draw students attention to the grammar box at the top of page 138. Play **Track 114** and tell students to follow in their books. Then play the track again, pausing after each set of sentences. Ask students to make a sentence with *there* plus *be* in the same tense as they heard it.

• Explain that the contraction *there's* can be used in the present tense – *there is* – or in the present perfect as a contracted form of *there has*.

Practise **1**

• **1** Read aloud the instructions. Say *To learn what tense we need, we can scan each sentence for clues.*

• **Model** Read aloud the first part of the dialogue. Say *Juan is asking Andrea about a festival that takes place in her country. He wants facts about the festival. When we're talking about facts, we use the present tense.*

Complete the first sentence and tell students to complete the remaining items independently. Invite pairs to perform the dialogue for the class.

Apply

- ② Read the instructions aloud and ask students to brainstorm a list of festivals in your region. Write the list on the board and write several characteristics next to each festival. Point to a festival's name and ask students to give details about it using *there* plus a form of *to be*.

- ② Say *In this activity, we're going to discuss a celebration. What type of celebrations do you have in your family?* Discuss how these events are celebrated.

- Put students into groups of three or four. Tell students to cut out the cards on page 175 and place them face down in a pile on the desk. Point out that one student will draw a card while the other group members compete against one another.

- **Model** Say *Let's talk about (birthdays)*. Take a card and say *This card says, 'There aren't going to be …'* Make a sentence by saying *There aren't going to be any clowns at my birthday party this year. My sentence is correct so I get a point.*

- Put students into small groups and tell them to take turns drawing cards. The remaining students in the group must compete against each other to slap the card first and make a correct sentence using the phrase on the card. If the sentence is correct, the student wins a point. The student with the most points at the end of the game wins.

Extend

- Tell small groups to use the cards from Activity 2 to play a guessing game. Tell students to remove the question cards from the pile and place the other cards face down on the desk. This time, students will take turns to choose a card and make a statement using the words on the card. For example, a student might say *There has been a chess club in our school for three years.* After a student makes a statement, each group member should guess if it's true or false.

- Hand out **Worksheet 1.8.5** to provide additional practice using *there + to be* to talk about existence at different points of time.

Consolidate

- Write the following sentence starters on the board:

> In the past, there was/were …
> There have/has always been …
> This year, there is/are …

- Say *Imagine you're planning a school dance. This dance happens every year. But this year, it will be a little different. Complete these sentences using your own ideas.* Invite several students to share their ideas with the class.

Grammar in Depth

There can be used with the verb *be* to talk about the existence of something. In sentences such as *There are 12 students,* the word *there* is the *subject*. It may be called the *preparatory subject* because it's not referring to a specific thing. The verb that follows *there* is singular or plural depending on the number of the noun that follows: *There is a student. There are 12 students.*

Teaching Tip

When there are consecutive pair- or group-work activities being assigned, review the activity content in advance. If the activities are similar, make sure students switch partners or groups to keep the conversation dynamic. However, if the activities are about very different topics, students may stay with the same partner or group. Let students know in advance how long they are expected to work with the given classmate(s).

Formative Assessment

Can students
- use *there + to be* to talk about existence?

  Ask students to talk about a traditional festival or celebration using *there* followed by two different tenses.

Workbook For additional practice, assign Workbook pages 84–85.

Online Workbook Grammar 2

WRITING

Objectives
Students will
- identify elements of a classification paragraph.
- analyse a model classification paragraph.
- write a classification paragraph about local festivals.

Writing Classification paragraph

Academic Language *classification, concluding, divide, topic*

Content Vocabulary *bonfire, maypole, reflect, solstice*

Resources Online Workbook/Workbook page 86; Process Writing Worksheets 1–5; Genre Writing Worksheet: Classification; Graphic Organiser: Word Web (Teacher's Resource CD-ROM/Website); CPT: Writing

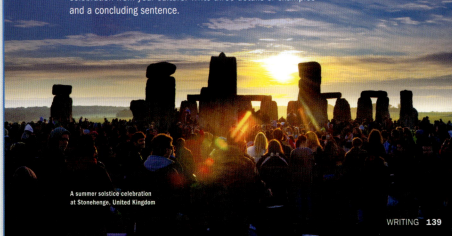

WRITING

When you write a classification paragraph, you divide your main topic into different parts. You give details and examples about each of the parts. When you finish, write a concluding sentence to connect the parts to the main topic.

1. **Read the model.** What is the main topic? How many parts does the writer divide the paragraph into? *summer solstice celebrations / three parts*

The summer solstice, the first day of summer, has always been a special day. There have been summer solstice celebrations since ancient times. Some of these are still celebrated today. In Sweden, people celebrate this, the longest day of the year, by singing, dancing around a maypole, and enjoying special food and drinks. Unlike Sweden, people in Spain don't dance around a maypole. Instead, they dance in the streets. There are fireworks and bonfires. Some people even jump over the bonfires. People in both Sweden and Spain celebrate the summer solstice at the end of the day. However, at Stonehenge, in the United Kingdom, thousands of people come together to celebrate the longest day of the year at sunrise. The sounds of beating drums fill the air at this celebration. People around the world celebrate the summer solstice in different ways that reflect their culture.

2. **Work in pairs.** What are the different parts of the paragraph? What does the writer describe in each part?

3. **Write.** Write a paragraph about a traditional festival or celebration from your culture. Write three details or examples and a concluding sentence.

A summer solstice celebration at Stonehenge, United Kingdom

Warm Up

- **Revisit** Say *In the last lesson, we discussed different festivals. Think of one of the festivals that we discussed. For example, we discussed* Inti Raymi. *Let's talk about the details of that festival, based on what we learnt.* Write the following on the board:

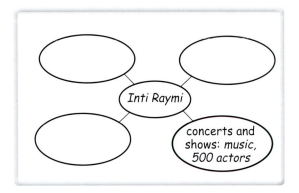

- Say *Today, you'll be asked to write a paragraph about a festival in your culture. You'll need to divide your topic into several parts with examples of what goes on there. Let's think about how we could do this for* Inti Raymi. Ask students to review Activity 1 on page 138 and give details and examples about the festival. Categorise the responses on the web. For example, write reasons for celebrating in one space and different ways of celebrating in other spaces. Leave the web on the board as a model.

Present

- **Explain** Ask students to open their books at page 139. Draw their attention to the green box at the top of the page. Read aloud the text. Say *We just described different parts of the* Inti Raymi *festival and we classified the information into different categories, such as* concerts and shows. *To write about* Inti Raymi, *we'd present these details together. Then we'd present another part of the celebration, such as food and keep those details together. When we finish explaining each part, we'd write a concluding sentence. A concluding sentence is the last sentence of the paragraph. It connects each of the parts we discussed back to the main topic.*

- Write and say a concluding sentence that reflects the details in the web from the Warm Up activity, such as the following:

> Inti Raymi is a traditional celebration that brings people together with delicious food, ceremonies and lively shows.

Read the Model

- Say *In a moment, we're going to read a model of a classification paragraph. First, let's look at the photo.* Draw students' attention to the photo on page 139. Ask *What are these people doing?* (celebrating) *Where are they?* (outdoors, in Stonehenge, UK) Say *The caption tells us that this is a summer solstice celebration. Have you ever seen this type of celebration?*

- **1** Read the instructions aloud. Say *As I read the paragraph, write a number above the first sentence of each part.* Read the paragraph aloud, slightly pausing after you read about each country's celebration. Pause just long enough for students to write a number, but not so long that it's too obvious. Then say *Now (Min) will re-read the paragraph aloud. When a new part begins, put your hand up.* Choose a student to re-read the paragraph. Then discuss the main topic and the number of parts the paragraph is divided into. (3)

- **2** Give students a copy of the Word Web graphic organiser and tell them to write *summer solstice celebration* in the centre. Tell them to cross out all but three outer circles on the web. Then put them into pairs to re-read the paragraph, taking notes on the topic and details for each of the three parts.

- As students work, walk around the room to make sure they put correct parts in the web (Sweden, Spain, England), as well as details for each part. Finally, discuss their ideas as a whole class.

- **Worksheet** If your students need a reminder of the elements of a classification essay, you may want to hand out **Genre Writing Worksheet: Classification** and review it together.

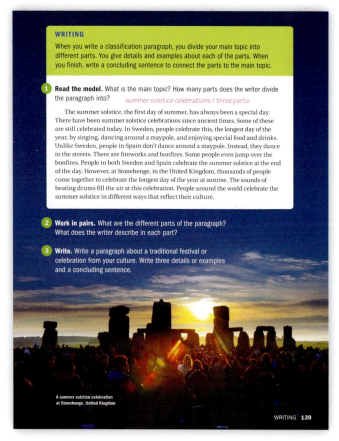

WRITING

When you write a classification paragraph, you divide your main topic into different parts. You give details and examples about each of the parts. When you finish, write a concluding sentence to connect the parts to the main topic.

1 **Read the model.** What is the main topic? How many parts does the writer divide the paragraph into? *summer solstice celebrations / three parts*

The summer solstice, the first day of summer, has always been a special day. There have been summer solstice celebrations since ancient times. Some of these are still celebrated today. In Sweden, people celebrate this, the longest day of the year, by singing, dancing around a maypole, and enjoying special food and drinks. Unlike Sweden, people in Spain don't dance around a maypole. Instead, they dance in the streets. There are fireworks and bonfires. Some people even jump over the bonfires. People in both Sweden and Spain celebrate the summer solstice at the end of the day. However, at Stonehenge, in the United Kingdom, thousands of people come together to celebrate the longest day of the year at sunrise. The sounds of beating drums fill the air at this celebration. People around the world celebrate the summer solstice in different ways that reflect their culture.

2 **Work in pairs.** What are the different parts of the paragraph? What does the writer describe in each part?

3 **Write.** Write a paragraph about a traditional festival or celebration from your culture. Write three details or examples and a concluding sentence.

A summer solstice celebration at Stonehenge, United Kingdom

WRITING **139**

- For pre-writing, give each student a copy of the Word Web graphic organiser and ask students to write the festival's name in the centre. Then tell them to identify and write different parts of the festival in the outer circles.

- **Worksheets** If your students need a reminder of any of the steps of process writing, hand out **Process Writing Worksheets 1–5** and review them together.

- **Workbook** Refer students to Workbook page 86 to help them organise and plan their writing.

Write

- After students have finished their pre-writing, tell them to work on their first drafts. If you haven't got enough time for students to complete the first draft in class, assign it as homework.

Revise

- After students finish their first drafts, ask them to review their writing for clarity and organisation. Ask students to consider the following: *Can I identify my main topic? Can I identify my three parts? Do I give enough examples and details for each of these parts? Do I have a good concluding sentence? What needs more work?*

Edit and Proofread

- Ask students to consider elements of style, such as sentence variety, parallelism and word choice. Then tell them to proofread for mistakes in grammar, punctuation, capitalisation and spelling.

Publish

- Publishing includes handing in pieces of writing to the teacher, sharing work with classmates, adding pieces to a class book, displaying pieces on a classroom wall or in a hallway and posting on the Internet.

Plan

- Say *Now you're going to write a classification paragraph about a celebration of your choice.* Refer students to the celebrations that were discussed in the previous lessons or tell them to go online to learn about a different festival that interests them.

- Say *Think about the different parts of the festival we discussed. In our discussion, we talked about what went on at the festival. In the model, we talked about how the festival was celebrated in different places. As you organise your ideas, you need to think about how you can organise your essay into parts.*

Writing Assessment

Use these guidelines to assess students' writing. You can add other aspects of their writing you'd like to assess at the bottom of the table.

4 = Excellent
3 = Good
2 = Needs improvement
1 = Re-do

	1	2	3	4
Writing Student's ideas are clear and well organised; paragraph has a main topic with three parts supported by details and examples of a concluding sentence.				
Grammar Student uses present perfect and *there + be* correctly.				
Vocabulary Student uses a variety of word choices, including words used in this unit.				

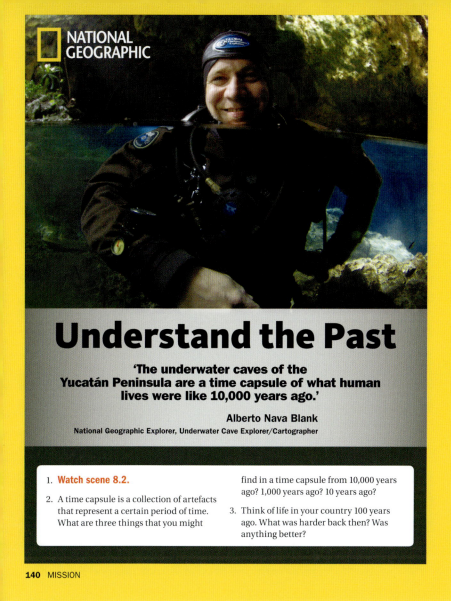

Understand the Past

'The underwater caves of the Yucatán Peninsula are a time capsule of what human lives were like 10,000 years ago.'

Alberto Nava Blank
National Geographic Explorer, Underwater Cave Explorer/Cartographer

1. **Watch scene 8.2.**

2. A time capsule is a collection of artefacts that represent a certain period of time. What are three things that you might find in a time capsule from 10,000 years ago? 1,000 years ago? 10 years ago?

3. Think of life in your country 100 years ago. What was harder back then? Was anything better?

MISSION

Objectives
Students will
- identify what artefacts represent different points in the past.
- explain what their lives would have been like 100 years ago.

Content Vocabulary *time capsule*

Resources Video scene 8.2 (DVD/ Website/CPT); Worksheet 1.8.6 (Teacher's Resource CD-ROM/ Website); Online Workbook: Meet the Explorer; CPT: Mission

BE THE EXPERT

Teaching Tip

Before showing videos, always watch them yourself. As you watch, take note of any information that you feel is especially important for understanding the video. Then, in class, preview that information with your students. This will give students a bit of background knowledge that will help them better understand the video's content.

Online Workbook Meet the Explorer

Mission

- Say *Open your books at page 140.* Ask a student to read aloud the mission. Say *In this unit, we've learnt that the past is more than what we see in history books. To really understand the past, we must look at both big events and daily life.* Ask students to review what aspects of daily life were presented in this unit. (games, work, celebrations)

- Ask a student to stand up and read Alberto Nava Blank's quote. Ask *What other explorer in our book studied caves?* (Guillermo de Anda) *Would you like to explore caves of the Yucatán? Why or why not?* Ask several students to answer these questions.

- **Activity 1** Say *Now let's watch a video about Alberto Nava Blank.* Play **Video scene 8.2**. Tell students to focus on the meaning of Alberto's discovery.

- **Activity 2** Read the question aloud. Explain what a *time capsule* is and ask students to think of objects they would include in a time capsule if they were to create one today. Put students into pairs and ask them to fold a piece of paper into three sections. They should write one of the following phrases at the top of each section: *10,000 years ago; 1,000 years ago; 10 years ago.* Give students examples for each section to get them started.

- **Activity 3** You may want to ask students to interview grandparents or other older relatives and ask them to share stories or memories. Invite students to discuss the questions in pairs. Then ask each pair to come to the front and summarise their conversation for the class.

- **Worksheet** Hand out **Worksheet 1.8.6**. Explain that students will use the worksheet to further discuss connections to the past.

Objective
Students will
• choose and complete a project related to the past.

Academic Language *biography, perform, rehearse*

Content Vocabulary *carton, costume, mancala, prop, sketch*

Resources Assessment: Unit 8 Quiz, Units 5–8 Mastery Test and Final Test; Workbook pages 87 and 96; Worksheet 1.8.7 (Teacher's Resource CD-ROM/Website); CPT: Make an Impact and Review Games

Materials empty egg cartons; seeds, beans or other small objects; poster board; historical props or costumes (supplied by students)

Assessment Go to pages 262–264.

Unit Review Assign Worksheet 1.8.7
Workbook Assign pages 87 and 96.
Online Workbook Now I can

Make an Impact

YOU DECIDE Choose a project.

1 Teach the class to play mancala.
· Research the history of mancala. Learn how to play. Write the instructions on a poster.
· Make mancala boards for your classmates. Use egg boxes. Bring in seeds or beans as pieces.
· Share your poster and teach classmates how to play mancala. Walk around to answer any questions as others play the game.

2 Make a biographical poster.
· Research a scientist who discovered something connected to our origins.
· Prepare a biography of that person. Include information on what he or she discovered and what it taught us about our origins.
· Create a poster and share the information with the class.

3 Perform a sketch.
· Choose a time period in the past and research what children did then.
· Write and rehearse a sketch showing what life was like for children at that time. Find costumes and props.
· Perform the sketch for your classmates.

Mancala

PROJECT **141**

Prepare

• **YOU DECIDE** Ask students to choose a project.

• **Activity 1** Explain that each space on a mancala board should hold four small objects. If students prepare a board with 12 spaces, make sure they count 48 objects for each board. Encourage students to make enough boards so there's one for each pair of students in the class.

• **Activity 2** Before students begin, revise the parts of a biography. Point out that students should include personal information about when and where the person was born, lived and studied. They should also include information about this person's professional accomplishments. If the subject of the biography is still active, suggest students research what projects he or she is working on now and, if possible, what the subject's plans are for the future.

• **Activity 3** Tell students to revisit the reading on pages 134–135 before they begin their projects. Remind them that they can develop their projects around information in the reading or they can choose children from a different era and region to focus on. Discuss groups' ideas from the start and guide each pair or group to focus on a different era and/or region so there is variety among the sketches.

Share

• Schedule time for students to present their final projects to the class. If necessary, bring in a projector to show students' presentations.

• **Modify** You may want to bring in a mancala board game with the instructions to give support to students who choose Activity 1. Give a list of names, including palaeoanthropologists such as Mary Leakey and Lee Berger, to students who choose Activity 2. If many students choose Activity 3, tell them to record their sketches and post the video on a class website.

Track 102 ① **Listen and read.** See Student's Book pages 128–129.

Track 103 ② **LEARN NEW WORDS** **adult** / Adults long ago didn't live as long as they do now. **ancestor** / Our ancestors long ago hunted and lived in caves. **believe** / Many people believe that scientists do important work. **bone** / There are more than two hundred bones in the human body. **civilisation** / We study ancient civilisations to learn about life long ago. **continue** / Humans will continue to change well into the future. **diet** / Some early species had a diet of nuts, seeds and roots. **discover** / Explorers often discover interesting things in caves. **origin** / Scientists want to learn more about the origin of the Nasca lines. **site** / Archaeologists are always looking for new sites to excavate. **skeleton** / Skeletons can help us learn about our ancestors. **skull** / The shape of human skulls has changed over time. **species** / Scientists believe there are still certain species to be discovered.

Track 104 ⑤ In 1991, hikers in the mountains of Italy, Europe, found the frozen body of Ötzi or Ice Man, half-buried in ice. Back in Ötzi's time, 5,000 years ago, this area was covered in ice. The cold and ice preserved Ötzi's body. This was helpful because scientists could study his body and learn more about him.

They learnt that Ötzi was male, walked long distances and carried tools, although they weren't as advanced as the tools we use today. He had more than sixty simple tattoos on his body. Scientists think the tattoos were for his health, not for decoration.

Ötzi may have died long ago, but he has descendants who are alive today. Recently, scientists discovered at least 19 living people connected with Ötzi and they expect to find many others.

Track 105 ⑤ **LEARN NEW WORDS** **advanced** / We are more advanced than our ancestors. **back** / The use of tools dates back more than three million years. **descendant** / Some of Ötzi's descendants are alive today. **helpful** / Ice is helpful in preserving things.

Track 106 **SPEAKING STRATEGY** See Student's Book page 131.

Track 107 ① **S1**: Hey, Lily. I'm writing an essay on Kabuki, an ancient style of Japanese theatre. **S2**: I've never heard of Kabuki, but I'm really into theatre. **S1**: I am, but I always thought that ancient styles of theatre were awful. You know, really boring. **S2**: What changed your mind? **S1**: Well, my family and I went to Japan on holiday. We saw a Kabuki performance and now I'm really into it. **S2**: Cool! What's different about it? **S1**: The actors wear amazing make-up and traditional clothing. They sing and dance, too. There's only one thing that I don't like. **S2**: What is it? **S1**: There are no female actors. Men play the role of women. I don't like that at all. **S2**: Well, it's OK. Things were different back then. But we certainly won't be doing a Kabuki play at school any time soon!

Track 108 **GRAMMAR** See Student's Book page 132.

Track 109 ① Mancala is a board game that people from many cultures have played since ancient times. It's a game of moving seeds from hole to hole. People have said that mancala is the world's oldest board game. Historians believe people began playing mancala in Egypt. Egypt is the place of origin for many other ancient games as well. Also, archaeologists found mancala boards carved into the roofs of Egyptian temples. This proves that Egyptians played mancala before the year 1400 BCE. In fact, players have enjoyed mancala in nearly every African country for centuries. When people went from place to place long ago, they took mancala along with them. Today mancala is played around the world.

Track 110 ④ **S1**: I've learnt a lot about the game of chess recently. Did you know that Christopher Columbus's first voyage to the Americas was mainly because of a game of chess? **S2**: What do you mean by that? **S1**: You know how Christopher Columbus asked King Ferdinand to give him money for a trip to find a new way to Asia? **S2**: Yeah. **S1**: Well, both King Ferdinand and Queen Isabella of Spain loved chess. And when Columbus arrived to get the King's answer about the money, King Ferdinand was playing chess with a friend and losing. **S2**: So? Then what? **S1**: Queen Isabella quietly gave the king some advice on his next move. He took her advice and won the game! He was so happy that he gave Columbus the money for his voyage. **S2**: Really? What a cool story. **S1**: Yes! Queen Isabella was very powerful. In modern chess, the name of one of the pieces changed to *queen* and became the most powerful piece on the board. People have said that Queen Isabella may have caused these changes.

Track 111 ④ **LEARN NEW WORDS** **advice** / Young people sometimes ask their parents for advice. **chess** / The game of chess has been popular for centuries. **king** / Some countries are ruled by a king. **piece** / Most board games have pieces that players move. **queen** / A queen is a country's ruler.

Track 112 ② **LEARN NEW WORDS** **age** / In most countries, you can learn to drive at the age of 17. **chore** / In the past children did a lot more chores at home. **education** / You go to school to get an education. **teenager** / Teenagers are older than children, but younger than adults.

Track 113 ③ **WHILE YOU READ** See Student's Book pages 134–135.

Track 114 **GRAMMAR** See Student's Book page 138.

Track 115 ① **Express Yourself** See Student's Book pages 142–143.

Objectives

Students will
• read and listen to a student's predictions for the future.
• connect ideas about the future and the past.

Academic Language *prediction*

Content Vocabulary *elevator, get around, include, pod, transportation, tunnel, vehicle*

Resources Workbook pages 88–89/ Online Workbook (Units 7–8 Review); Worksheet 1.8.8 (Teacher's Resource CD-ROM/Website); Track 115 (Audio CD/Website/CPT); CPT: Express Yourself Units 7–8

Materials shoebox *(optional)*

Express Yourself

1 Read and listen to a student's predictions for the future. 🎧 115

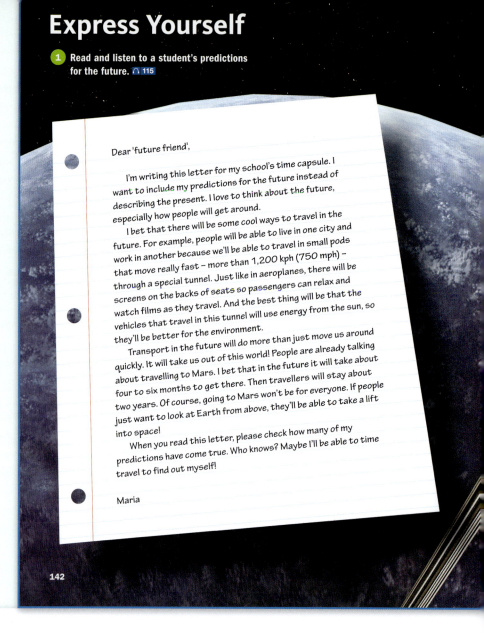

Dear 'future friend',

I'm writing this letter for my school's time capsule. I want to include my predictions for the future instead of describing the present. I love to think about the future, especially how people will get around.

I bet that there will be some cool ways to travel in the future. For example, people will be able to live in one city and work in another because we'll be able to travel in small pods that move really fast – more than 1,200 kph (750 mph) – through a special tunnel. Just like in aeroplanes, there will be screens on the backs of seats so passengers can relax and watch films as they travel. And the best thing will be that the vehicles that travel in this tunnel will use energy from the sun, so they'll be better for the environment.

Transport in the future will do more than just move us around quickly. It will take us out of this world! People are already talking about travelling to Mars. I bet that in the future it will take about four to six months to get there. Then travellers will stay about two years. Of course, going to Mars won't be for everyone. If people just want to look at Earth from above, they'll be able to take a lift into space!

When you read this letter, please check how many of my predictions have come true. Who knows? Maybe I'll be able to time travel to find out myself!

Maria

142

Present

• **Preview** Ask students to turn to pages 142–143. Say *Look at the photo.* Ask *What do you think this is?* (a space lift)

• **1** **Read together** Say *We're going to listen to and read a letter. A student wrote this letter to share her predictions for the future. She wrote the letter for a time capsule – a collection of things that represents a certain time.* Play **Track 115**. Then ask the following questions for discussion:

  What topic is she making predictions about?
  What predictions does she make?

• Ask *Which prediction does the photo show?* (the space elevator) *Do you think this prediction will come true?* Say *Maria's other prediction is that we'll be able to travel between cities in small pods.* Ask *Do you think this prediction will come true? What predictions have you made for how we'll get around in the future?*

Practise

• **2** **Discuss** Put students into groups. If students have never seen a time capsule, ask them to consider what time period is most interesting to them. Then ask them to think about artefacts that might be found in a time capsule from that period.

• You may want to ask students to actually create a time capsule. Give them a shoebox and ask students to choose things – or photos of things – to put inside. Check to see if there is a place where the capsule could be hidden within the building or find another place in your community to put the capsule.

• After students discuss their preferences regarding Maria's predictions, tell them to revisit their predictions about transportation in the future and then express their preferences about them.

A space lift

2 Discuss in groups.

1. Have you ever seen a time capsule? If so, what was in it? If not, would you be interested in one? Why or why not?

2. What would you put in a time capsule to be opened in 100 years?

3. Which forms of transport that Maria mentions would you like to take? Why?

3 Connect ideas. In Unit 7, you learnt about life with modern gadgets. In Unit 8, you learnt about people, tools and games from long ago. What connection can you see between the two units?

4 YOU DECIDE Choose an activity.

1. Choose a topic:
   • tools and games of today and tomorrow
   • tools and games of the past

2. Choose a way to express yourself:
   • a letter for a time capsule
   • a video presentation
   • a sketch

3. Present your work.

143

Connect 3

• 3 Read Activity 3 aloud. Say *As you discuss the question, think about changes to gadgets and tools in your own lifetime. What is different now from five years ago? What do you think will change? Will you still use computers in ten years?* Invite pairs to come to the front of the class to summarise their discussions.

Prepare 4

• Read the instructions for Activity 4. You may want to assign this activity in advance so that students have time to work on it in class or at home.

• 4 **Activity 1** Put students into small groups and tell them to choose a topic: either tools and games of today and tomorrow, or tools and games of the past.

• **Activity 2** Remind students who choose to write a letter that they can use the letter on page 142 as a model.

• Guide students who choose the second option to select useful tools and games to present in the video. They might choose contemporary tools or find photos or drawings of items from the past.

• Encourage students who choose to present a sketch to bring in props and costumes from home. If students prefer, they can perform their sketches outside class time and record them to share with classmates.

Share

• **Activity 3** Set aside time for sharing students' work with the class. Remind students to listen actively by focusing on the speaker or presenter. Tell students to write at least one question they want to ask the presenter. Then allow several minutes for questions and answers.

Resources Unit 1 Quiz (*ExamView®*)

Testing Tip

Help students become comfortable with assessments by treating tests as part of the course. For example, create review worksheets and study guides with content, style and formats that are similar to what students will see on an assessment. This allows them to gain familiarity with the materials and prepare for tests at the same time.

Projecting a positive attitude toward test taking and making it routine will help students approach assessments with constructive feelings.

Unit 1 Quiz

Before the Quiz

1. To generate the quiz, go to *ExamView® Test Generator* and select *Create a new test using a wizard*.

2. Give your quiz a title (for example: Unit 1 Quiz).

3. Select the Unit 1 question bank and select all items. Quizzes include questions that assess comprehension of vocabulary and grammar, as well as skills in these four areas: *listening, speaking, reading* and *writing*.

• You may choose to customise this quiz or create your own.

4. Print the quiz. Then make copies for each student in your class.

• For additional review, use the end-of-unit games in the **Classroom Presentation Tool**.

Giving the Quiz

• Hand out the quiz and tell students to read the instructions. Clarify instructions if necessary.

• For the listening comprehension activities, play **Track 002** or read the audio script available on the *ExamView®* CD-ROM, and also on the Teacher's Resource Website.

• For the speaking section of the assessment, use the questions on *ExamView®* and these additional questions:

Would you prefer to live in a large city, a small town or somewhere else? Why?

Think about two interesting places you've visited. What do you like about those places?

Do you spend a lot of time outdoors? Why or why not? What do you like to do when you are outdoors?

Unit 2 Quiz

Before the Quiz

1. To generate the quiz, go to *ExamView® Test Generator* and select *Create a new test using a wizard*.

2. Give your quiz a title (for example: Unit 2 Quiz).

3. Select the Unit 2 question bank and select all items. Quizzes include questions that assess comprehension of vocabulary and grammar, as well as skills in these four areas: *listening, speaking, reading* and *writing*.

• You may choose to customise this quiz or create your own.

4. Print the quiz. Then make copies for each student in your class.

• For additional review, use the end-of-unit games in the **Classroom Presentation Tool**.

Giving the Quiz

• Hand out the quiz and tell students to read the instructions. Clarify instructions if necessary.

• For the listening comprehension activities, play **Track 003** or read the audio script available on the *ExamView®* CD-ROM, and also on the Teacher's Resource Website.

• For the speaking section of the assessment, use the questions on *ExamView®* and these additional questions:

Would you prefer to work indoors, outdoors or both? Why?

If you could design your own job, what would it be? What sort of things would you combine in your work?

Think of a person you know about who has an interesting job. What does he or she do for work? What's interesting or unusual about that job?

Resources Unit 2 Quiz *(ExamView®)*

BE THE EXPERT

Testing Tip

Before a test, think about what will be needed. For example, have extra pencils, paper and rubbers ready. Be prepared with an activity for students who are early finishers, such as providing them with magazines or other reading materials in English. Before the testing session begins, write all of the instructions on the board and read them aloud. Answer any questions, so that students have a clear understanding of the testing procedure.

BE THE EXPERT

Testing Tip

Help students to manage their time efficiently during a test. Tell students to first answer easier questions before going on to more challenging questions. Remind students to allow themselves additional time to answer essay questions or questions with greater scores. Explain that students should avoid rushing to complete the test and should instead try to keep a steady pace.

Unit 3 Quiz

Before the Quiz

1. To generate the quiz, go to *ExamView® Test Generator* and select *Create a new test using a wizard*.

2. Give your quiz a title (for example: Unit 3 Quiz).

3. Select the Unit 3 question bank and select all items. Quizzes include questions that assess comprehension of vocabulary and grammar, as well as skills in these four areas: *listening, speaking, reading* and *writing*.

• You may choose to customise this quiz or create your own.

4. Print the quiz. Then make copies for each student in your class.

• For additional review, use the end-of-unit games in the **Classroom Presentation Tool**.

Giving the Quiz

• Hand out the quiz and tell students to read the instructions. Clarify instructions if necessary.

• For the listening comprehension activities, play **Track 004** or read the audio script available on the *ExamView®* CD-ROM, and also on the Teacher's Resource Website.

• For the speaking section of the assessment, use the questions on *ExamView®* and these additional questions:

What would you like about living in the dark for two months? What wouldn't you like?

Think of a city in a time zone different from yours. What time is it there now? What do you think is happening in that city right now?

What do you usually do on Monday after school? Name at least three things, and describe where and when you do them.

Unit 4 Quiz

Before the Quiz

1. To generate the quiz, go to *ExamView® Test Generator* and select *Create a new test using a wizard*.

2. Give your quiz a title (for example: Unit 4 Quiz).

3. Select the Unit 4 question bank and select all items. Quizzes include questions that assess comprehension of vocabulary and grammar, as well as skills in these four areas: *listening, speaking, reading* and *writing*.

• You may choose to customise this quiz or create your own.

4. Print the quiz. Then make copies for each student in your class.

• For additional review, use the end-of-unit games in the **Classroom Presentation Tool**.

Giving the Quiz

• Hand out the quiz and tell students to read the instructions. Clarify instructions if necessary.

• For the listening comprehension activities, play **Track 005** or read the audio script available on the *ExamView®* CD-ROM, and also on the Teacher's Resource Website.

• For the speaking section of the assessment, use the questions on *ExamView®* and these additional questions:

Can you give two reasons for conflicts between humans and animals?

Are any animals in your country losing their habitat? What is happening to them?

Do you think it's important to help protect wildlife? Why or why not?

Resources Unit 4 Quiz *(ExamView®)*

BE THE EXPERT

Testing Tip

Make sure that you give meaningful feedback to students. Offer praise on sections where students did exceptionally well. For errors, offer helpful information so that students can understand what they did wrong. For example, instead of just marking an *X* near an incorrect answer, write a word or phrase that hints at the problem (e.g. *preposition*, *spelling*, etc.)

If time allows, schedule a few moments to discuss the results of each assessment with students. During this time, re-teach information as necessary, and offer tips on how to handle similar questions on the Mastery Test.

Resources Units 1–4 Mastery Test
(ExamView®)

BE THE EXPERT

Testing Tip
Review test-taking strategies for a variety
of question types.

· For multiple-choice items, remind
students to read all the answer choices
before choosing one. Some choices
that appear correct at first glance turn
out to be wrong upon a closer look.
· For true or false items, suggest that
students underline or circle key words
in the question.
· For fill-in-the-blank items, students can
look for clues in the sentence structure
to work out what type of word is
needed, for example, a verb, a noun or
an adjective.

Units 1–4 Mastery Test

Before the Test

1. To generate the test, go to *ExamView® Test Generator* and select
Create a new test using a wizard.

2. Give your test a title (for example: Units 1–4 Mastery Test).

3. Select the Units 1–4 Mastery Test question bank and select all
items. Tests include questions that assess comprehension of
vocabulary and grammar, as well as skills in these four areas:
listening, speaking, reading and *writing*.

• You may choose to customise this test or create your own.

4. Print the test. Then make copies for each student in your class.

• For additional review, use the end-of-unit games in the **Classroom
Presentation Tool**.

Giving the Test

• Hand out the test and tell students to read the instructions. Clarify
instructions if necessary.

• For the listening comprehension activities, play **Track 010** or read
the audio script available on the *ExamView®* CD-ROM, and also on
the Teacher's Resource Website.

• For the speaking section of the assessment, use the questions on
ExamView® and these additional questions:

*Compare the city of Astana to the area where you live. How are they
the same? How are they different?*

*Do you think you would enjoy having a job that includes outdoor
adventures and physical activity? Why or why not?*

*Would you like living in a place where it's light all day for two
months every year? Why or why not?*

*Are there wild animals where you live or near where you live?
Are there conflicts between humans and animals in any of those
places? Describe them.*

Unit 5 Quiz

Before the Quiz

1. To generate the quiz, go to *ExamView® Test Generator* and select *Create a new test using a wizard*.

2. Give your quiz a title (for example: Unit 5 Quiz).

3. Select the Unit 5 question bank and select all items. Quizzes include questions that assess comprehension of vocabulary and grammar, as well as skills in these four areas: *listening, speaking, reading* and *writing*.

• You may choose to customise this quiz or create your own.

4. Print the quiz. Then make copies for each student in your class.

• For additional review, use the end-of-unit games in the **Classroom Presentation Tool**.

Giving the Quiz

• Hand out the quiz and tell students to read the instructions. Clarify instructions if necessary.

• For the listening comprehension activities, play **Track 006** or read the audio script available on the *ExamView®* CD-ROM, and also on the Teacher's Resource Website.

• For the speaking section of the assessment, use the questions on *ExamView®* and these additional questions:

What do you usually wear to school on a normal day? Why do you dress that way?

Do you think school uniforms are a good idea? Why or why not?

How does our environment affect what we wear? Give at least three examples.

Resources Unit 5 Quiz *(ExamView®)*

Testing Tip

Create a positive classroom atmosphere by encouraging students to give their best efforts. Remind students to focus on what they know, and to come back to difficult or challenging questions at the end of an assessment. Explain that it's OK if they're unable to answer a question.

Encourage students to stay relaxed during a test by periodically taking a few deep breaths.

Resources Unit 6 Quiz (ExamView®)

Testing Tip

Tell students to make a habit of taking time at the end of a quiz or test to review their answers. Students can check for careless mistakes, such as writing a correct answer in the wrong place, or skipping over a question. For multiple-choice items, students might check that they've marked only one response to each question. For short answer items, students can re-read their written responses for sense, to correct grammar and usage, and to determine whether the response fully answers the question.

Unit 6 Quiz

Before the Quiz

1. To generate the quiz, go to *ExamView® Test Generator* and select *Create a new test using a wizard*.

2. Give your quiz a title (for example: Unit 6 Quiz).

3. Select the Unit 6 question bank and select all items. Quizzes include questions that assess comprehension of vocabulary and grammar, as well as skills in these four areas: *listening, speaking, reading* and *writing*.

• You may choose to customise this quiz or create your own.

4. Print the quiz. Then make copies for each student in your class.

• For additional review, use the end-of-unit games in the **Classroom Presentation Tool**.

Giving the Quiz

• Hand out the quiz and tell students to read the instructions. Clarify instructions if necessary.

• For the listening comprehension activities, play **Track 007** or read the audio script available on the *ExamView®* CD-ROM, and also on the Teacher's Resource Website.

• For the speaking section of the assessment, use the questions on *ExamView®* and these additional questions:

> *Think of two things you could put together for a mash-up (food, music, etc.). What are they, and what would the mash-up be?*

> *What two games do you enjoy playing? Compare the two.*

> *Have you ever tasted food that was a combination of foods from different cultures? Describe it. If not, do you think you'd like to try some? Why or why not?*

Unit 7 Quiz

Before the Quiz

1. To generate the quiz, go to *ExamView® Test Generator* and select *Create a new test using a wizard*.

2. Give your quiz a title (for example: Unit 7 Quiz).

3. Select the Unit 7 question bank and select all items. Quizzes include questions that assess comprehension of vocabulary and grammar, as well as skills in these four areas: *listening, speaking, reading* and *writing*.

• You may choose to customise this quiz or create your own.

4. Print the quiz. Then make copies for each student in your class.

• For additional review, use the end-of-unit games in the **Classroom Presentation Tool**.

Giving the Quiz

• Hand out the quiz and tell students to read the instructions. Clarify instructions if necessary.

• For the listening comprehension activities, play **Track 008** or read the audio script available on the *ExamView®* CD-ROM, and also on the Teacher's Resource Website.

• For the speaking section of the assessment, use the questions on *ExamView®* and these additional questions:

What apps or gadgets do you use every day? What do you use them for?

What apps or gadgets do you think are the most or least interesting? the most or least useful? Why?

What sort of apps or gadgets do you think people will use in the future? What will they use them for?

Resources Unit 7 Quiz *(ExamView®)*

BE THE EXPERT

Testing Tip

Remind students to write complete sentences when answering questions or completing a writing task. When completing writing tasks, students should carefully read a question so that they can be sure to answer appropriately. Students can then restate the question in the topic sentence of their response. For speaking tasks, remind students to also answer with complete sentences.

Resources Unit 8 Quiz (*ExamView®*)

Testing Tip

During assessment, one of the key things to remember is that the first question might not be the best place to start. Sometimes, a student will look at the first question on an assessment and panic, thinking he or she knows nothing. That can derail the rest of the assessment. Instead, help students take a holistic approach by spending time scanning the entire assessment, and looking for positive entry points where they feel most confident.

Unit 8 Quiz

Before the Quiz

1. To generate the quiz, go to *ExamView® Test Generator* and select *Create a new test using a wizard*.

2. Give your quiz a title (for example: Unit 8 Quiz).

3. Select the Unit 8 question bank and select all items. Quizzes include questions that assess comprehension of vocabulary and grammar, as well as skills in these four areas: *listening, speaking, reading* and *writing*.

• You may choose to customise this quiz or create your own.

4. Print the quiz. Then make copies for each student in your class.

• For additional review, use the end-of-unit games in the **Classroom Presentation Tool**.

Giving the Quiz

• Hand out the quiz and tell students to read the instructions. Clarify instructions if necessary.

• For the listening comprehension activities, play **Track 009** or read the audio script available on the *ExamView®* CD-ROM, and also on the Teacher's Resource Website.

• For the speaking section of the assessment, use the questions on *ExamView®* and these additional questions:

> *Are you interested in learning about cultures that came before yours? Why or why not? If so, what cultures are you most interested in?*
>
> *Is there a game in your culture that people have played for many years? Describe it. Do you know how to play it?*
>
> *What was life like in your area 100 years ago? What has changed? What has remained the same?*

Units 5–8 Mastery Test

Before the Test

1. To generate the test, go to *ExamView® Test Generator* and select *Create a new test using a wizard*.

2. Give your test a title (for example: Units 5–8 Mastery Test).

3. Select the Units 5–8 Mastery Test question bank and select all items. Tests include questions that assess comprehension of vocabulary and grammar, as well as skills in these four areas: *listening, speaking, reading* and *writing*.

- You may choose to customise this test or create your own.

4. Print the test. Then make copies for each student in your class.

- For additional review, use the end-of-unit games in the **Classroom Presentation Tool**.

Giving the Test

- Hand out the test and tell students to read the instructions. Clarify instructions if necessary.

- For the listening comprehension activities, play **Track 011** or read the audio script available on the *ExamView®* CD-ROM, and also on the Teacher's Resource Website.

- For the speaking section of the assessment, use the questions on *ExamView®* and these additional questions:

  Describe the clothes you're wearing right now. Why are you wearing them?

  Do you like mash-ups? Why or why not? Describe a mash-up that you like or don't like, and explain your ideas.

  What app or gadget would you like to have that you don't have now? What would you use it for?

  Why do you think people try to understand the past?

ASSESSMENT

Resources Unit 5–8 Mastery Test (*ExamView®*)

BE THE EXPERT

Testing Tip

Look for patterns of errors to help students identify areas where they can improve. If students have left questions blank because of a lack of time, they can practise estimating how much time they need for particular tasks and improve their ability to pace themselves. If they have made errors because they didn't follow instructions, students can read more carefully and circle or underline important words that may lead them to the correct answer.

Resources Final Test *(ExamView®)*

BE THE EXPERT

Testing Tip

Review content regularly in class to help reinforce learning and to better prepare students for quizzes and tests. Periodically recognise and reward successful students. Encourage students to take notes on their own to help them review topics with which they feel less comfortable. Students might use different colour highlighting to help them differentiate important vocabulary or grammar topics.

Consider providing students with grading criteria or assessment guidelines before they take a test so they understand how the test will be marked and how each portion of a test contributes to the whole.

Final Test

Before the Test

1. To generate the test, go to *ExamView® Test Generator* and select *Create a new test using a wizard*.

2. Give your test a title (for example: Units 1–8 Final Test).

3. Select the Units 1–8 Final Test question bank and select all items. Tests include questions that assess comprehension of vocabulary and grammar, as well as skills in these four areas: *listening, speaking, reading* and *writing*.

• You may choose to customise this test or create your own.

4. Print the test. Then make copies for each student in your class.

• For additional review, use the end-of-unit games in the **Classroom Presentation Tool**.

Giving the Test

• Hand out the test and tell students to read the instructions. Clarify instructions if necessary.

• For the listening comprehension activities, play **Track 012** or read the audio script available on the *ExamView®* CD-ROM, and also on the Teacher's Resource Website.

• For the speaking section of the assessment, use the questions on *ExamView®* and these additional questions:

How are unusual places and unusual jobs connected? Give two examples from what you learnt in Units 1 and 2.

How are humans and wild animals connected? Think about what people and animals do during the day and at night, and give two examples from what you learnt in Units 3 and 4.

How are clothing and mash-ups connected? Give at least two examples from what you learnt in Units 5 and 6.

How are modern apps and gadgets, tools and games from the past connected? Give at least two examples from what you learnt in Units 7 and 8.

WORKBOOK

Unit 1
Life in the City

1 Find ten vocabulary words. Then write the correct words to complete each sentence.

opankskyscrapersnubckbuniquenvkvufkvkfvunusual/kbebfbcapitaluffjfilujlf
urbannmbdhwfulitruralubsjjshapeyeplangubbodesigninbotrtowernosid

1. People often talk about the differences between _____rural / urban_____ life and _____urban / rural_____ life. My friend is _____unusual_____ because she lives for six months in the city and six months in the countryside.

2. I have another friend who has a very special window in his bedroom. The window is in the roof and is the _____shape_____ of a star. It's like sleeping under the stars! The _____design_____ is _____unique_____ because he made it himself – nobody else has one like it!

3. Living in a _____capital_____ city is exciting. When I get a job, I _____plan_____ to live in Paris or Ottawa or Rome.

4. Is there a city in the world that doesn't have tall buildings or _____skyscrapers_____? Maybe, but every airport must have a communications _____tower_____ to help planes.

2 Listen. Write the number of the sentence that goes with each picture. 🔊002

a. `3` b. `2` c. `4`

d. `1` e. `6` f. `5`

3 Listen. Then read and tick **T** for *True* or **F** for *False*. Rewrite the false statements to make them true. 🔊003

	T	F
1. Renato is an architect.	✓	
2. He designs skyscrapers.		✓
3. Renato's design for a city has areas only for people.		✓
4. In Renato's city, cars travel above residents' heads.	✓	
5. Renato's design is only for older people.		✓
6. Renato's city design is safe for the residents.	✓	
7. The bicycle tracks are high up with the cars.		✓
8. Renato's city is expensive to build.	✓	

GRAMMAR

Present simple: General statements

Architects **design** new buildings for cities.	She **studies** the plans for the new capital.
The city's design **includes** a lot of green spaces.	The road **goes** next to an indoor park.
This tall tower **doesn't look** new.	The skyscraper **has** a garden inside.

To form the present simple, use the infinitive without *to*. *I/You/We/They* **design** unusual buildings. Note that with *he/she/it*, we add **-s** to the verb: *He/She* **designs** a new skyscraper. *It* **looks** amazing. To make a negative sentence, use *don't* or *doesn't*.

The spelling of some verbs changes after adding **-s** or **-es**. Add **-es** to verbs such as *cross* → *crosses*, *wash* → *washes*, *watch* → *watches*. For verbs that end in *y*, drop the *y* and add **-ies**: *study* → *studies*.

Some verbs are irregular: *go* → *goes*, *do* → *does*, *have* → *has*.

1 Listen. Circle the verb you hear. Then listen again to check your answers. 🔊004

1. Capital cities **has** / **have** large public areas.
2. Children often **play** / **plays** in city parks.
3. An architect **teach** / **teaches** how to design buildings.
4. People **doesn't** / **don't** walk on this pavement.
5. Huge mountains **surround** / **surrounds** the capital city.
6. In winter the city park **closes** / **close** early.
7. She **study** / **studies** unusual architecture in Denmark.
8. The bridge **doesn't** / **don't** go to the sports centre.

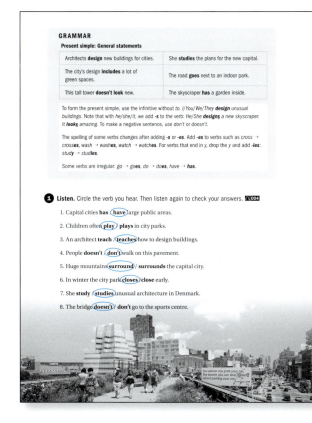

2 Write. Fill in the blanks with the correct present simple form.

1. In Bogotá, people sometimes _____ride_____ (ride) their bikes on the motorway.
2. Residents _____like_____ (like) to relax by the stream.
3. Architects _____don't design_____ (not design) skyscrapers for rural areas.
4. A new bridge _____crosses_____ (cross) the motorway.
5. People _____need_____ (need) green spaces in capital cities.
6. Sometimes architects _____plan_____ (plan) buildings with parks on the roof.
7. In urban areas, people _____don't enjoy_____ (not enjoy) crowded pavements.
8. My village _____has_____ (have) a water tower.
9. A major motorway _____connects_____ (connect) two big cities.
10. The stream _____doesn't go_____ (not go) through the city.

3 Write about a city you know. Use some of the words in the box.

Things:	architecture	bridge	motorway shape	pavement	skyscraper	tower
Descriptive words:	concrete	indoor	outdoor rural	unique	unusual	urban
Verbs:	be	construct	cross design	have	need	plan

Answers will vary.

4 Draw a plan of your city. Use a separate piece of paper. Practise talking about the details of your plan with your classmates or teacher.

5

WORKBOOK **265**

1
Listen and read. As you read, notice the separate paragraphs. Why does the writer start new paragraphs? 🔊 005

Desire* Paths

*desire v. to want something
n. the feeling of wanting something

¹Everybody has seen one, most people have walked on one, and perhaps you started a new one. We may not know the name, but these paths are called 'desire paths'. These are paths, tracks, or pavements made by people or animals walking on the grass to move quickly from one concrete pavement to another. For example, we see these paths in urban spaces where people don't use the pavements, but take a shortcut through green land, parks and gardens.

²So why do people decide to walk on the green grass and not on the pavements? Sometimes the architect's plan for urban spaces isn't the best. Residents, people like you and me, who use the outdoor areas every day, know the best and quickest way to walk from one place to another.

³The problem is that we destroy the grass when we make a desire path. Also, these new tracks get wet and dirty easily. Concrete is cleaner. We know that we need to protect our green spaces, but we also need to move from place to place quickly.

⁴Perhaps we need better designers and architects to plan our pavements and urban green spaces. They should ask local people and pay attention to what residents want.

2
Answer the questions. Write the number of the paragraph on the line.

___1___ 1. Which paragraph gives us a definition of desire paths?
___3___ 2. Which paragraph tells us about problems with desire paths?
___2___ 3. Which paragraph describes the reasons for desire paths?
___4___ 4. Which paragraph discusses possible solutions to the problems?

3
Complete the diagram. Read the text again and make notes in the boxes.

Desire paths

Reasons
1. best/fastest way between two places
2. concrete pavements are not well planned

Problems
1. grass is destroyed
2. dirty

4
Think about the information from the texts in this unit. You've read about desire paths and a plan to make London into a new type of national park. Read the sentences. Do you agree with these ideas? Tick (✓) the boxes if you agree. Write a question mark (?) if you're not sure. Write (X) if you don't agree.   *Answers will vary.*

1. There's a lot of green space where I live. ☐
2. We need to protect green spaces in cities. ☐
3. I use desire paths. ☐
4. Concrete pavements are important. ☐
5. I feel happier when I spend time outdoors. ☐
6. The walk to my nearest park is too long. ☐
7. Architects should ask city residents about their ideas for green spaces. ☐
8. People haven't got enough information about nature in urban areas. ☐

GRAMMAR

In and on: Expressing location

People walk **on** the grass and make new paths.	There aren't enough trees **in** cities.
There's a restaurant **on** top of the skyscraper.	We need more green spaces **in** urban areas.
I walk my dog **on** the pavement.	I like to relax **in** the park.

We use *in* and *on* to say where something is. Use *in* to give the idea that things are inside something or in an area; for example, in buildings, cities and countries. *People live in skyscrapers. There are many beaches in Rio de Janeiro. Rio de Janeiro is in Brazil. Brazil is a country in South America.*

Use *on* to say that something is on the surface or on top of something else. We also use *on* with streets and roads. *They live on an island. Their house is on Broad Street. They often walk on the beach.*

1
Circle the correct preposition.

1. Cars don't go **on** / in pavements.
2. There are a lot of skyscrapers **in** / on big cities.
3. The Statue of Liberty is **on** / in an island.
4. You can find lot of green areas **in** / on the countryside.
5. Moscow is **in** / on Russia.
6. The Taj Mahal is on / **in** India.
7. The most popular Internet café is on / **in** Main Street.
8. The architect lives **in** / on Los Angeles.
9. Many residents of Rio de Janeiro like to relax **on** / in the beach.
10. There's a new restaurant **on** / in top of the building.

2
Listen. Draw a dot *in* or *on* each box according to the sentence you hear. 🔊 006

1.   2.   3.   4.

5.   6.   7.   8.

3
Write. Marta is in her first year at college. This is an e-mail to her younger brother. Read and fill in the blanks with *in* or *on*.

Hi Seba,

How are you? I'm fine now after two days (1) __in__ my new room at college. It's really cool here. Everybody can find me easily because my name is (2) __on__ the door!

I don't know the town very well yet, but my building is (3) __on__ Main Street, so everything is close. I see that there's a new park near my building. Guess what? It has a skateboard track (4) __in__ the middle! So bring your skateboard when you come. I think you can fit it (5) __in__ your bag, can't you? Here's a photo of the park.

I'm thinking of joining a club that does something called 'Parkour'. Have you heard of it? They also call it 'urban free running' – running (6) __in__ cities. Look it up on the Internet. There are some amazing videos!

Say hi to Mum and Dad, and see if you can visit me soon.

Bye for now!

Marta

4
Think about the design of the neighbourhood where you live. Write at least six sentences using *in* and *on* and the words from the box. Practise talking about your neighbourhood with your classmates or teacher.   *Answers will vary.*

bridge	motorway	park	river	shopping centre	pavement	skyscraper

I live in a skyscraper in Hong Kong.

_____
_____
_____
_____

6   7   8   9

WRITING

When we want to tell someone about a person, a place or a thing, we often use descriptive words. Words such as *dirty*, *busy* and *wet* are adjectives that go with nouns to paint a better picture in our mind. Notice how these descriptive words create different pictures in our mind.
- *Alexis skates on the **dirty** pavement.*
- *Alexis skates on the **busy** pavement.*
- *Alexis skates on the **wet** pavement.*

❶ Organise.

1. Your topic is a place that needs changing. Think of a place you know that has a problem. Maybe it's very small, too dry or wet, or maybe there's a lot of rubbish there.

   In the first column, list three things you don't like about the place. Then, in the second column, think of how you can change each thing. Use descriptive words.

A place I don't like	My changes
school playground – broken bench	new, wooden bench

   Read your two lists and add more descriptive adjectives. Use a dictionary to help.

2. Plan your writing. You need an opening statement that describes the place and what the problem is. This will be your topic sentence. It helps the readers understand your idea. Write your topic sentence here:

   _____

   Next, you'll need a paragraph describing what the problem is, and a paragraph about what the place looks like after the change. Remember to use descriptive words to create a picture in your readers' minds.

❷ Write.

1. Go to page 21 in your book. Re-read the model text and the descriptive words.
2. Write your first draft. Check for organisation, content, punctuation, capitalisation and spelling.
3. Write your final draft. Share it with your teacher and classmates.

10

Now I can ...

· **talk about cities and different types of life in the city.**

☐ Yes, I can!
☐ I think I can.
☐ I need more practice.

Write two sentences about urban life.

_____
_____

Write two sentences about green spaces in cities.

_____
_____

· **use the present simple to talk about general statements.**

☐ Yes, I can!
☐ I think I can.
☐ I need more practice.

Write four sentences using the present simple form of any of the verbs from the box. Two of your sentences should be negative.

construct	design	explore	find	grow	live	need	pay	plan	use	walk

_____
_____
_____
_____

· **use *in* and *on* to express location.**

☐ Yes, I can!
☐ I think I can.
☐ I need more practice.

Write four sentences about a place you know. Use *in* and *on*.

_____
_____
_____
_____

· **write a description of a place in my neighbourhood.**

☐ Yes, I can!
☐ I think I can.
☐ I need more practice.

Use four or more descriptive words to write about a real place.

_____
_____
_____

YOU DECIDE Choose an activity. Go to page 90.

11

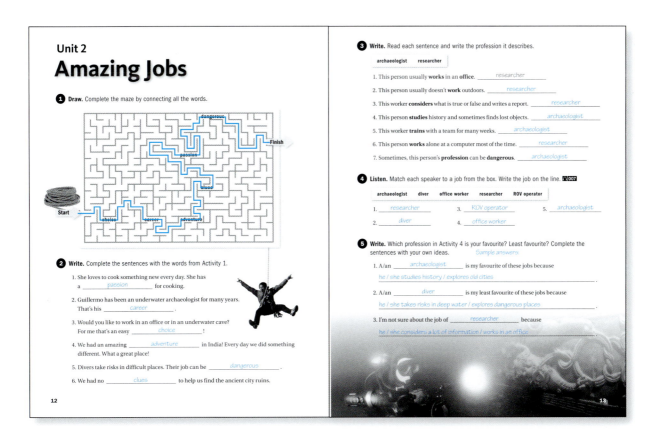

Unit 2
Amazing Jobs

❶ Draw. Complete the maze by connecting all the words.

dangerous

Finish

passion

clues

Start

choice   career   adventure

❷ Write. Complete the sentences with the words from Activity 1.

1. She loves to cook something new every day. She has a _____passion_____ for cooking.

2. Guillermo has been an underwater archaeologist for many years. That's his _____career_____ .

3. Would you like to work in an office or in an underwater cave? For me that's an easy _____choice_____ !

4. We had an amazing _____adventure_____ in India! Every day we did something different. What a great place!

5. Divers take risks in difficult places. Their job can be _____dangerous_____ .

6. We had no _____clues_____ to help us find the ancient city ruins.

12

❸ Write. Read each sentence and write the profession it describes.

archaeologist	researcher

1. This person usually **works** in an **office**. _____researcher_____
2. This person usually doesn't **work** outdoors. _____researcher_____
3. This worker **considers** what is true or false and writes a report. _____researcher_____
4. This person **studies** history and sometimes finds lost objects. _____archaeologist_____
5. This worker **trains** with a team for many weeks. _____archaeologist_____
6. This person **works** alone at a computer most of the time. _____researcher_____
7. Sometimes, this person's **profession** can be **dangerous**. _____archaeologist_____

❹ Listen. Match each speaker to a job from the box. Write the job on the line. 🔊007

archaeologist	diver	office worker	researcher	ROV operator

1. _____researcher_____   3. _____ROV operator_____   5. _____archaeologist_____
2. _____diver_____   4. _____office worker_____

❺ Write. Which profession in Activity 4 is your favourite? Least favourite? Complete the sentences with your own ideas.   Sample answers

1. A/an _____archaeologist_____ is my favourite of these jobs because *he / she studies history / explores old cities* .

2. A/an _____diver_____ is my least favourite of these jobs because *he / she takes risks in deep water / explores dangerous places* .

3. I'm not sure about the job of _____researcher_____ because *he / she considers a lot of information / works in an office* .

13

GRAMMAR

Present simple questions and answers: Talking about routines

Does a water slide tester **travel** to different countries?	**Yes**, he **does**. / **No**, he **doesn't**.
Do water slide testers **get** any money?	**Yes**, they **do**. / **No**, they **don't**.
Do you **know** when a water slide isn't good?	**Yes**, I **do**. Sometimes the water **doesn't go** on some parts of the slide, or the design is not perfect, so I **stop** in the middle.
Where do water slide testers **work**?	We **work** in places such as hotels, theme parks and cruise ships.

To form questions in the present simple, use **do/does** and the verb (infinitive without *to*). A short answer to these questions starts with **Yes** or **No**, and we repeat **do/does** or **doesn't/don't** but not the verb. **Does** an underwater explorer **have** a dangerous job? **Yes**, he **does**. Sometimes, we give additional information. **Do** you **like** your office? **No**, I **don't**. It's too small.

When we look for specific information, we start the questions with questions words (*where*, *what*, *when*, *why* and so on). **Where do** researchers **work**? They **work** in an office.

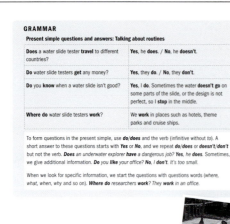

1 Read and match the questions with the answers.
Write the letter on the line.

b 1. Does this man like his job?   a. about $30,000 a year
d 2. Do people really do this job?   b. Yes, he does! He enjoys it a lot.
a 3. How much money does he earn?   c. No, he doesn't. He just needs to be fit.
e 4. Why do designers need to test slides?   d. Yes, they do!
c 5. Does he need special physical training?   e. because water slides have to be safe and fun

2 Listen. Then complete the short answers. 008
1. Yes, I do. 3. No, she doesn't. 5. No, they don't.
2. Yes, he does. 4. Yes, we do. 6. Yes, it does.

14

3 Write. Use the words to ask questions.
1. he / speak / many languages — Does he speak many languages?
2. you / have / accidents — Do you have accidents?
3. when / you / usually / work — When do you usually work?
4. he / need / interview — Does he need an interview?
5. where / you / apply for / job — Where do you apply for the job?
6. what / he / like / about his job — What does he like about his job?

4 Write. Think about these unusual jobs. Imagine the answers to the questions.
1. What does a pet food tester do? *Sample answers:*
He tests the flavour of new cat food.
She smells the food.
2. What does a dog surfing instructor do?
He helps the dog stand on the surfboard. / He pulls the surfboard. /
He catches the dog when it falls.
3. What does a golf ball diver do?
She waits for a golf ball to go in the water. / He looks for the lost ball. /
She dives in the water.

5 Choose one unusual job from this unit. Imagine you have an interview for that career. Ask and answer two questions. *Sample answers:*
Question: What do underwater archaeologists do?
Answer: They study objects and places from the past, under water!
Question 1: Do I have to wear a uniform?
Answer: Yes, you do.
Question 2: What hours do I have to work?
Answer: You work from 11 a.m. until 7 p.m.

15

1 Listen and read. As you read, think what each paragraph is about. 009

Unlucky Days at Work

¹When you choose an unusual career, like I did, you don't expect everything to be easy. I'm an underwater archaeologist, and things can go wrong. That's normal. Sometimes an advisor says that we might find bones in a cave, for example, but we arrive and it's empty. That tells me nobody lived there. So now we ask – why didn't anybody live in that cave? In this way we create new research and change a bad situation into something positive.

²When we explore an underwater cave, we work hard. We get up early, check our equipment, and drive for many hours. Then we get out and walk, carrying our heavy ropes and diving equipment. Like most people, we have to follow a schedule carefully. We can't spend too many hours diving.

³One time we got our measurements wrong. I went down into a cave on a 50-metre rope to check the cave. When I got near the bottom, the rope wasn't long enough. And then I saw that there was almost no water in the cave! I looked very funny with all my expensive diving equipment in a cave with no water! Anyway, underwater archaeology is my passion, and it's better than commuting to an office.

1. Give an example from paragraph 1 of a problem that the author had.
He expected to find bones in a cave but there were none.
2. How are underwater archaeologists like many people? Give two examples.
They have to follow a schedule. Things sometimes don't go to plan.
3. What is one problem the author describes in paragraph 3?
Incorrect measurements can cause problems.

16

2 Read the text again. Complete the table for paragraph 1.

Paragraph 1	
Topic Sentence	
Supporting Details	
Concluding Sentence	

3 Think about the information in this unit. You've read about a photographer, a space scientist and an underwater archaeologist. If you agree, tick (✔) the sentence. If you don't agree, change the sentence so that it's true for you. *Answers will vary.*

1. I want to be a professional photographer who works in the Himalayas.
I don't want to be a professional photographer in the Himalayas. OR
I want to be a professional photographer in the Caribbean.
2. Space science costs too much money. We don't need to learn about other planets.
3. Diving in a cave is probably the coolest job in the world.
4. Taking risks for your career is a bad idea.
5. Learning about the past helps us plan our future.
6. Explorers are important because we need to know more about our planet.

17

GRAMMAR

Possessives: Showing ownership

The **camera's** lens is broken.	**My** camera isn't working.
Thomas's dad is a photographer.	Is **his** mum a photographer, too?
NASA's new space telescope takes great pictures.	**Its** name is Hubble.
The **children's** / **boys'** password is new.	**Their** new password is 'adventure'.

To show that something belongs to a person or thing, we use these words: *my, your, his, her, its, our, their.*

We can also show possession by adding **'s** to a singular noun or to plural nouns that don't end in **s**: *The **diver's** job is interesting. **Women's** passion for diving isn't unusual.*

Add only an apostrophe (') to plural nouns that end in **s**: *photographers' cameras*. Add **'s** to words that end in **s**: *Mr **Dickens's** house.*

1 **Listen for the possessives.** Circle the word you hear. 🔊 010

1. (**Jupiter's**) / Jupiter moon might have water.
2. The (**doctors'**) / doctor plane is like a flying hospital.
3. Are these (**your**) / yours oxygen tanks?
4. The (**photographer's**) / photographer camera is expensive.
5. All three researcher / (**researchers'**) data needs to be in one report.
6. The bicycle has lost (**its**) / his wheel.
7. Please order three children / (**children's**) meals.

2 **Write the possessive form for each noun.**

1. researcher	*researcher's*	5. office	*office's*	
2. women	*women's*	6. Dickens	*Dickens's*	
3. bicycle	*bicycle's*	7. puppies	*puppies'*	
4. advisors	*advisors'*	8. house	*house's*	

18

3 **Complete the sentences.** Use the correct words from the box.

my	your	his	her	its	our	their

1. Would you like to borrow __my__ dictionary?
2. Oh no, __our__ flight is late. We'll miss the connection in Madrid.
3. Excuse me, you dropped __your__ ticket.
4. The divers carry __their__ oxygen tanks.
5. Dr Emily Park has to change __her__ schedule this week.
6. His laptop isn't working now, so he has to recharge __its__ battery.
7. Tony loves __his__ work. He's an underwater photographer.

4 **Listen.** Then read and tick **T** for *True* and **F** for *False*. Rewrite any false sentences to make them true. 🔊 011

	T	F
1. Judy's job is to explore mountains.	☐	☑
2. Judy finds cool places in Dublin where animals also live.	☑	☐
3. Street art can change an ugly urban space into a more positive environment.	☑	☐
4. Animals need green spaces in cities.	☑	☐
5. A lot of young people in Dublin go to parks.	☐	☑
6. Judy wants young people to have fun and also experience nature.	☑	☐

1. *Judy's job is to explore cities.*

5. *Young Dubliners stay indoors a lot and don't often visit parks.*

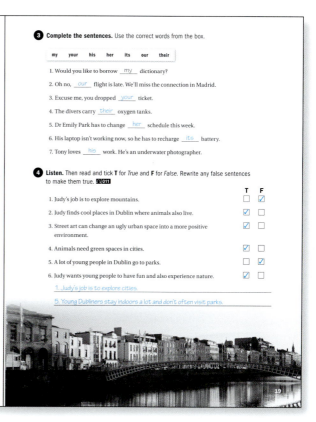

19

WRITING

When we write good descriptive paragraphs, we want our readers to understand our ideas clearly. So, each paragraph needs a topic sentence, some details, and a concluding sentence.

steeplejack *–n.* a person who climbs tall buildings to clean, paint or repair them

1 **Organise.**

1. Your task is to write a description of someone's daily routine for an unusual profession. Look through the unit for ideas on unusual jobs or do some research on the Internet. For example, you can write about the steeplejack in the photo.

2. Plan your writing. Your paragraph needs a title and should start with a topic sentence that describes the unusual job. Then, write a few sentences about the daily routine of the person who has this unusual job. Finally, you will need a concluding sentence.

   Use the table to help you plan and list the important details of your paragraph. Think about details such as where the person works, what kind of equipment he or she needs to do the job, and what he or she does from day to day.

ropes · hard hat · gloves · belt · bucket

Title	
Topic Sentence	
Supporting Details	
Concluding Sentence	

2 **Write.**

1. Go to page 37 in your book. Re-read the model text and the writing prompt.
2. Write your first draft. Check for organisation, punctuation, capitalisation and spelling.
3. Check your final draft. Share it with your teacher and classmates.

20

Now I can ...

· **talk about unusual careers.**

Describe one of these unusual careers.

☐ Yes, I can!
☐ I think I can.
☐ I need more practice.

pet food tester | golf ball diver

_____
_____
_____

· **use the present simple to ask and answer questions about routines.**

☐ Yes, I can!
☐ I think I can.
☐ I need more practice.

Complete the questions and answers with *do* or *does*, and a verb.

My uncle is a fortune cookie writer.

__Does__ he work every day? Yes, he __does__ . / No, he __doesn't__ .

__Do__ you get cookies from him? Yes, I __do__ . / No, I __don't__ .

Where __does__ he __work__ (work)? He __works__ at home.

· **use possessives to show ownership.**

☐ Yes, I can!
☐ I think I can.
☐ I need more practice.

Change the nouns to possessives.

1. (Kenji) __Kenji's__ advisor is a scientist. __His__ advisor is a scientist.
2. (the dog) __The dog's__ food is very tasty. __Its__ food is very tasty.
3. (the men) __The men's__ restaurant is underwater. __Their__ restaurant is underwater.

· **write a description of someone's daily routine.**

☐ Yes, I can!
☐ I think I can.
☐ I need more practice.

Title: _____

Topic sentence: _____

Details: _____

Conclusion: _____

YOU DECIDE **Choose an activity.** Go to page 91.

21

WORKBOOK

Units 1–2 Review

1 Read. Choose the word that best completes the sentences.

1. Tammy's brothers and sisters don't like snakes, but she does. Her mother says that she's _____ in her family.
   a. unique   b. similar   c. normal

2. Tim goes to bed at 6 a.m. and wakes up at lunchtime. He works most nights. He's _____ because most people work during the day.
   a. unusual   b. common   c. normal

3. Ivan asks the photographer some questions. He's _____ her for his blog.
   a. researching   b. interviewing   c. considering

4. There are lots of parks and outdoor spaces in my city. I like living in a(n) _____ area.
   a. rural   b. urban   c. countryside

5. I love history, so I know what profession I want to study in college. I want to be an _____ .
   a. architect   b. animal researcher   c. archaeologist

6. Katerina climbs towers and skyscrapers in her work. She _____ every day.
   a. takes risks   b. applies for   c. constructs

2 Listen. Match each teenager to a career he or she might like. Write the number on the line. 🎧 012

_5_ a. Steeplejack – travel the country; clean, repair tall buildings

_4_ b. Dog walker – outdoor spaces and parks; take dogs for walks

_1_ c. Personal trainer – sports centre; help people keep fit, learn sports

_3_ d. Underwater photographer – seas around the world; taking photos

_2_ e. Researcher – home; collect information, interview, write reports

22

---

3 Read. Decide which answer (**a**, **b**, **c**, or **d**) best fits each blank space.

A Twenty-first Century Place to Live

My home is in Yangon, the old capital of Myanmar. Yangon (1) _a_ city centre is changing fast; (2) _d_ old buildings are being replaced by new skyscrapers. People walk on new concrete pavements. The city (3) _c_ modern architecture is amazing. There are three new motorways and tall bridges over the river.

Many years ago (4) _a_ family bought an apartment on Strand Road, next to the river. We could see boats from every room. Now (5) _a_ kitchen only has a view of a new skyscraper. When we sit in our living room, we can see (6) _c_ favourite cinema.

1. a. 's   b. s'   c. its   d. his
2. a. his   b. 's   c. their   d. its
3. a. his   b. its   c. 's   d. s'
4. a. my   b. his   c. 's   d. her
5. a. our   b. their   c. its   d. s'
6. a. your   b. s'   c. our   d. its

4 Read the sentences. Circle the correct word.

1. The motorway **don't** / **doesn't** cross the river.
2. **Do** / **Does** children play in the park?
3. Why **don't** / **doesn't** you like working in an office?
4. Maya and her daughter **plans** / **plan** a visit to the water tower.
5. **Does** / **Do** we have any clues about the unusual symbols on that wall?
6. Before Coco can go to live **in** / **on** the jungle, she must learn how to climb.
7. Commuting to the city centre is more tiring **in** / **on** a bicycle.
8. My cousin's profession is unusual. She tests pet food **in** / **on** a scientist's laboratory!
9. Architects design our pavements but they don't think about the people who walk **in** / **on** them.
10. Her brother's friend works **in** / **on** Saudi Arabia as a photographer.

23

Unit 3
Secrets of the Dark

1 Read. Decide whether each sentence describes picture A or B. Write *A* or *B*.

A

B

_B_ 1. The boy is very active.
_A_ 2. The boy is going to sleep.
_A_ 3. It's after sunset.
_B_ 4. It's daylight.

_A_ 5. The streetlight is lit up.
_B_ 6. The streetlight isn't lit up.
_A_ 7. It's dark outside.
_B_ 8. It's after sunrise.

2 Listen. Then circle the best answers. 🎧 013

1. Ella walks to school in **darkness** / **daylight**.
2. The students see the **sunrise** / **sunset**.
3. The playground is **lit up** / **not lit up**.
4. When Ella walks home from school, cars drive with **headlights on** / **headlights off**.
5. People in Stockholm **go to sleep** / **are active** when it's dark early.

24

---

3 Read. Then match the sentence halves about daylight hours in Stockholm. Write the letters.

In Stockholm, Sweden, there are 18 hours of daylight during the month of June. However, in December, there are only five hours. This causes some health problems. People need the sun's vitamin D for healthy bones and skin. So the residents add extra vitamin D to their winter diet by eating more yoghurt and drinking extra milk. Also, they usually take two holidays a year to enjoy the sun.

There are other problems, too. People feel sad, lose energy, and go out to festivals less often. In the city centre, tall buildings block the sunlight from reaching the pavements, so sometimes offices and homes get less than 5 hours of light a day. However, when it snows, the city looks brighter because streetlights and cars' headlights light up the snow.

_e_ 1. In the city centre, tall buildings
_a_ 2. Eating more milk products
_d_ 3. Some people feel unhappy
_b_ 4. Although Stockholm has very few hours of sunlight in the winter,
_c_ 5. One good thing is that when it snows

a. helps people be healthy in the winter months.
b. it has fewer hours of darkness in the summer.
c. the city appears lighter because of the streetlights shining on the snow.
d. when they don't have enough daylight.
e. block the sun, so it's dark.

4 Write. Look at the picture and write sentences. Use vocabulary words from the word box.

| active | darkness | streetlights | sunset |

Sample answers:
1. People are walking in the darkness.
2. The streetlights are lit up.
3. It's after sunset.
4. It's dark, but people are still active.

25

GRAMMAR

Present continuous: Saying what is happening now

Non-action verbs	Action verbs
We **understand** your idea.	She**'s wearing** snow boots.
She **doesn't think** it's expensive.	I**'m ice-skating** on the lake.
They **stay** at their grandmother's house in the summer.	You**'re learning** about time zones.
You **look** healthy.	They**'re making** a green glowing light.

Some verbs describe actions: *learn, skate, sing, grow, climb*. We can use the *be + –ing* form with these verbs. *Now we **are learning**. I'm **skating**. They're **singing**.*

Other verbs don't describe actions. We use them to describe situations, feelings and ideas: *be, live, believe, understand, have, hear, want*. We don't often use the *be + –ing* form with these verbs.

Some non-action verbs can become action verbs with a change in meaning; for example: *think, have. I **think** this sunset is beautiful. I **am thinking** of the sunset I saw yesterday.*

1 **Choose the correct verb to complete each sentence.** Think about if the sentence describes something happening now (*action verb*) or something that is always true (*non-action verb*).

1. She (**is wearing**) / wears a hat and gloves when it is cold at night.
2. He (**believes**) / is believing there's life on Mars.
3. Animals that glow in the dark (**include**) / are including fireflies and jellyfish.
4. David Gruber often (**surfs**) / is surfing when he goes on holiday.
5. Scientists (**are learning**) / learn that more underwater creatures glow in the dark.
6. Kids (**love**) / are loving unusual animals.
7. I'm busy right now. I (**am working**) / work on my report.

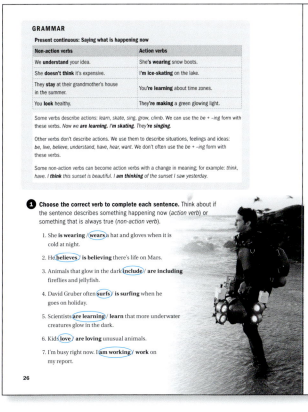

26

2 **Listen.** Circle **A** for *Action* and **NA** for *Non-action*. 🔊 014

1. A (NA)   3. A (NA)   5. A (NA)   7. A (NA)   9. A (NA)
2. (A) NA   4. (A) NA   6. (A) NA   8. (A) NA   10. (A) NA

3 **Write.** Put each word under *Day* (sun) or *Night* (moon). Add more words using your own ideas. Then write five sentences using the words from the lists.

awake   car headlights   dark   darkness   daylight   go to sleep   streetlight   sunset

Day ☀	Night ☾
awake sunrise daylight	asleep sunset darkness
lunchtime school sports	midnight streetlight
	dark car headlights
	go to sleep

1. Answers will vary.
2. _____
3. _____
4. _____
5. _____

4 **Finish these sentences.** Use vocabulary from this unit. Don't forget to use negatives.

1. During the day, a DJ goes to sleep because he works at night .
2. We use streetlights so we can see in the dark .
3. In Stockholm, people don't go to sleep at sunset .
4. At sunset tonight, they plan/are planning to take pictures of the sky .
5. People in many countries use fireworks when they celebrate light festivals .
6. Today, we are learning about time zones .

27

1 **Listen and read.** As you read, underline the words in bold type from pages 44–45 of your student's book. The first word is done for you. 🔊 015

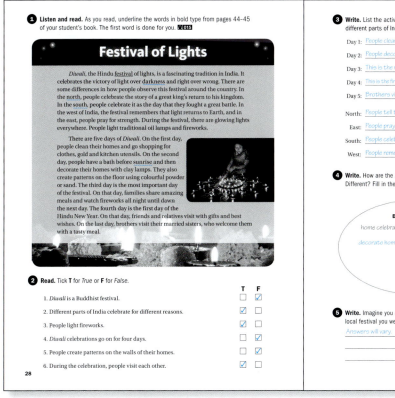

Festival of Lights

Diwali, the Hindu <u>festival</u> of lights, is a fascinating tradition in India. It celebrates the victory of light over darkness and right over wrong. There are some differences in how people observe this festival around the country. In the <u>north</u>, people celebrate the story of a great king's return to his kingdom. In the <u>south</u>, people celebrate it as the day that they fought a great battle. In the west of India, the festival remembers that light returns to Earth, and in the east, people pray for strength. During the festival, there are glowing lights everywhere. People light traditional oil lamps and fireworks.

There are five days of *Diwali*. On the first day, people clean their homes and go shopping for clothes, gold and kitchen utensils. On the second day, people have a bath before <u>sunrise</u> and then decorate their homes with clay lamps. They also create patterns on the floor using colourful powder or sand. The third day is the most important day of the festival. On that day, families share amazing meals and watch fireworks all night until dawn the next day. The fourth day is the first day of the Hindu New Year. On that day, friends and relatives visit with gifts and best wishes. On the last day, brothers visit their married sisters, who welcome them with a tasty meal.

2 **Read.** Tick **T** for *True* or **F** for *False*.

	T	F
1. *Diwali* is a Buddhist festival.	☐	☑
2. Different parts of India celebrate for different reasons.	☑	☐
3. People light fireworks.	☑	☐
4. *Diwali* celebrations go on for four days.	☐	☑
5. People create patterns on the walls of their homes.	☐	☑
6. During the celebration, people visit each other.	☑	☐

28

3 **Write.** List the activities for the five days of *Diwali* and the reasons people celebrate it in different parts of India.

Day 1: People clean their homes and go shopping for gold and kitchen utensils.
Day 2: People decorate their homes with clay lamps and patterns of powder.
Day 3: This is the main day of the festival when families eat together and watch fireworks.
Day 4: This is the first day of the Hindu New Year. Friends and relatives visit with gifts and best wishes.
Day 5: Brothers visit their married sisters for a tasty meal.

North: People tell the story of a great king's return.
East: People pray for strength.
South: People celebrate a battle.
West: People remember that light returns to Earth.

4 **Write.** How are the *Diwali* festival of lights and the Chinese Lantern Festival similar? Different? Fill in the Venn diagram.

Diwali
home celebration
decorate homes

Both
bright lights
fireworks
families eat together

Chinese Lantern Festival
street celebration
parades / dance

5 **Write.** Imagine you are a writer for your school website blog. Write a few sentences about a local festival you went to.

Answers will vary.
_____
_____

29

GRAMMAR

At, on and in: Saying when things happen

Our New Year starts **on** 1st January.	There's no school **on** Thursday. It's a holiday!
Stockholm has only five hours of daylight **in** November.	**In** the evenings, my brother is less active.
During the *Diwali* festival, people have a bath **at** dawn.	The sun rises at 9.30 **in** the morning.

We use *on* for days of the week and for specific dates: **on** *Tuesday (morning)*, **on** *6th June*.

We use *in* with months, years, seasons and periods of time: **in** *February*, **in** *2017*, **in** *(the) winter*, **in** *the morning*, **in** *a minute*.

We use *at* with exact times and certain expressions: **at** *sunset*, **at** *lunchtime*, **at** *3.45 p.m.*

1 **Listen.** Circle *in*, *on* or *at*. 🔊016

1. Many plants grow (**in** / **on** / **at**) night.
2. The Chinese New Year festival is usually (**in** / **on** / **at**) February.
3. My parents eat lunch (**in** / **on** / **at**) 12.30 p.m.
4. DJs usually work (**in** / **on** / **at**) the weekend.
5. People have a bath (**in** / **on** / **at**) sunrise during the *Diwali* festival.
6. I was born (**in** / **on** / **at**) 2004.
7. These festivals start (**in** / **on** / **at**) the evening.
8. See you (**in** / **on** / **at**) Tuesday morning.
9. Birds are very active (**in** / **on** / **at**) dawn.
10. Don't forget his birthday! It's (**in** / **on** / **at**) 1st April, too!

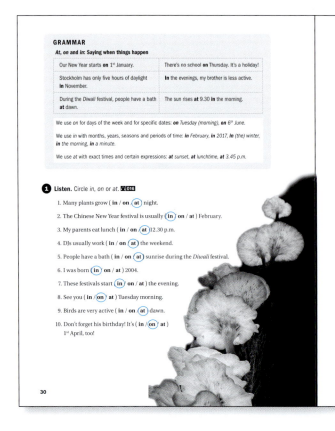

2 **Read Carlos's blog.** Then answer the questions using *at*, *on* or *in*.

Day 1: Iceland's unique landscape, with its snowy mountains and frozen lakes, is a perfect place for photographers like me. It's mid-winter, and I hear that all over the country you can see the famous Northern Lights, or *Aurora Borealis*. I'm looking forward to seeing the night sky lit up with green, red, yellow and purple light. The best view is around midnight, they say. So, here I am! I checked into my hotel. My camera battery is charging, and I'm waiting for the sunset! See you tomorrow!

Gallery

1. What time of year are the Northern Lights visible?
   They're visible in mid-winter.
2. What time of day or night gives the best view of the Northern Lights?
   The best view is at midnight.
3. When is the photographer going outdoors to take a photograph?
   He's going out at sunset.

3 **Read Carlos's blog from Day 2.** Complete the sentences with *at*, *on* or *in*.

Incredible! I can't believe how beautiful the sky was last night. I left my hotel (1) _at_ 3.30 (2) _in_ the afternoon. The sunset was soon after that, (3) _at_ around 4.00. The weather here is freezing. It's 23 degrees Fahrenheit (-5 C) (4) _at_ sunset. I don't like standing around outside (5) _in_ winter, so I decided to go back into the hotel.

(6) _At_ about 8.00 (7) _in_ the evening, I put on my hat and went outside again. Perfect timing! An amazing green light glowed in the sky in front of me, with lines of purple and red. Wow! More people were outside by now, watching in silence. Click on the gallery link to see my photos. More tomorrow! Flying home (8) _on_ Tuesday.

WRITING

We can talk about an event using the five senses as we describe what we see, hear, taste, smell and feel. With sensory words, our readers imagine that they are there at the event.

1 **Organise.**

1. Your task is to describe a colourful event, for example, a festival, fireworks, a sunset or watching a wood fire.
2. Plan your writing. Your paragraph should start with an introductory sentence that describes the colourful event. Use the hand below to write three or more sensory words to describe what you see, hear, taste, smell and feel. If needed, use a dictionary to help.

   Write your introductory sentence here:

   _____

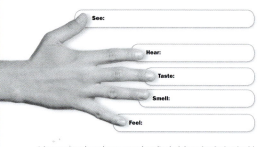

- See:
- Hear:
- Taste:
- Smell:
- Feel:

3. In your paragraph, use the sensory words you listed to help you describe the colourful event. Finish your paragraph with a brief statement of why this event is special and how you feel about it.

2 **Write.**

1. Go to page 55 in your book. Re-read the model and writing prompt.
2. Write your first draft. Check for organisation, content, punctuation, capitalisation and spelling.
3. Write your final draft. Share it with your teacher and classmates.

Now I can ...

- **talk about night, darkness and nocturnal activities.**
  ☐ Yes, I can! ☐ I think I can. ☐ I need more practice.

  Choose a nocturnal animal and a light festival. Write two sentences about each.
  Sample answers:
  1. Sharks live 500 m. (1640 feet) under the sea.
     Sharks glow in the dark.
  2. During the Chinese New Year festival, people use expensive fireworks.
     At night, people dance in the streets.

- **use non-action and action verbs.**
  ☐ Yes, I can! ☐ I think I can. ☐ I need more practice.

  Write two sentences using action verbs and two sentences using non-action verbs.

  | believe | feel | glow | shine | understand | watch |

  1. The sun is glowing on the horizon.
  2. They are watching a wildlife programme.
  3. You understand time zones.
  4. The photographer feels cold at sunset.

- **use *at*, *on* and *in* to say when things happen.**
  ☐ Yes, I can! ☐ I think I can. ☐ I need more practice.

  Write sentences using the following information.

  1. morning / watch / sunrise — In the morning, we watch the sunrise.
  2. weekend / ride a bike / park — At weekends, I ride a bike to the park.
  3. observe / animal / night — He observes animals at night.

- **write a description of an event using adjectives and the five senses.**
  ☐ Yes, I can! ☐ I think I can. ☐ I need more practice.

  Use sensory words to describe your experience at a fireworks show.
  Answers will vary.
  _____
  _____

YOU DECIDE **Choose an activity.** Go to page 92.

WORKBOOK

Unit 4
Living Together

1 Read the clues. Then complete the words.

1. w i l d l i f e — Animals that live in their natural setting
2. c o n f l i c t s — Fights, disagreements
3. d i s a p p e a r — To go away so we can't see something
4. m i s t r e a t — To injure, hurt or be unkind to someone or something
5. a c c e s s — A way in
6. h a b i t a t — Animals' natural homes

2 Read. Complete each sentence with a word from **Activity 1**.

1. At sunset, wild animals come close to the tent, and then they __disappear__ .
2. People who don't take care of their pets __mistreat__ them.
3. Amy Dickman studies __conflicts__ between wild animals and humans.
4. We had __access__ to the mountain area to observe the wild cats.
5. The snow leopard's __habitat__ is in cold, mountainous areas.
6. There's a special relationship between people and __wildlife__ .

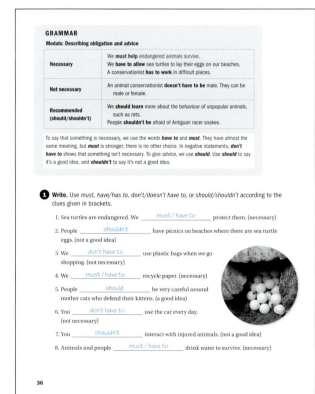

3 Listen. Then tick **T** for *True* or **F** for *False*. Rewrite the false sentences to make them true. 🎧 017

	T	F
1. The programme was about animals.	✓	
2. He thinks that dogs are wild.	✓	
3. She thinks that Siamese crocodiles aren't very clever.		✓
4. The crocodiles' habitat doesn't have any water.		✓
5. We can't live without water.	✓	
6. Little animals catch crocodiles.		✓

3. She thinks that Siamese crocodiles are clever.
4. Crocodiles live in wet, muddy places.
6. Crocodiles hunt little animals.

4 Read. Number the sentences in order.

5 We want to educate the villagers so that they can learn safe ways to live with the wildcats.
3 To help them, we need to find $2,000 to spend on saving the wildcats in my grandfather's village.
2 It's called 'Save the Wildcats' because we want to help the survival of these animals in Peru.
1 Good morning, everyone. I want to explain our project to you.
6 Please give money or your time to help wildlife live together with local people. Thank you for listening!
4 People living in the mountains frighten the wildcats away when they use the land for their farms.

Peruvian wildcat

5 Write. Complete the notes about the project in Activity 4.

1. In Peru, some villagers are afraid of the wildcats .
2. The busy farms frighten the cats away .
3. At the moment, people don't want to help the cats because they are afraid of them .
4. This project can help people learn how to live together with wildcats .
5. I think I should give some money / time to help this project .

35

GRAMMAR
Modals: Describing obligation and advice

Necessary	We **must help** endangered animals survive. We **have to allow** sea turtles to lay their eggs on our beaches. A conservationist **has to work** in difficult places.
Not necessary	An animal conservationist **doesn't have to be** male. They can be male or female.
Recommended (should/shouldn't)	We **should learn** more about the behaviour of unpopular animals, such as rats. People **shouldn't be** afraid of Antiguan racer snakes.

To say that something is necessary, we use the words **have to** and **must**. They have almost the same meaning, but **must** is stronger; there is no other choice. In negative statements, **don't have to** shows that something isn't necessary. To give advice, we use **should**. Use **should** to say it's a good idea, and **shouldn't** to say it's not a good idea.

1 Write. Use *must, have/has to, don't/doesn't have to,* or *should/shouldn't* according to the clues given in brackets.

1. Sea turtles are endangered. We __must / have to__ protect them. (necessary)
2. People __shouldn't__ have picnics on beaches where there are sea turtle eggs. (not a good idea)
3. We __don't have to__ use plastic bags when we go shopping. (not necessary)
4. We __must / have to__ recycle paper. (necessary)
5. People __should__ be very careful around mother cats who defend their kittens. (a good idea)
6. You __don't have to__ use the car every day. (not necessary)
7. You __shouldn't__ interact with injured animals. (not a good idea)
8. Animals and people __must / have to__ drink water to survive. (necessary)

36

2 Listen. Is the idea *necessary, not necessary,* or *recommended*? Tick the correct answer. 🎧 018

	Necessary	Not necessary	Recommended
1.	✓		
2.			✓
3.	✓		
4.	✓		
5.			✓
6.	✓		
7.		✓	
8.	✓		

3 Write. Look at the pictures. Use the clues and *must, has/have to, doesn't/don't have to,* or *should/shouldn't* in your sentences.

Sample answers

1. snake handler / gloves
   A snake handler must wear gloves.

2. lion / circus
   We shouldn't use lions or other wild animals in a circus.

3. bird of prey / fish
   A bird of prey doesn't have to eat fish.

4. turtle / plastic bags
   We shouldn't throw plastic bags into the sea. / We must protect turtles from plastic bags.

37

1 Listen and read. While you read, notice the problems (causes) and the big result (effect). 🔊 019

Stop the boat party –
Lamma Island's sea turtles are in danger!

When you think of Hong Kong, you probably don't think of **wildlife**, do you? But one of Hong Kong's islands, Lamma Island, is also home to endangered green sea turtles. Between June and October, they come to the island's Sham Wan beach to lay their eggs.

Special nature police must keep people away from the turtles. At nesting time, you shouldn't go near the beach. If the police see you, you have to pay a fine, **which** can be a lot of money. However, the police aren't always there to protect the area. The biggest problem is human **behaviour**. Boat parties play loud music, and tourists go swimming and have picnics, which **frightens** the turtles away. Scientists and conservationist groups say we **need** a bigger restricted* area to help the turtles **survive**.

Experts agree that green sea turtles in Hong Kong are in danger. The turtles are **disappearing**. One scientist said, 'When a turtle is **afraid of** going onto the beach, it has to lay its eggs underwater, where they die.' In 2006, there were 14 records of nesting turtles in Sham Wan beach but only two after that, and not a single turtle has been seen since 2012. Another expert said that the number of turtles should increase in the future because now people are working on creating a better **relationship** with the turtles.

restricted adj. with limits, closed-off

38

2 Read the text again. Find four problems (causes) that contribute to a result (effect) for the green sea turtles.

Cause 1	Cause 2	Cause 3	Cause 4
Nature police not there all the time	Boat parties, loud music	Swimming	Picnics

Effect
Turtles are frightened away; no turtles have been seen nesting since 2012.

3 Summarise the text. Tell someone about the Hong Kong green sea turtles. Write sentences about the problems, the results and a possible solution.

1. One problem for the turtles is that people have parties on the beach
2. Another problem for the turtles is that people swim in the sea
3. A third problem for the turtles is that nature police are not there all the time
4. Conservationists think that turtles need a bigger area protected from people
5. One solution is to have more nature police

4 Write. Think about the information from the texts in this unit. You have read about different problems between humans and animals. Complete the list of advice.

At home: We shouldn't leave food around for wild animals
At the beach: People shouldn't go to beaches when turtles lay eggs
In the mountains: Villagers should follow the experts' advice

39

GRAMMAR

Modals: Describing ability in present and past

Crocodiles **can sleep** with one eye open.	At that time, turtles **could lay** their eggs on the beaches.
Most domestic animals **can't survive** in the wild.	Conservation groups **couldn't rescue** all the birds.
Why **can't we interact** with wildlife easily in a city?	The injured deer **couldn't avoid** the predators.

We use *can/can't* to talk about ability in the present. We use *could/couldn't* to talk about ability in the past.

1 Listen. Circle the word you hear. 🔊 020

1. The baby panda **can / can't** see people.
2. They **could / couldn't** understand animals before.
3. Trained dogs **can / can't** sniff for chemicals.
4. They **can / can't** drive to the injured snow leopard.
5. They **could / couldn't** save all the birds.
6. We **can / can't** avoid using plastic bags.
7. The turtles **could / couldn't** lay their eggs.

40

2 Read. Underline the phrases with *can*, *can't*, *could* or *couldn't*. Then circle the correct word to complete the sentence.

The Survival of the Antiguan Racer Snake

The Antiguan racer is probably the world's least known snake. It's not dangerous and it can't kill you. However, these snakes are slowly disappearing from Bird Island, a small island off the coast of Antigua. How can we save these racers?

Conservationist Jenny Daltry studies the snakes, so we can now understand the Antiguan racers' habitat and behaviour. During her five-year project, they have removed the racers' biggest predators, black rats, from the island. Now the rats can't prey on the snakes' eggs. However, the snakes can still die because of hurricanes or bad weather conditions, other predators and tourists.

Sadly, there's also another problem. Bird Island is so small that only about 100 racer snakes could survive there. Jenny's team hopes that they can introduce racers to other nearby islands. They have already saved the Antiguan racer; we can be sure that, without this project, this snake would disappear.

You can read about Jenny's project in an article on the Internet.

Because of this project, more racer snakes **can / can't** survive on Bird Island.

3 Read the article again. Complete these sentences using *can*, *can't*, *could* or *couldn't*.

1. The Antiguan racer snakes could die / couldn't survive
2. Black rats could kill the snakes / can't prey on the snakes
3. Jenny and her team can introduce the snakes to other islands / can help the snakes find new habitats
4. The five-year project can / could save / rescue the snakes
5. Hurricanes, predators and tourists can kill the snakes
6. Researchers hope that the snakes can survive on other islands, too
7. This project means that now people can interact with / find the rare snakes
8. You can read about the project on the Internet.

41

WORKBOOK

WRITING

After you write, you need to read your work and check it. Ask yourself some questions: Is my writing organised? Are the ideas clear? Circle any spelling and grammar mistakes. Finally, rewrite your work and proofread it for any last changes.

1 Organise.

1. Your topic is a relationship between a person and an animal. Think of a relationship you know, have read about, or seen in a film. How would you describe the relationship? Make a list of your ideas in the table.

Person	Animal

2. Plan your writing. You'll need an introductory paragraph with a topic sentence. Your topic sentence will state the relationship between the person and the animal. Write your topic sentence here:

_____

Next, you'll need a paragraph to describe the relationship and how the person and animal interact. Explain the situation with a few details.

Remember to finish your paragraph with a brief statement of why this relationship is special.

2 Write.

1. Go to page 37 in your book. Re-read the model and writing prompt.
2. Write your first draft. Check for organisation, content, punctuation, capitalisation and spelling.
3. Write your final draft. Share it with your teacher and classmates.

42

Now I can ...

· **talk about interactions between animals and humans.**

☐ Yes, I can!
☐ I think I can.
☐ I need more practice.

Describe the relationship of the man and the baby elephant. Write two or three sentences.

The relationship is very friendly. The man is happy because he helps the elephant. The baby elephant is playful.

_____

· **use modals to describe obligation and advice.**

☐ Yes, I can!
☐ I think I can.
☐ I need more practice.

Complete the sentences according to the clues. Use *must, has/have to, doesn't/don't have to* or *should/shouldn't*.

1. I _____must_____ help this injured animal, so it can survive. (very necessary)
2. Animals have feelings, too. You _____shouldn't_____ mistreat them. (advice)
3. We _____have to_____ keep the seas free of plastic bags. (necessary)

· **use modals to describe ability in the present and past.**

☐ Yes, I can!
☐ I think I can.
☐ I need more practice.

Complete the sentences with *can/could* or *can't/couldn't*.

1. A mountain lion _____can_____ climb over a 12-foot wall.
2. When it was born, the baby panda's eyes were closed. It _____couldn't_____ see.
3. Yesterday, they _____could_____ rescue some sea turtles.

· **write a description of a special relationship between an animal and a human.**

☐ Yes, I can!
☐ I think I can.
☐ I need more practice.

Describe a situation in which an animal interacts with a human.
Answers will vary.

_____

YOU DECIDE Choose an activity. Go to page 93.

43

Units 3–4 Review

1 Read. Then choose the correct words.

A
Please don't call me today. I'm not feeling very well and (1) **I'm staying** / I stay in bed. Call me (2) **on** / at about 10.00 tomorrow morning. I (2) **want** / am wanting to check our science project before class (3) **on** / at Monday.

B
After our meeting today, I had another idea. I can't (1) **go to sleep** / asleep without telling you. I think we can ask teachers to talk to students about how important it is to (2) **interact** / rescue with wildlife and learn about the animals' behavior and habitat. We can write a letter (3) **in** / at the morning to local schools. What do you think?

C
Are you (1) observe / **observing** wildlife? Don't forget to take photographs of the birds, mice, rabbits and insects around your home (2) **on** / in the weekend! Get up early both days, (3) **on** / at sunrise. Bring your photos to Monday's club meeting (4) at / **on** 1 p.m.

2 Listen. Then choose the best answer. 🔊 021

1. Cars __b__.
   a. stop to rescue salamanders
   b. kill salamanders in the darkness
   c. with headlights help salamanders

2. The speakers agree that __b__.
   a. salamanders are very clever
   b. salamanders are afraid of cars
   c. salamanders should move faster

3. Snakes __a__.
   a. hunt salamanders
   b. don't hunt salamanders
   c. eat insects

44

3 Read. Choose the best answer for each blank.

A conservation magazine reports that we must try to (1) __a__ the destruction of our planet. When people cut down trees to construct new buildings, they are destroying animals' (2) __c__. Forests are homes to thousands of (3) __b__ animals. Now these animals (4) __a__ find new places to live. Some animals go into towns and villages because they can't (5) __c__ for food in the forests. It (6) __a__ dangerous in North Canada, for example. While people are (7) __a__, wild bears have easy access to waste food in rubbish bins. Our relationship with animals (8) __c__ change if we want to share our planet.

1. **a.** avoid   b. keep   c. not
2. a. horizon   b. time zones   **c.** habitats
3. a. tame   **b.** wild   c. clever
4. **a.** have to   b. need   c. should
5. a. observe   b. defend   **c.** hunt
6. **a.** is becoming   b. are becoming   c. should becoming
7. **a.** asleep   b. awake   c. injured
8. a. couldn't   b. shouldn't   **c.** must

4 Read the sentences. Use the words in the box to complete the second sentence so that the meaning is the same as the first sentence. Use no more than one word for each blank.

at	couldn't	mistreat	observe	predator	relationship	sunrise	sunset

1. While people are asleep, wild bears hunt for food in North Canada. Wild bears sniff around the rubbish bins in North Canada _____at_____ night.
2. When it's early morning in Europe, it's 12.30 p.m. in India. When I see the _____sunrise_____ here in Spain, my friend in India is finishing her lunch!
3. I think the sky is more beautiful when the sun goes down. I believe _____sunset_____ is more beautiful.
4. The world of insects fascinates me. I love to _____observe_____ ants, spiders and tiny animals.
5. People interact with domestic animals. Pets, such as cats and dogs, are easy to have a _____relationship_____ with.
6. Snakes eat mice and salamanders. Salamanders and mice have the same _____predator_____ – snakes.
7. Reports say that aquatic parks treat dolphins and whales very well. I hope that aquatic parks don't _____mistreat_____ their sea creatures.
8. Yesterday the rats were not able to sniff any of the landmines. The rats _____couldn't_____ find any landmines yesterday.

45

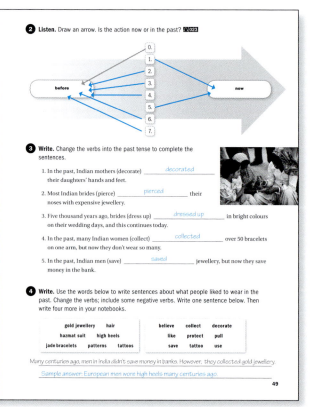

Unit 5
What We Wear

1 **Organise the clothes.** Decide if the clothes are practical, formal or casual. Write P, F or C.

C/P   P   C/P   F   C/F

F   F   C   F

2 **Write.** Put words that describe the images in Activity 1 into the puzzle. Then answer the question.

| business suit | denim jacket | firefighter's uniform | high heels | jeans |
| shirt | trainers | trousers | sweatshirt | tie |

F I R E F I G H T E R ' S   U N I F O R M

Write the letters from the numbered boxes. Then unscramble the letters to find which 19th-century practical fabric is now a 21st-century fashion fabric.

N I E M D   DENIM

46

3 **Listen.** Complete the student's survey. Then write your answers in the last row. 022

Interviewees	What are you wearing today?	What do you wear at the weekend?
Martin	sweatshirt, white denim jeans	different jeans and sweatshirt
Mrs Gardener	suit	casual shirt and trousers or skirt
Fiona	tights, high-heel trainers, shorts and sweatshirt	dress and jacket
You		

4 **Draw.** Listen to 022 again. Draw the clothes in your notebook. Talk about them in class.

5 **Write.** Survey your friends and classmates. Use words from this unit and your own questions.

Example questions: Do you like to dress up for a party? Which formal clothes do you wear?

| casual | denim | dress up | formal | heels | jeans |
| practical | suit | sweatshirt | tie | tights | uniform |

Answers will vary.

Interviewees		

47

GRAMMAR

Past simple: Saying what happened

Ami photograph**ed** people in Kenya and India.
They dress**ed up** for the wedding party.
He **didn't dress up** for school.
They **didn't wear** high heels.

Questions:
Did the women paint their hands?
Why **did** they tattoo their faces?

Verbs change when we talk about past events. Most verbs add -ed (protect → protect**ed**)
Be careful with spelling! Verbs ending in e add -d (love → love**d**)
Some verbs double the final letter, then add -ed (stop → sto**pped**)

1 **Read.** These facts are about the tattoos of Maoris from New Zealand and the Chin people from Myanmar. Are the facts the same (**S**) or different (**D**)? Write **S** or **D**. Then complete the sentences about the Maori and Chin people.

___S___ 1. Maori men and women decorated their faces with tattoos. Chin women painted tattoos on their faces.

___S___ 2. Maoris used tattoos to show people from other villages or tribes where they lived. Chin women's tattoos showed their village group or tribe.

___D___ 3. The government stopped the Chin people putting tattoos on their faces. Maori people didn't stop using tattoos because of the government.

1. In the past, Chin and Maori people both _had tattoos on their faces._

2. Before, Chin women _used tattoos to identify their villages._

3. The New Zealand government _still allows face tattoos._

48

2 **Listen.** Draw an arrow. Is the action now or in the past? 023

0.
1.
2.
3.
before   4.   now
5.
6.
7.

3 **Write.** Change the verbs into the past tense to complete the sentences.

1. In the past, Indian mothers (decorate) _decorated_ their daughters' hands and feet.

2. Most Indian brides (pierce) _pierced_ their noses with expensive jewellery.

3. Five thousand years ago, brides (dress up) _dressed up_ in bright colours on their wedding days, and this continues today.

4. In the past, many Indian women (collect) _collected_ over 50 bracelets on one arm, but now they don't wear so many.

5. In the past, Indian men (save) _saved_ jewellery, but now they save money in the bank.

4 **Write.** Use the words below to write sentences about what people liked to wear in the past. Change the verbs; include some negative verbs. Write one sentence below. Then write four more in your notebooks.

gold jewellery	hair		believe	collect	decorate
hazmat suit	high heels		like	protect	pull
jade bracelets	patterns	tattoos	save	tattoo	use

Many centuries ago, men in India didn't save money in banks. However, they collected gold jewellery.

Sample answer: European men wore high heels many centuries ago.

49

1 Listen and read. While you read the article, notice the events in the past and the events in the present. Answer the questions. 🔊024

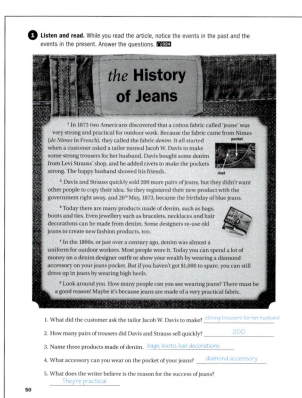

the History of Jeans

¹ In 1873 two Americans discovered that a cotton fabric called 'jeane' was very strong and practical for outdoor work. Because the fabric came from Nimes (*de Nimes* in French), they called the fabric *denim*. It all started when a customer asked a tailor named Jacob W. Davis to make some strong trousers for her husband. Davis bought some denim from Levi Strauss' shop, and he added rivets to make the pockets strong. The happy husband showed his friends.

² Davis and Strauss quickly sold 200 more pairs of jeans, but they didn't want other people to copy their idea. So they registered their new product with the government right away, and 20ᵗʰ May, 1873, became the birthday of blue jeans.

³ Today there are many products made of denim, such as bags, boots and ties. Even jewellery such as bracelets, necklaces and hair decorations can be made from denim. Some designers re-use old jeans to create new fashion products, too.

⁴ In the 1800s, or just over a century ago, denim was almost a uniform for outdoor workers. Most people wore it. Today you can spend a lot of money on a denim designer outfit or show your wealth by wearing a diamond accessory on your jeans pocket. But if you haven't got $1,000 to spare, you can still dress up in jeans by wearing high heels.

⁵ Look around you. How many people can you see wearing jeans? There must be a good reason! Maybe it's because jeans are made of a very practical fabric.

1. What did the customer ask the tailor Jacob W. Davis to make? _strong trousers for her husband_

2. How many pairs of trousers did Davis and Strauss sell quickly? _200_

3. Name three products made of denim. _bags, boots, hair decorations_

4. What accessory can you wear on the pocket of your jeans? _diamond accessory_

5. What does the writer believe is the reason for the success of jeans? _They're practical._

50

---

2 Read again. Find verbs in the past simple tense. Write the events they describe under **In the past**. Write present-day actions in the **Now** column.

In the past	Now
Two Americans discovered jeans.	We have accessories made of denim.
A customer asked the tailor, Jacob Davis, to make strong trousers for her husband.	Designers re-use jeans and make new products.
Davis bought denim from Levi Strauss.	You can spend a lot of money on designer denim outfits.
He made the trousers and added rivets.	You can buy jeans with a diamond accessory on the pocket.
They quickly sold 200 pairs of jeans.	We can dress up in jeans.
They registered the product in 1873.	Jeans are practical and many people wear them.
Denim was almost a uniform for workers because most workers wore them.	

3 Read the summary. Write the words from the box in the blanks. Practise telling a classmate or teacher about the history of jeans.

added	denim	fabric	jeans	practical	wanted

'Jeane' was a strong, cotton (1) _fabric_ sold in America 200 years ago.

A woman (2) _wanted_ new trousers for her husband.

Jacob Davis bought some (3) _denim_ from Levi Strauss.

He (4) _added_ rivets to make the pockets strong.

Many workers liked the jeans because they were (5) _practical_.

Davis and Strauss registered their new trousers in 1873 so that nobody could copy their (6) _jeans_.

4 Read again. You have read about the history of football uniforms and jeans. Make new sentences about how your clothes have changed over time. Use verbs in the past simple.

Answers will vary

_____

_____

_____

_____

51

GRAMMAR

Past simple: Describing what happened

You **were** in the clothes shop.	She **kept** extra tights in her bag.
I **was** in the shoe shop.	We **left** our jackets at the door.
He **had** a denim jacket in his hand.	Shops **sold** thousands of pairs of jeans.
They **put** their mobile phones in their pockets.	I **brought** your sweatshirt for you.
I **began** jewellery classes last year.	

Questions

To form questions with be:
Were you in the clothes shop this morning? **Was** she in the shoe shop?

All other verbs begin with did/didn't:
Didn't you **see** the fashion show? **Did** they **do** exercises to keep healthy?

Some verbs in the past simple do not add -ed. They are irregular verbs: be, begin, bring, buy, do, eat, get, give, have, keep, leave, make, mean, put, see, sell, think, wear. These past-tense verbs are used often. We must memorise them!

These verbs don't change forms in the past simple: I (you/he/she/it/we/you/they) **wore** new shoes.

The verb be changes when used in the past simple: I **was** (you **were**, he/she/it **was**, we/you/they **were**) in the shoe shop.

1 Write. Look at the photos. Write the verbs in the middle column to complete the sentences.

became	bought	meant	sold	was	were	wore

Ski fashion	was	different in the past.
The clothes	were	thick and loose.
People	wore	wool and cotton trousers and jackets.
In the 1970s new fabric	became	available.
Shops	sold	lightweight jackets.
Advanced technology	meant	that fabric changed.
Skiers	bought	colourful all-in-one suits.

52

---

2 Listen. Circle the correct past simple verb. 🔊025

1. (thought) / bought
2. was / (had)
3. was / (were)
4. got / (put)
5. sold / (got)
6. (gave) / had

3 Read the interview. Write similar questions to interview an older person you know. Show your survey questions in class. If possible, ask your interview questions.

Interviewer:	Good morning, Mr Daniels. Thank you for speaking to us today.
Mr Daniels:	No problem. How can I help?
Interviewer:	Could you tell us about how school clothes were different when you were a boy?
Mr Daniels:	Oh, well, in my school the uniform was very formal. We wore short, heavy wool trousers. I had a hat and tie, too.

Question _When did you buy your first pair of jeans?_

Answer _____

Sample questions:

Question _Were your clothes formal or casual?_

Answer _____

Question _Did your parents buy your clothes for you?_

Answer _____

Question _How did you choose your clothes?_

Answer _____

Question _Did you wear a sports kit?_

Answer _____

53

WRITING

The last stage in writing is publishing. When you publish your work, you let other people read it. But first, you need to make sure it is as good as it can be. You know how to write, review and proofread your work. Do one last check before you show a classmate or teacher.

1 Organise.

1. Your task is to write an essay about a uniform that has changed over time. Think about different types of uniforms, how they are used now, and how they were used in the past. Decide on one type of uniform to research. List changes in clothes, styles, materials and decorations.
2. Plan your ideas. Decide who your readers are. Decide where to publish your paragraph.

Uniform	
Before	
Now	
My readers	
Place for publishing	
Topic sentence	

2 Write.

1. Go to page 89 in your book. Re-read the history of football uniforms.

2. In your notebook, write the first draft of your paragraph about how a uniform has changed over time. Proofread your work. Check your past simple verbs.

3. Write your final draft. Check it one last time, and publish it for your readers.

54

Now I can ...

· **talk about fashion changes through history.**

Write about how some clothes have changed over time. Write four sentences.

☐ Yes, I can!
☐ I think I can.
☐ I need more practice.

Sample answers:
1. In the past, _Some men wore high heels._
2. Now, _many men wear trainers or formal shoes._
3. In the past, _ski suits were heavy._
4. Now, _ski suits are light._

· **use regular past simple verbs.**

Write sentences using the past tense of some of these words.

☐ Yes, I can!
☐ I think I can.
☐ I need more practice.

attach	colour	decorate	dress up	look	mix	pierce	prefer	protect	use

1. _Women in ancient Greece coloured their hair with henna._
2. _Some people pierced their babies' ears._
3. _Artists decorated the bride's hands and feet._

· **use irregular past simple verbs.**

Choose words from the box to write sentences using the past tense.

☐ Yes, I can!
☐ I think I can.
☐ I need more practice.

begin	bring	buy	eat	get	give	keep	leave	put	see	sell	think

1. _Doctors thought the special suits gave them protection from the plague._
2. _After 1870 football players began to wear uniforms._
3. _Men gave their wives jewellery made of metal rings._

· **write and share my description of clothes that changed over time.**

Write two sentences about your personal fashion changes. Share your description with a classmate or teacher.

☐ Yes, I can!
☐ I think I can.
☐ I need more practice.

Answers will vary.

YOU DECIDE Choose an activity. Go to page 94.

55

Unit 6
Mix and Mash

1 Find the new vocabulary words. Look again at pages 94–96 in your book. Find a word that begins with each letter. X = no word.

A _audio_   B _bands_   C _cool / combine_   D _download_
E _electronic / edit_   F _fan_   G Gokh-Bi System
H _hit_   I _include_   J Japanese   K -x-   L -x-
M _mix_   N _no_   O _opinion_   P _perform_
Q -x-   R _record / recording_   S _song_   T _traditional_
U _urban_   V _video_   W West Africa
X -x-   Y _you_   Z -x-

2 Write. Cross out the word that doesn't connect to the people. Then choose from the remaining words to complete the sentences. Circle the letter – is it picture A, B or C?

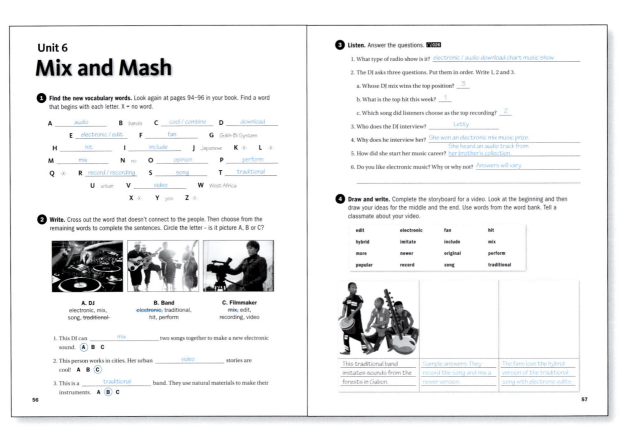

A. DJ
electronic, mix, song, ~~traditional~~

B. Band
~~electronic,~~ traditional, hit, perform

C. Filmmaker
~~mix,~~ edit, recording, video

1. This DJ can ____mix____ two songs together to make a new electronic sound. (A) B C

2. This person works in cities. Her urban ____video____ stories are cool! A B (C)

3. This is a ____traditional____ band. They use natural materials to make their instruments. A (B) C

56

3 Listen. Answer the questions. ▶026

1. What type of radio show is it? _electronic / audio download chart music show_

2. The DJ asks three questions. Put them in order. Write 1, 2 and 3.
   a. Whose DJ mix wins the top position? _3_
   b. What is the top hit this week? _1_
   c. Which song did listeners choose as the top recording? _2_

3. Who does the DJ interview? _Letty_

4. Why does he interview her? _She won an electronic mix music prize._

5. How did she start her music career? _She heard an audio track from her brother's collection._

6. Do you like electronic music? Why or why not? _Answers will vary._

4 Draw and write. Complete the storyboard for a video. Look at the beginning and then draw your ideas for the middle and the end. Use words from the word bank. Tell a classmate about your video.

edit	electronic	fan	hit
hybrid	imitate	include	mix
more	newer	original	perform
popular	record	song	traditional

This traditional band imitates sounds from the forests in Gabon.	Sample answers: They record the song and mix a newer version.	The fans love the hybrid version of the traditional song with electronic edits.

57

GRAMMAR

Adjectives: Comparing two or more things

The band didn't perform their **older** hits.	It's **more difficult** to buy tickets this year.
The light show was **as cool as** last year.	Modern dance is **less tiring than** traditional dance.
The fans are **noisier** tonight than last week!	In my opinion, CDs are **better than** downloads.
The song from the film *Spectre* was a **bigger** hit than other Bond film songs.	The sound quality is **worse** with downloads.

We use comparatives to compare two things. Use *more* before adjectives that have two or more syllables. Add *-er* to adjectives that have just one syllable. With two-syllable adjectives that end in *y*, both options are possible (**more noisy** or **noisier**). Remember to change *y* to *i* before adding *-er*.

Some adjectives have irregular comparative forms: *good* → **better**; *bad* → **worse**

We use *as ... as ...* to describe how things are similar or the same.

1 Complete the conversation. Think of the opposites of the words in bold and compare the two things.

Gustav: These new hybrid sports are not **bad**. What do you think? I know you can't play many sports, so which one is (1) _____ better _____ for you?

Katia: Disc golf isn't **difficult**, is it? I think it's a little (2) _____ easier _____ than traditional golf. Do you agree?

Gustav: Sure. It uses **soft** plastic discs, not balls. Those plastic discs are not as (3) _____ hard _____ as golf balls when you make a mistake!

Katia: Also there aren't any **heavy** golf clubs. Discs are (4) _____ lighter _____ .

Gustav: That's true. And disc golf is **cheap**. My parents say that their golf membership is (5) _____ more expensive _____ every year!

Katia: But isn't golf **boring**? Let's try something (6) _____ more exciting _____ ! What do you think of volcano boarding?

58

2 Read. Find the differences in the musician's notes about two recordings. Change the words in the box to finish the sentences.

Version 1: 12/11/2016
Track 1: Drums – volume high
Bass guitar – comes in too late.
Piano OK – but slow in the middle.
Guitar – OK

Version 2: 17/11/2016
Track 1: Drums – volume low
Bass guitar – much better now.
Piano – love it!
Guitar – can't hear it!

early	fast	loud	old	quiet

1. Version 1, from 12ᵗʰ November, is _____ older _____ than Version 2.
2. The drums on Version 1 are _____ louder _____ than the drums on Version 2.
3. In Version 2, the bass guitar comes in _____ earlier _____ than in Version 1.
4. The piano is _____ faster _____ in the middle of Version 2.
5. In Version 2, the guitar is _____ quieter / more quiet _____ .

3 Listen. Which picture is the speaker describing, in your opinion? Circle A or B. Then complete the sentences. 🔊 027

1. I love these hybrid lamps! Lamp A / B is (cool) _____ cooler _____ than lamp A / B because _____ .
2. I think lamp A / B is (useful) _____ more useful _____ than lamp A / B because _____ .
3. Which version is good? Lamp A / B is (good/bad) _____ better _____ than lamp A / B because _____ .
4. Lamp A / B is (bright) _____ brighter _____ than lamp A / B because _____ .

59

1 Listen and read. While you read, notice the differences between the traditional and the modern activities. 🔊 028

Skipping Filipino Style

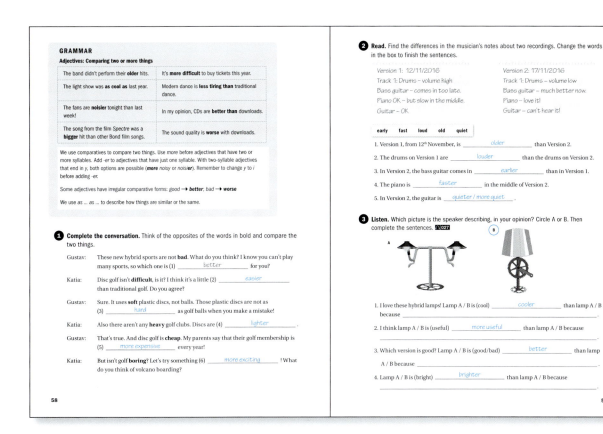

1. Mix the past with the present and you get a traditional dance from the Philippines plus a cool new type of sports activity! Tinikling is a fun form of exercise that combines rhythm with fast foot- and legwork. The original sport began in central Philippines and imitates the tikling bird walking carefully through grass and bamboo. Tinikling improves awareness of space and includes skills similar to skipping. Every year young people perform it in school shows all over the Philippines, and audiences love it.

2. Tinikling is a type of dance that involves two people hitting bamboo poles together and on the ground. This makes the beat or rhythm. At the same time, one or more dancers step over and in between the poles. It's not easy, especially for girls who wear long traditional dresses! In the traditional dance, bamboo poles make the beat along with music from a type of string instrument. Today's 21ˢᵗ century version uses simpler, four-beat electronic dance music.

3. There are many tinikling products available now, such as tinikling songs on CDs and audio downloads, dance-step instruction videos, and tinikling sticks made of bamboo or plastic. For the traditional version, you must find thick bamboo poles, but be careful – just imagine the pain if you make a mistake!

60

2 Read the article again. Answer the questions.

1. What activity is tinikling similar to?
   skipping

2. What are the dancers and the bamboo poles imitating?
   Tikling bird walking through grass and bamboo

3. What modern-day products can we buy for tinikling?
   Video, CDs, audio downloads

3 Re-read the article. Compare the differences and similarities between the traditional dance and the sport of today. Practise telling a classmate or your teacher about tinikling.

Tinikling traditional dance	Both	Today's sport
string instrument, imitates the bird	jump between poles, combine music and dance, bamboo poles	four-beat electronic music, videos, audio downloads, CDs, plastic poles

4 Write. Read the text again. Write two new sentences about changes in this traditional dance.

Example: *The traditional music for the dance was more complex than today's four-beat rhythm.*

61

GRAMMAR

Countable and uncountable nouns: Talking about amounts

Countable nouns	Uncountable nouns
Many / **Some** / **A lot of** / **A few** cultures have a traditional dance.	**Some** / **A little** / **A lot of** / modern dance mixes words, too.
They perform **a few** traditional songs.	Listening to **a little** music before the show is a good idea.
She saw **a couple of** shows last month.	There is **too much** information on fan websites.

Questions	Questions
How **many** downloads were there?	How **much** money do we need?
Were there **many** fans outside the door?	Did they make **much** noise?

Countable nouns are nouns we can count (*one song, two songs*). Uncountable nouns are nouns we can't count (*music, time*). They don't have a plural form. We can't use *a/an* or numbers before uncountable nouns. Use *a few/many* to talk about countable nouns and *a little/much* to talk about uncountable nouns.

1 Read. Look at the nouns in **bold** and circle *UC* (uncountable nouns) or *C* (countable nouns).

1. Hiro is planning his birthday meal, so he's checking how much **food** he has ready. ((UC) / C)

2. Is there enough **juice**? ((UC) / C)

3. Hiro needs to buy two or three more **bottles** of juice. (UC / (C))

4. He wants to share a birthday **pizza**. A sushi-pizza! (UC / (C))

5. Eight people need some **pizza**. ((UC) / C)

6. Everyone will probably eat at least one **piece** of sushi-pizza. (UC / (C))

7. Hiro only bought two **boxes** of sushi-pizza. (UC / (C))

8. His friends all love sushi-pizza. Hiro has to buy more **pizza**. ((UC) / C)

2 Write. Look at this menu. Sort the food in **bold** into countable and uncountable nouns.

Viva Tacos! Traditional Mexican flour and corn tortillas

Original Classic tacos

Shrimp taco: Two fresh, grilled **shrimps** with sauce and lime **juice** in a soft tortilla

Chicken tacos: Two medium, soft, corn **tortillas**, wrapped around **slices** of chicken

Beef taco: Minced **beef** in a thick tomato sauce, wrapped in a soft tortilla made of **corn**

Vegetarian dishes

Black bean or roast vegetable tacos

Salad

Black **rice** salad, green salad, tomato salad, green tomato salad

Salsa

Cheese **sauce**, spicy tomato sauce, lemon **mayonnaise**, spicy green sauce

American fast-food style

Fried tortillas: Replace the soft tortilla with a USA crispy version.

Nachos: Fried corn **chips** with your choice of salsa

Countable nouns	Uncountable nouns
tacos, shrimps, tortillas, slices, dishes, chips	*juice, beef, corn, salad, rice, sauce, mayonnaise*

3 Listen. What do the friends choose to eat? 🎧 029

Choice 1: *Chicken tacos*

Choice 2: *Green tomato salad, spicy green sauce, shrimp tacos*

Choice 3: *Original Mexican beef taco, American-style nachos*

4 Write. Read the menu again. Write questions about some of the food in the box.

black rice	chicken slices	lemon mayonnaise
roast vegetable tacos	spicy tomato sauce	corn tortillas

How many: *How many chicken slices are there?*

How much: *How much black rice is in the salad?*

Are there: *Are there a lot of tomatoes in the spicy tomato sauce?*

Is there: *Is there much lemon in the lemon mayonnaise?*

WRITING

A good paragraph of exemplification introduces your idea and uses examples to support that idea. We use *for example, another example* and *such as* to introduce these supporting sentences.

1 Organise.

1. Your task is to write a paragraph about your own unique ani-mix. Think of two or more animals and mix them together. Draw your animal in your notebook. You need to imagine its name and write examples of how it is unique.

2. Plan your ideas in the table. Research your chosen animals, their appearance and what they can do. If possible, create a photo of your chosen ani-mix to go with your paragraph.

	Animal 1	Animal 2	Animal 3
Name			
Size and appearance			
Body parts (legs, wings)			
Abilities (climbs, swims)			

2 Write.

1. Go to page 105 in your book. Re-read the model and writing prompt.

2. Write your first draft. Check for organisation, content, punctuation, capitalisation and spelling.

3. Write your final draft. Share it with your teacher and classmates.

Now I can ...

· **talk about how two things combine to make something new.**

☐ Yes, I can!
☐ I think I can.
☐ I need more practice.

Write three sentences about how artists combine ideas.

1. _____
2. _____
3. _____

· **compare two or more things.**

☐ Yes, I can!
☐ I think I can.
☐ I need more practice.

Complete the sentences using the given words.

1. Tinikling is ___*cooler*___ (cool) than skipping.

2. Mash-up music is ___*more difficult*___ (difficult) to perform than many people think.

3. I think cooking fried rice is ___*easier*___ (easy) than baking cakes.

· **use countable and uncountable nouns.**

☐ Yes, I can!
☐ I think I can.
☐ I need more practice.

Write sentences using these words. food   meat   songs   videos

1. *Answers will vary.*
2. _____
3. _____
4. _____

· **write a paragraph of exemplification.**

☐ Yes, I can!
☐ I think I can.
☐ I need more practice.

Write about your idea for a new mix of art, sports or music. Support your idea with examples. Plan and check your paragraph. Present it to your classmates and teacher.

_____
_____
_____

YOU DECIDE Choose an activity. Go to page 95.

62

63

64

65

Units 5–6 Review

1 Read. Choose the correct word to complete the sentences.

1. Wei doesn't like formal clothes.

   He takes off his school ____ as soon as he gets home.
   a. uniform **b.** jeans **c.** tights

2. The DJ preferred the second version of the song.

   He thought the newer mix was ____ than the first one.
   a. worse **b.** better **c.** noisier

3. I like to include stars in all my paintings.

   I ____ stars into all my art work.
   a. mix **b.** perform **c.** record

4. What type of ____ was the singer wearing on her arms and wrists?
   a. necklace **b.** tie **c.** bracelet

5. My mother works in a laboratory.

   She has to wear a special suit, for ____ reasons.
   a. practical **b.** formal **c.** casual

6. Video game designers have to be more creative every year. They have to

   ____ cool, new ideas that nobody has tried.
   a. combine **b.** imitate **c.** imagine

2 Listen. Decide if the sentences are *True* (T) or *False* (F). 🔊030

1. The original recording was from the 1980s. ___T___
2. He doesn't like formal clothes. ___T___
3. She thinks her friend looks good. ___T___
4. The girl asks for her mother's opinion about her hair. ___F___
5. The boy prefers traditional guitar music. ___F___

66

3 Read. Choose the best answer to the questions.

1. The wimple was a popular head covering for women in Europe from the 12ᵗʰ to the 15ᵗʰ century. Wimples were usually made of cotton or silk. They provided protection from the weather, and they were a way to dress up for formal occasions. Sometimes the wimple covered the top of the head and shoulders, and went around the neck, finishing up at the chin.

2. Wealthy women sometimes used the wimple to display their jewellery. They decorated the cloth before placing it on their head. Sometimes a circle of fabric or metal, like a queen's crown, was placed on the head to hold the wimple in place.

3. Head covering is an ancient fashion for both women and men. Many centuries ago, men and women in Ancient Greece, Rome and China covered their heads for a variety of reasons. Today people from countries around the Mediterranean still wear similar coverings to protect them from the strong sun and to dress up on formal occasions.

1. What was the wimple made from?
   a. wool **b.** denim **c.** cotton

2. For how many centuries was the wimple in fashion in Europe?
   a. six **b.** four **c.** one

3. Which part of the body did the wimple not cover?
   a. shoulders **b.** hands **c.** neck

4. What did some women add to their wimple to show their wealth?
   a. jewellery **b.** paint **c.** flowers

4 Read the sentences. Circle the correct word.

1. My sweatshirt looks cleaner than yours because I **wash** / **washed** it last week.
2. **Some** / **Much** brides in Morocco still **paint** / **painted** their hands, and in this way they keep the tradition alive.
3. **Many** / **Much** Indian women **pierce** / **pierced** their noses when they got married.
4. Today **a few** / **a little** young Maoris still **wear** / **wore** tattoos on their faces.
5. When she was a teenager, my mum **loves** / **loved** hybrid songs.
6. Last year my neighbour **hates** / **hated** my favourite type of music, but now she likes **much** / **many** of it!

67

Unit 7
Cool Apps and Gadgets

1 Write. Find four vocabulary words or phrases from this unit on the screen. Then use them to complete the text message.

nbsdigjglookupegkgxhl
osmartphoneooauhtsfrb
ngamescbwgnInternetbi
klou

Can you please _look up some smartphone games on the Internet?_

2 Write. Use words from the word bank to send a message. Write on the smartphone.

apps	chat	connect	incredible	mobile	possible	search
send	share	tablet	text	useful	Wi-Fi	

My new app is really useful.
Do you want to chat on
your new tablet? Please
share the photo from last
night.

3 Read. Match the words with the definitions. Write the letter on the line.

___e___ 1. chat   a. to allow another person to use something too
___a___ 2. share   b. able to move from place to place
___b___ 3. mobile   c. to join two things together
___c___ 4. connect   d. about computer technology
___d___ 5. digital   e. to talk

68

4 Listen. Match each speaker to his or her words. Write the name on the line. 🔊031

1. _Vijaya or V_ — I love using mobile apps to chat with my friends.

2. _Rose_ — It's easier to send a text than to walk upstairs to my room, says my mum!

3. _Pablo_ — Sorry, I need help with my photo-sharing app.

4. _Tom_ — Share my gadget webpage!

5 Complete the responses. Use words from the box and your own ideas.

gadgets	Internet	look up	share	smartphone	useful

1. I'll send everybody the coolest photo from the party – this is my favourite!

   Please don't _share the photo of me dancing!_

2. I'll send a text when I get on the train. It's the easiest way to talk to you.

   Did you _look up the best train on the Internet?_

3. My brother's going to ask for a tablet as a birthday present. He needs to search the Internet and wants to play games, but a basic version is OK.

   Lucky him! For my next birthday, _I'm going to ask for a smartphone._

4. Are you going to finish your electricity project before Friday? I'm not! Can you please send me some useful images?

   We need to search for _images of useful gadgets that use electricity and a battery._

69

GRAMMAR

Superlatives: Talking about extremes

| **The scariest** part of the film is at the beginning. |
| This dictionary app is **the most useful** one I have. |
| This game scores **the highest** in this year's reviews, but it's my least favourite. |
| That café on the corner has **the worst** Wi-Fi connection in town. |

We use superlatives to compare one thing in a group to the rest of the group. Superlatives always take *the*.
Use *most* before adjectives that have two or more syllables:
It's **the most difficult** computer game.
Add *-est* to adjectives that have just one syllable:
This is **the loudest** setting on my mobile phone.
With two-syllable adjectives that end in *y*, both options are possible: *the scariest* or *the most scary*. (Remember to change *y* to *i*.)
Use *least* with any adjective: *the **least** difficult*, *the **least** scary*, *the **least** loud*.
Some adjectives have their own superlative form: *good/bad* → *the **best**/the **worst**.*

1 Read. Circle the correct words. Complete the reviews.

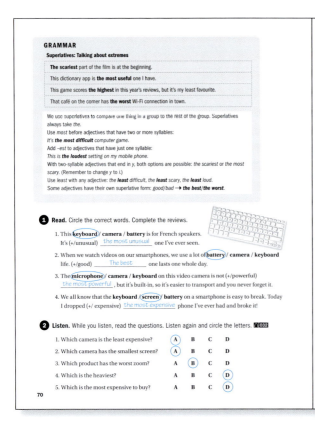

1. This (keyboard) / camera / battery is for French speakers. It's (+/unusual) ___the most unusual___ one I've ever seen.
2. When we watch videos on our smartphones, we use a lot of (battery) / camera / keyboard life. (+/good) ___The best___ one lasts one whole day.
3. The (microphone) / camera / keyboard on this video camera is not (+/powerful) ___the most powerful___ , but it's built-in, so it's easier to transport and you never forget it.
4. We all know that the keyboard / (screen) / battery on a smartphone is easy to break. Today I dropped (+/ expensive) ___the most expensive___ phone I've ever had and broke it!

2 Listen. While you listen, read the questions. Listen again and circle the letters. 🎧032

1. Which camera is the least expensive? (A) B C D
2. Which camera has the smallest screen? (A) B C D
3. Which product has the worst zoom? A (B) C D
4. Which is the heaviest? A B C (D)
5. Which is the most expensive to buy? A B C (D)

70

3 Write. Match the opposites. Then change the pairs to their superlatives. Choose one word from the pair to complete the statements.

| easy | good | high | loud |

| bad | difficult | low | quiet |

___easiest___	___most difficult___
___best___	___worst___
___highest___	___lowest___
___loudest___	___most quiet___

1. I finished in two minutes! This computer game puzzle is ___the easiest___ we have tried this term.
2. You're amazing! Your score is ___the highest OR best___ ever!
3. Which smartphone has ___the worst OR lowest___ volume control?
4. My old phone had ___the worst___ screen quality! I couldn't see any texts at night!
5. That free download app is ___the most difficult___ I have ever tried – I can't get past level one!

4 Read the e-mail. Write a reply.

> Hi!
>   I'm doing a survey about computer games, websites and apps.
> Can you please take a moment to answer these questions?
>   What are the best / worst / funniest / most useful / least exciting computer games, websites and apps that you know? Please explain why.
> Thank you!
> JJ

___Answers will vary.___

71

1 Listen and read. As you read, notice the main idea and the details. 🎧033

Mobile Magic!

[1]What connects government offices in Nigeria, doctors in Malawi and farmers in El Salvador? The answer is ... useful mobile phone software invented by Ken Banks. In Africa, Ken noticed that people in rural areas travelled for hours to share information. Because people there are not connected to the Internet, he decided mobile phones could help.

[2]All you need is a laptop computer and a mobile phone. It doesn't have to be the newest smartphone. An old or recycled phone is fine. 'After downloading the free software, you never need the Internet again,' Ken explains. Attach your phone to the laptop, type your message on the computer keyboard, select the people you want to contact, and hit 'Send'. The message goes to mobile phones as a text!

[3]So what do people send messages about? One good example is in Malawi. Ken sent a hundred recycled phones and a laptop with his software downloaded. After training for two weeks, doctors in the city can communicate with rural villages to decide which medical supplies to bring on their visits. These texts save time and thousands of dollars in travel costs. Even more importantly, a group of doctors in Malawi can now help the highest number of patients ever.

[4]Ken tells us, 'We need to help people recognise that you can do useful things without lots of money or expensive technology.'

2 Read. Answer the questions.

1. Which continent gave Ken the idea to design mobile phone software?
   ___Africa___
2. How many times do you need to connect to the Internet to access this service?
   ___Only once___
3. Give two examples of how Ken's invention can help people in Africa.
   ___Saving time, money; helping more patients___

72

3 Write. Choose the main idea for each paragraph, and write it in the table. Then complete the table with the details A–F. Write the letters in the spaces.

| How it works | Ken's message | One example | Introduction |

A. Type a message on the laptop.
B. Africans travel for hours to share information.
C. Thousands of hours and travel costs are saved, and many more patients are helped.
D. They are not connected to the Internet, but phones might help.
E. Click 'Send' and the message goes to mobile phones in a text.
F. Doctors send messages to mobile phones in rural villages.

	Main idea	Details
Paragraph 1	Introduction	1. Nigeria, Malawi, El Salvador use Ken's text software. 2. _B_ 3. _D_
Paragraph 2	How it works	1. Connect phone to laptop. 2. _A_ 3. _E_
Paragraph 3	One example	1. Malawi doctors received 100 phones, 1 laptop and training. 2. _F_ 3. _C_
Concluding sentence	Ken's message	We don't need a lot of money or technology to be useful.

4 Think about the information from the reading text. You've read about a useful text message service. Tick (✓) the sentences that are true.

☐ Only two or three countries can use the text service.
☑ Someone needs to type a message on a laptop.
☑ It saves people a lot of travelling time.
☐ It's only useful for doctors.
☑ Mobile phones can receive text messages.

73

GRAMMAR

Will and going to: Talking about the future

Schools **will have** chat rooms where students can ask questions online to teachers.	Wi-Fi **is going to speed up** in developing countries.
Smartphones **won't cost** so much money.	The Internet **isn't going to replace** teachers.
Will there **be** more female computer game designers? **Yes,** I think there **will be**.	**Are** our screens **going to affect** our eyesight? We're **going to need** better eye tests.

To make predictions about the future, we use *will* or *going to*.
Will + verb: *will be, will go, will cost*
present form of *be* + *going to* + verb: *am/is/are going to have*
will not = *won't*
will = *'ll*

1 **Listen.** Circle the form of the verb that you hear. 🎧034

1. South Korea **is going to be** / (**will be**) a world leader in digital technology.
2. India (**is going to build**) / **will build** many new Wi-Fi towers.
3. Estonia (**will continue to be**) / **is going to be** very involved in the digital age.
4. Some experts say that many more countries **will enter** / (**are going to enter**) the race for the best designs in mobile technology.
5. Village farmers **are going to pay for** / (**will pay for**) services with their smartphones.
6. More people (**are going to use**) / **will use** taxis because it's easier to order one through the Internet.

2 **Listen.** Tick the pictures that are in the description you hear. 🎧035

1. ☐ 2. ☑ 3. ☑
4. ☐ 5. ☑ 6. ☑

3 **Read the blog.** Circle the correct answers.

¹ Learning from our own mistakes is useful, but learning from another country's mistakes is going to be the fastest way to develop, I say.

² India has been developing its technology for many years. Other countries may have started before us, but today they often still have old technology – for example, unmodernised telephone systems. We can learn from this. First, we need to look at the original technology. We'll look at the problems but keep the best designs. But then we'll search for the latest ideas, and create something similar but better. Countries like India are catching up. But there's competition! Some experts say that Estonia is going to be the most creative country for gadgets, and India will jump ahead with mobile phone technology.

³ How will India jump in front? For example, now most people in India go shopping in street markets and small, local shops. There aren't any large supermarkets in rural areas, so people have to travel to buy more expensive products. But soon we'll start to buy things using the Internet on our smartphones. We're still going to use our small shops and markets, but we'll 'jump' over the need for supermarkets. Get ready – change will come fast!

1. What does the writer think is going to be the best way to improve her country?
   (a.) Learning from another country's mistakes   b. Making mistakes
   c. Copying old technology
2. How will countries like India design new gadgets and technology?
   a. They will keep the same old technology.
   (b.) They will copy and improve on existing technology.
   c. They won't spend any time on new ideas.
3. According to the blog, which country is going to design the most creative gadgets?
   (a.) Estonia   b. India   c. Britain
4. How will India 'jump in front' of more developed countries?
   a. India will spend more money on travel.
   b. Indians won't use the Internet.
   (c.) Indians will use technology to develop smart solutions to everyday problems.

4 **Write.** Read the text in Activity 3 again. Write about some of the ideas in the text in your own words, using *will* and *going to*. Answers will vary.

Estonia will be the most creative country for gadgets.

India will have more digital shopping.

Indian villagers are not going to need supermarkets.

WRITING

To write a good review of a product, we need descriptive words. We want our readers to imagine the product clearly. Details are important, so remember to list good and bad things about the product, and give examples of each.

1 **Organise.**

1. Your task is to write a review of a product that you have used. Look through the unit for product ideas, or do some research on the Internet, then think of similar products you have used.

2. Plan your writing. Your review needs examples of good and bad points. Finish with your opinion and the reasons that support it.

Use the table to help you plan. List the examples you will use in your review.

Product	
Good points	
Bad points	
Your opinion and reasons	

2 **Write.**

1. Go to page 123 in your book. Re-read the model and writing prompt.
2. Write your first draft. Check for organisation, content, punctuation, capitalisation and spelling.
3. Write your final draft. Share it with your teacher and classmates.

Now I can …

- **talk about cool apps and gadgets.**   ☐ Yes, I can! ☐ I think I can. ☐ I need more practice.

  Write two sentences about apps and gadgets. Give examples of what they can do.
  My smartphone came with a cool weather app that shows the temperature every hour. There's a great device for cycling now. You can connect to the Internet to show your friends your route and your average speed.

- **use superlatives to talk about extremes.**   ☐ Yes, I can! ☐ I think I can. ☐ I need more practice.

  Complete the conversation with the superlatives.
  Example: Your music app is (+/cool) ___the coolest___ I have seen!

  Pietro: Have you heard (+/new) ___the newest___ download from this band?
  Camilla: No! Do you think it's their (+/good) ___best___ version?
  Pietro: Well, we could look up a review to see (+/high) ___the highest___ rated downloads.
  Camilla: OK, but that band is my (-/favourite) ___least favourite___. Can we look up this other band as well?

- **talk about the future using *will* and *going to*.**   ☐ Yes, I can! ☐ I think I can. ☐ I need more practice.

  Write about the photo using *will* and *going to*.

  The dog is going to eat the biscuit. The girl will talk to the dog.
  The dog will be excited / won't be lonely.

- **write a review.**   ☐ Yes, I can! ☐ I think I can. ☐ I need more practice.

  Write about a product. Include examples of its good and bad points, as well as your opinion about the product.
  Answers will vary.

YOU DECIDE Choose an activity. Go to page 96.

Unit 8
Into the Past

1 **Write.** Combine the words in the bones to make a question. Write the question on the first line. Answer the question using two of the words from the word bank. Write your answer on the second line.

15,000	believe	site	discover

1. *discover*   *where did archaeologists*   *bones from adult skeletons*

   Where did archaeologists discover bones from adult skeletons?

   Archaeologists discovered the bones from the adult skeletons at the site.

2. *do the sites*   *go back in time*   *how many years*

   How many years do the sites go back in time?

   Archaeologists believe the sites go back 2,300 years.

2 **Write.** Match the words and phrases with similar meanings. Then use the words or phrases to complete the sentences.

1. bones — a. ancestors
2. continue to think — b. skull
3. origins — c. still believe

Experts put together a human (1) _____skull_____ and some skeletal
(2) _____bones_____ .

Some scientists (3) continue to think / still believe that the (4) ____ancestors / origins____
of American people are Asian, but others (5) still believe / continue to think a different
story about their (6) ____ancestors / origins____ .

3 **Listen.** Complete the summary using the words in the box. 🔊 036

adult	advanced	ancestors	believe
bones	discovered	skeleton	skull

Scientists _____believe_____ that they
have _____discovered_____ the origins of
the American people.

The answer came from a nearly complete
_____skeleton_____ and
_____bones_____ found in the sea near
Mexico. It belonged to a young woman, almost
an _____adult_____ . Scientists used
_____advanced_____ computers to make a
model head from the _____skull_____
bones and now think that the common
_____ancestors_____ of the first Americans
may have come from Asia.

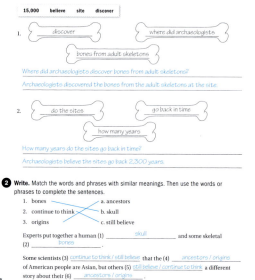

4 **Write.** Use the words from Activity 3 and the box below to make sentences.

there + be	has/have + discover/believe

Sample answers:

They have discovered a human skull.

There was a skeleton at the bottom of the sea.

_____

_____

_____

GRAMMAR

Present perfect: Describing a past action that still continues

Chess **has been** popular for hundreds of years.

I **have played** chess for five years.

My brother **hasn't played** board games since he started playing video games.

Have you always **liked** video games? Yes, I **have**.

How long **have** you **played** video games?

We use the present perfect to talk about actions that began in the past but continue in the present.
To form the present perfect, use *have* or *has* and a past participle of the verb. Most verbs form the past participle by adding *-ed*, but some verbs are irregular. (be → been, go → gone)
We use *for* with the present perfect to talk about how long it has been from the moment an action or situation began until the present moment.
For + period of time: **for** two years, **for** five days, **for** a very long time
We use *since* with the present perfect to talk about when an action or situation began.
Since + a point in time: **since** last week, **since** 2015, **since** I arrived

1 **Complete the sentences.** Write the correct form of the verb in brackets and select *for* or *since*.

1. My father ____has played____ (play) chess ____for____ (for / since) 40 years.

2. My two brothers ____have played____ (play) chess ____since____ (for / since) they were little, too.

3. I ____have played____ (play) chess ____for____ (for / since) just one year, but it ____has become____ (become) my favourite game!

4. My father ____has____ never ____liked____ (like) video games, but my mother ____has____ always ____loved____ (love) them.

5. I've never liked video games, but that ____has changed____ (change) ____since____ (for / since) last week. I ____'ve discovered____ (discover) a really cool video game about ancient Rome.

6. I only started to play a week ago, but I ____have completed____ (complete) all levels!

2 **Listen.** Circle the sentence with the present perfect form. 🔊 037

1.
   a. They discovered bones in a cave.
   b. They've drawn a map showing the bones in the cave. ⃝
   c. They show the map of the cave to the newspapers.

2.
   a. Scientists have studied early civilizations similar to our ancestors. ⃝
   b. Scientists believe that modern humans are less healthy.
   c. Our ancestors slept better than us.

3.
   a. Rajiv moved his queen three squares closer to Amena's king.
   b. Amena hasn't forgotten that the queen is a powerful chess piece. ⃝
   c. Amena blocks Rajiv's queen with another piece.

3 **Listen again.** Complete the sentences with the present perfect form of the verb. 🔊 037

1. First, they found bones in the cave. Next, they drew a map of the cave to show the newspapers. The journalists (see) ____have seen____ the map now.

2. Our ancestors slept very well. Modern humans don't sleep very well. Scientists (find) ____have found____ that early civilizations can help us understand our sleep problems.

3. Rajiv moved his queen closer to Amena's king. Amena knows that the queen is a powerful chess piece. Rajiv (not win) ____hasn't won____ the chess game yet.

4 **Write.** Use the words to make sentences using the present perfect.

1. Experts are looking for descendants of the last King of India. They / find / some descendants / in Myanmar and Pakistan / but / most / live / India all their lives.
   They have found some descendants in Myanmar and Pakistan, but most have lived in India all their lives.

2. Archaeologists in Russia / discover / unusually long skulls / site named Arkaim.
   Archaeologists in Russia have discovered unusually long skulls at the site named Arkaim.

1 Listen and read. As you read, think about what scientists have learnt about ancient civilizations. 🔊038

My History Page

Wait – change the history books!
Which is the oldest civilization in Southeast Asia?

¹ For many years, scientists have thought that the oldest human civilization in Southeast Asia was from India, because humans have lived there for at least 10,000 years. Scientists believed that those early people moved east, and that their descendants populated other countries, such as my country, Sri Lanka. So this is what our education system has always taught teenagers like me.

² But new technology shows that there has been civilization in ancient Sri Lanka for much longer, dating back 30,000 years. Since the 1980s, archaeologists have studied skeletons that show cultures have survived almost three times longer than we previously believed. Finger bones and skulls discovered in archaeological sites in dry caves show that the ancestors of modern Sri Lankans were advanced enough to make their homes in caves 30,000 years ago. That's 20,000 years before people in Europe did this!

³ So Sri Lankans now have new information about our origins. We have learnt that our ancestors were almost the first humans to use tools to cut stone and hunt animals. I say 'almost the first' because Sri Lankans are not the oldest civilization in the world. That prize goes to South Africa, where people have lived for an amazing 50,000 years! As technology improves, scientists must keep looking to see if they really have discovered the oldest sites in your country, too.

2 Read again. Answer the questions.

1. Which country did experts think had the oldest human civilization in Southeast Asia?
   India

2. How many years have civilizations lived in Sri Lanka? _30,000_

3. What were the ancient Sri Lankans doing 20,000 years before the Europeans?
   Living in caves, using stone tools, hunting.

4. Which country has the oldest civilization in the world? _South Africa_

82

3 Read. Match the cause with the effect. Write the number on the line.

Cause	Effect
1. Experts thought that India was the oldest civilization in Southeast Asia.	_3_ Now, there are plans to search for older sites in other countries, too.
2. Scientists discovered bones from 30,000 years ago in Sri Lanka.	_1_ So, schools taught that Sri Lankans were descendants of Indians.
3. Scientists used modern technology to find the age of the bones.	_2_ So, now we know there have been Sri Lankan civilizations for much longer.

4 Write. Read the text again. Write the cause and three possible effects in the graphic organiser. Write the letters in the spaces.

A. Archaeologists might search for older sites in other countries, too.

B. Scientists discovered 30,000-year-old bones in Sri Lanka.

C. Sri Lankan school books may need rewriting!

D. Europeans have learnt that their ancestors are younger than Sri Lankans' ancestors.

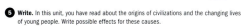

cause B → effect A / effect C / effect D

5 Write. In this unit, you have read about the origins of civilizations and the changing lives of young people. Write possible effects for these causes.

1. Cause: The Aztec education system taught boys and girls separate subjects.
   Effect: _Aztec boys and girls had different skills and did different work._

2. Cause: Archaeologists don't always use the most modern technology in every country.
   Effect: _Some countries don't know how old their cultures are._

3. Cause: Many centuries ago, most adults could not read or write.
   Effect: _Most children didn't learn to read or write from their parents. / Parents taught their children practical skills._

4. Cause: Some poor teenagers worked in factories in England in the 1800s.
   Effect: _Some teenagers had no free time to meet their friends._

83

GRAMMAR

There + to be: Expressing existence at different points of time

There was going to be a talk about teenage art and culture tonight.	But unfortunately, **there isn't** anybody available to speak at the moment.
In any teenager's life **there are** always good times and bad times.	**Were there** difficult times for you, too? Yes, **there've been** many!
At the camp **there'll be** jobs for us to do every day.	**There's been** a tradition that the teachers all cook breakfast for us.

To show that something exists in our world we use there + be: there is/was, there are/were, there has/have been, there will be, there is/are going to be, etc.
There can be followed by a singular or plural form of the verb be. The choice of singular or plural depends on the noun that comes after the verb.
For questions, the form of be is placed before there.

1 Listen. Circle the correct form of be. 🔊039

1. There **is** / **are** / **were** a lot of missing pieces in this chess set.
2. There **were** / **will be** / **are** too many people at the festival.
3. Did you say there **will be** / **was** / **is** a traditional dance?
4. In next year's exhibition there **will be** / **are going to be** / **have been** some bones from 2,000 years ago!
5. There **have been** / **are** / **will be** giant stones here for ages!
6. Someone has moved my pieces. There **was** / **is** / **were** an empty space here before!
7. You said there **aren't** / **won't be** / **weren't** any pieces for this game, but I've found some!
8. The king's descendants are still alive. There **were** / **is** / **are** six grandchildren in India.

2 Read. Match the graph to the sentence. Write A, B, or C.

A. There was very little education for girls one hundred years ago.

B. There has been an increase in primary-school-aged girls in school.

C. In the future we hope that there will be more girls in schools.

_B_

2003	
2012	

0 10 20 30 40 50 60 70 80
Girls of primary school age out of school (millions)

84

3 Write. Read the conversations and write there + the correct form of be in the spaces.

1. Is there a spinner for this game?
   Yes, _there's_ a special spinner with pictures instead of numbers.

2. Are there any ancient sites here?
   No, unfortunately _there aren't_ any ancient sites to visit.

3. Has there been any interest from the newspapers about this new site?
   There's been a little. _There have been / are / were_ a few questions from a local magazine, but we haven't contacted all of the newspapers yet.

4 Read and listen. Tick **T** for True and **F** for False. 🔊040

Carrom: An ancient game

The board Carrom is a game that's played on a smooth, flat, wooden board. In each corner there's a circular hole about 2 in. (5 cm.) in diameter, and underneath each hole there's a net pocket to catch the pieces.

The pieces Each player has a 'striker' piece about 2 in. in diameter. There are also nine dark pieces and nine light pieces, plus a red piece called the 'Queen'. People often have their own strikers, which are sometimes made of bone and so are heavier than the wooden pieces.

Preparation The Queen is placed in the centre of the board. Six pieces form a circle around the Queen. The remaining 12 pieces go around the first circle of six pieces.

Objective Players choose their colour and then take turns pushing their striker piece against the other pieces. The goal is to get your pieces into the corner pockets. The winner is the player who has put all his or her pieces in the pockets first. However, it's not just a simple race. Neither player wins until one player has put the Queen in a pocket, too.

	T	F
1. On a Carrom board there are round holes in each corner.	✓	☐
2. There are 20 pieces, including two strikers and the Queen.	☐	✓
3. The heaviest piece in Carrom is the striker.	✓	☐
4. Players use their strikers to push their pieces into the holes at the corners.	✓	☐
5. The game ends when there are no pieces on the board but the Queen.	☐	✓

5 Write. Re-read the description of Carrom. Then write a short paragraph describing a board game you know and enjoy playing.

85

WRITING

When you write a classification paragraph – one on festivals, for example – it's a good idea to separate it into parts, such as: *festival music, food, origins.* Start with a topic sentence to introduce your paragraph. Describe each part using different details and examples. When you finish, write a concluding sentence to connect the separate parts back to the first topic sentence.

1 Organise.

1. Your task is to describe a traditional festival or celebration from your culture. Decide on your topic. Decide how to divide your topic into two or three parts.

2. Plan your writing. Research the topic. You'll need an introductory topic sentence. Your topic sentence will describe the festival or celebration. Write your topic sentence here:

_____

Next, you'll need to add details for each part of your paragraph. Make a list of details for each part.

_____
_____
_____
_____

Remember to finish your paragraph with a conclusion. Write your concluding sentence here:

_____
_____

2 Write.

1. Go to page 139 in your book. Re-read the model and writing prompt.

2. Write your first draft. Check for organisation, content, punctuation, capitalisation and spelling.

3. Write your final draft. Share it with your teacher and classmates.

86

Now I can ...

· **talk about events in the past.**
☐ Yes, I can!
☐ I think I can.
☐ I need more practice.

Describe something that happened last month or last year. Write two or three sentences.

<u>Answers will vary</u>
_____
_____

· **describe actions that started in the past and continue into the present.**
☐ Yes, I can!
☐ I think I can.
☐ I need more practice.

Complete the sentences using verbs in the present perfect form.

1. Many people from Kenya (continue) <u>have continued</u> winning prizes in international sports competitions.

2. One researcher (discover) <u>has discovered</u> that teaching chess is helpful in many areas of education.

3. Surprisingly, when observing less advanced civilizations, we (learn) <u>have learnt / learnt</u> more about our own culture.

· **express existence at different points of time using *there + to be.***
☐ Yes, I can!
☐ I think I can.
☐ I need more practice.

Complete the sentences with *there + to be.*

1. We saw that <u>there were</u> bones from adult skeletons at the site.

2. I have a question: <u>will there be / are there going to be</u> any jobs to do at the education camp next week?

3. I don't think <u>there is</u> a black queen piece in this old chess set.

· **write a classification paragraph.**
☐ Yes, I can!
☐ I think I can.
☐ I need more practice.

Describe a game.

<u>Answers will vary.</u>
_____
_____
_____

YOU DECIDE Choose an activity. Go to page 96.

87

Units 7–8 Review

1 Read. Choose the correct word to complete the sentences.

1. I've looked up the word ____ on the Internet, and it says it's a blood relative, for example a child born to a parent, connected to older ancestors.
   a. 'advanced'   b. 'civilization'   c. 'descendant'

2. Can you please ____ the game? I've waited five minutes for my turn already!
   a. discover   b. continue   c. believe

3. Can you believe the Wi-Fi here? I've downloaded the complete video already! It's the ____ Internet access in town!
   a. fast   b. faster   c. fastest

4. These gadgets use too much power. My ____ has died already after only an hour!
   a. microphone   b. battery   c. screen

5. My art project ____ fun. We'll design new king and queen chess pieces.
   a. is going to be   b. are going to be   c. will

6. Have you seen the smartphones with the Chinese ____ app? You can type in Chinese.
   a. find   b. camera   c. keyboard

2 Listen. Number the pictures in the order you hear them described in the radio show. Then listen again and answer the questions. 🎧 041

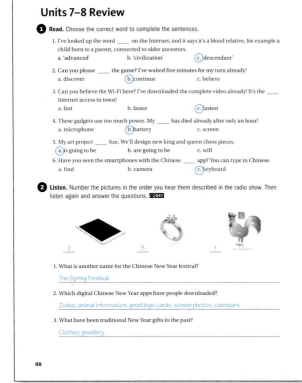

2   3   1

1. What is another name for the Chinese New Year festival?

<u>The Spring Festival</u>

2. Which digital Chinese New Year apps have people downloaded?

<u>Zodiac animal information, greetings cards, screen photos, calendars</u>

3. What have been traditional New Year gifts in the past?

<u>Clothes, jewellery</u>

88

---

3 Read. Decide which answer (*a*, *b* or *c*) is <u>not</u> true. Circle the letter.

> Dear Barbara,
>
> There's going to be a festival in our village next summer! Will you be free to visit? I've joined the festival planning group, so it'll be more exciting for teenagers. Before, only adults decided on the food and music, and there weren't any games. I've started to search the Internet for the most interesting festival games and music. Last year there was a local band. They weren't the best but they were fun. This year the music is going to be even better – I'm the DJ! Please send any helpful advice you have, and any suggestions for music downloads!
>
> Check your calendar – it's going to be incredible!
>
> Hope to see you soon,
>
> Mike

1. Mike asks his friend Barbara
   a. to visit his village festival next summer.
   b. to be a DJ at the festival.
   c. to help him choose music.

2. Last year
   a. there weren't any games.
   b. the adults chose the entertainment.
   c. there was Mexican food.

3. Mike thinks that
   a. the local band was the worst thing at the festival.
   b. DJ music will be more exciting for teenagers.
   c. the festival will be better next summer.

4. Barbara
   a. was asked to send ideas about the music.
   b. was asked to give advice to Mike.
   c. is going to be in the festival planning group.

4 Write. Re-read Mike's e-mail in Activity 3 and write a reply. Ask questions about the events last year and the events planned for this year. Use the present perfect, *will* and *going to* questions.

<u>Possible answer: Hi Mike, What date is the festival going to be? Are you going to be the</u>
<u>DJ all day and night? Will we have time to talk, too? Is the food going to be hot or cold?</u>
<u>Have you heard of the game 'Catch the Flag'?</u>

89

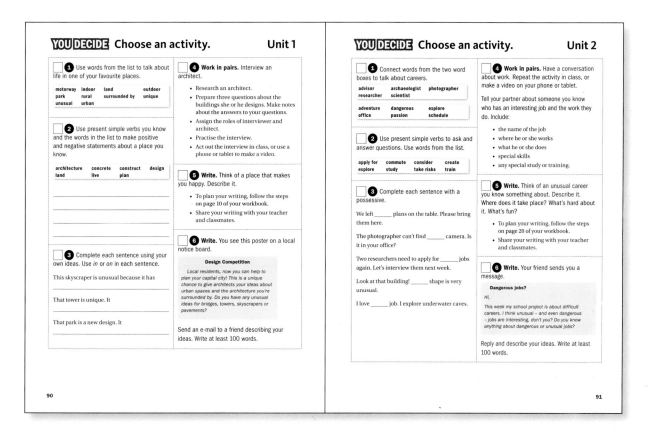

YOU DECIDE Choose an activity. Unit 1

1 Use words from the list to talk about life in one of your favourite places.

motorway	indoor	land	outdoor
park	rural	surrounded by	unique
unusual	urban		

2 Use present simple verbs you know and the words in the list to make positive and negative statements about a place you know.

| architecture | concrete | construct | design |
| land | live | plan | |

_____

_____

_____

_____

3 Complete each sentence using your own ideas. Use *in* or *on* in each sentence.

This skyscraper is unusual because it has _____

That tower is unique. It _____

That park is a new design. It _____

4 **Work in pairs.** Interview an architect.

- Research an architect.
- Prepare three questions about the buildings she or he designs. Make notes about the answers to your questions.
- Assign the roles of interviewer and architect.
- Practise the interview.
- Act out the interview in class, or use a phone or tablet to make a video.

5 **Write.** Think of a place that makes you happy. Describe it.

- To plan your writing, follow the steps on page 10 of your workbook.
- Share your writing with your teacher and classmates.

6 **Write.** You see this poster on a local notice board.

Design Competition

Local residents, now you can help to plan your capital city! This is a unique chance to give architects your ideas about urban spaces and the architecture you're surrounded by. Do you have any unusual ideas for bridges, towers, skyscrapers or pavements?

Send an e-mail to a friend describing your ideas. Write at least 100 words.

90

YOU DECIDE Choose an activity. Unit 2

1 Connect words from the two word boxes to talk about careers.

| advisor | archaeologist | photographer |
| researcher | scientist | |

| adventure | dangerous | explore |
| office | passion | schedule |

2 Use present simple verbs to ask and answer questions. Use words from the list.

| apply for | commute | consider | create |
| explore | study | take risks | train |

3 Complete each sentence with a possessive.

We left _____ plans on the table. Please bring them here.

The photographer can't find _____ camera. Is it in your office?

Two researchers need to apply for _____ jobs again. Let's interview them next week.

Look at that building! _____ shape is very unusual.

I love _____ job. I explore underwater caves.

4 **Work in pairs.** Have a conversation about work. Repeat the activity in class, or make a video on your phone or tablet.

Tell your partner about someone you know who has an interesting job and the work they do. Include:

- the name of the job
- where he or she works
- what he or she does
- special skills
- any special study or training.

5 **Write.** Think of an unusual career you know something about. Describe it. Where does it take place? What's hard about it. What's fun?

- To plan your writing, follow the steps on page 20 of your workbook.
- Share your writing with your teacher and classmates.

6 **Write.** Your friend sends you a message.

Dangerous jobs?

Hi,
This week my school project is about difficult careers. I think unusual – and even dangerous – jobs are interesting, don't you? Do you know anything about dangerous or unusual jobs?

Reply and describe your ideas. Write at least 100 words.

91

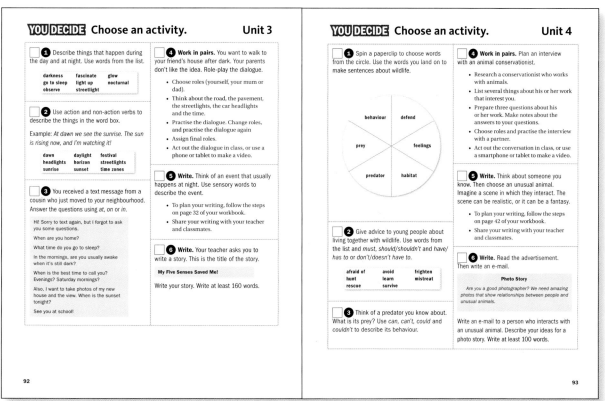

YOU DECIDE Choose an activity. Unit 3

1 Describe things that happen during the day and at night. Use words from the list.

darkness	fascinate	glow
go to sleep	light up	nocturnal
observe	streetlight	

2 Use action and non-action verbs to describe the things in the word box.

Example: *At dawn we see the sunrise. The sun is rising now, and I'm watching it!*

dawn	daylight	festival
headlights	horizon	streetlights
sunrise	sunset	time zones

3 You received a text message from a cousin who just moved to your neighbourhood. Answer the questions using *at*, *on* or *in*.

Hi! Sorry to text again, but I forgot to ask you some questions.

When are you home?

What time do you go to sleep?

In the mornings, are you usually awake when it's still dark?

When is the best time to call you? Evenings? Saturday mornings?

Also, I want to take photos of my new house and the view. When is the sunset tonight?

See you at school!

4 **Work in pairs.** You want to walk to your friend's house after dark. Your parents don't like the idea. Role-play the dialogue.

- Choose roles (yourself, your mum or dad).
- Think about the road, the pavement, the streetlights, the car headlights and the time.
- Practise the dialogue. Change roles, and practise the dialogue again.
- Assign final roles.
- Act out the dialogue in class, or use a phone or tablet to make a video.

5 **Write.** Think of an event that usually happens at night. Use sensory words to describe the event.

- To plan your writing, follow the steps on page 32 of your workbook.
- Share your writing with your teacher and classmates.

6 **Write.** Your teacher asks you to write a story. This is the title of the story.

My Five Senses Saved Me!

Write your story. Write at least 160 words.

92

YOU DECIDE Choose an activity. Unit 4

1 Spin a paperclip to choose words from the circle. Use the words you land on to make sentences about wildlife.

behaviour defend
prey feelings
predator habitat

2 Give advice to young people about living together with wildlife. Use words from the list and *must*, *should/shouldn't* and *have/ has to* or *don't/doesn't have to*.

afraid of	avoid	frighten
hunt	learn	mistreat
rescue	survive	

3 Think of a predator you know about. What is its prey? Use *can*, *can't*, *could* and *couldn't* to describe its behaviour.

4 **Work in pairs.** Plan an interview with an animal conservationist.

- Research a conservationist who works with animals.
- List several things about his or her work that interest you.
- Prepare three questions about his or her work. Make notes about the answers to your questions.
- Choose roles and practise the interview with a partner.
- Act out the conversation in class, or use a smartphone or tablet to make a video.

5 **Write.** Think about someone you know. Then choose an unusual animal. Imagine a scene in which they interact. The scene can be realistic, or it can be a fantasy.

- To plan your writing, follow the steps on page 42 of your workbook.
- Share your writing with your teacher and classmates.

6 **Write.** Read the advertisement. Then write an e-mail.

Photo Story

Are you a good photographer? We need amazing photos that show relationships between people and unusual animals.

Write an e-mail to a person who interacts with an unusual animal. Describe your ideas for a photo story. Write at least 100 words.

93

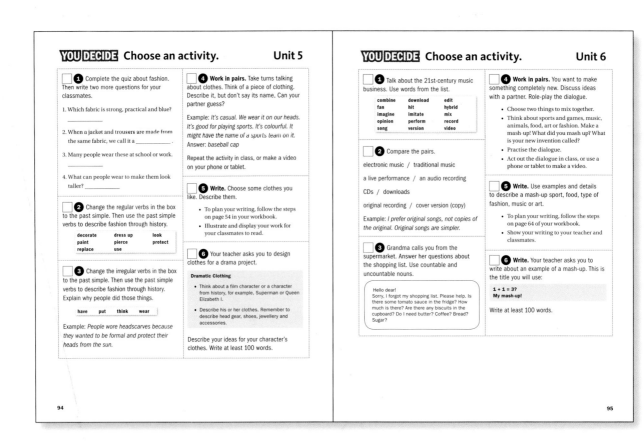

YOU DECIDE Choose an activity. Unit 5

1 Complete the quiz about fashion. Then write two more questions for your classmates.

1. Which fabric is strong, practical and blue?

_____

2. When a jacket and trousers are made from the same fabric, we call it a _____.

3. Many people wear these at school or work.

_____

4. What can people wear to make them look taller? _____

2 Change the regular verbs in the box to the past simple. Then use the past simple verbs to describe fashion through history.

decorate	dress up	look
paint	pierce	protect
replace	use	

3 Change the irregular verbs in the box to the past simple. Then use the past simple verbs to describe fashion through history. Explain why people did those things.

have	put	think	wear

Example: *People wore headscarves because they wanted to be formal and protect their heads from the sun.*

4 **Work in pairs.** Take turns talking about clothes. Think of a piece of clothing. Describe it, but don't say its name. Can your partner guess?

Example: *It's casual. We wear it on our heads. It's good for playing sports. It's colourful. It might have the name of a sports team on it.* Answer: *baseball cap*

Repeat the activity in class, or make a video on your phone or tablet.

5 **Write.** Choose some clothes you like. Describe them.

- To plan your writing, follow the steps on page 54 in your workbook.
- Illustrate and display your work for your classmates to read.

6 Your teacher asks you to design clothes for a drama project.

Dramatic Clothing

- Think about a film character or a character from history, for example, Superman or Queen Elizabeth I.
- Describe his or her clothes. Remember to describe head gear, shoes, jewellery and accessories.

Describe your ideas for your character's clothes. Write at least 100 words.

94

YOU DECIDE Choose an activity. Unit 6

1 Talk about the 21st-century music business. Use words from the list.

combine	download	edit
fan	hit	hybrid
imagine	imitate	mix
opinion	perform	record
song	version	video

2 Compare the pairs.

electronic music / traditional music

a live performance / an audio recording

CDs / downloads

original recording / cover version (copy)

Example: *I prefer original songs, not copies of the original. Original songs are simpler.*

3 Grandma calls you from the supermarket. Answer her questions about the shopping list. Use countable and uncountable nouns.

Hello dear!
Sorry, I forgot my shopping list. Please help. Is there some tomato sauce in the fridge? How much is there? Are there any biscuits in the cupboard? Do I need butter? Coffee? Bread? Sugar?

4 **Work in pairs.** You want to make something completely new. Discuss ideas with a partner. Role-play the dialogue.

- Choose two things to mix together.
- Think about sports and games, music, animals, food, art or fashion. Make a mash up! What did you mash up? What is your new invention called?
- Practise the dialogue.
- Act out the dialogue in class, or use a phone or tablet to make a video.

5 **Write.** Use examples and details to describe a mash-up sport, food, type of fashion, music or art.

- To plan your writing, follow the steps on page 64 of your workbook.
- Show your writing to your teacher and classmates.

6 **Write.** Your teacher asks you to write about an example of a mash-up. This is the title you will use:

1 + 1 = 3?
My mash-up!

Write at least 100 words.

95

YOU DECIDE Choose an activity. Units 7–8

1 **Work in pairs.** Put the words in the box in order from 1 to 5. (1 = the coolest and 5 = the least cool.) Explain your choices to a partner.

a computer game	a sports gadget	a music app
a tablet	a smartphone	

Now put the things in order of practicality, from the most to the least practical. Explain your thinking.

2 List several activities you plan to do next week. Are you going to do anything practical or interesting? Or maybe something incredible?

practical	interesting	incredible

3 **Write.** Choose a product that has positive and negative points. Describe its good and bad points, and then give your opinion.

- To plan your writing, follow the steps on page 76 of your workbook.
- Share your writing with your teacher and classmates.

4 **Write.** Below is part of a letter from an English-speaking friend.

When I come to visit you, I want to buy something from your country. Maybe you can help me think of an idea. I want something interesting and unusual. It doesn't have to be perfect! If you think of anything, please tell me about the good and bad points. Then I can choose the best thing to buy.

Respond to the letter. Write at least 100 words.

1 How have archaeologists helped us learn about our world? Use words from the list. Make sentences using present perfect verbs.

Example: *They have discovered bones under the sea.*

advanced	ancestors	bones	civilization
descendant	origins	site	skeleton
skull	species		

2 **Work in pairs.** Choose a word from Activity 1. Have a conversation about it using *there + be*. Repeat the activity in class, or make a video on a phone or tablet.

3 **Write.** Choose a game that you enjoy playing. Describe it in detail. Classify the different parts of the game.

- To plan your writing, follow the steps on page 86 in your workbook.
- Share your writing with your teacher and classmates.

4 Below is part of an e-mail you received from an Australian friend.

Hello,
I'm writing a blog about Internet games for teenagers. Do you know any cool games? I'm thinking about games related to education or culture. I'm also interested in games that help with maths, or maybe language learning. I DON'T want to write about games that involve racing or fighting. Can you please help me by explaining your favourite educational Internet game?

Write a reply. Write at least 100 words.

96